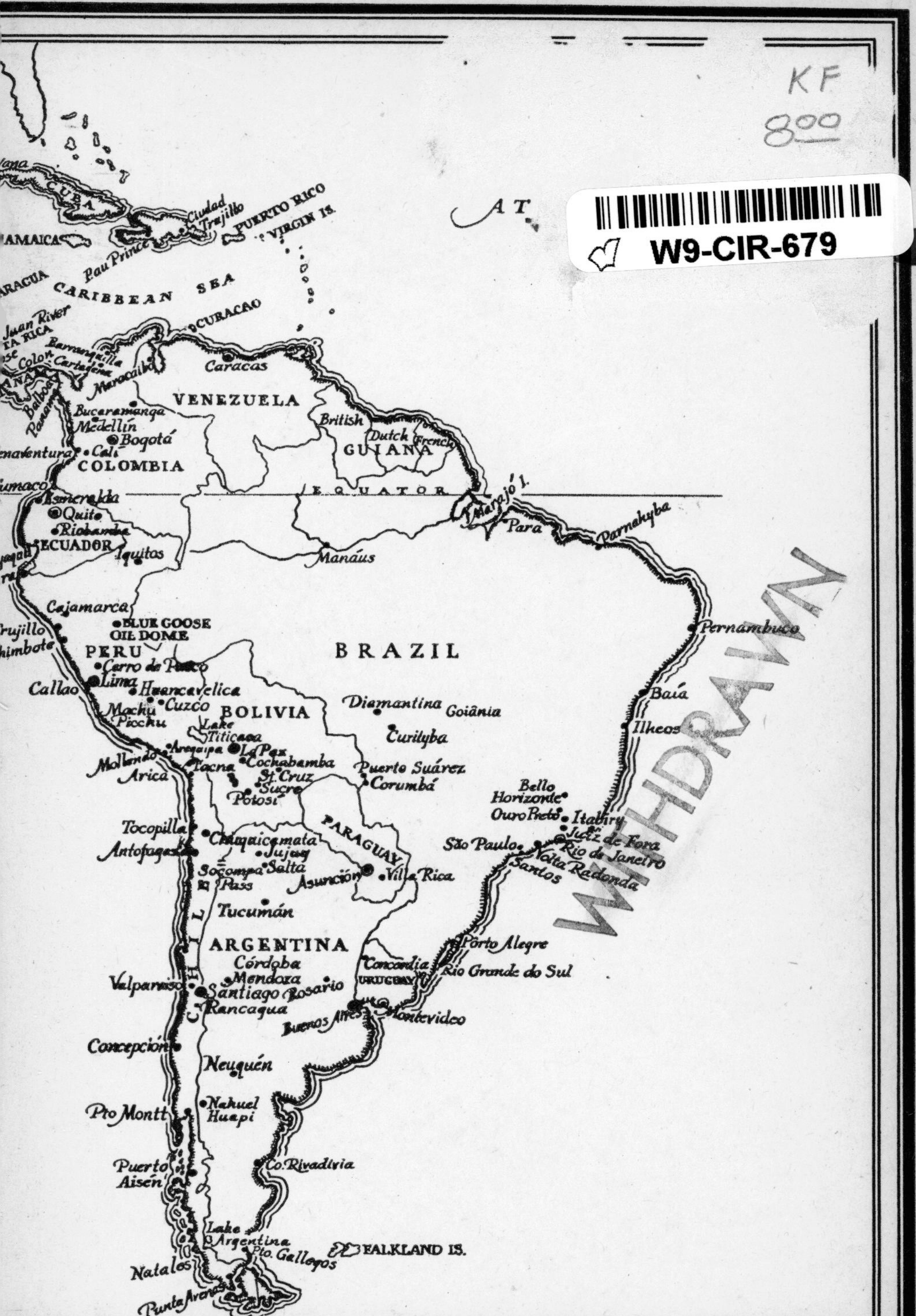
CUBA
JAMAICA
Pau Prince
Ciudad Trujillo
PUERTO RICO
VIRGIN IS.
AT
CARIBBEAN SEA
CURACAO
Juan River
Barranquilla
Colon
Cartagena
Balboa
Panama
Maracaibo
Caracas
VENEZUELA
Bucaramanga
Medellín
Bogotá
Cali
COLOMBIA
British
Dutch
French
GUIANA
EQUATOR
Marajó I.
Para
Parnahyba
Esmeralda
Quito
Riobamba
ECUADOR
Iquitos
Manáus
Cajamarca
BLUE GOOSE OIL DOME
PERU
Cerro de Pasco
Callao
Lima
Huancavelica
Cuzco
Machu Picchu
BRAZIL
Pernambuco
BOLIVIA
Lake Titicaca
Arequipa
La Paz
Cochabamba
Mollendo
Arica
Tacna
St. Cruz
Sucre
Potosi
Diamantina
Goiânia
Curityba
Puerto Suárez
Corumbá
Baía
Ilheos
Bello Horizonte
Ouro Preto
Itabira
Juiz de Fora
Rio de Janeiro
Volta Redonda
São Paulo
Santos
Tocopilla
Chuquicamata
Antofagasta
Jujuy
Salta
Socompa Pass
PARAGUAY
Asunción
Villa Rica
Tucumán
ARGENTINA
Córdoba
Mendoza
CHILE
Valparaiso
Santiago
Rosario
Rancagua
Concordia
URUGUAY
Porto Alegre
Rio Grande do Sul
Buenos Aires
Montevideo
Concepción
Neuquén
Pto Montt
Nahuel Huapi
Puerto Aisén
Co. Rivadivia
Lake Argentina
Pto. Gallegos
FALKLAND IS.
Natales
Punta Arenas
C.V.J.

LANDS OF THE DAWNING MORROW

By CARLETON BEALS

LANDS OF THE DAWNING MORROW

RIO GRANDE TO CAPE HORN

DAWN OVER THE AMAZON

PANAMERICA

THE GREAT CIRCLE

AMERICAN EARTH: THE BIOGRAPHY OF A NATION

AMERICA SOUTH

GLASS HOUSES

THE COMING STRUGGLE FOR LATIN AMERICA

THE STONES AWAKE

THE STORY OF HUEY P. LONG

FIRE ON THE ANDES

THE CRIME OF CUBA

BLACK RIVER

PORFIRIO DIAZ: DICTATOR OF MEXICO

BANANA GOLD

BRIMSTONE AND CHILI

DESTROYING VICTOR

ROME OR DEATH: THE STORY OF FASCISM

MEXICO: AN INTERPRETATION

LANDS OF
THE DAWNING MORROW

The Awakening from
Rio Grande to Cape Horn

By CARLETON BEALS

THE BOBBS-MERRILL COMPANY

PUBLISHERS

INDIANAPOLIS-NEW YORK

First Edition

To Mother

TABLE OF CONTENTS

LANDS OF THE DAWNING MORROW

Memories of the Future

Lands of Tomorrow

In Mexico City, a pulque shop called *El Porvenir*—The Future—closed down. Dust gathered on its thick green mugs, and the patrons looked for another spot to drink their frothy white beer.

One day the shop reopened with the grand new sign: *Recuerdos del Porvenir*—Memories of the Future.

This is more than droll Mexican humor. Latin America has had many dreams of the future and many hard battles to win the future—mostly unrealized. Nearly all have turned into mere "memories of the future."

Thus the oft-repeated phrase, Mañana Lands—Lands of Tomorrow—has far deeper meaning than mere sun squatting. It long spelled the tragedy of peoples deprived of their liberties, but now it begins to spell hope, for that "tomorrow" is knocking at the door. The future is at last catching up with the present. The awakening of the sunlands is here.

In few parts of the world has the word "future" always been used so constantly, with such eager emphasis, as in the twenty divergent republics to the south. It is true that "shall" and "will" are words nonexistent in the Spanish language—spoken by all the countries except Brazil and Haiti—but the verb endings of the future tense are always sprinkled plentifully in newspaper headlines, orations and books. This is merely another way of saying that the destiny of the continent is still in the making, that these are still Mañana Lands—Lands of Tomorrow.

Though abuses by many dictatorial regimes long blocked the way to larger freedoms and still do in a few countries, everywhere there are wide horizons which in most of the world have now been closed off. None of the countries has been exhausted by war or shattered by war. Wealth and confidence have not been drained away or destroyed. Nearly all, these war years, have grown rapidly in stature. Compared with twenty years ago the growth has been truly astounding. The phrase is being turned around: the future is now a memory.

11

Thus opportunities pulse stronger than in most of our war-torn militarized world. Many of those opportunities are now being grasped.

Some time ago an Argentine leader in Paris spoke of the serious problems of his country. The French premier retorted: "You people in the New World, you have no problems. You don't know what difficulties are. We French are forty million people in a matchbox; you are only fourteen million in a vast empire nearly as big as all Europe outside Russia. If you have troubles, it is because you make them, not because you are obliged to have them."

For in the southland world, man in general has a far better chance at Nature. He reaches out his hand more easily, if he cares to do so, for the fruits of life. It is a world in progress, an expanding, not a war-torn or contracting world, but one still eager to reach maturity in modern ways.

Go directly from Europe to any Latin American port—such glittering magnificent cities as Buenos Aires or Rio, or to shabbier rag-tail places steaming in the tropic sun—and immediately, from the bearing of the people, you will know beyond any doubt that you have arrived in the New World and nowhere else on earth. This was even true in Europe's brighter days before it was reduced to impotence and ruin and caught in the giant nutcrackers of two great Powers. Whatever the particular American government of the moment, instantly you sense a more zestful air of freedom and confidence, a brighter eye, a bolder step. Man is not so crowded, so bowed down by intimate rules and regulations. Most of the Americas are not yet a fenced-in world, but a world in the making.

True, the gaps of wealth and poverty are wide. During long centuries —under colonial rule, military dictatorship and revolutionary regimes— many struggles for popular freedom have been thwarted. Progress has been repeatedly aborted. And though many battles have been won and a great culture has grown into being, until lately most of the lands have been held back from the threshold of modern life.

This backwardness still peers out on many sides. Social evils there are aplenty. Raw cruelty is sometimes close to the surface. Graft and disorder are not always strikingly absent. Often lack of education, even of good health, holds many people back. But the faith and energy exist to face and rectify these shortcomings. The people, now, everywhere are awakening, and already new types of governments are beginning to tackle such ills in a determined and original spirit.

The swift developments of the last few decades are by no means confined to purely material advances in industry and trade. They include education, health, politics, science, the arts—all fields of human endeavor.

This new Latin America now growing up so rapidly, destined in a few years to surpass Europe in wealth and power, is worth knowing for its fascinating history and for its great and varied achievements in art, literature and human relationships.

The extraordinary beauty and majesty of its great mountains and forests, lakes and rivers, the gleaming islands and harbors, tell even the most casual visitor that this whole region has been fashioned in true grandeur for heroic purposes where the spirit and courage of man must ever rise to great deeds.

Already it has witnessed some of the most remarkable feats in the annals of mankind. Empires rose and died there even before the British were skin-clad savages eating raw meat by the dismal North Sea. Empires rose and died there long before Emperor Caligula tore the wings off flies. Great stone monuments were built on the lofty highlands of Bolivia twenty centuries before Xanthippe chased Socrates around the public square of Athens—in a dim past nearly ten times the span of what we call recorded literary history.

And has the stupendous Spanish conquest of the Americas ever been equaled by any race of any clime in any age?

The Independence of the Thirteen Colonies was a trifling skirmish compared with the decades of war in the southlands, the marching of great armies over a continent and a half: the epic strategy of Morelos and Bolivar, San Martín and Sucre. The march of San Martín across the Andes was one of the great military feats of all time. During the hundred years that followed, few areas of the world have known such high-ticking drama.

Travelers who learn the language and grow more intimate with the various lands will soon cherish the admirable talented folk of Latin America, people so strongly individualistic, yet so kindly and generous, not yet regimented into automata of thought and deed by mass production, neither slave of the machine nor of the State; not yet driven into abdication of their moral and mental integrity as individuals by the brutal sterile race for world power, nor broken by the disasters and tragedies of the war years. In general the Latin American people, even on the humblest levels, are more intuitive, sensitive and artistic than most. They know a grace of living that few countries have ever enjoyed.

Not the least of the excitement of this new Latin America in the making is due to what the Mexican educator, José Vasconcelos, has called "the cosmic race." The melting pot to the south is not merely one of many nationalities, like the United States, but of many races, mingling, working together, growing together, becoming one new race, and each making its unique contributions in an unfettered manner to what—precisely because of these rich divergent sources—will eventually become one of the most original and splendid cultures ever achieved by man. From this our harsh race-divided United States could learn much. If class divisions are still sharp and unjust in much of Latin America, race prejudices are few, and those exist mostly where North Americans have intruded. A Brazilian remarked to me, "Down here when we look at a human being, we don't see the color of his skin. We simply don't see it. We look right inside him and see the human being."

All told, Latin America is one of the more exciting and exuberant regions of the world, and today, growing, pulsing with new life, it stands on the threshold of achievements greater than ever before in its history.

Today the peoples of the whole world seek a new formula that will repudiate the degenerate fatal power-struggle shaping up before our eyes; for a way of life that repudiates the harsh extremes of monopoly capitalism and of Soviet Communism—reactionary forces now leading the world straight to disaster. Life is greater than any such struggle— all the frontiers of Nature, science, art, the human soul, stretch far beyond such a narrow trap. Man is greater than that. The whole world is looking for a way of life which will revitalize the freedom of creative individual expression and bring forth greater security, happiness and peace, in relation to industry and government, in relation to the daily task of gaining a livelihood and to the expanding claims of militarism and the State. That is the path Latin America is seeking, and which in some places it may have found.

Recently the leader of Peru's popular movement, Haya de la Torre, declared: "We do not want bread without freedom; and we do not want freedom without bread."

Unless some such open route of escape is found for mankind away from the struggle of colossal opposing powers, unless some superior synthesis supersedes both warring ideologies, unless some better answer is found than the present dull bellow of lying official propaganda from all quarters, than this repeated hurried "bum's rush" of whole peoples into ill-advised and dangerous foreign adventures, civilization will be destroyed along with the millions who compose it, in endless misery for most of the world.

The present experiments in industry, government and social relationships in the newly expanding world of Latin America seem to provide at least some partial answers to the present dilemma. A different, more human sort of system is growing up there in the shadow of the blind Old World struggle for power that so engrosses our thought and emotions. There, in that developing region of the south, a new vigorous life is sprouting under the hard crust of the world's present militarism.

Looking over the Shoulder

For centuries Latin America mostly looked over its shoulder at faded colonial and feudal glories, a sort of romantic gold-braid conception of existence. Like Lot's wife it was salted down in its tracks.

Perhaps the delightful easygoing way of life of the southern peoples may partly have accounted for their long indifference to what North Americans are pleased to call progress. There have been many more valid reasons for the slower tempo of the south countries: long-standing cultural conflicts, historical circumstance, the feudal institutions left by the Spanish Conquest, geographical handicaps, nineteenth-century imperialism, trade monopolies, cartels, colonialism, lack of techniques and capital. The recent foreign control of most natural resources—now being broken in nearly all the southland countries—prevented rounded development and industrialization, forced the southern lands to sell their highly competitive materials at the lowest possible prices abroad and to buy consumers' goods in high markets—a squeeze that kept them impoverished, illiterate and unsanitary. From this blind curse they are now emerging.

Until recently nearly all Latin America lay to one side of the main east-west Atlantic and Pacific trade routes carved out by the rise of England and the United States to power. This brought the Hispanic lands only the eddies of modern progress, denied them full material and spiritual growth in the modern world. It imposed on them disproportionately high carrying costs and impeded their industrial development.

Today those prewar routes have lost much of their exclusive importance. The wrecking of the major industrial plants of Europe and the Orient, the decline of Great Britain, the rise of Australia and southern Asia, the growth of South Africa, the new industrial potential of Canada, the industrial upsurge in Argentina and Brazil plus growth in most of Latin America, are pulling the world's commerce in many new directions. Old travel and commercial channels have been partly silted up; new ones are flowing.

North-south routes are rapidly becoming more important. The Inter-American Highway is considerably more than either a system of hemisphere defense or sentimental good-neighborliness—motives which got the enterprise started. But, in spite of the unfortunate wartime graft and bungling that marred our efforts in that direction, this land route is part of a significant realignment of all America and of the world. Such new routes—land, sea and air—not only have meaning for the sturdier integration of the Western Hemisphere, they are a part of a new global flow in which for the moment the Soviet Union and its satellites stand apart like a bitter lost island.

Today northeast Brazil, which long languished in sleepy isolation, has become one of the world's pivotal air centers, and all along the Bulge charming Rip Van Winkle cities have been growing quickly into new modern metropolises. Tomorrow the shortest route from South America to Australia and southern Asia is likely to be via Antarctica, which will make historic Magellan Straits at the tip of the continent—already stirring with new oil and mineral discoveries—once more one of the busy emporiums of international trade and travel.

Other barriers have long blocked man in the lands south. In spite of so much latent wealth, that area has always faced stupendous natural difficulties. Man there long resigned himself to fatalistic subordination to Nature: a prayerful supplicant, not its master. He was caught in the tight coils of Nature like some agonizing Greek statue; he was unable to harness Nature.

Until yesterday the jungles, full of fabulous riches, were fanged areas of death and danger. They kept men out. They kept men apart. Men who did thread those intricate green hells grew hard and savage or died.

Until yesterday the great snow-clad Andes stood as an almost impassable barrier, cutting all South America into two separate worlds, the Atlantic and Pacific regions, and isolating men, villages, valleys, regions, whole countries. Men lived there in the free Andes, breathed the crisp upland air gratefully, but remained enclosed in their own particular stone-walled valley. The cost of escape, of joining hands with the men of coast or jungle, even with those of the next valley, was usually too great to contemplate. They not only lived apart. Actually they were of different race and culture. And when they did encounter lowland folk, they often fought bloodily—as they fought in the Chaco, as the Peruvian-Bolivian Confederation twice fought Chile, as the highland men of Quito in Ecuador battle the coast men of Guayaquil for control of the country.

During four centuries eighty per cent of South America's population remained within two hundred miles of the coast, unable to penetrate in any large numbers far inland, unable to master the forests and mountains, unable therefore to grasp the pulsing heart of the continent and its real wealth and power, even its full meaning. Only when South Americans really tame their continent—and they are doing so now— will adequate hemisphere defense be achieved. This cannot be accomplished by loading them down with the second-rate war surpluses that are often sent to half-baked militarists, the curse of the southern lands for thirty generations, whom they are now trying to ease out of power.

"What we need, and urgently," a Chilean statesman told me, "is not armaments but industrial potential: schools, sanitation, machinery, factories. We've always had too many priests, too many strutting generals, too many idle aristocrats, too many glib lawyers and bureaucrats; what we need now is engineers, scientists and builders. After World War I you northerners dumped your outworn armaments onto us, and what was the outcome: defense against Germany? Not at all. No, progress was halted. Continental disorder became the rule. The Chaco War. The Leticia conflict. The Peru-Ecuador battle. The Beagle Canal dispute. Bloody revolutions all over the lot. We don't want to be handcuffed once more to rancid military systems we are just beginning to escape. That will merely make us an easier prey to Fifth Columnists, Communists and any other outside power. What our people need now is a prosperity worth fighting for, a prosperity that will provide the real sinews of defense. That is true Hemisphere Defense. Without that there is no defense. Send us tractors and dynamos, then send us some more of them."

The instruments for this nobler continental conquest are available. Only the United States' preoccupation with Europe, its diversion of so much productive power, machinery and goods to that one lone ruined alley of the world, slows up the march. But new weapons and instruments, new medicines and techniques, new ideas and prospects have come unexpectedly into the hands and minds of Latin American men, and a new era has struck as swiftly as lightning on the crags. Until the last few decades the technical means for fully subduing the inner continent, such as sanitation, air cooling, aviation, etc., scarcely existed. Only the last few years have certain dread tropical maladies even been studied. Only during the recent war was effective mass prophylaxis devised.

Yesterday the men who built the fantastic Madeira railroad through the inner Brazilian jungle died like flies. They would not do so today. Yesterday the men who built Peru's first lofty Andean railroad burst apart in agony from the dread *verruga* disease. Today the constructors of the new Santa River power project, which will soon supply the electricity needs of half the country and drive the wheels of new factories, enjoy the best of health though they work right in the *verruga* belt. DDT has eliminated the night-flying insect that spread the malady.

Today British, Argentine, Brazilian and United States pressure-cabin planes bounce right over the highest Andean crests from Buenos Aires to Santiago in three hours. Today oil wells are gushing from the Blue Goose dome of the inner Amazon foothills, a region only ten years ago almost beyond man's reach. Clear down on Tierra del Fuego—Fire Land—within a stone's throw of Cape Horn and hard by the Straits of Magellan—there where the early Portuguese mariner almost had to eat his sails in order not to perish—other wells are being drilled. Today the snow packs are being blasted off yesterday's inaccessible ridges to get out newly discovered uranium and the rich coal deposits of inner Patagonia. Today men are surging into the deep inner Matto Grosso plateau in Brazil, into the Chaco wilderness, into the great Petén jungle of Guatemala—to start new farms, new industries, build new roads and new cities.

Though most southern countries have predominantly temperate-zone climates, central Brazil is mostly hot, but man subdued northern climes by mechanizing the production of heat, and it will prove little more costly and return perhaps greater profits to air-cool dwellings in necessary places in the sunlands and thus bring one of the richest empires on earth, the great Amazon basin, into general use. The development of the Amazonas has attracted a full-scale study by the United Nations. Had not the inefficiency and graft in our wartime seeking of rubber there been so great the area might even now be more advanced. But in spite of them, new oil wells, new airfields, new roads, better medical standards were introduced, and in the not distant future great new populous cities will arise there and all along the balmy delightful eastern Andean foothills—right in the heart of the continent. Brazil—next to the Soviet Union endowed with the greatest resources of any country— is destined to become one of the most prosperous nations in the history of man.

The awakening pokes fingers into many remote humble places, even in corners isolated for centuries. Caribbean islands that slumbered for four hundred years now find themselves suddenly in the main current of everyday travel. Silver wings sweep in from the sky with the hum of the world's new power. Overnight their peoples have rubbed their eyes and have looked about, and now are demanding freedoms and decencies long denied them by bungling backward imperial rule.

'Way up among the Oaxaca peaks in Mexico we visited an Indian village where only three persons spoke Spanish. The people had long resisted efforts to set up a school. Now they have built their own and imported their own teacher.

"Once," said a village elder, "we could learn everything from Nature and needed and wanted nothing more. Only half a dozen of us have ever been down to the nearest railroad town. We have been a happy folk and wish things could always have stayed that way.

"Now they are going to dam the big river near here and make light and power, something we have never even seen. Now a railroad is pushing up the valley below us. We have heard what that will mean. Unless our children are taught to read and write, unless they learn the ways of the builders of railroads, cunning men will soon steal their lands; cunning men will steal our crops and the work of our hands. When the first airplane flew over, our people fell on their knees in adoration and terror. They burned candles to the Holy Virgin and swore they had seen Jesus Christ fly through the air. Now they ask, 'When will the planes land in the village?' Yes, Señor, our children must go to school now. There is no other way."

In the long run retarded development in the southlands may prove to have been very lucky. Now earlier failures and mistakes of other countries are in plain view. Slower tempo has permitted industrial change to be absorbed more gracefully, with more emphasis on national and social welfare, with less disruption of the rich and cultural and artistic heritage. The southern lands have had more time for sound planning. Perhaps this delay may salvage some of the valuable culture of various surviving pre-Spanish populations and permit their remarkable arts and handicrafts to continue to enrich the life and color of many of the countries. Perhaps, too, some of the love of leisure, so characteristic of all Latin America (without which no truly great culture can ever be achieved), will also be salvaged—that zestful capacity of the people to love and enjoy the immediate moment so fully.

We United Statesians often battle and toil all life long for a leisure we are then unable to enjoy properly. The Latin American insists on enjoying himself along the road, savoring the delights, the poetry, the beauty and the wisdom of all the scenery en route.

Recently at a UN conference, a Guatemalan statesman was chided for his dilatory attitude. He retorted: "We Latins know that the end of every human life is—death! We simply refuse to hurry toward that end."

Delayed development may also prove a boon to all mankind. Resources, recklessly drained away in the rest of the world, will still be available. About the time the United States' iron reserves approach dangerous exhaustion (thirty-five years hence, sooner if another war hits us) Brazilian steel production, now getting under way on a considerable scale, will likely be at peak levels—and in that land are a fourth of the world's known iron deposits.

And so the future, always a golden dream in the Mañana Lands, advances upon the present with longer, swifter strides than ever before, something to be grasped, now, quickly and well. The changes sweeping over Latin America are numerous and startling. Industry, institutions and ideas—all are in flux. A new spirit of progress prevails. The mileposts click by faster now.

War and Change

To nearly all Latin America the war years have brought remarkable growth. The rapid transformations in our half-wrecked universe jolted the countries south in many new ways. Although less directly involved in the world conflict than people of other continents, all the American lands were deeply affected, both favorably and unfavorably. They are still being jostled into new lines of endeavor.

War threw all the national economies out of gear, either by excessive prosperity or by actual privation. All sorts of stress and strain showed up and still operate. In some places—for instance Puerto Rico and Venezuela—there were almost famine food shortages. Largely at the behest of the United States wages everywhere were pretty well frozen. Most strikes were barred. Even whole labor movements were outlawed, although the cost of living for people already chained to pitifully low, almost hunger standards, soared nearly everywhere. As all the countries have been overdependent on outside consumer goods, this has meant almost universal hardship. Today, except in Argentina, inflation is a terrible whiplash on the backs of the people. Problems are complex and many, and even those nations which enjoyed epochal prosperity, such as Brazil, Guatemala, Mexico and Argentina, were hit by various shortages.

All such difficulties, however, had their bright side. Totalitarian war elsewhere, causing serious lack of commodity goods and machinery, obliged all the countries to try better to meet their own requirements and those of their neighbors, to manufacture more of their own goods, to lay long-range plans never to be caught so short again by depression or war, calamities which three times in thirty-odd years have had such disastrous effects. In spite of the difficulty of getting machinery, the continent is now dotted with textile and steel mills, processing plants, shipyards, highways, chemical and electrical establishments, paper mills, airfields and so on, which did not exist when war started.

Walk down Ahumada Street, the main business thoroughfare of Santiago de Chile, and window-shop for metal office furniture, hardware, gas and electric stoves, radio sets, electric refrigerators, electric washing machines—just to mention a few items. Ten years ago those products would have borne only British, United States or German trademarks. Today they bear the names of firms in Chile, Brazil and Argentina.

Several years ago the number of workers in industry in Argentina barely surpassed those in agriculture; now it is nearly double. Before the war Brazil was not only predominantly an agricultural but a coffee country. Today its industrial output is valued at two and a half times farm production.

Such developments have brought about new kinds of interchange in new directions. South American trade with South Africa and Australia has increased considerably. During the war, trade among the Latin American countries themselves soared to levels never before believed possible. Just before the war Ecuador exported mostly to the United

States, Germany and the United Kingdom. Germany now takes nothing; the United Kingdom almost nothing. Ecuador's second largest market, due in part to shifts in the type of products, is now Cuba. Before the war most of Peru's imports came from the same big Powers, but today her second source is Argentina. Brazil used to be a great British market. Today England supplies only four per cent; Argentina, more than a fourth. Today Colombia's big market in Germany is gone. Canada, Mexico and Venezuela have taken its place. Before the war Argentina sold little to Colombia; now it sends her almost as much as Great Britain does, and a barter deal promises to put the Plata country far ahead.

Wartime upsets, the closing off of old markets and sources of supply, led the southern countries to push far-reaching projects for industrial expansion, greater self-sufficiency, better over-all utilization of home resources. Goals sought have been greater economic independence, elimination of foreign absenteeism, wider employment, improved living standards, better internal communication. A determination has grown up on all sides to strengthen home economies to insure against being so badly crippled by future disasters beyond their borders, by depressions and wars.

During the Napoleonic wars the southern lands were cast adrift to shift for themselves and thereby achieved both independence and greater self-reliance. Today also, while the major Powers grappled in life-death struggle, Latin Americans moved toward greater economic freedom. They have polished their shields with greater pride in local achievements, greater faith in their own capacities and futures. The countries south are definitely, if painfully, emerging from colonialism.

The same spirit is abroad, be it in backward, tyrannized Nicaragua or in great, civilized Argentina. "Nicaragua for the Nicaraguans!" "Argentina for Argentineans!" "Latin America for Latin Americans!" These are living, fighting slogans.

The Four Freedoms, to many North Americans mere wartime propaganda to be forgotten afterward as soon as possible, moved the hearts and minds of the southlands deeply and still do. Denied most of those freedoms, the Latin American people found them revolutionary doctrines. Already dictators have been driven out by outraged peoples, personal freedoms have broadened, and now fuller national freedom on the basis of wider industry and prosperity is everywhere a goal and a hope.

It is a seesaw battle, gains made, gains lost, but a new Latin America is in the making.

Problems and difficulties are great, often staggering. The economic disaster of the world, lack of machinery and capital, the swift postwar curtailment of United States aid, inability even to obtain needed materials, do not smooth the road. On top of this, the clash of conflicting interests, classes, ideas—these twist progress out of a straight line. Many struggles loom ahead. Many setbacks are to be expected. Free government is built up one place and perishes another. At the moment there is in fact a real danger that the fight against Communism now being staged will not promote democracy but will serve dictatorial and fascist forces to resort to reaction, militarism, dictatorship and a destruction of democracy and human rights. Many countries, especially dictatorial lands, will be hit by serious revolutions before they join the general progress of the continent.

Communism, socialism, fascism, democracy, capitalism in its various phases, collectivism—these, plus old-time feudalism and militarism, are making Latin America, as the rest of the world, a most unreasonable battleground. As elsewhere a race is on between the forces of growth and freedom and the forces of disaster, and perhaps not all the countries south are able yet to meet any such challenge.

But in spite of all, Latin America is awakening. It is on the march: its people, its industries, its governments, its culture. It is no exaggeration to say that these twenty years have witnessed in the lands south the most tremendous revolutionary change, in methods of production, institutions, government, that has occurred in all the hundred years since Independence.

This is a dramatic hour in the life of our New World neighbors. The outcome of that growth and change will shape much of the world we are to live in tomorrow.

Tale of the Cities

Mirrors of Growth

Nothing has been quite so startling during the last ten years as the rapid growth of Latin American cities. Spared the ravages of war, all the countries, now bulging with new wealth and energy, have been hit by large population shifts and urbanization. Major centers have been rapidly transformed from placid colonial communities into great rushing metropolises. In city planning, design, comfort and architecture, some take the lead over nearly all places in the world.

Most southern communities are older than any United States city, having been founded well before the middle of the sixteenth century. They were a product of the amazing burst of human energy that swept out of Spain with the Counter Reformation to subdue a continent and a half and which, in a few decades, threw up hundreds of new cities and tens of thousands of churches.

Thanks to wise Spanish city planning, with its great spiritual and moral idealism, its welding of practical, aesthetic and soul-aspiring human needs, plus also the still earlier planning of the Incas and Aztecs in such places as Cuzco and Mexico, the Hispano-American cities have always been among the most handsome in the world.

But well into this century, whatever their size, most were still semi-rural places, living on past glories rather than moving ahead in the central stream of progress. Cows, chickens, goats often rustled around within stone's throw of the main plaza. But more than a decade ago, Mexico City, for sanitary reasons, banned all horse-drawn vehicles.

By 1910 Latin America began to have major trunk-line rail systems, and new urban growth steadily gathered headway. Momentum increased with autos and roads. Now the airplane has swept even the most isolated localities into its net. Brazil has actually constructed a handsome brand-new jungle city, the new capital of Goiaz Province, with no rail or road connections, only air services.

24

Really big expansion has come with the war and since the war. The oldest New World cities now often wear the garb of the newest cities of the globe. Not all changes have been happy. Sentiment makes one regret much that is falling by the wayside. But "the revolution of the cities" is in full swing.

Before the war Guatemala City, except for one de luxe hotel, was a bedraggled little hole. Today it is a busy, sparkling community of paved streets, handsomely landscaped boulevards, fine new buildings, attractive residential districts—all kept so clean you hesitate even to toss your cigarette butt into the gutter. New public health and dental clinics have been set up and one of the finest large modern hospitals in the Americas is rising.

Before the war lofty La Paz, capital of Bolivia, was a filthy if super-picturesque cobbled mountain town, sans sewers. It is now the butterfly of the high Andes. In a few short years it has spread showy wings against the snow peaks as one of the most beautiful modernized cities of the two continents. A new skyscraper university may not spell beauty, but through the main draw of the deep canyon where the city nestles a boiling Andean river has been channeled and covered over for a broad central boulevard. New garden avenues in more open meadows below have been laid out with attractive modern office buildings, apartment houses and fine homes.

The older, hill-twisting alleys still teem with Aimará and Quechua venders of handicrafts, herbs, primitive charms, flaming textiles—a busy jovial folk in bright costumes. The short Aimará women wear white stovepipe hats, some nearly two feet high, at every jaunty angle. That native part of La Paz is comparable only to some buzzing North African bazaars in congestion, poverty and flaming colors. Here the old and the new still elbow each other in startling contrast.

The city, set in that deep slot in the upland plateau, beneath the grandest snow-clad mountain giants on earth, always has had the most gorgeous setting of any city on the continent. Now it is spreading out, climbing up and down, to become ultramodern and supersplendid.

Lima, Peru, these past ten years, has stretched out gracefully clear to distant bathing beaches. Callao and Lima, with broad handsome connecting avenues, have merged into one city of green bowers and palaces. In the other direction, building has pushed right up against the Andean sand hills, soon to be utilized as additional municipal gardens. It has become one of the most charming, livable cities of South

America. The Popular Party has elaborated plans for even greater amplification and beautification. All one evening Haya de la Torre told us in detail of the program to make Lima the best-organized as well as the most superb city of the Americas.

The extraordinary growth has produced a startling change in the population. Lima was originally a conquest barracks city, then the center of colonial rule, cultured and luxurious, but always, even in the days of the Republic, ruthlessly ruling the rest of the country. Even after Independence it remained predominately a "White" European city in structure and outlook, with little sympathy for the rest of the land. Today with new roads and air services threading the interior, even beyond the Andes to Amazon headwaters, the gates have opened wide for back-country folk to come to Lima easily.

Formerly, to visit the capital of his own country, the citizen of Iquitos on the Amazon had to muleback six weeks through frightful jungles, or spend months going down the Amazon, then around Cape Horn or through the Panama Canal. It was much easier to go to Europe. That situation persisted as late as 1940. Now folk from Iquitos can get to Lima by river boat and highway in three days or by air in a few hours. As a result, Lima's population is no longer an island of Europeans and White Creoles, but represents a racial cross-section of the whole country. Like Mexico City it has rapidly developed into a mestizo, or as they say in Peru, a cholo city. Hence it has become an agency, not for selfish rule, but for the new unification and development of the whole country. It is really part of the country now in a way it never was even twenty years ago. It is a mirror of the new, more democratic, more industrialized Peru in the making.

The list of new or made-over metropolises in South America is astonishing. There is the beautiful well-planned growth of Bogotá, of Medellín, Cartagena, Barranquilla and other Colombian centers in a land today developing as fast, or faster, than any other New World country. Caracas is going through a great revamping that seems more bizarre than graceful. The stately if steadier growth of Santiago, Chile, has produced fine new parks and boulevards, its impressive gray-granite skyscraper Civic Center, its miles of new workers' housing. Concepción, Chile, mostly rebuilt after the 1938 earthquake, stretches along its magnificent rivers with modern architecture, and a whole new white university city gleams against the evergreen hills. Even remote Asunción in Paraguay has been shaken out of centuries of primitive isolation. Before the war it did not even have a sewer or modern water system, a hospital, paved streets. The United States poured a lot of money into Paraguay to start some of these services. The rich injection of dollars, democratic propaganda, Lend-Lease, the extravagant spending of a big corps of North American bureaucrats, threw the whole political and economic balance out. One product was the recent bloody civil war. But, as cities go, Asunción has greatly changed and expanded.

Montevideo has pushed out on all sides. For one thing, Uruguay has had to make room for the quarter of a million rich Argentine tourists who make the city their playground every year. It has built low-cost housing for its humbler citizens.

Rosario in Argentina has burst like a flower on the pampas into a city of nearly a million inhabitants.

The major growth and planning of Buenos Aires started much earlier than in most cities of the continent, and "the Paris of America" went through a major civic revamping long before the war. But during the war and since, if its development has been less spectacular—building materials have been scarcer than in even some smaller countries—the city has grown tremendously with new apartment houses, de luxe hotels, industries, workers' housing. A wildcat boom was nipped when the government decreed no old buildings could be torn down unless tenants were provided with quarters similar in price and quality. The beautification of this handsome city has gone on steadily and, compared with a few years back, seems even startling.

One local Buenos Aires daily, giving a résumé of the nation's wartime industrial boom, "unequaled in all Argentina's history," said in its January 1, 1943, issue: "An extensive indication of prosperity is the increase of de luxe buildings of all kinds; without exaggeration one may say that nowhere in the world such luxurious apartment houses and retail stores are being built as in Buenos Aires."

Probably today, next to large North American cities, no other city in the world can match Buenos Aires' fine new building equipment, its fashionable mercantile establishments, its broad new avenues. With its busy but easy life, it is one of the most graceful, splendid cities the world over, much like Paris in the heyday of its love of culture and pleasure. The broad tree-shaded Ramblas, even in the business heart of the city, are like those of Barcelona, Spain. Its ever-crowded sidewalk cafés are like those of Paris and Rome of yesteryear. Nearly all its restaurants have the tingle of real epicurean food. The window displays on fashionable Calle Florida surpass those of Fifth Avenue in up-to-the-minute artistry. For blocks on end Lavalle Street is solid with de luxe movie houses where one may see the latest Hollywood production as soon as Broadway. Since monopoly has not narrowed down the cultural horizon, one may also see, any night of the year, the movies of Argentina, Chile, Mexico, France and England.

It is a city reconditioned for the modern era; with an intricate far-flung system of comfortable subways. Its famous Ninth of July Avenue, widest in the world, a sixteen-lane boulevard with a show of gardens and trees, cuts through the center of the city. Enormous underground parking lots take care of rush traffic. The harbor facilities not only do not mar the beauty of the city, they are among the most modern in the world and make those of New York look like an old junk heap. There are few slums, for Buenos Aires pioneered as early as 1910 with low-cost public housing, some of the finest and most attractive anywhere. Beautiful open parks spread through all sections of the city.

The growth of Brazilian cities, with that country's rapid wartime industrial expansion, has been the most amazing on the whole continent.

Since 1920 São Paulo's population has more than doubled, is moving up to the two-million mark, promising soon to surpass that of Rio.

The city has a more zestful climate than warm Rio. At times it is blustering cold. It is set on a green plateau, flanked by purple mountains, and is reaching out on all sides. Skyscraper hotels, office buildings and apartment houses, fine movies and theaters, factories, workers' homes are rising everywhere. Whole blocks rattle down for new avenues and plazas. Factories now stretch along the railway clear to the great coffee port of Santos the other side of the mountains. In the state of São Paulo today is half the country's industrial production. It has become the greatest industrial center south of the United States and is matched in few other continents.

This is not just war boom. It is solid growth based on the rise of new industrial power, and São Paulo, the beautiful, is its capital. It has much the massive drive Chicago once displayed and much of the same initial ugliness. But the later phase of São Paulo's growth has been conditioned by better planning, with wide parkways, flying overhead viaducts, double-tunnel tubes, all with more determined respect for spaciousness, grace and beauty, with more concern for recreation, social welfare and the good life of its citizens.

One outstanding Brazilian development has been the entirely new capital, Goiãnia, of the rich mining state of Goiaz. This city was planted right in virgin jungle where only a few primitive naked Indians lived. There, flanked by deep wooded ravines, has been constructed a modern comfortable metropolis. From the spacious civic plaza, flanked with parks, lakes, stately public buildings and the Grand Executive Palace, seven tree-lined diagonal avenues sweep out to intersections with various landscaped boulevards that encircle the whole city. It is a hub-spoke-rim, spoke-rim, spoke-rim city, French style. From rich to poor, today the dwellers of Goiãnia—there in the remote jungle—are among the best-housed folk of any city.

The chain of beautiful Latin American metropolises, from Mexico and Havana, clear to charming Valdivia in Chile, is set with many jewels.

Let us look more closely at three typical centers: one outstanding for its modern architecture; another, lost in the folds of the Andes, which is still little changed by converging modern forces, but which even now, as in the past, is a symbol of continental unity; and finally one of the fastest growing cities in the New World, teeming with a million new dwellers, driving ahead with dizzy speed to keep up with national growth.

Rio: the Beautiful

The Federal District, in which Rio, the capital of Brazil, is set, has nearly four thousand species of butterflies. As you walk along the promenades in the parks and beside the sea, on the pavements beneath your feet you will see some of those exquisite tropical wings copied in marble mosaics. And along fashionable Rua Ouvidor you will see more butterflies in jewelers' windows—patterned in gold and platinum and fretted silver, outlined in precious stones set in gleaming enamel.

Rio itself is a jeweled city, set in the prongs of a hundred forested hills, bordered by an emerald and sapphire sea—a glistening city of gold and green and white, with bands of flaming flowers and vivid fruits, a place where even stone and steel and concrete seem to turn into precious metal and grow fluid and radiant.

It is the glowing capital of the only important independent tropical civilization on earth, the fourth largest country of the world, larger than the main continental United States. In spite of all its achievements, it has scarcely begun yet to use its vast resources. Exciting future possibilities unfold on every hand.

Rio, an expression of the more modern Brazil, is a city of fervent but leisurely and friendly people, who are proud of the beauty that is Rio. Its life seems focused, not on the miles of piers, tucked out of sight so skillfully that four thousand ships a year slip in and out almost unnoticed; not on its magnificent modern business skyscrapers, hotels and apartments facing the sea—"one may wallow in luxury in Rio"—but on the parks, along the high panorama boulevards, on the sidewalk cafés, on the bright umbrella-dotted beaches—eight miles of gleaming white sand—on the vegetable and flower markets: the *feira livre*, they are called. What other port on earth has so splendidly utilized and beautified the unusual natural beauty with which it is endowed?

The city's name is "River of January"—so the early Portuguese discoverer called the vast purple harbor—but it is known as the "Play City of the New World." It is a city that lives outdoors in eternal warm spring, at sport and boating and fishing clubs; a city which grows excited and bets wildly over horse racing and polo matches, basket and volleyball, golf and tennis, swimming and yachting. Only in Chile and Mexico are people more sports-minded.

The Rioenses love outdoor concerts too. They jam the great opera house. There, long ago, Toscanini, at the age of nineteen, conducted his first symphony. It is an eager city that rushes to the National Art Museum or into the latest exhibit, perhaps to see Candido Portinari's most recent painting of São Paulo coffee pickers. It is the center, next to Buenos Aires, of the greatest literary life on the American continents, the capital of a country that has already produced one of the world's most remarkable literatures and some of the great books of all time.

Rio folk, too poor for some of these diversions, crowd the flamboyant movie palaces, or they make their own music and dance the vigorous *samba* or the *macumba* in dozens of street festivals that swirl, brightly costumed, about the churches set on every hill and in all the hollows that only a few years back were open valleys of sugar cane and flowering orchards. Now they swarm with tinted flat-roofed dwellings set among palms and bananas and scarlet bougainvillaea and purple orchids.

First, Rio must be seen as a whole, in all its majestic beauty and power—perhaps from the Corcovado (Hunchback) or from Sugar Loaf or from the Hill of Glory, or any one of a dozen eminences.

Pitch your tent on lofty Hunchback, with its great white statue of the Saviour two thousand feet up. At daybreak white mist rolls from the forest, and the sun rises gold and rose in the northeast. At sunset gold glows on tinted wall and the harbor, which turns slowly to deep purple, then to ink. At night the lights ripple along the beach promenades clear to Copacabana and along the great Avenida Branco, and in and out among the hills, like festoons of chile peppers, on the glistening sands, in the suburbs, ten miles across the water.

From Hunchback you may easily see the 365 jungle-clad mountains rising on every side: the Five Fingers of God towering up from the lofty Organo range, hard by to the west. Pão de Assucar—Sugar Loaf Hill—at the inner harbor entrance, also provides breath-taking vistas of sea, city and mountain. It is reached by cables swung high above the mighty forest and the water.

Few ports can in any way be compared with Rio: perhaps San Francisco, Valparaiso, Naples, Algiers. But in none does Nature provide quite such a majestic setting, such vivid contrasts, and no other port city has made such artistic and enjoyable use of what Nature has provided.

Here the centuries jostle, old and new. Do not search for the buildings on the tall hill where the Portuguese planted their first fort and settlement in 1555. That whole height has been sluiced down into the sea to make the Santos Dumont super-airport. But the old palaces of emperor and viceroy and noble dot the city—Itarnarati, now the office of Foreign Relations; Guanabara, former home of Princess Isabela, now of Brazilian Presidents. And in Praça Quinze de Novembro, once the center of colonial Rio, still stands the tall obelisk fountain of Emperor Dom João VI, where Negro slaves used to tote water on their heads, where the sailors of all nations still lounge before what was once the palace of early government, then the haunt of grandees in velvet breeches, lace sleeves, gold braid and bejeweled swords. Here, now, is the wholesale market, piled high with silver fish, squawking poultry, golden heaps of papayas, bananas and pineapples. Around about are cubbyhole restaurants, each with its special sea delicacy, but the coffee of Brazil is the same in each—steaming, ink-black, fragrant.

The line of poorer cafés finally ends in the Mangue (Mud) district of the Ruas Carno Neto and Abilea Cavalcantu, with gleaming female eyes peering out with sordid invitations from between horizontal bars.

Like every other great city, in spite of its great sunburst of super-modernistic architecture, Rio still has plenty of ugly slums—its *favellas*—its low dives and hangouts for thieves and ruffians—*jaguncos*. And yet, with so much sun, with yellow fruit hanging from every branch, those tawdry districts seem gayer, less oppressive than in gloomier climates. Gradually they are being replaced by new sanitary centers.

The new expanding Rio displays more architectural experimentation and originality than perhaps any other city in the world. In this respect, Rio, like some other Latin American cities, goes far in advance of anything attempted in the United States for a long time. The unusual angles and planes of glass, the flying, soaring concrete, the daring adaptations to tropical sunlight—many such startling and often beautiful innovations are purely Brazilian ingenuity.

What is more magnificent than the exciting modern skyscraper architecture that has made Dos Nacões Avenue one of the most beautiful and inspiring thoroughfares in the world? Take one look at it and you will realize why visiting Brazilians are nearly always disappointed with the drabness and lack of originality of cities in the United States. The eighteen-story educational building, set in the air on great reinforced concrete pillars, is like a sandwich between two tall slices of almost solid glass. Its interior walls have been enriched with frescoes by Brazil's leading modern painter, Candido Portinari.

Above all, few cities have achieved such healthful, comfortable and dignified community living. Few cities are so wholeheartedly dedicated to beauty and culture or are so sensitive to fresh ideas from all the world—a trait that more powerful nations, with their strength, smugness and feelings of superiority, seem to be losing. In few other cities do music and dancing play such an integrated part in daily living. The people of Rio really enjoy themselves. At the same time, in a way not known even ten years ago, the new power of this metropolis is driving ahead into the modern life of a great expanding nation.

Cuzco: City of Condors

In the brief twilight along a narrow curving street, cut a thousand years ago from the flank of the "Copper Mountains," sandaled feet whisk along the flagstones. Whiffs of roasting lamb fat float out on the thin crisp air. Small herds of llamas and alpacas, bedecked with blue and red tassels and tiny copper bells, tinkle past—golden-brown, black, or snow-white—with quick mincing steps (almost like chic girls wearing French heels), their heads proudly arched. Above, in colorful carved balconies, brown women lean ample bosoms against overhanging balustrades in soft pliable patience, with an aura of eternal expectation. It is the hour of repose between daytime tasks and nighttime freedom.

The dark drops swiftly in this upland Andean world, and the soft musical lilt of the Quechua tongue drifts out from ancient stone doorways, from little candlelit shops scooped out of masonry laid up perhaps when England was still only a land of warring tribes. The gentle voices and quiet laughter float out with flower petals from inner patios of fragrant vines and trees growing against the hodgepodge of nearly two thousand years of building on building. Quechua was probably spoken hereabouts when the first stone was tooled and fitted; it is still the living language of millions of people in half a dozen countries all along the great valleys and plateaus of the Andes. It is the speech of handsome folk whose big chests have a lung capacity twenty-five per cent greater than that of other mortals—a biological adaptation to the high altitudes that must have gone on for at least fifteen or twenty thousand years.

Lofty Cuzco, the magnificent capital of the mighty Inca Empire, was the last glory of this people, for after the Spanish Conquest the Quechuas—"the Spring Valley folk"—fell on evil days. Many of their palaces and temples, fine roads and irrigation systems hewn out of living stone, their endless tiers of stone-faced farming terraces, fell into ruin or were wantonly destroyed.

Even four centuries of subjugation have been but a splinter of time in the historical cycle of this strongly rooted race, and their beautiful city atop the Andes still glows with color and artistry. It is still the pride of the folk, "the golden dream," the living capital, now, of a more invisible empire. Because most Cuzco citizens still talk Quechua, travelers from jungle recesses, from the great Marañón gateway to the Amazon, from the frozen heights of Ecuador and Bolivia, feel at home here, and come, often on foot, a thousand miles or more across the mightiest ravines of earth to visit the great fairs, the splendid religious fiestas of bright costumes, waving plumes and wailing music—or merely to pat the sacred earth of the great square. . . .

Cuzco—"the eternal city of a hundred births and deaths and soul transmigrations," "the Rome of South America," with similar grandeur, antiquity and continuity—was once the center of an empire whose land area was greater than Rome's, an area more difficult to traverse, organize and rule.

The Inca roads or trails—often bored through solid rock, cut out of living precipices, passing over great suspension bridges thousands of feet above swirling torrents—represented more colossal energy and ingenuity than the famous Roman roads.

Cuzco was the center of all this effort, the center of an empire with "civic rights," moral precepts and concern for general welfare far superior to ancient Rome. Here was a people that knew much of law and real justice, who used gold and silver not for greed but to decorate their temples, to make jewelry, for public statues, for the great gold chain annually sunk in Lake Titicaca as a tribute to the life-giving Sun, for the gold plow symbolically used by the Emperor in person to start each season's turning of the furrows.

No man dare say just when the megalithic stones of some of Cuzco's construction and of the huge zigzag north wall of Sacsahuamán (the fortress acropolis perched above the city) were quarried and trundled into place. There is some doubt whether even the later Quechua and Aimará dwellers in Cuzco and in great Tiahuanaco in Bolivia knew who had thrown up the first great walls. At Sacsahuamán huge stone blocks, some weighing a hundred and fifty tons, some 38x18x6 feet (as measured by Spanish chronicler José de Acosta), were tailored each to each meticulously with intricate angles, often as snugly as a modern automobile cylinder. How many centuries even before those walls were erected was the flower-decked valley below settled?

But apparently anywhere from eight hundred to fifteen hundred years ago the first Inca—Manco Capac, the original "Son of the Sun"—appeared, clad in shining armor like a being from heaven at the door of a cave in a hill just east of the present city, and there sank his golden staff of authority into good productive soil. With his sister-wife, Mama Ocllo, he founded a long dynasty that lasted more centuries than Rome and still claims descendants.

The form and proportions of the city came to match the full majesty of growing empire. The huge central Weeping Square, to this day one of the largest in South America, was laid out with pomp, the earth for it supplied from the "Four Quarters" of the empire in repeated acts of civic splendor and obedience, a never-ending corner-stone laying. Four broad avenues led out toward the Four Quarters—to the coast; to the eastern jungles; to Bolivia, Argentina and Chile; to Ecuador and Colombia—and these four avenues still rule the city. Each street had its wayside shrines. Spanish Vice-Regal Adviser Polo de Ondegardo counted three hundred twenty of them. Around the square and along those avenues rose not only the rounded apse of the Temple of the Sun, its inner walls sheathed with gold and silver, but the various government buildings—the gymnasium, the archive rooms of knotted chords (which recorded the detailed statistics of the empire, "down to the last pair of sandals"), the University City or "Teachers House," schools founded by one of the first Incas; the House of Holy Sun Virgins, the *Ñustas*, chosen as the most beautiful girls from all parts of the empire—an early version of Miss America rites but considerably more sacred.

The mighty hill fort, Sacsahuamán, was constructed even more impressively, with commanding towers. In the long peace of the empire it served as an arsenal, training school and parade grounds. There the Inca and his nobles, provided with large carved stone seats on an adjacent hill, reviewed troops in colorful civic fiestas. Sacsahuamán became the Incan West Point.

The Spaniards merely grafted onto that part of the old Inca city they did not destroy. In some palaces gold dust had been used in the mortar. These, of course, the conquerors tore apart with the fury of madmen. The Cassana, or big gymnasium, and the Viracocha temple were tumbled down to get stones for the cathedral, which after about a century rose as the richest, most impressive religious edifice in the Americas, a place of golden treasure, of art and beauty, of eternal mysticism in the soft twilight and incense under its soaring dark green pillars.

The House of Holy Virgins became the House of the Brides of Christ, the Santa Catalina convent—as inaccessible to the modern traveler as the Inca convent had been to the layman of the old days.

The Sun Temple, Coricancha, with its subordinate shrines of the Silver Moon, Red Lightning, Dark Thunder, Golden Stars, now wears Christian cross and saints in the superimposed church and monastery of Santo Domingo, one of the finest Spanish constructions in all America. Airy balconies and columns embrace the inner flower-and-fountain patio circled with unusually fine frescoes.

Part of the present-day beauty of Cuzco is due to the mingling of the two cultures and talents. After the Conquest, the limber, inlaid blades from far-off Toledo and the clanking armor of Don Quixote flashed with the flaming Inca tunics—right in the Plaza of the Sun. The permanent hangman's scaffold, stuck up in the Weeping Square, was also a complete innovation. But little by little both peoples combined to initiate a new era in the city's long history. Thereafter horse and ass, later cattle and sheep, jostled with llama and alpaca. But even the horse was never one third as fleet as the flying *chasquis*, the trained relay messengers of the Emperor, who brought fresh fish up from the coast in two days, who dashed day and night over the ridge roads, the snow roads, the deep ravine roads, fifteen hundred miles north to Ecuador in less than a week. According to chronicler Garcilaso, "neither storms nor anything whatsoever held up the Royal mail service even in the wildest stretches."

The later Spanish edifices, though born of the universality of Spanish spirit and the crusading flavor of the Counter Reformation, were subtly reshaped and decorated, infused throughout also by native spirit and artistry—so that all are indistinguishably Cuzco temples. They could have been built nowhere else on earth.

Except for a few more substantial Spanish constructions, lighter stones, bricks and adobes were tacked right onto the massive old walls, giving the solemn imperial city a note in places almost of frippery, just as the Spaniards also brought in, among more solid and astute traits, loquacity, airy recklessness, laughter and adventure. By all accounts Quechua humor, then as now, leaned on the droll, dry side, and their etiquette was often more patterned and formal. And so both Spanish architecture and character rested on solid Incan foundations. All the new slanting tile roofs with their two-foot eaves lie over casements cut through Inca stones. Often a wooden balcony, gaily carved and painted, juts out from a massive Inca wall, like a dangling gilt bird cage.

The conquerors narrowed down several of the wide Cuzco avenues, just as they narrowed down the achievements and opportunities of the Quechuas; and modern Peru is now put to the expense of restoring those thoroughfares to their original Inca width to make room for modern traffic, just as it is also put to the expense of restoring the isolated persistent native folk to a functional place in the modern society of the nation.

From those central avenues the same Inca hill-climbing streets and open terraces and alleys still spread about. Some lanes are so narrow you can touch either house wall. One twilight we leaped frantically into an open doorway to escape a herd of bellowing steers rushing pell-mell single file down a street so tight their broad horns scraped splinters from the doorways on either side.

And so today the pattern of the old city and Quechua culture still lies athwart all the Spanish growths above the stone of empire. Behind doors framed with massive Inca stones, today are grocery stores, barbershops, a poolroom, the dwellings of the poor and many not so poor. An Inca aqueduct is in use after a thousand years. The city was never wholly dominated, never entirely beaten down by the sword of destruction, still stands as a symbol of the rebirth into modern ways of many of the pre-Spanish peoples.

Today, facing the secondary plaza, the "Joy Terrace," laid out by the Incas a step away from their main "Weeping Terrace," rises the brand new Hotel Cuzco, a luxury establishment, but built inside and out in harmony with the architecture of earlier edifices. Now the newly paved south Avenue of the Incas runs out to railroad station and airfield.

Cuzco still lies at the very core of South America—physically and in many spiritual ways. Old traditions remain strong. Elements in the Tucumán Independence Congress early last century wanted to set up all Argentina, plus the highland area, as a hereditary monarchy under a descendent of the Inca dynasty—this after three hundred years of Spanish rule, of executions and attempted cultural eradication. Had this happened the whole course of South America would have been radically different. Present Peruvian school texts hail martyred Inca Tupac Amaru as the first independence patriot: "the colossus of the American revolution." The Inca sun still blazes forth on the shield and national flag of modern Peru. Peruvian officers are required to learn Quechua, and an annual Sun ceremony is celebrated by the armed forces.

Cuzco thus still conserves much of its power, a great message for modern times. Scarcely a contemporary writer, rhapsodizing on this "wonder city of the Americas," does not aver that it will recover its onetime greatness; that Cuzco and the Andean people will return to freedom and importance and help shape the destinies of the southern world. "Someday," writes J. Uriel García, "we will reconstruct Cuzco as the capital of the Empire. It is the hope of all America."

Maybe this is unadulterated romanticism, but the hope is one of basic Americanism—respect for all submerged races and classes, the creation of a world where they can really function and contribute their remarkable talents.

Certainly today the reactivation of the Inca world is part and parcel of the program of Peru's great Popular Party, the Apra, the majority party led by Haya de la Torre. Apra constantly preaches adoption of the term "Indo-América" to replace conventional dry "Latin America" with its stale implications of Spanish Conquest and disregard for the cultural heritage of ten million New World people who speak no Latin tongue, only pre-Spanish tongues; of those many more millions who are bilingual; and of the overwhelming majority of the continent made up of mestizos, men of mixed blood. All this is part of the new march of the submerged folk of the southlands, the revindication of all the races and all the cultures of the Americas, and the free participation of all as free men in the life of tomorrow.

Furthermore, Cuzco is once more becoming a key highland center as modern roads and air services create a new economic unity of South America, a unity unknown except partially in Incan times. Cuzco Valley gains fresh importance as the rich inner foothill region of the Andes once more comes into use and grows more significant with the discovery of oil and uranium deposits.

Cuzco, the "oldest" corner of the New World, is the only place in the Americas where the life of every age still lives on side by side—from paleolithic cave painting in the shadows of Sacsahuamán to the meadow-moving shadow of the latest fifty-passenger plane dropping down into its big modern airport. All past eras are not only recorded, they still flourish in the culture of contemporary men. In its great walls Cuzco holds the spiritual treasure of a hundred vivid epochs—a city "crowned a thousand times." Every stone "palpitates" with tradition, writes a Peruvian, "and all are alive in some way or other."

The Sun City of the Andes, the so-called "City of Condors," holds the clue to much of the resurrection of the continent and its races and cultures, to all the bolder freedoms of tomorrow—quite as much as do the driving pistons of mechanical progress.

Mexico City: City of the Eagles

The war transformed Mexico City. Much of the old-time sleepy "City of Palaces," the city of colonial towers and blue-and-gold cupolas, has been all but obliterated—not by bombs but by feverish progress. The ancient rose-colored palaces of volcanic *tezontle* stone with their carved white sandstone trimming, are now overshadowed by tall, severely modernistic buildings of reinforced concrete, much horizontal glass, much black marble. Even a new broad avenue has been cut through old adobe and brick right into the great central square, the Zócalo, where once stood Aztec temples and palaces, where now stand the massive colonial cathedral, the beautiful red-stone Sagraro, the National and Municipal Palaces and other gems of architecture, with handsome sidewalk arcades—mostly early Spanish.

For the new twentieth-century Mexico, the filthy, primitive but picturesque market area behind the square is earmarked for prompt demolition. Everywhere the sky line is being reshaped by swank banks and business offices, factories, fine hotels, movie palaces, luxurious tall apartment houses. The new "Monument to the Revolution," though so recently finished, is already dwarfed by big insurance and bank buildings.

The block busting has been going on at a dizzy pace. At every step old brick walls rattle down in clouds of dust. Sidewalks everywhere are blocked with scaffolding. Whole blocks have been ripped out, new avenues slashed through. Now and then one of these modern park-adorned boulevards divides in a flow of busy two-way traffic around some survival of Churriguerresque art, which not even the vandalism of progress wishes to destroy. Steam shovels dip deep into filled-in lake bottom on which Mexico City, with the name Tenochtitlán, was originally founded in 1325 (or earlier) and often bring up artifacts of civilizations even more ancient than the Aztec. Cranes lift steel girders story on story toward the sky.

Mexico, with its more than two million inhabitants, has become a rushing torrent of humanity, one of the great populous cities of the world. It is the second city of Latin America, the fourth city of all the Americas.

But to those knowing the older, more delightful Mexico City, recent changes, all the clang and bang, bring regrets and at moments disgust at this new crass commercialism, the graft and greed now visible at every turn, traits previously subordinated to courtesy, generosity and friendliness. Yet when the trend is over and the great boom bursts, as booms always do, Mexico City, thanks to this belated "Robber Baron" era, this rise to power of the new "Millionaire Socialists" of the Revolution, will have become one of the greatest, most beautiful, modern cities of the New World.

Mexicans, who love satirical jokes, have revamped an old story for the new era. Peering up at a skyscraper, a tourist, who had been loudly boasting how rapidly things were done in the United States, asked a taxi driver, "When did they put that up?"

"I don't know, Señor. When I drove past here this morning there was only a vacant lot."

The modern growth of Mexico City began with the 1910 Revolution when the countryside became unsafe and people sought refuge in cities, when land was being expropriated for the peasants and rural investments became risky. But urban expansion reached its present dizzy pace during the late war.

Escape capital from Europe, Asia and the United States has flowed in. Enormous amounts of Mexican capital, driven abroad during the more violent revolutionary period, returned to the now safer Mexican homeland. Immigrants from abroad, refugees from the terrors of Franco Spain, of Nazism, Communism, war, have brought not only their funds but their skills.

American Lend-Lease, United States gold and silver purchasing at inflated prices, expanded wartime demand for minerals and materials. This plus war loans, the presence of thousands of wartime American experts in the country, probably piled much more than a billion dollars into Mexico. Still another billion of private United States capital has come in to participate in starting new basic industries.

Tourists, unable to visit Europe or Asia, crowded in. Right after the war, this movement became a torrent almost too great to handle. Overnight, modern hotels have soared toward the clouds. The tourist business has become Mexico's second largest industry and, in return for sunshine, curios and services, earns nearly half a billion pesos annually.

Thus for some years, the Mexican capital has received more of everything than could be digested well—although the appetite and results have been prodigious. Whenever the highland Mexican stirs from the coma of his lower body pressure, he is never a halfway soul.

The radical alteration of the city is also the product of prior municipal planning. Thus, fortunately, the sudden stupendous expansion of the city has been well-guided toward a master plan of beautification, functional utility, social welfare and livability often far superior to similar, earlier developments in the United States.

Yet even this supermodern planning has been basically conditioned—except where new areas have been invaded—by the early city planning of the Aztecs, who drove the first piles into the marshes hereabouts more than six centuries ago. Early Tenochtitlán was founded in accordance

with the command of War God Mexitli at a spot where the migrating
Mexicans (People of the War God) would come upon a cactus-perched
eagle with a serpent in his beak. This is the modern emblem of Mexico
(Place of the War God) depicted on the national shield and in the
center of the Mexican flag.

Mexitli means Navel of the Maguey, the heart of the plant that for
Aztec Mexico and modern Mexico has been all-important for life and
joy. It provides the milky pulque or native beer served at green tables
in wall-frescoed shops. Its fibers served for cordage and thread; its
parchment for paper; its thorns for needles and for blood-letting pen-
nance; its honey-water sap for vitamins and medicines. No male, it is
claimed, who drinks *aguamiel,* the maguey sap, will ever suffer from
prostate trouble; and today it is canned and dealt out by prescription in
United States drugstores. Maguey leaves spread out like a huge green
fleshy rosebud. The sap flows from the cut-off central stem like the
eternal fountain of youth. In ancient days fields were laid out in mystic
blocks of eight, with much recondite numerology and consultation with
the gods. Maguey fields have always been part of the highland contour
of Mexico—as much as the sharp volcanic cones, the pyramids, the
peaked sombrero. They circle the present highland metropolis.

The Zócalo in this city is the same large quadrangle where once stood
the magnificent carved-snake wall and pyramid temple to Mexitli and to
the God of Rain, Tlaloc, along with some forty other shrines, and the
enormous Palace of Montezuma. The stones of these Aztec structures
were subsequently utilized to build the rose-colored colonial government
building, now the National Palace, and other notable sixteenth-century
edifices still standing. The only direct evidence of prior Aztec occu-
pancy that now survives is found in commemorating frescoes and
statues in the public buildings, in the big stone coils of feathered snakes
that lie on a lower level near the cathedral, and in the massive stone
gods and the superb Calendar Stone in the National Museum of the
Palace.

The Aztec City was a Venice, with canals for streets, but from this
square four great avenues rayed out—causeways filled in solid with earth
and masonry. The south causeway, over which the Spaniards first rode
in to greet Emperor Montezuma and his nobles, was so wide eight horsemen could ride abreast. It came in near Ixtapalapa, now an integral part
of the newer city, at the foot of the Hill of the Star where every fifty-
two years the Aztecs celebrated their impressive New Fire ceremony.

The early thoroughfare went past the royal botanical and zoological gardens and crossed a moat drawbridge under a ten-foot stone wall beside the massive Xoloc fortress, then led right to the main pyramid-temple on the site of which now stands the cathedral.

The Aztec capital, ampler and more splendid, according to Cortés and Bernal Díaz, than any city in Spain, is said to have had a population of two hundred thousand, and a public market bigger than that of Salamanca. After the Conquest it took several centuries for it to regain that number of inhabitants. It took several more centuries for it to creep up to the half-million mark. A major engineering feat was required to tunnel through the mountains to drain off the valley lakes and marshlands and make modern living possible. Then during the two decades of the wilder revolutionary epoch the city jumped to a million. Now, in a decade, it has topped two million and is still growing fast. When I was there early in 1946, countryfolk were coming into the new booming city in great caravans.

As a result, in less than a decade it has done more building than in all the previous six centuries or more of its existence. Towns formerly an hour's distance by interurban have been swallowed up by the tide of new construction. The city has flowed on beyond its former suburbs relentlessly. Corn and maguey fields have disappeared. Only a few years ago the government expropriated private estates around Ixtapalapa to give the villagers communal lands. Today the government has expropriated the village commons to provide for municipal expansion.

The wealthier sections that have sprung up rival the swankiest suburbs of American cities. The greater palaces are quite the peer—in good taste and bad taste—of those of our own *nouveaux riches* along the Florida gold coast. There on the Chapultepec Heights (Grasshopper Hill) near the former summer home of the Aztec Emperors and the beautiful castle started by Cortés and remodeled by Maximilian, now stands the colossal mansion of a former Minister of Agriculture—somewhat beyond the scale of living of the peasants he was supposedly aiding. There stands the private palace of the founder of the National Revolutionary Party. There stands the great feudal castle, like some miraculous Arabian Nights dream, of the brother of a late President, a man renowned for his reckless speculation, who in wartime won the sobriquet of "Lend-Lease millionaire." There rise the many palaces of the once uncouth generals of the Revolution who have now parked their pistols (temporarily or permanently?) in the lower drawers of mahogany desks as presidents of new industrial concerns. One gaudy residence is owned by a once ragged vendor of lottery tickets who hit on a pooling scheme and so became wealthy. Most of these various benefactors of the commonwealth have other palaces in the eternal flower-draped Spring of Cuernavaca, and in Acapulco, along Mexico's new sparkling Riviera, places that have expanded with almost the same dizzy pace as Mexico City. The showy owners of many of those showy palaces are "the Barons of the Revolution," "the Millionaire Socialists," who once rode the crest of earlier days out in the armed countryside and now ride the broncos of war—and postwar—speculation in the forward surge of industrial expansion. They are the new group running Mexican affairs with a curious combination of nationalism, socialism and rugged individualism. They are the moguls of Mexico's belated industrial revolution now getting under way, and the splendor of their achievement is this new wonder capital of the Americas.

Not all is of stone and steel and greed. The great new Plaza Hotel bears the latest frescoes of Diego Rivera, Mexico's most renowned painter. New books bubble off the presses.

Ballet dancing, concerts, symphonies, all sorts of musical entertainment are available. As of old, orchestra and band programs are given in public parks. In beautiful Chapultepec Park—on Sundays filled with elegant (and not so elegant) promenaders, slow-moving autos and horsemen tricked out in gold and silver cowboy costumes and huge blazing sombreros—the famous Charro Typical Orchestra plays under the tall old ahuehuetle trees that rival the California red groves in size and which were planted there by the Montezumas long before the Spaniards arrived four centuries ago. One cannot sit long in any balcony restaurant or bar before a street-wandering marimba or mariachi orchestra plays and passes the hat.

Both bull rings (most seats topping New York wartime theater prices) are sold out months in advance. The new super-ring in the brand new Sport City stands alongside a new super-stadium—the largest gathering places, according to local pride, in all Latin America, and you are sometimes told "in the whole world." Anyway, they wear long pants. A new million-dollar baseball park, with theater-cushioned seats to accommodate fifty thousand is being built, and the Mexican leagues now try to compete for crack American ballplayers. The great two-million-dollar Hippodrome is always jammed, and betting runs into millions. Grandstand reviews of *charros* are often staged.

Other sports are equally popular: soccer, polo, wrestling, prize fights, basketball, tennis, golf. The university has a football team that challenges smaller Southern colleges in the United States, an enterprise started and aided for many years by Arthur Constantine, veteran American news correspondent. A new combination court, dance hall, restaurant and cabaret has been built for that king of sports, *jai alai*, where the betting is as fast as the flash of the ball around the three walls. It is probably the world's hardest, fastest game, and American ideas will get a jolt when the professional players, who earn fancy salaries, toss down glasses of fiery tequila between games.

Formerly Mexican stores rang down their iron shutters by eight at night, and the business center then became a solid iron canyon, dismal, ill-lighted. Now a large proportion of the show windows are illuminated all night. Now the city, which except for a few hot spots used to roll up its sidewalks by ten o'clock, wears an aspect of all-night gaiety, of blazing light. The avenue fountains no longer spray up humbly in the light of clear starlit nights but glow with artificial colors that spread the far flame of perpetual gaudy carnival. Neon lights glow everywhere, sometimes even on the pulque shops of the poor.

Mexico has a unique and fascinating culture, more complex than anything this side the Orient; and even in this new era of factory building and city growth, the patterns being worked out, even when they imitate Hollywood or New York or Paris, are indistinguishably Mexican, different from anywhere else in the New World. The flamboyant new growth now is a symbol of rapid changes in the entire country.

What Price City?

Few great cities in the United States can quite match most new—or even old—Latin American cities in their beautification of harbor and river frontage, their use of hillsides and valleys for civic purposes. Modern Santiago de Chile with its handsome Forestal Park along the Mapocho River and its central hill garden of Santa Lucía, the whole provided with a backdrop of snow fire on the highest mountains of the whole Andean chain, is a city long to remember. It is also a city to live in and to enjoy.

On the other hand, for all the stressing of artistic, religious and cultural values—rather than unrestricted commercialism—which so features South American municipalities, one problem in that world for generations has been the overdevelopment of its cities in relation to the countryside. The all-absorbing cities usually drew off the resources and best talents of the rest of the country without properly promoting new enterprise in the interior. Relatively small portions of the public revenues were ever applied to outlying places and their needs. The cities, pumped up quite out of proportion to national income and the low standards of rural living, in spite of their beauty were long animated by the grasping spirit of the Spanish Conquest. They lived off the countryside rather than with the countryside. In good part they were parasitic, with much luxury and harshly contrasting slums, places for a small upper class to rule and enjoy, plunder and splurge in, with little regard for general welfare.

Today they have expanded more than ever, in many instances have grown more in a decade than in all their past histories. Is this mushroom growth, mostly so magnificently executed, merely a fever of abnormal wartimes, of speculation, a symbol of the new get-rich-quick class that springs from the blood and mud of all wars? Will it mean still greater overhead for countries lacking a sufficiently broad economic base? Or are the new cities real expression of greater and sounder national prosperity, of real industrial and social growth?

Opinions differ. Those gazing openmouthed at the colossal expansion of Mexico City have mixed emotions. Behind the marble and stone, some see only the speculation and graft, the bad inflation, the draining away of rural man power, and declare that the new Mexico City is merely a horrible cancer sapping the very lifeblood of the country and will bring more revolution, death and ruin. But others see in the new palaces of "the City of Palaces" an expression of the rapid widening of Mexico's whole productive life.

Undoubtedly Brazil, one of the most illiterate countries in the world, about on the level of Haiti and India, needs a hundred thousand little red schoolhouses more than it did the magnificent administrative building in Rio for splurging bureaucrats, but the shame of contrast may drive some of those bureaucrats to erase the strident discrepancy.

Visitors gape admiringly at the magnificent new architecture of Rio, but leftist Gilberto Freyre, premier Brazilian novelist, cries out: "Of what use to Brazil is her prosperity. . . ? What does it matter that the luxurious sections of Rio resemble New York, or that São Paolo rivals Chicago, when in the interior there are provinces like those in the interior of China, more miserable than those of India or Abyssinia?"

Probably no clear-cut answer can be given yet. Probably the truth lies somewhere between. Certainly the democratic trends of the countries south have in most places forced a new outlook on cities and governments, a greater concern for more balanced national development. The more representative population in the cities of today has had much influence in this salutary direction. Civic pride has increased remarkably. In nearly all the cities, old and new, political rule has broadened and social welfare is ever more stressed.

Slums and glaring contrasts there still are. The hovels of Mexico City, in spite of wholesale demolition and the building of modern sanitary dwellings, have spread out quite as far in new directions and are quite as filthy as what was torn away. If anything, the area is now greater. Santiago de Chile still has mile on mile of slums, these unsanitary, unheated, unlighted *conventillos* that breed so much tuberculosis, pneumonia, syphilis, immorality and despair. It has mile and mile also of new low-cost government housing, both duplex homes with gardens and huge cream-colored concrete modernistic apartment houses, with long open sunlit galleries and curving ramps.

Only a few years ago nobody bothered or cared, but today slums continue to be attacked, health conditions have been improved until nearly all the cities are as safe to live in as those elsewhere. In city planning the southern countries are mostly far ahead of the United States, and today there is far more respect for the average man, the worker, the expanding middle class, just beginning to demand its place in the sun and rapidly becoming the directing force in the new cities.

Also, part of the democratic upsurge in each country has been toward forcing the capital metropolis to make concessions to the rest of the land and help build up the whole nation. This was inherent in recent governmental changes in Guatemala and Venezuela, and as a result the back country in each is humming as never before. Part of the popular movement that put Perón into office in Argentina was precisely this rural demand that the economic balance between Buenos Aires and the rest of the country be redressed. This, in turn, has given all the cities more body and a truer economic function.

Moreover, many of the biggest new cities are themselves interior cities —an indication of resettlement and a rapidly developing countryside: places like Rosario, Medellín, Goriãnia, Belém, some of the south cities in Chile. In Mexico the boom has also hit more distant places, as Monterrey, the steel and iron center, and Vera Cruz, the Gulf port.

Tapachula, a small coffee and banana city 'way down on the Guatemalan border, ten years ago was a sleepy cobbled forgotten place. Now it is busily paving streets, putting in new candy-bar gas stations, sewers, water mains, an air-conditioned movie, a new hotel.

In any case, the fate of present large cities and the happiness of their inhabitants greatly depend on an over-all national prosperity. Certainly the better utilization of national resources, the new industries, new roads, railroads, air lines, can alone provide a sure foundation for the new cities. In good part they do reflect this new growth. The final tally sheet has not been cast yet, but in many ways the modern Latin American city is the bright show window of countries rapidly reaching maturity in many new directions.

‖‖ Green World

Where Chlorophyll Is King

SOUTH AMERICA has been called the Green Continent. The same adjective describes most of the Caribbean, Central America and the south of Mexico.

The Amazon River—with the world's biggest drainage system and five times the volume of the Mississippi—navigable by ocean liners for nearly two thousand miles up to the old rubber port of Manáos, is the greatest green empire on earth. From Manáos large river boats go up a thousand miles more to Iquitos in Peru. Motorboats carry on for another thousand miles up various tributaries. Nearly everywhere this mighty region, probably larger than the total main area of the United States, is filled with forests and great meadows, one of them larger than the whole area of Texas. The virgin, almost unused territory stretches into five other countries besides Brazil and pushes right up to the borders of the three Guianas. Where else is there such a vast solid expanse of chlorophyll?

South America has other enormous jungle areas in the Orinoco and Paraguay basins. Add to this the lush green country along the Magdalena in Colombia, the great grass llanos of Colombia and Venezuela; the mighty pampas of Uruguay and Argentina; the plantation lands of lower Bolivia; the rich coastal valleys of Peru like moving green snakes in the sloughed-off hides of the desert; the inner green-clad foothills of the eastern slopes of the Andes up and down the length of the continent; the fertile Vales of Paradise in Chile. Even in cold south Chile, because of heavy year-round rainfall, are dense jungles, with pine, lofty evergreen beeches and enormous alerce trees, right up to the snow line.

Add also to this vast green world, the extensive coast jungles of Central America and Mexico, the hot inland jungle of Petén in Guatemala, whence comes most of our chewing gum, and the lush semitropical world of the entire Caribbean.

But in spite of such prolific vegetation, the proportion of good farming areas is considerably smaller than in most of the United States. The towering Andean cordillera usurps much of the continent. The Sierra Madre in Mexico, a southward continuation of the Rockies, is a lofty tangled affair that fills out most of the land or else cuts off rain from the dry northern plateau. The extensive coast jungles, though they provide valuable forest products, also prevent ordinary farming.

Many times I have stood in little jungle clearings, where the gigantic trees, the looping lianas, the greedy vegetation folds in on the fields and cabins with the least slackening of toil, and I have marveled at the persistence of folk seeking life and freedom against such odds. Dwellings left vacant for a while are broken into by jungle animals and rodents and ants. Spiders weave a fog of gray. The pages of books are soon bored through and through. The curtains are gnawed away. Yet in other places, where men have stood together and not as isolated frontiersman, large islands have been cleared and made livable, and the corn on such black soil really reaches right up to the elephant's eye, not once, but sometimes in three crops, a year.

The west-coast deserts of Peru limit farming, and yet much of that region of restless sands will undoubtedly someday be used, for the eternal water of the Andes lies above it, waiting for the magic wand to bring it down and give exuberant life to the desolation. But most of the barren nitrate fields of Chile are beyond all farm use by man.

In spite of such limitations, and though in Argentine and Brazil the value of manufactured and processed products has surpassed that of agriculture, the Green Continent is still predominantly a farming continent. Most men make their living from the soil.

Latin America produces most of the coffee and cacao of the world. It is coming back into its own as a producer of rubber and quinine. It is the world's greatest source of vegetable oils, fibres, many unique drugs. Brazil and other countries have become great cotton growers. Cuba rivals Java as the world's sugar warehouse, and its tobacco surpasses the quality of that of the Near East. Bananas, pineapples, citrus fruit, avocados, papayas pour into the holds of the world's commerce. The coconuts of Nicaragua and Brazil make a great deal of the glycerin, the munitions, the gas masks of the Great Powers. Chilean wines rival the best. The Guianas and Ecuador have become the rice bowls of the New World.

Argentina at times has exported more wheat than the entire North American continent, particularly during the Wallace scarcity program.

It sends abroad three fourths of all the world's exported corn. It is the world's greatest meat exporter and, next to the Australian continent, the largest wool exporter. It is the greatest source of linseed and of yerba mate, which provides the tea drunk by ten million people.

No one has really known rural hospitality in Chile, Argentina, Paraguay, Bolivia or southern Brazil until he has joined a friendly circle sucking mate through silver-tipped tubes out of hand-carved gourd bowls.

Since agriculture—despite industrial gains in many places—remains the chief occupation of the most people, farm methods and the kinds of crops are all-important for the progress and happiness of the southern folk.

Everywhere the pattern is different from United States farming. The nature of the land, the people, the type of early village holdings and the feudal nature of the Conquest produced a different system. Our small pioneer farmer, who got free lands and who opened up and built the West, was never much in evidence in Latin America.

A few small ranches were created in Mexico, Chile and elsewhere, but mostly these were soon squeezed out by feudal encroachment and by the closed-market operation of both the feudal and communal systems.

In more recent years Chile's new frontier to the south has been settled in good part by small landowners. Many of the vineyards around Mendoza in Argentina and the new citrus belt in northern Mexico are owned by small growers. Also some individualistic farming has sprung up around large modern cities. But frontier settlement, North American fashion, was never possible except in limited areas.

Except in Argentina and Uruguay there was never much free unoccupied land. Individual Spaniards who tried to open up the hot jungles or the upland plateaus could not stand the climate or the excessive altitudes; they perished from strange diseases. Besides, the Spaniards had not come to the New World with any idea of sweating it out on farms but to find gold and quick wealth. Only reluctantly did they turn to the soil. Rather did they conquer existing cities or else founded new ones near by and simply took over existing farm areas with the people as serfs. They either continued the village communal system or grafted on their own feudal setup. They worked land only where they could get slaves and, except for mining sectors, opened up few new frontiers.

Only in late years, with new techniques and health controls, with far-reaching group or government aid, have new frontier movements come about; only now is a true conquest of the continent being pushed. But it is being done by big companies or by governments, for the small frontiersman cannot individually overcome preliminary obstacles.

Wherever the original population managed to hang onto lands in the interior of Mexico, Guatemala, a small part of Salvador, Colombia, Venezuela, the highlands of Ecuador, Peru and Boliva, and in Araucano and in Andacollo villages along the Andes, a communal system, featured by varying degrees of individualism, persisted.

We visited several of these prosperous communities around Temuco and Nueva Imperial, near the scene of one of the greatest early victories of the native folk against the Spaniards. The people in these villages of thatched *rucas* still speak Mapuche; the women still wear their heavy necklace plates of silver.

In some rural communities the Spaniards grafted on their own communal aspects already centuries old in Mother Spain: common village timber and pasturage lands, common water rights. In many places, the Spaniards concentrated dispersed populations into such communal villages the better to control them and have a labor supply—on the pretext of Christianizing them.

The Jesuits in Paraguay concentrated the Guaranís into missions on a fraternal communal basis where they were taught Christianity, new skills and trades.

Most communal farming has been and is on a subsistence, not a commercial footing. But the nature of many crops, such as sugar, henequen, cacao, coffee and, in later days, wheat, rice and cotton, made both communal and small independent farming unrealistic and unprofitable. These called for big plantations.

Thus the major over-all pattern of Latin America landholding has been and is today both feudal and communal, two contradictory ways of life living on side by side.

Stick Farming

All day in the dust and tropic sun at the end of the dry season of southeast Mexico we struggled up the face of a mountain toward a divide between two sharp peaks. There above us a man blew on a conch shell, and a knot of people in bright serapes and big straw sombreros gathered.

With immense gravity the elders of the tiny village on the mountain saddle examined our papers, listened to our reasons for wishing to visit Mazateca country, then bade us welcome.

Still high above us, about the very crown of the needle peak, were circles of thatched houses and corn patches on slopes so steep it was difficult to imagine how they had been planted.

Women, with blue *rebozos* around their full brown cheeks, pattered down like a flock of bright birds with baskets of warm food, *tortillas*, chicken and chile. We ate in front of the little schoolhouse. Its benches and desks had been hand-hewn out of solid mahogany from forests stretching through eastern valleys.

Our wide, well-made trail wound along sheer cliffs through a stupendous region. All the enormous inner ravine was cultivated—from peaks often mantled in snow down to hot jungle country. Everywhere thatched houses perched on the steepest slopes and gave the landscape a Japanese quality. But palm trees, red-flowering matapalos and other growths soon dispelled the illusion. Up at the top, down below, everywhere, cornfields sprouted. In the middle zone were also beans and tomatoes, cucumbers, squash and melons; below, chile vines, bananas, pineapples, silver-green cane. Side canyons were pocketed with heavy timber. The shy, almost tongue-tied folk were burning off patches to plant corn—the same way the United States was originally cleared and settled.

One of Hitler's chemists said that in the war the German people if necessary would eat their trees, and he served a repast concocted out of chemically treated pulp. But the simple Mazatecans have not yet learned how to eat their trees, so they burn them to produce potash, and plant corn by poking a pointed stick among the stumps. It was sad to see handsome mahogany trees going down before machete and fire, but it was good to see corn sprouting.

Only in richer, flatter valley stretches did we observe any plows, iron-tipped wood drawn by oxen, yoked by their heads, ancient Egyptian style. Something must be said for stick planting and straight shallow plows; the latest theory is that the deep curved plow has well-nigh ruined the soil over whole areas of modern civilization. A University of California expert recently stated that for the steeper portions of Mexico ancient stick planting is the most efficient method yet devised, that more modern methods have merely resulted in great stretches of Mexico being lost forever to farm use.

The vertical farm pattern of the rich Mazateca region is repeated over and over through areas of Mexico and Guatemala. On the Inter-American Highway near Tamazanchale (to Americans "Thomas and Charlie") even casual visitors can see some of these corn patches tilted against the sky. Local legend has it that sometimes farmers roll off and get killed.

"How on earth," an American schoolteacher exclaimed, "do they get those fields planted?"

A fellow-traveler, a French-Mexican business man replied, a twinkle in his eyes, "Very simple, Señorita. They merely stand below and shoot the corn in with double-barreled shotguns."

Some of the primitive farming of such difficult places is older than the Spanish Conquest. More often it is the aftermath of the driving off of the early peoples, refusing to be enslaved, from richer valley lands seized by feudal estates. The vertical farming of Mexico attests to the unflagging industry and stubborn independence of ancient peoples, their love for the soil and old village communalism.

Stone Terraces

The Incan peoples not only cultivated but irrigated the very crags with their artificial stone canals, their Quencos or "Zigzags." Wherever you travel up the Marañón, along the Vilcanota, through the Urubamba gorge, rise—tier on tier—the laboriously built stone-faced terraces of the ancients, many still in use, bubbling with scarlet Flowers of the Inca, the crinkly leaves of the coca plant, golden tassels of corn, white potato blossoms. Often the stone walls are overhung with peach and plum trees. Less familiar plants are also grown: the *quinúa*, a cereal, and *oca*, a vegetable. The orange blossoms of the quishuar tree are ground up for saffron flavoring. The hard green balls of the yareta-tree foliage are chopped into chunks for fuel; to this day they are carted down to Chilean mining regions to heat bunk rooms and offices at freezing altitudes.

For miles on end along the narrow-gauge line from Cuzco down the Urubamba, carefully laid terraces, dating back to pre-Conquest times, rise up thousands of feet on either side. Far above stretch the bleaker early pasture lands of alpacas and vicuñas. Still higher, mounting in august majesty, tower the solid Andean snow walls: great violet glaciers flashing in the sun, huge buttress of icy fire-flame, the massive shoulders of never-melting snow packs.

Here and there a peak rises far above in solitary grandeur, notching the close deep-blue sky, and higher than any mountain in main continental United States. There stands majestic Apu Sallcantai, "Lord of the Mountains," the Holy Height of the Inca gods, eighteen thousand feet aloft, circled by winging condors, swept by mighty storms, roaring with thunder and lightning. Near here is Vilcanota Knot, a great tangle of even loftier peaks where the various Andean chains mingle before separating on south about the broad upland Bolivian mesa.

Against this awe-inspiring backdrop the Quechuas, "the Spring Valley" folk, built their terraces and plowed their fields throughout an era many times longer than the whole history of the United States. In many places their fields lie above the clouds. One chill dawn in northern Peru I stood at fourteen thousand feet in potato and corn patches, looking down on a billowing sea of white.

As in most of the Americas the Inca farm system was semicommunal. Each adult, male and female, and each child was entitled to enough land to guarantee comfortable livelihood. The alpaca and llama herds, mostly owned by the Emperor, were cared for by skilled herdsmen, whose talents aroused the respect of the conquerors. Each year the fleece was equitably distributed to the villagers. Part was woven for use by the Incas. Newlyweds were always given a house and a royal dowry of new clothes.

Henry Wallace's tepid attempts to work out AAA, resettlement, crop insurance, an ever-normal granary, seem fumbling and half-baked in comparison with Inca practices. In the Andean highland empire those reforms were an integral functioning system for many centuries, though never involved in willful destruction of products or animals. When land became insufficient in any community—careful statistics based on an annual census were kept—part of the population was resettled on land similar in quality and at approximately the same altitude. Compare that with the ragged disorderly hegira of the *Grapes of Wrath* folk during our dust-bowl crisis. At close intervals, along every road, *tambos*, which served as inns and storehouses for the seven lean years, were stocked with wool, potatoes, cereals and other supplies. The Spaniards lived off those accumulations for years after the Conquest. More land was cultivated in ancient Peru than in present-day Peru.

The early peoples knew considerable about farming. In the Santiago de Chile National Museum of History we looked over the tools of the Andacollos and allied mountain folk. They had every kind of handy garden tool found in any New England home—hammers, adzes, axes, drills, shovels of every size and shape, rakes, hoes, special foot plows, also the curved machete, and not a few other implements that look so efficient they might well be copied by modern factories. One does not need to be an anthropologist or soil expert to know how much the early people loved the soil, how well and energetically they worked it.

Soil conservation, through terracing, crop-rotation, protection of top-soil, was more universally practiced than it is today in the United States.

In broken fashion this early system lives on in remoter parts of the Andes. After the Conquest the Children of the Sun were able to hold on to only the most difficult areas. The richer bottom lands were seized for feudal estates, but those mountain stretches still astonish every traveler for the energy, skill and good sense they represent.

To mention only two of many lofty Andean areas we have revisited, the trip down the Urubamba and the Apurimac, as down other inner valleys, is thrilling: life going on much as it did thousands of years ago, aloft on the same old terraces, close to earth, close to sky. Here and there, where the jungle has crept back upon the fields, may be glimpsed outlines of long-forgotten stone cities, slowly strangled now by the tangle of lianas and the big orange quishuar trees.

Ollantaytambo, halfway down the Urubamba rail line, is set among such terraces and many abandoned stone settlements. It is one very ancient city that has survived, though now it is a mestizo town with less historical continuity than Cuzco, its folk little aware of old traditions. Near by is one of the ancient Inca suspension bridges, fiber cables now replaced with steel, but still using the same ancient stone towers and big stone pier in the center of the river. The conductor obligingly stopped the train while we got out and took pictures of it.

Downstream, on the nose of a three-thousand-foot cliff above the boiling river, stands the ghost city Machu-Picchu, the Three Window place of earlier migrations. Some claim that it is older than Cuzco. Opposite, on another stone nose, still higher is Huayna Picchu, a lookout fort with more terraces, a place so difficult to reach now, since the old Inca zigzag trail up the face of the solid stone cliff has been broken by earthquake, that even alpine climbers have lost their lives.

Machu-Picchu—one of dozens of such settlements—stands in lonely stone majesty, commanding the river in both directions. The green-white swirling waters can be seen directly below the cliff from the impregnable ramparts. Now and then a loaded truck passes along the gorge-carved highroad on its way to the Bolivian jungles. Temples, dwellings, storehouses, council chambers, barracks, sport fields, are set beside a wide curve of farming terraces. In ancient days, when these were bright with crops and flowers and fruit trees, it must have been fantastically spectacular and beautiful. Intricate stone conduits, often drilled through living rock for long stretches, fed the numerous bathing rooms, drinking fountains, the pools and the lofty fields. One royal bathroom carved out of solid rock has modernistic design, with an angle cross seat and scooped-out wall handholds and niches, presumably for soap and cosmetics. All told, Machu-Picchu is one of the most astonishing and sublime achievements in the history of man. Its majesty rose right out of the stone farm terraces of the humble farmers. Many such still shape the farm life of inner Peru.

Feudalism

Feudal landholding in the Americas is based mostly on original grants made by conquering Spanish captains to favorites, grants subsequently ratified by the Crown and expanded.

A grant that included Indian serfs or slaves "to be Christianized" was an *encomienda*. Early British Crown grants on the Atlantic seaboard also often included the obligation to "Christianize" the Indians. A simple Spanish Crown land grant not conveying human beings was known as a *repartimiento*.

The Spanish hacienda, based on Indian, then Negro, slavery, later carried on by serfdom, debt enslavement or various forms of share cropping and tenantry, had few labor costs and hence little incentive to introduce machinery or better methods. Each hacienda became a petty closed empire, almost self-sufficient, providing nearly all its own needs—timber, wool, adobes, building materials, food, homespun clothing. The owner was complete master over his serfs, could enjoy their daughters, punish them even up to death. Schools were rarely maintained, although the priest might teach some bright boy, so the Latin American farm workers were and are universally illiterate.

With this self-sufficient (and insufficient) physical and moral life, everything sold outside—over and above what was necessary to buy simple tools and manufactured articles or improve the breed of animals—became pure gravy, one hundred per cent profit.

With this easy income, the owners, who lived on their estates only during more pleasant months and then splurged at first in Paris and later in Lima, Santiago or Buenos Aires, were the most lavish spenders on earth. It was an ideal if semiparasitical existence, a rare combination of healthful outdoor life and of urban luxury and sophistication. However limited in his ideas and his comprehension of the modern world the hacienda owner was and is, by and large he remains one of the most virile and cultured types ever produced by any society—gracious socially, steeped in literature, art, music, particularly of Paris.

The other side of the coin was not always so pretty. Until a few years ago Guatemalan highland villagers were rounded up by the army, tied together by the necks with ropes and led off to German coffee *fincas* to work for a few cents a day. And even these meager wages were often pocketed by the army officer. Similar abuses were committed in Ecuador, Peru and Bolivia. Even now in some corners one will find backward brutal owners (*gamonales*) who still flog their serfs (*yanacones*) and rule their estates and adjacent villages with little restraint from outside. They control the local officials, the federal inspectors, bribe the local garrison officer, hold the local priest to their will.

A few years ago in one of the most aristocratic households of Peru, the Señora, noted for her pious charity work, grew angered at a servant girl's slowness and brutally yanked one of her eyelids. This girl brought down from the highland hacienda, received no wages at all and had no inkling of her rights.

"You see," the Señora told me, "I have to treat her just as I would on the hacienda so she will understand."

But in most places over the continent the enchanting world of the feudal *hacendado*, be he backward or enlightened, has crashed about him. In general, the medieval estate set up in the New World by the Conquest brought in various new crops, animals and techniques. But in the long run it did not always tend toward so much efficiency and certainly did not provide such equitable distribution as the old communal system. Nor later did the feudal system meet the growing demand of a commercial era for mass food crops. As in Europe much earlier, it became unable to match the needs of modern industry and the modern city.

Thus, the hacienda, which so patterned colonial and modern times, has been challenged in every direction—by scientific agriculture, by changing national needs, by the demands of the cities for ever larger food supplies, by serfs and workers, by new doctrines of social welfare.

That challenge has ranged from terrifying revolution in Mexico to schemes of subdivision and resettlement, from State ownership as in Guatemala to Perón's new "Law for Peons" in Argentina. The peasants everywhere have awakened. Today in most places crueler old-time feudal lords have disappeared. Except in remoter interior areas of the highlands, in parts of Chile and in most of Brazil, the more inhuman medieval privileges have largely vanished. Not that the peasants or seasonal workers anywhere enjoy what we would call a decent civilized existence. But then neither do they in the United States.

But serfdom where the peon was tied his life long to the land—so prevalent even a few years ago—has increasingly been eliminated by peasant unions and by revolt, by welfare agencies, by State protective laws and by all more enlightened owners. The greatest reforms have occurred in Mexico, Guatemala, Argentina, Colombia and Uruguay, to some extent along the coast of Peru. Decided improvement has taken place under the new Venezuelan Betancourt regime. Slight gains have been made in parts of Ecuador and Brazil.

Feudalism: Modern Style

A far cry in most ways from the old *gamonal*, ruling undisputed and cruelly, are the Larco Herreras of the rich Chicama Valley on the coast of Peru, who own a big sugar estate, one of the most modern in the country.

The public-spirited Larcos have been millionaire benefactors—witness a million-dollar insane asylum, various fully equipped hospitals, a fine archaeological museum in Lima. They have served as mayors, congressmen, diplomats; one was Vice-President. They long controlled the Lima daily newspaper, *La Crónica*, and others elsewhere. Few great landowners anywhere have been so active, so interested in education, art, science.

The coast of Peru, where their buildings lie, is a rainless desert, cut through by fertile valleys, where streams flow down from Andean snows. One of the richest of these valleys, Chicama, now devoted chiefly to sugar cane, some fruit and cotton, was densely inhabited long before the Incas held sway there, was already flourishing at least five thousand years ago. In the foothills are remains of a great pre-Spanish aqueduct that required the moving of millions of tons of earth. More area was cultivated in olden times than during the colony or even today with modern machinery.

There in Chicama, before the time of Christ, the Mochicans built up a remarkable culture—some of the most splendid art known to the world.

In Moche, a settlement of hybrid descendants of the forgotten folk, we ate small sea crabs in red sauce, drank chicha beer from huge glass beakers and danced the marinera. Though old-time Mochican greatness is gone, they till communal lands still in a tiny corner of the valley.

After the Mochicans came the Chimús, a more stately organizing people. The tangled remains of the great Chimú capital, Chan-Chan, with its lofty triple encircling walls, lies crumbling away hard by modern Trujillo, the third city of Peru, an old colonial place of beautifully carved balconies.

A few years back, the great Chimú (as the pre-Spanish monarch was called) was the elder Larco Herrera. "The Larcos own Trujillo" was the saying. But in the last decade, with social change knocking on the door, this became no longer true.

Several members of the family drove us out through the smiling sun-kissed countryside of adobe walls, false pepper trees, scarlet jacarandas and bougainvillaea, to their estate.

The low rambling Casa Grande, set in the Grange or small adobe workers' village, is a cool sprawling colonial structure. One wing is dedicated to a private archaeological museum. The dwelling has been furnished with the expensive hodgepodge of the world, a valuable Chinese vase beside a Grand Rapids quickie settee or an Italian porcelain Madonna, all rich but conforming to no known ideas of interior decoration. The paintings are conservative and banal. The Larcos, though great art patrons, will have no truck with anything modernistic or too realistic. The fine work of such Peruvian moderns as José Sabogal, Julia Codesido, Camilo Blas and others arouse their contempt—perhaps also their fear.

The Larcos, educated abroad—several at Princeton—pride themselves on following the latest scientific farm methods with the most modern equipment and for looking after the welfare of their workers. Although the homes of the peons, one or two-room adobe affairs, have no modern conveniences or running water, the workers were paid about twenty-five cents a day as compared to twenty elsewhere. The Larcos also maintain a school, clinic, swimming pool, sports club and community center and demand that their workers go to bed not later than ten o'clock, for a twelve to sixteen-hour day is the rule. These benevolent undertakings, when first introduced, aroused the fury of other landholders. Now most such things are required by law.

Enemies of the Larcos on the other end of the social scale argued that this paternalism was merely to keep workers docile, to pile up bigger profits—that in any case this could be no generalized solution for the serious land problem of all Peru. They argued that the three big Chicama estates (one is owned by an absentee North American company; another by a naturalized German family) deliberately strangled Trujillo, preventing growth and modernization, that they shut out industries to insure a large supply of cheap floating labor.

Certainly the Larco benefactions have been chiefly for Lima where they blaze better in the public eye, not for Trujillo. Lima has the great University of San Marcos, the oldest in the Americas, flourishing a century before Plymouth Rock. But the equipment of the famous and also venerable University of Trujillo scarcely comes up to that of a third-rate high school in the United States, even though in spirit, courage and civic consciousness it has stood squarely on traditions of freedom in a manner not particularly characteristic of most North American universities.

In spite of the Larcos' benevolence, it was precisely in the shadow of their empire that Peru's first modern students' and peasants' revolt started under the leadership of young Haya de la Torre, who has since become Peru's most outstanding public figure. Part of the program of the People's Party, known as Apra, which he heads and which has the overwhelming support of most Peruvians, is to provide lands for the people.

As we drove back to Trujillo from the Larco estate, after a luncheon served in formal state manner, one of the Larcos waved his hand at the signs daubed on every wall and rock: "Apra will save Peru!" and sighed deeply. "Once," he said, "Trujillo was a quiet, contented little town with peace in its heart. Where did all this class hate come from?"

Hate there certainly was. On an earlier trip to Trujillo in 1934 we had seen the fresh blood of scores of students and peasants that still stained the old throne walls in Chan-Chan where the unfortunate victims had been dragged by the soldiery of Dictator Sánchez Cerro and massacred with machine guns. It is not a pleasant thing to see mashed brains smeared over a chauffeur's cap or a grinning face half gone. This was but one of a number of such slaughterings.

Since that day the Apra movement (which now has a Congressional majority, though it does not yet control the government) through persistent education and organization has created an alert public opinion and brought much progress after so many decades of dictatorial rule.

The change is vividly reflected in Trujillo. Today, outwardly at least, the city again enjoys peace—and something more. Under more popular rule, plus wartime prosperity, much of its picturesque decay of yesterday has disappeared. Paved streets, new buildings, public monuments, a de luxe hotel have appeared. In 1934 the hotel was a dirty creaking trap; the plaza, an abandoned weed-grown square. Few autos bumped over the cobbled streets. Now the city has been improved, is well kept. Better-dressed folk walk the streets. With a few industries and more democratic control Trujillo has blossomed into a more bustling community.

Chilean Fundo

Señor Ignacio Bravo, a masterful, spiky-haired little man, picked me up at the Hotel Bidault in Santiago de Chile—a humble hostelry that filled him with some qualms as to our being quite the distinguished foreigners he had belived us to be. He whisked us out in his Packard to his great *fundo* or estate southeast of the capital.

Bravo is the direct descendant of the original Spanish captain who received the property from Pedro de Valdivia, the Spanish conqueror of Chile, the brilliant and daring leader who, with his mistress, Inez Suárez, clanked across snow passes and deserts 'way back in 1540 to add Chile to the Spanish empire.

Soon after Valdivia had founded Santiago and subdued the country as far south as he could against the unflagging resistance of the fierce Araucanos, he divided all the land into some seventy strips extending from the sea clear to the Andes—the entire width of the country—and gave these holdings with their inhabitants to his captains. Some of those great colonial *fundos* are still almost intact in spite of Chile's paucity of good soil in that strangely elongated empire of deserts, crags, forests and antarctic snows.

These captains became the first citizens, the new nobility, that soon bought titles from the Spanish Crown. They and their descendants, a handful of powerful families, governed Chile for four hundred years.

Not until the popular electoral revolt, led by Arturo Alessandri, kingpin of the Liberal Party, produced the more democratic constitution of 1925, was the landholders' tight monopoly broken. New types then entered the halls of government—businessmen, professors, engineers, middle class, even Socialists and Communists.

Even so, the landholding aristocracy has been more enlightened than similar groups in neighboring lands, more so than the Peruvian Civilistas, who are ugly, conspiratorial, divorced from any taint of modern ideas or progress. Many Chilean Conservatives quickly adjusted themselves to the popular change, even took the lead in carrying out far-reaching reforms.

The cynical charged that this was to prevent the new dispensation in Chile from bettering the lot of the *inquilinos* or serfs and block any revolutionary land program. In spite of the leftist flavor of recent Chilean governments, the peasants there remain among the most miserably paid, the most vilely treated in all South America.

Señor Bravo himself is a ramrod of the Agrarian Labor Party, a group of landlords (with about four seats in Congress) who consider the salvation of the country dependent on modern farm technology. They are closely affiliated with the Liberals and Conservatives.

That morning as we rode through the Chilean countryside the air was crisp, the ground still soggy from winter rains, but the first breath of spring came with awakening fruit buds. Neat tiled houses with pleasant flower gardens stood behind thick adobe walls topped by small tile roofs. Ahead of us rose the great Andean giants, a mighty wall of snow. Tupungato thrust a bare white shoulder against the pale blue sky.

Soon we were headed across the rich Maipó Valley where occurred the crucial battle of Independence. Today it is one of the richest farming regions anywhere, part of Chile's central Vales of Paradise.

We swung past a lake dense with wild fowl. Our concrete road gave way to macadam, presently to gravel, then packed earth. After some hours we climbed rolling hills, then turned through a big gate and rode along a mile of driveway between stiff poplars to Bravo's home.

Several *inquilinos* passed us in old-fashioned buggies. The men wore rough homespun black wool and funny little felt hats; the women, thick black shawls, heel-length black skirts, awkward shoes—they possessed none of the color most Latin American countryfolk have. Picturesqueness was monopolized by the wheeling cowboys or *huasos*. As they galloped about, their short tan ponchos whirled up to show wide red sashes, large *corvo* knives and baggy trousers. The last, similar to those of the Argentine gaucho, originally were derived from the Araucano Indians whose blood flows in the veins of nearly all Chileans to make them a stocky, big-nosed race of fierce, matter-of-fact purposefulness.

Señor Bravo's *fundo* has about two hundred fifty families, or one thousand resident dwellers. Their dwellings were built by Bravo, and since he is a man of modern enlightenment, his housing is superior. Though no house has any plumbing, running water or toilets, all have concrete floors and walls, tiled roofs and windows.

The concrete, some peasants protested, was overly damp. The windows, quite an innovation, were also opposed. In winter icy blasts whip down from Andean snows, and as peasants nowhere have heat, even during freezing spells, windows, many argued, would increase drafts and cold.

Each house has two small square rooms (on most *fundos* only one) and at the side a thatched roof on poles under which the family cooking is done over stones or on tin braziers. As some families have ten or more children plus relatives, even Bravo's fine housing is scarcely adequate.

But each family has its own small plot of ground for vegetables, cultivated by the women and children, since the men and boys must work steadily in the fields during planting, cultivating and harvesting. For each day worked the peon is paid the equivalent of twenty-five cents, double the wage in vogue elsewhere. Day workers, called in at harvesttime, receive as much as seventy cents a day (on other *fundos* only fifty-five cents) and two meals consisting of *locro*, a what-have-you vegetable stew, and a small hunk of bread. At Bravo's they get meat on Sundays, though most estates, especially wheat farms, give out no meat until a general feast day at the end of harvest. Señor Bravo also maintains a clinic and school. All told, he represents the most up-to-date trend in colonial Chilean landholding.

Don Ignacio's own flat-roofed house was built centuries ago but has been added to and modernized. Elevated corridors with interlaced brick balustrades run around the patios, which are connected by a low barrel-vaulted passageway. Behind the house, inside a ten-foot adobe wall, is a large orchard of peaches, apples, plums, cherries, a corral for riding horses, chicken coops and a tiled swimming pool shaded by poplars and evergreen beeches.

For the owner and his family, life is leisurely though each day is full. When they tire of it here, they fly off to Santiago, Viña del Mar or Buenos Aires, though in former days they more often went to Paris.

There is an early horseback ride, a dip in the pool, then coffee under a ramada or grape arbor. Those who prefer may have breakfast in bed.

Señora Celestina Bravo was no lie-a-bed. She was already dressed in the shiny black satin, very tight and bulgy in front, that she loves to wear at all hours of the day, and already bedecked with costly, glittering jewels on ears, neck, bosom and fingers.

As in all Chile breakfast consisted of a pot of coffee essence, a pot of hot water, several slices of dark bread, marmalade, but no butter. Since we were foreigners, we could order ham and eggs and cereal, although Señora Bravo told me with a shake of her head, a warning gleam in her large black eyes and a superior smile, that it was not wise to break the night's fast with too much food. Maybe that was why all North Americans had such burpy digestions and must chew gum like ruminating cows.

Her peppery frankness is typical of nearly all Chileans, despite their own touchy anger at the slightest criticism of anything Chilean. When we gloomed about the rain the second day we were there, Señora Bravo flared up: "Naturally it never rains in *your* country!"

The heavy meal of the day, served about two o'clock, consisted of six courses with different wines. It dragged on until nearly four.

Then there was a siesta, more horseback riding and swimming.

Tea, obligatory as any meal and almost as heavy, was served at 6:30. It is called *once*, which means "eleven," no one seems to know why, and consisted of paper-thin sandwiches of enormous dimensions, toast, marmalade, jellies, cake, pastry, cookies, candy and fruit. It was the one time in the day that butter was served—great towering mounds of it.

The evening meal, identical with that at midday minus one course, was likewise served with wines. It started at nine and continued, with sparkling conversation, until nearly eleven.

Afterward a *huaso* came in with his guitar and sang:

My life, if I should wish,
If I should wish a firefly,
The firefly of your eyes,
I would wish it.

I would wish it, ay, yes,
All my life,
To light my life in them—
Flower of my Life. . . .

The "ay, yes" rose in a wild upward shout, and the handsome *huaso*, eyes shining, teeth shining, almost broke his elbow in an appropriate upward sweep of his arm.

At Eastertime, which comes in autumn after crops are in, a whole week of special religious revivals is held—gala occasions, all day and night prayers, flagellation or other discomforts, fasting, then much feasting. Visitors are invited to listen to some priest renowned for his eloquence. A few more faithful hard-working *inquilinos* and their wives are also picked out to attend. Thereby they get a respite from labor and receive wages besides. Usually they pray harder than they ever work, though Chileans are no shirkers. Until the final feasts the celebrants are supposed to cover their heads with kerchiefs, keep their eyes downcast and not exchange a single word with anybody. After fasting they get more food and drink than all the rest of the year put together. These annual religious observances, Señor Bravo noted to me, greatly reduce petty thieving on the estate and are always followed by a wave of belated Church marriages.

Sugar Paradise

A twentieth-century phenomenon, particularly in the Caribbean, has been the growth of "capitalist" absenteeism for large-scale crops with an international market, such as sugar, bananas, coffee, cotton, tobacco, etc.

Foreign-owned plantations, though using modern machinery and efficiency, at first largely followed the existing feudal pattern. In some places they proved harsher than the feudalism, more disruptive of the social order, for mostly they did away with the individual plots that had

given the workers some all-year security. They depended almost entirely
on seasonal labor. In the Cuban sugar industry workers were even forbidden to grow vegetables or have animals at the company houses in
order to make them more thoroughly dependent on their wages. Even
though higher wages might be paid for a few months, since other industries in such lands are too undeveloped to absorb labor between harvests,
much misery and unemployment resulted.

Cuba, sugar paradise owned by absentee landlords, used to look prosperous during the *zafra* or harvest period. The rest of the year Havana
and other cities were crowded with destitute beggars, whole families
sleeping on the streets. This is still the general picture throughout the
colonial sugar regions of the Caribbean.

In 1933, when Gerardo Machado was dictator and the country was
engulfed in official terrorism, the author, sitting at a sidewalk café, invited a ragged fellow at the curb to have a drink.

Politely he replied, "I'd rather have a dime—just one dime." He
held it up dramatically between thumb and forefinger. "This would be
what I'd earn working like a dog in the sizzling sun from can-do to
can't-do. Is it not more sensible to loaf in Havana?"

Most of the arable land in the country, since soon after Independence
in 1898, has been owned or controlled by foreign individuals or companies. During the *zafra*, those brutal Machado days, we visited a vast
sugar estate near Camagüey.

The silver-green cane filled the whole river bottom and rolled on over
soft hills around the neat screened-in bungalows of the foreign employees.

Down in a hollow we visited one of the workers' barracks, a single
room, 150 x 20 feet, with thatched roof and sides. A terrible stench hit
our nostrils. Everything was in a tangle of confusion; crisscross clothes-
lines; mangy dogs; women cooking, scrubbing, washing or just gabbing;
rampaging, bawling children mostly naked; sick folk lying on rags. Each
family had a small space, heaped with rags, utensils, boxes, an occasional
cowhide trunk. Here and there mirrors had been tacked to posts above
some cloth-covered box to hold toilet articles. The interior was smoky
from little tin stoves. No family had any privacy; they were all dumped
in together.

The chief stench was from an open ditch at one end of the barracks
which served as combination latrine and garbage dump. Not even
screened off, it had one low narrow rail for squatting purposes.

When we exclaimed with horror, the Cuban overseer shrugged. "They are animals. They wouldn't appreciate anything better."

"Surely you can't get much work out of such people," we remarked, looking around at sufferers from malaria, yaws, tuberculosis, skin diseases, syphilis, malnutrition.

"They aren't paid more than they are worth."

After harvest these folk would be tossed back upon the towns and cities to spread their diseases, beg, steal, hang out at soup kitchens.

This was about the most extreme case we found. Some other companies, even then, had fairly decent housing, though everywhere wages were down to a few cents a day. Such conditions brought about the revolution of 1933 that overthrew Machado. The new provisional people's President, Grau San Martín, though opposed by Ambassador Sumner Welles, managed to implant a seventy-five-cent minimum wage. Later this was upped to a dollar and a half. Grau enforced health regulations, started housing, promoted diversified crops, distributed a few acres of land. This general trend continued through the dictatorship of Mendieta and Fulgencio Batista, became even stronger when Grau returned to the Presidency in a free election.

During those troubled times the Camagüey estate passed through some bad moments. For a few days the workers barricaded the foreign administrators in their bungalows, cut off their outside communications and water and demanded better wages and housing.

Today this same estate, under more intelligent administration and obliged to conform to recent laws, has good-model screened housing and sanitary outhouses. It now pays better than the minimum wage, maintains a clinic, dispenses medicine free, provides each worker with a plot of ground. It is making more money. Output per worker has increased.

The eager new overseer, a Cuban this time, showed us the improvements. "It took a lot to convince these people to plant gardens, but little by little they are taking to it. . . ."

Gradually the picture on all such estates has brightened, not only in Cuba but also in Central America. Due to the same pressures as those affecting the backward native feudal owner, plus growing nationalism and resentment against foreigners, such absentee enterprises have become more enlightened, if for no other reason than to avoid expropriation, as occurred in Mexico, which now prohibits all foreign absenteeism in agriculture.

Today in all the countries plantations owned by North Americans usually pay the best wages, have better housing and other conditions, and are 'way ahead of their neighbors in technical efficiency. You would be hard put to it to suggest any improvements on one fine modern foreign-owned banana plantation we visited in Guatemala where there was pleasant housing and the highest rural wage paid in the country. Oddly enough, in Honduras, where the dictatorship remains unchallenged, and even fruit company lawyers sit in the cabinet, this same company has kept on with shocking old-time conditions. But in general in the last ten years everything on most such plantations and in most regions has changed marvelously for the better.

On the other hand, local critics contend, since all profits go out of the country, such absenteeism, even when generous and paternalistic, does little to build up new industries or bring about public improvements. The economic independence and growth of the countries where they operate by so much are obstructed. Of course, part of this anti-foreign, almost Boxer, attitude frequently is fostered by old-line Simon Legree feudalists who resent the improved working conditions that have taken place on foreign-owned plantations.

The inevitable trend in all Latin America is for the land—the meadows, the farms, the plantations—eventually to go back to home-citizen ownership, as happened earlier in the United States in the case of large British holdings. In Chile the millions of acres of government grazing land in Patagonia and Tierra del Fuego, so long controlled by four dominant British companies, have now been opened up to small Chilean sheep raisers. The war pretty much wiped out German and Japanese landholdings in many countries. Everywhere the cry of the peoples, as in the Mexican revolution, is for land—land, water and schools.

IV Rebirth of the Land

THE reorganization of feudal landholding, the elimination or control of land absenteeism, land distribution, resettlement, the opening up of new frontiers, the development of new crops, the improvement of peasant working standards—all this means the rebirth of Latin American farming on a new and broader scale.

Attempts have been made, not only to modernize the feudal hacienda, but to modernize the ancient communal system, chiefly in Mexico, but in a minor degree in Guatemala, Peru and Bolivia.

In Mexico land reform was the very core of the 1911 Madero revolution. After the 1920 "Revindicating Revolution" of Obregón and Calles, but especially under President Lázaro Cárdenas (1934-40), the village commons, or *ejidos*, became the pivot of the revolutionary land system.

The main causes of the revolution against Porfirio Díaz had been the pauperism of the rural inhabitants, the harsh serfdom of large landowners, the mounted rurales who "shot first and inquired afterward." With the revolution, estates were broken up, serfdom abolished, lands restored to the *ejidos*. New legislation protected rural workers with better housing, sanitation and medical care, special maternity provisions. Company stores were abolished. Land distribution was accompanied as far as possible by rural schools, farm institutes, co-operative centers, co-operative or State marketing, water systems, health care, etc. The whole economic and political foundations of Mexican life were forever altered.

Success of the revolutionary program has varied according to village, region, crop, the amount of government aid. Sometimes show places were built up for visiting investigators, and other communities neglected.

Some years ago, on an extensive horseback trip in inner Oaxaca, we observed many flourishing *ejidos*. Others within a few miles were sunk in deplorable abandon and poverty. In one low-lying village, its fields weed-grown, nearly all the inhabitants were infected with malaria, yaws (tropical syphilis) and pinto (a hot-country depigmentation blood disease). But a village only ten miles away, on higher ground, had a

69

healthy population, and its fields were beautifully cultivated with loving care. It had built a new plaza grandstand, a new school, a new community center and an outdoor theater. Why in one village should there be fine alert leaders; in another, close by, with apparently the same conditions, apathetic or dishonest leaders? In more prosperous *ejidos* we found a contagious spirit of hope and gaiety previously unknown.

Enemies of the land reform even charge that now government bureaucrats have replaced the former *hacendados*; that villagers are as badly off as before, their new freedom illusory, their labor eaten up by graft, costly overhead and maladministration. Certainly most revolutionary generals and leading bureaucrats themselves have become great landholders. Certainly rural Mexico is still enmeshed in extreme poverty. And now, hard hit by inflation, the peasant is a long way from pie in the sky.

In some regions—as in Yucatán where henequén is grown, and in sugar-cane country—land was broken up that could not be profitably farmed in small units. A valuable commercial crop was lost by the growing of corn on land better suited for other products. Often, too, age-old enslavement and ignorance prevented proper utilization of the soil.

The gap between farm production and demands due to rapid urbanization now poses one of the most serious problems the country must face. The inefficient feudal hacienda did not meet such needs. Neither has the free *ejido*, although here and there, as in the big cotton coöperatives in the Lagunilla district of Coahuila, increasing acreage, efficiency, bigger output have steadily added to Mexico's production so that it now has an excess for export. New modern plantations are coming in inevitably. Mechanized corn production in the most up-to-date Iowa manner has brought results in Nayarit. In general, farm production, which was partly paralyzed during the transition period of the breakup of the estates and armed disorders, has stepped far beyond what it was half a dozen years ago. And after all the pros and cons seventy percent of Mexico's farm crops are harvested on the *ejidos* or village commons.

And whatever the pros and cons, the Mexican peasant is a far freer man than a few decades ago, even though his standard of living may not have risen greatly. His village has lands. In that village he has his own home. The extensive development of farm schools, the spread of technical knowledge, more use of implements and machinery—all this is beginning to bear fruit now. In addition, the peasant enjoys more personal liberty, security against forced labor or being seized by the army. Serfdom is gone for good. His women enjoy respect. He has better health conditions. In the past twenty years smallpox has been practically stamped out in all Mexico. Various regions have been cleared of malaria. Drives have been made against many diseases. The peasant's children now go to school. He has a better chance of getting justice in the courts and can no longer be cheated out of his wages or held in slavery for debt.

Land Colonization and Resettlement

Government land colonization is not new. Argentine has a long tradition of developing the country by organized land settlement with immigrants. A fine account of this is given in Mark Jefferson's *Peopling the Argentine Pampas*. Every so often in interior Argentina one comes on a little corner of Bohemia, of Switzerland, of Russia, of Italy—the slant of the roofs, the vine-covered picket fences, the porches, the flare of skirt and blouse, the tilt of odd headgear.

Right after Independence, Bernardo O'Higgins of Chile tried to promote European immigration to frontier areas. As early as 1850 the government began bringing Germans and Jugoslavs into south Chile, where they were allowed to homestead.

Once more Chile is making new vigorous efforts to open up all its south clear to Tierra del Fuego in a combination of government aid and free homesteading, particularly around Puerto Aisén, Natales and on intermediate channels and fiords. Frequent regular steamship service is maintained through all the maze of islands and water passages. New roads have been pushed clear through into Argentina, swamps drained, schools built. Hotels have been subsidized. Harbors have been improved or built from scratch.

In beautiful half-moon Puerto Montt, set on a great inland bay of densely wooded hills, this busy southward urge quivers along the water front of high-stacked lumber. The harbor is always full of vessels. Those from "around the Horn" have a weather-beaten but jaunty appearance, yardarms stained by storms and the albatross which fly by here for hours on end.

The sturdy ninety-passenger *Tenglo*, one of a fleet of six government vessels constantly plying south channels, rides high at the dock on the crest of the forty-foot tide. Even its decks are stacked with lobster pots, marine engines, drums of petroleum, waterproof alerce timbers, bed-springs, a knocked-down windmill. The vessel is bound for one of the regular twice-a-week runs these boats make to southern settlements and farms, Chiloé Island, the famous Chonos Archipelago, and Puerto Aisén. Next run, the vessel will go clear south to Lake San Rafael, with its blue glaciers crashing into foaming waters, and its swank hotel on the Oquí Isthmus. Steam shovels are now slicing through the Isthmus to make an all-inland waterway clear to the Straits of Magellan.

A third of the *Tenglo* passengers are new settlers. The American Geographic Society maps of the region, published less than twenty years ago, do not even show the now flourishing little cities of Puerto Aisén and Natales. In the last few years tens of thousands of settlers have taken up millions of acres in homesteads, and the green back country is now full of log cabins, stump fields, cattle, sheep, new roads, new schools. Sawmills buzz. Fifteen thousand miners are urgently needed for new mines.

A *roto*, or Chilean seasonal worker, hangs over the *Tenglo* rail with wife, six children, two dogs and bundles. He was shaken out of Concepción in that bad 1938 quake and has never taken root since.

A Puerto Aisén storekeeper has been north buying hardware, kerosene lamps, rayons, calicoes and satin wedding gowns.

"Our young folk are getting married now. That means they are rooted, have found homes down there for keeps. That's good."

He himself is dressed in heavy woolens, *bombachos*, looking like a cross between golf knickers and gaucho pants. "I came in six years back, lived two winters in a shack without even a stove. Now Aisén has fine docks and streets and parks, and I have a big store. The city now has three mighty good—well, kind of good—hotels and up at Coyahique in the back country there are three more. You should see the beautiful lakes, the fine streams, black with ducks and twelve-pound trout."

Back from Aisén the main highway follows the new split-rail fences along beautiful dancing Simpson River up the thrilling Snail Grade through stupendous forests, past gorgeous lakes and Virgin Falls. To this name a local Irish wag, who loves showing strangers around, always appends the phrase, "Sooner or Later." Natales, farther south, now a place of ten thousand, has also felt the boom.

From 1945 to 1947 Chile spent three billion pesos on land coloniza-tion; three hundred millions more on rural housing; one hundred fifty millions on clearing frontier areas, including the lake region; five billions on rural roads and bridges, not to mention great sums on new irrigation and power projects. Two of these are located in the valleys back of the northernmost port, Arica, to make it agriculturally self-sufficient.

Brazil is opening up in a big way the inland Matto Grosso plateau. Venezuela and Colombia are making herculean efforts to develop and settle their vast interior pampa and jungle country.

In Colombia only twenty-five per cent of the arable land is under cultivation because of poor methods, inadequate transportation and geographical obstacles. Lofty mountains divide the country. But now many new areas are being tapped with organized colonization, thanks to new roads, railroads and one of the most extensive air services on the whole continent.

Venezuela is trying to recover from the long neglect of agriculture under Gómez due to land monopoly and depending solely on petroleum exports to procure food abroad. In 1947 the Institute of Immigration and Colonization brought in fifty thousand European "D.P.'s," will bring in one hundred thousand in 1948, hopes to double the country's population in ten years and really open up the now mostly unpopulated but incredibly rich south country of mountains, jungles and plains. Big land co-ops are being started for these people, with mechanical equipment, to produce corn, potatoes, beans, sugar, rice, coffee and tobacco.

State colonization, partly for political purposes, has been made by Dictator Trujillo in the Dominican Republic with "D.P." Jews and Spanish refugees to prevent infiltration of Haitian Negroes from the overcrowded neighbor country. This will undoubtedly prove more constructive than slaughtering them by thousands as Trujillo did some years back.

In Guatemala the Arévalo government is pushing development of the difficult but rich northeast Petén region. Because of jungle, bad health conditions, poor transportation and lack of a sea outlet, due to Great Britain having grabbed Belize, Petén is only sparsely inhabited by Indian villagers, chicle gatherers and lumber campers.

In good, fairly healthful high-ground country the government has just set up a large new farm colony, with a central town enjoying simple but modern conveniences. Nearly a million dollars are being spent to put a road through to Golfo Dulce on the Caribbean Sea. Both Guatemalan and foreign settlers are sought. It is expected this area will soon liberate Guatemala from import of cereals and other foodstuffs and even provide a surplus for the Atlantic coast of neighboring Honduras.

When I talked with President José Arévalo, he had just flown back from a visit to the settlement. Petén, a fifth of Guatemala's area, is the richest fifth in resources, but barriers to its development have kept it mostly unused for centuries.

"Our task," the President told me, "is a new conquest, the opening of roads, towns, industries, the completion of a historical process begun by the Spanish adelantados but long interrupted."

"But your conquest," I ventured, "will scarcely be in the same spirit as that of the early Spaniards."

He replied: "I have just been reading the Spanish Laws of the Indies. Those regulations regarding settlement were practical, wise and constructive and can still serve as a guide for many things we are trying to do."

Resettlement is also carried out increasingly in most countries. Government land distribution and resettlement in Mexico were practiced on a gigantic nation-wide scale with little pretense of recompensing former owners. But customarily, in Argentina, Peru, Guatemala, Chile and Brazil, either government land is utilized or remuneration made to private owners.

On January 19, 1946, the Argentine government thus expropriated for resettlement, a 421,350-acre ranch (larger than Rhode Island) owned by wealthy Conservative Robustiano Costas, the country's biggest landowner, whose treatment of peons on his numerous estates, particularly in the quebracho and mate tea industries, had long aroused adverse comment. On the same date the government also expropriated a 506,250-acre estate on the Bolivian border.

These days in Argentina whole caravans of peasants come trotting down to Buenos Aires to ask the government for lands, irrigation, schoolhouses, loans, improvements. A few years ago they would have been shot. While we were there in 1946 a troop of Indian villagers from above Jujuy started walking two thousand miles south to protest against the encroachments of a big landowner. Before, they would have been killed. Instead, this time they were greeted en route like heroes and fed by the various communities. The publicity grew and the government finally brought them on in by train.

For some time Chile has been one of the most active countries with resettlement. In El Noviciado, near Santiago de Chile—to cite only one of scores of such efforts—a hundred families have been placed on ten thousand acres in government row-type housing, with an administrative center, school and sports field—as the Chileans call it, a *cancha*, a Quechua word, which means a court or open square.

State-Owned Lands

Another significant detail in the over-all land pattern for the continent is the new use being made of State-owned lands. All governments, including the United States—and doubly so since the recent war—are big landholders, because of parks, mineral and forest reserves, military and naval defense, and because large areas often have no immediate profitable use.

As a result of confiscation of Axis properties, the Guatemalan government came into possession of sixty per cent of the developed plantation land of the country. According to the new 1945 constitution this cannot be alienated or disposed of to private citizens or companies.

These properties are now being run: (A) Directly by the State. Wages and living conditions have slightly improved. No forced labor, as previously, has been used. According to official statement, a larger profit has accrued to the public treasury than was ever earned by previous German owners. (B) By the Army, to provide its own food, reduce army costs and provide conscripts with technical farm training to take back to their villages. (C) By co-operatives. (D) By lease to private companies.

Costa Rica has handled her confiscated German and Japanese farm properties largely through co-operatives. In Nicaragua and Honduras, they have been mostly grabbed in faked auctions by high bureaucrats around the two dictators who run those two lands with such brutal selfishness. Salvador has not yet outlined a policy, but some properties apparently have already been "stolen."

Chile has large experimental farms run by a State-owned corporation, which has also turned its attention to developing new crops, lumbering, improving plants and seeds, reforestation, fighting diseases and pests. More than a billion pesos have been invested directly in these various undertakings.

In Haiti, United States government money and officials attempted large-scale planting of a rubber shrub. This resulted in complete loss to everybody concerned except the bureaucrats. It saddled Haiti with a relatively huge debt and caused about a hundred thousand persons in a desperately overcrowded land to lose their farms and homes. The area is now abandoned, eroded, an eyesore. All told only about five tons of doubtful-quality rubber were ever produced. It was one of the blunders, and it has not set well with the Haitians.

Co-operative Land Enterprises

Land co-ops are relatively advanced in Argentina, Chile and Colombia, not to mention the nation-wide *ejido* experiment in Mexico. In 1945-46 the Betancourt government of Venezuela launched 300 new co-operatives, and this method is being used now with European immigrants to develop the back country. In Brazil Dictator Vargas promoted considerable co-operative land farming. From 231 co-ops in the whole country in 1933, the total rose to over two thousand in 1944, and many were farmer groups. Around São Paulo, the large industrial and coffee center, over a hundred and twenty thousand farmers are tilling land co-operatively. A strong National Farm Workers Co-operative Federation has branches in most of the country.

Some effort has been made in Peru to put old communal Incan *ayllus*, or village commons, on a co-operative basis. Co-operatives are not greatly advanced in Bolivia, although the law relieves them of most taxes, and they enjoy a twenty-five per cent discount on railroads.

In Chile most dairy farms are in a co-operative setup. One co-op there is a million-dollar concern, with the most modern plants for canning and dehydrating milk. Fruit co-operatives have proved popular and successful, particularly to provide capital for the long period before trees mature.

Improved Standards

Over the last few decades rural working conditions have improved almost everywhere. The South American peasant, long held down to a coolie level, steeped in despair and ignorance, is beginning to emerge as a human being. The change has been brought about by peasant unrest and organization, even open revolt; by new wage, housing and sanitary legislation; and by more enlightened owners.

Much credit must be given to the international labor bureau of the old League of Nations which brought about the adoption in nearly all Latin American countries of standard farm labor laws.

But the greatest impetus was given by the Mexican Revolution. The new regulations governing farm-working conditions, written into the 1917 constitution and implemented by detailed legislation providing for minimum wage, health and educational standards, have been studied and widely adopted by other countries.

Forced labor existed in Guatemala from colonial days on. Even up to 1944 private owners could call on the army to round up village workers at the point of the bayonet and deliver them during harvesttime. Dictator Jorge Ubico made a big fanfare of abolishing this abuse but merely legalized it by a vagabondage law forcing all rural inhabitants to work three months on public works for a pittance. Army officers and contractors then farmed them out to private estates.

The fine green-stone National Palace, the new pink wedding-cake post office, Ubico's many large handsome police and army barracks, were largely built by such bayonet labor. Workers on the Inter-American Highway were thus recruited, and the Dictator protested vehemently when United States officials tried to pay slightly better wages.

Following Ubico's overthrow in 1944 the new government headed by Arévalo completely abolished all such coercion and set up many new standards for farm workers. Good rural housing was then required by law. Government specifications called for one of three types of concrete and tile construction for (a) hot lowlands, (b) highlands, (c) malarial areas.

On this the owners fought the government bitterly but they were tactfully won over. The government assisted them in every way to comply at the lowest possible expenditure. It provided machinery for mixing concrete or making cinder blocks. A drastic price reduction for all cement was secured from private companies. The railroads reduced tariffs considerably for all materials shipped. The government also provides ten-year low-interest loans to owners unable to bear the immediate outlay.

Extensive rural housing is being pushed in Venezuela and Colombia.

Chile, though its farm workers are in a deplorable condition even compared with low Latin American standards, was one of the first to tackle rural housing. Since 1938 the Caja de Colonización Agrícola has built about a thousand houses, and other government agencies have built large workers' *colectivos* or apartment houses. These have every modern convenience. We visited them in several towns. Always with a cream-colored exterior even in smaller communities, they loom as the tallest and best edifice on the landscape. The program of the Caja calls for building three thousand more houses and fifty new rural schools by 1948.

Argentine Estancia

Señor Diego Rosales invited me to Teja Verde (Green Tile), his big wheat and cattle *estancia* near Sante Fé—one of the largest and finest in all Argentina.

It is impossible to say whether Hollywood imitates a rich Argentina *estancia* or vice versa. Certainly the tiled swimming pool, with its garden appurtenances, seemed right out of the latest song-and-dance film of the movie city. The proportion of stunning women (and blondes, natural and synthetic) was quite as large, and the bathing halters were nearly down to minimum requirements.

To one side of the palatial rambling ranch house, shaded by ombus and eucalyptus, were whitewashed corrals where thoroughbred horses are raised. On all sides stretched level green acres of alfalfa and wheat clear to the lonely horizon—the great flat circle that spells so much of the interior of Argentina—the vast Pampa.

After-dinner conversation, with cigars and liquers, dealt angrily with the new peasants' protective law of Juan Perón—the *Ley de Peón*.

President Perón, the latest master of the loaves and fishes, is today the man most hated—and most often admired—by the great wheat and cattle barons. He represents the new industrial revolution in Argentina, a new kind of progress—the fight for national independence, freedom from improper British and North American "economic imperialism," the promotion of public works, the drive for new roads, railroads and air lines, the building up of the industrial potential, the spread of health and sanitation through the back country, the improvement of interior towns and cities. He has fought consistently for better living conditions for the people.

The wheat and cattle barons have never wanted Argentina's economic independence from Great Britain, historically their best customer. When in control of the government they were always willing to make deals forbidding the building of roads or the establishment of industries frowned on by the British. Treaties blocking such industry and such roads were even signed. The wheat growers were never interested—since they already could get their produce to market over the British railroads—in new roads and better transportation. To them sanitation, education, public works merely meant higher taxes. Above all they did not want adjacent towns built up. New industries near by would have led to competition for labor. Having their own palatial homes, they did not live in such towns, did not get supplies from them.

"Why worry about Rio Cuarto when there's Paris?" But Paris and Europe have been "gone" now these nine years.

According to our conversation at Señor Rosales', the big estates are now threatened with a triple squeeze, on the selling, buying and labor ends.

To meet wartime buying by the governments of the United States and Great Britain, Argentina had to bargain nationally to get a good price for her wheat, meat, hides, linseed, wool, etc. So all surplus agricultural exports came to be handled by the government, much as they are today by the United States with far less profit. England and nearly all other governments still have nationalized buying for most essential products, and the United States has many wartime holdover contracts still in effect. Argentina handles all such export goods through the government Institute for Promotion of Trade (IAPI).

This system was originally implanted by the wheat and meat barons themselves when they largely controlled public affairs. All the folk at Rosales' place agreed such steps had been necessary and inevitable if Argentina was not to get the short end of the stick. But they are now uneasy. Although, despite their hatred for Perón, they are getting larger profits than ever before in the history of the country, they complain pretty steadily about the great revenue the government skims off every transaction.

Also, they fear the rising cost of machinery and supplies will wipe out their present superprosperous position. They are very angry at the United States about that. The famine of needed machinery and the excessive prices call out a bitter cry everywhere from the Rio Grande to Cape Horn.

In October 1947 Miguel Miranda, head of IAPI, told the United States Army corn-buying mission: "Send me gasoline, trucks, locomotives and freight cars, and I'll be able to send you the food you want." And he told the public: "They give us nothing, but still ask us to produce more. What benefit is it to us, to the world, if our grain rots because we can't move it?"

In 1946 Herbert Hoover toured Latin America to find out what the various countries could contribute to the feeding of Europe. One wonders why such findings have been ignored, why no sensible system of economic co-operation has been worked out with the southern countries, why we refused even to discuss this at the Rio Conference. Argentina, if she had not been boycotted so long and if she were not still blocked on getting machinery and other materials, if she were not being prevented from buying gasoline, could easily supply the extra quantities of grain that can now be supplied by the United States only through mounting prices, soap-opera meatless and chickenless days, and sacrifice. Why have such possibilities not been properly explored? Why are Americans needlessly and ruthlessly thrown out of work as in the distilling industry? Are not those Americans quite as good as Frenchmen and Italians overseas? Is not the proper co-ordination of the Western Hemisphere quite as important as that of Europe?

To combat foreign monopoly Perón has pooled all machinery and farm equipment in the National Institute. By forcing competitive bids and buying in mass quantities he has been able to get what machinery there is to be had—mostly from England and Sweden, some from Spain, Italy and France—at the lowest possible price. Thereby he has also insured a market for Argentina products. But the landowners fear this soon may prove too easy a way for the government to get income, that they may have to pay even higher prices. They favor it, if——

Now, with all United States surpluses going to Europe, perhaps later on to the Orient, Latin America fears it may have to go without for years on end, while its dollar balances are used up in fripperies. This would mean considerable setback to industry, transportation and living standards. As a result, though the landed proprietors still hate Perón, now, because of lack of machinery for the great mechanized *estancias*, they are gradually falling into line behind his efforts to build factories.

As one man at the Rosales estate put it: "You people are up to your neck in Europe, and we can't sit around years and years waiting for you to come across. Besides, your prices were always too steep for us anyway."

But the real gripe about Perón from this aristocratic quarter, which all evening caused the guests to speculate in conspiratorial whispers how this or that general could be bribed to overthrow him, was over his labor and peasant laws. Whatever else he might do, that forever made him unpalatable.

"Why doesn't he just stick to his factories and roads?" groaned one member of the party.

Perón's *Ley de Peón* filled the Rosales smoking room with Stygian gloom.

Until Perón came along Argentina in all its history had passed only twenty-five innocuous labor laws—one of the few large countries without a modern labor code. Previous dictatorial regimes had failed to adopt model Geneva legislation. Within six months Perón put across more labor legislation than had ever before been adopted.

His peasant law establishes minimum wages per living costs, local conditions and skills. It provides for proper housing. In most places, prior to the 1943 revolution, Argentina workers and their families had to sleep in stables or pens, often on hard open ground even in winter. Under the Perón law, three adequate meals a day replaced the previous two-meal crust-of-bread diet. The new legislation calls for three daily rest periods, two weeks' vacation with pay, free medical and hospitalization for the worker and his family, collective bargaining, signed contracts, social insurance, workers' compensation. The standards set are far in advance of those for migratory workers in the United States.

"That law elected Perón," grudgingly admitted one owner over his strong Mendoza cognac.

Just as after the Civil War in the United States Southern cotton growers used to vote their Negroes en masse, so the big Argentine proprietor used always to ride into the election booth and announce that all his *inquilinos* voted for Fulano de Tal, whereupon the corresponding ballots were stuffed in. But in 1946 for the first time the right of farmers and peasants to vote was sternly enforced. Even the big proprietors —as do all opposition parties—ruefully admit that technically at least, whatever the preliminary campaign abuses, the voting was the most honest ever staged. Ninety per cent of all peasants voted for Perón.

"And that," remarked Señor Rosales grimly, "is precisely why democracy is no good for Argentina—not yet." He gave me a condescending smile. "For us, for the time being, the Franco system in Spain would best answer our needs."

"Many people in the United States call Perón a fascist."

Don Diego snorted. "And since when have the people of the United States ever tried to understand Argentina?" . . .

September 12, 1947, Miguel Miranda declared: "Other governments accumulate gold, but we have to accumulate something better—food.

Since so many nations need food and cannot eat gold, our economy today is one of the healthiest in the world."

He might have added that for the first time in the country's history the peasants and farmers who produced that food were beginning to eat and live a bit more decently.

Making New Land

Ever since the Calles government (1924-28) Mexico has been investing increasingly large sums in irrigation and power projects. The big Calles dam irrigated a large coastal fruit and sugar-cane region in Tamaulipas. The present Mexican Six-Year Plan has set aside a billion and a half pesos to increase irrigated areas by about three million acres.

Preliminary work has been started on a superproject that is expected to take twelve years, a great TVA electrical and farm development of the Papaloapam, the River of Butterflies, which flows down from the great Oaxaca mountain gorges, through mighty mahogany forests and the Zapotec farming villages, to the vast undeveloped lake harbor of Tequepán on the Vera Cruz coast—an enormous stretch of sun-drenched bay surrounded by jungles and purple mountains. The river passes through Mexico's richest tobacco region, which rivals the best of Cuba, the famous Valle Nacional, where men were flogged to toil, despair and death in the early Porfirio Díaz period, and on through the finest banana groves of the land. Finally, winding in great silver loops, it moves across the plains between coconut trees and big sugar estates.

At the quaint sand-dune settlement of Puerto Alvarado, I took one of the regular little freight and passenger launches that chug up to the various river towns—rather dilapidated places these late years—the thatched houses and church tower of Güendulain, the stately peeling columns of Tlacotalpan where Pofirio Díaz once lived, the bower of fruit and gourds of Tuxpán.

Later for days on end I horsebacked through the giant canyons of the upper reaches of the stream where it is known as the Quiotepec, under great red sandstone bluffs and cactus pincushion mountains, through Indian towns and steep cornfields.

All told, this river drains one of the richest, most magnificent areas of Mexico.

Already the Medical Sanitation Board of the Secretary of Hydraulic Resources, Adolfo Oribe Alba, has been stamping out malaria in the meadows and making a general health survey. As the region is brought under sanitary control, roads, river docks, irrigation, drainage canals, flood control will be attacked. Eventually four main dams and two small dams will be constructed. About half a million farm acres will be opened up, and some two hundred thousand kilowatts of electricity will be generated by two plants. A wide range of food processing and metallurgical industries are planned.

Brazil has eight replicas of the Tennessee Valley in the works, including that on the San Francisco River, known as "the Life Artery of Brazil." Early in 1947 the United States Export-Import Bank put up $7,500,000 toward the hydraulic development of the Vale de Rio Doce, where are located rich iron mines.

Uruguay is pushing the big Rio Negro dam, 150 miles from Montevideo, with a $12,000,000 Export-Import loan. Over a million dollars are being spent to irrigate nearly twenty thousand acres in the Arroyo Metaojo de Solís region.

Argentina, now making an aerial survey of over-all hydroelectric possibilities, is already going ahead with dozens of plans. It is also co-operating with Chile in building plants west of the Andes which will transmit part of their power across the border to Argentina. In April 1947 the governments of Argentina and Uruguay drew up final plans for jointly harnessing the majestic Salto Grande Falls on the Uruguay River in one of the world's largest hydroelectric projects. Plans call for a quarter-mile-long dam and an artificial lake of 230 square miles. This will cause a big development of Salto, already growing fast and now Uruguay's second city, in a cattle, citrus and honeybee belt, and of Concordia, one of the most progressive cities of Argentina in what is known as the Mesopotamia, an exceedingly fertile area. In Venezuela the government Corporación de Fomento is building the El Cenego dam to irrigate 80,000 acres of new land.

Peru is working out a big Tennessee Valley project in Duck Canyon on the Santa River in the northern coastal area. Not only will the controlled water provide enough power for nearly half the country, make possible big metallurgical, fertilizer, refining and chemical works, but it will also irrigate a large section of the coast desert where anything will grow provided water is available.

A new town called Hydroelectra has come into being 4,300 feet up in the Andes. Here the big Santa River drops down from the snows of Mount Huascarán, towering 22,185 feet into the southern skies, and from other mighty white hyperthyroid giants of the great Cerro de Pasco Knot where the Andean chains tangle together.

At Hydroelectra the river plunges through narrow stone Duck Canyon, and here is going forward (to be completed in 1949) one of the unique and most important South American power projects.

The place is reached via the little port of Chimbote on the Inter-American Highway. This lies on the edge of the desert, quite narrow here, and on the one really good but undeveloped ocean harbor in all Peru, a natural deep-water bay big enough to hold the navies of the world. Before the war it was an abandoned shore, although Japanese settlers had cannily bought up surrounding acreage. Today there are a fine modern dock, coal chutes for the high-grade anthracite now mined in the vicinity, and a cluster of modern homes. In a few years it will probably be a great industrial center, for here are to be located the big processing and manufacturing plants.

The new highway to Hydroelectra crosses the desolate rainless plain and winds up through barren sand mountains. Only along the river itself, one of the biggest and steadiest of Peru's west-coast streams, is vegetation lush, and a few farms are seen.

The power site was discovered and development conceived by a brilliant Peruvian engineer. Work is now going forward under the direction of Dr. Barton Jones, former Tennessee Valley man. It is unique, an inexpensive project, though it calls for plenty of stone boring. Only one small dam, easily constructed between the pinched-together Duck Canyon walls, is required to shunt the river through solid inner stone channels for a drop down concealed stone shafts that will give a fall eight times that of Niagara. Turbines and generators, buried deep in the mountain, will provide 125,000 kilowatts. Subsequently other dams lower down will break the 4,000-foot flight of water to low country to provide an additional 100,000 kilowatts and irrigate a great coastal garden that eventually will surround the steel and other plants at Chimbote.

The project, although a $25,000,000 Export-Import loan was offered, is being financed wholly by the government Corporación Peruana del Santa, which will also supervise industrial development. The initial cost to get power flowing in the main plant will come to only about $3,500,000, over half of which had been expended by the end of 1947. The cost per kilowatt hour will be only a mil, far less than that in the Tennessee Valley.

Along the slopes and crests of the mighty Andes above Hydroelectra runs one of the old Inca main roads, north from Cuzco to the royal Cajamarca baths and on to Quito in Ecuador. Curiously, the unusual nature of the Santa project, with its inner stone conduits, has striking similarity in method and spirit to Incan engineering feats. The early people, too, sometimes bored through stone mountains for their elaborate "Zigzag" conduits and irrigation systems.

The Santa development is going to revolutionize the whole Peruvian economy and make possible the rapid development, long delayed, of much of the country.

The Curse of Cain

One great blight in much of Latin America has been the one-crop or one-product system. A country largely dependent for its prosperity and independence on a single major export is unhealthy and unstable. Nearly always this has thrown up one-crop government—dictatorship—a totalitarian one-man system.

Since most southern countries are more highly geared for foreign trade than more developed lands, the consequences of the one-crop system have been doubly serious. Normally more than forty per cent, sometimes even sixty per cent, of Chile's entire production has been exported. Nearly ninety per cent of this used to be nitrates and copper.

After World War I sales of those products dropped off so abruptly that millions of tons were stacked at mine, port warehouse and dock—frozen in perpetual stench. With synthetic nitrates pushing into even near-by Bolivia cheaper than the natural product could be scraped off the Chilean desert and refined, Chile collapsed.

Whole towns were depopulated. Stores put up their shutters forever. Unemployment, hunger, a wild exodus from the nitrate coast to the disorderly public plazas of Santiago and Valparaiso resulted. A revolutionary period clawed the unhappy country.

Even today, along that bleak rainless northern coast, the traveler comes on ghost town after ghost town: huge excavators kneeling in drifting sand like prehistoric dinosaurs, closed dust-covered nitrate *oficinas*, railroad spurs disappearing under piles of white nitrate. Iquique, formerly a flourishing nitrate port, still keeps up a brave show of artificially watered public gardens. It has found some other industries, a little more diversified mining, is pushing some tourist facilities, but it has not been painted in twenty years, and on the sand hills about is a horrifying conglomeration of filthy slum shacks unparalleled anywhere—debris of the great collapse, part of the human and physical wreckage left behind.

At best such one-product conditions can bring only periods of exaggerated prosperity, followed by terrible slumps. Stability is impossible, either in industry or politics. What security has any nation if it must depend entirely on outside markets, prices set in far-off New York or London?

In some cases a single push button beside a mahogany desk in downtown New York could spell prosperity or suffering not merely for workers and owners in a given industry but for a whole nation and its millions. That push button reflected, not the needs and hopes of a particular country, but the quickly changing figures on a blackboard in the speculative stock market, or supply and demand in far corners of the globe, or the passing alarms of war. Or perhaps the push button was the all-powerful gadget of a world-wide cartel. The producing country or countries rarely had any say in the matter.

Besides that, the whole raw-product scramble brought much trouble. It helped occasion the rule of force, not the rule of the people. By-products were militarism, tyranny, sharp class divisions, lack of education and sanitation, unrest, revolution, Marine interventions, wars. Several Caribbean countries still revolve in that vicious circle.

Chile's long War of the Pacific against Peru and Bolivia was to grab the nitrate fields, mostly already British-owned. The armed uprising toward the end of last century against Chile's great Liberal President Balmaceda, financed by foreign nitrate and railway companies, was known as "the nitrate revolt." Oil played the main part in the long bloody Chaco War. Oil, gold and other potential resources were involved in the bloody disputes between Ecuador and Peru. Some years ago rival foreign banana companies whipped up a Central American boundary dispute that would have brought certain war had not one company bought the other out.

Fortunately the situation has greatly changed everywhere in the past few decades. In most countries remarkable gains have been made in broadening out the national economies. More push buttons at home make the single far-off push button less potent.

Twenty years ago Mexico depended on oil for nearly seventy per cent of her exports and her federal revenues—oil entirely in foreign hands. What economic health could exist? How could anything result but disorder and revolution? Oil, then the very lifeblood of Mexico, played its sinister role in corrupting officials, in producing banditry, disorder, civil war, and international ill will that came close to war. Oil, now in government hands, still is a corrupting influence, as witness the 1946 scandals over thieving officials and labor leaders. But what is really important is that oil is now a relatively insignificant item in Mexico's over-all productive picture. Even tourists and movie production have become more important, provide more wealth and income. Today Cantinflas, the great Mexican comedian, probably grosses as much as a whole flock of oil wells. In return for sunshine, colorful peasants, colonial ruins, scenery and service, tourists have been dropping a million pesos a day in Mexico.

Several decades ago, about seventy per cent of Brazil's exports was coffee—that magnificent coffee growing from the deep red soil, the *terra rosa*, of the south-coast foothills. Today coffee, though exports are as large as ever, provides only a little over thirty per cent of the total, is expected to drop as low as seventeen per cent.

Venezuela, which under the atrocious Vicente Gómez dictatorship put all eggs in the petroleum basket, is now carrying out a far-reaching program of farm and factory diversification. So long as oil in foreign hands accounted for ninety per cent of the country's revenues, the people could hope for little democracy, education, decent living standards or any permanent stability.

In Cuba, when the great sugar "dance of the millions" collapsed after World War I and Dictator Machado was finally driven out, strenuous efforts were made by Grau, Mendieta and Batista to diversify agriculture, grow more foodstuffs, build up small industries, exploit the rich iron, copper and manganese deposits and get away from complete dependence on sugar. Since at best sugar is a sweatshop industry, unless it be greatly supplemented by other production, it brings low living standards, seasonal starvation and periodic boom and bust. The bust each time brings about revolutionary conditions and dictatorship and, in the recent past, Marine interventions.

Argentina has been working for years on a survey of all resources and new industrial possibilities—plans now really getting into high gear under Perón.

This general Latin American trend has required the development of new lands through irrigation and power projects, the opening up of new frontiers, and above all the starting of new farm crops.

New Crops

A. MEXICO

We motored from Mexico City north over the Inter-American Highway, greatly improved since first opened, magnificent for its scenery, comfort and roadside facilities. After crossing the upland plateau through vast ravines, the road drops down to hot country at Tamazanchale, climbs a mountain spur, then hits real hot country at Valle.

From here on, the rolling foothill countryside has been completely transformed. The last time we made this trip (1937), except for a sugar-cane belt near El Mante, the road was flanked only by sagebrush and chaparral. Today on both sides for a whole day of long driving are new glistening citrus groves—oranges, lemons, grapefruit. Already Mexico is the chief producer of limes in the Western Hemisphere, and this new region enjoys the great advantage of being wholly free from frosts. Near towns the highway is lined with fragrant fruit stands. Land never before used in human history has been cleared and made over into a garden spot, perhaps now the world's greatest single unbroken citrus belt.

This is merely one small picture of the new crop diversification in Mexico and the continent. Mexico in the past has been more fortunate than some countries, for it has long had a varied list: corn, beans (production doubled since 1937), rice (greatly expanded), coffee (up fifty per cent over ten years ago), sugar cane (up fifty per cent), tobacco, vanilla beans, cacao. In the past few years around Fortín, Vera Cruz, have been built up some of the most modern and efficient coffee *fincas* on the whole hemisphere. Spices, sesame, castor-oil, beans, indigo, waxes, gums, vegetable oils are increasingly important. Mexico is the producer of such important industrial fibers as *ixtli* hemp, henequén, pita, *zacate* and a dozen others. In more recent years, bananas (for a time badly hit by floods and the sigataka blight), pineapples, avocados, papayas and other fruits have pushed into the picture. Probably when improper United States fruit restrictions protecting privileged groups are eventually abolished, the American public will be able, thanks to rapid modern transportation, to enjoy a dozen different kinds of tropical fruits we are not allowed even to smell though they pile high and golden in the markets of the country right next door.

Wheat, now grown in the highlands, has reached half a million tons, not a large amount, but partly relieving need for foreign currency. Cotton production, more than doubled in less than ten years, is now three times the amount required by Mexican textile mills. Thanks to the irrigation of the rich northwest Yaqui Valley, chick-pea output (standard daily food in Spain) has tripled in ten years. Tomato production, much of which is exported to the United States, has also tripled. Cattle growing, ruined by the revolution, has staged a big comeback, though the hoof-and-mouth disease, which hit in 1946, was akin to a national tragedy.

About a million rubber trees have been set out—new sturdy strains. Tung-oil plantations have been started. Other special Far Eastern products, spices, fibers, oils, drugs, hit "for a loop" by war, are now finding a new home on Mexican soil.

B. Argentina

Few countries have so rapidly diversified farm production as Argentina, long the world's great exporter of wheat, corn, mate and linseed. Fruit also is now entering the picture in a big way. At the beginning of this century Argentina produced only a few thousand tons of peanuts. Now a quarter of a million are grubbed out. In 1930 only a thousand tons of sunflower seed were grown; now, over a million. At the beginning of the century only a thousand tons of cotton seed were produced; now, nearly a quarter million. Linseed output has reached as much as two million tons a year. The olive crop has been increased fivefold since 1943; and late in 1946 cheaper grades of oil were selling in Buenos Aires stores for ten cents a quart.

This general increase showing in vegetable oils has been remarkable—tenfold from 1930 to 1942 and now even greater. By 1942, although Argentina's consumption had increased threefold, one hundred thousand tons were exported. This was twice as much as Argentina herself had had to import prior to the war. It was equal to fifty per cent of the entire world's net imports of all such oils. Spanish, Italian and Greek economies will be hard hit from now on.

C. PANAMA

For decades a smoldering feud, concealed by coldly polite interchanges or silence, then becoming vocal and featured by petty retaliations, went on between our Canal Zone authorities and Panama. The author happened to be in an Ancón movie house on the Zone when a newsreel showed President Harmodio Arias being entertained at the White House in Washington. The audience, made up mostly of White Zone employees, whistled and jeered, "Monkey!"

It was always easier for North Americans to boss Jamaican Negroes, speaking English and docilely accepting "silver" wages and Jim Crow regulations, than for our civil servants to learn Spanish. In practice most Panamanian products were boycotted by the Zone commissaries.

Panamanian development was thereby retarded. The interior, almost devoid of highways, was largely abandoned to primitive agriculture. Education and sanitation were woefully lacking. The center of the country along the canal was reduced to a tourist-circus place of curio shops and endless side-show brothels, such as famed Coconut Grove. The United States Government, via the Panama Railroad, still owned nearly the whole area of the city of Colón in Panama and so at that time was probably the greatest slum and whorehouse landlord on earth. The Panamanian municipal authorities could collect no taxes on real estate save for a few blocks owned by Panamanians; nevertheless they were obliged to maintain police, fire-department, street-cleaning corps, schools and other public services.

Even along the Canal Panamanian merchants had a hard time competing with the Zone canteen stores, at that time open to all comers, not merely to Zone employees. Zone goods came in on government bottoms with minimum freight charges, were mostly free of excise taxes, paid no Panama duties, were sold at cost. No Panamanian merchant could compete with seven-cent cigarettes, fifty-cent Japanese tennis rackets, sixty-cent men's shirts. At the same time most goods from nearby Panama were taboo in Zone canteens.

Although a few typical Zone brass hats used to try to solve everything in adjacent Panama by sending in troops whenever there was a dogfight, a few high military men were deeply concerned about this situation. This writer talked with one high officer who volubly cursed the whole setup.

The smallest common sense, he insisted, indicated that proper Canal

Zone defense required the fullest possible development of all Panama's resources, plus a large technically trained Panama labor supply. Should the Canal be cut off in wartime (and how close we came to this!), adequate food supplies and trained men should be available close at hand. Proper Panamanian transportation facilities would permit quick mobilization to any menaced coastal point.

Little by little a dent was made in the attitude of the Zone's civil employees, most of whom, particularly the unionized workers, seem to have violent and ignorant race prejudices. Before the war the old hostile attitude, partly because of the good-neighbor policy, was on the way out, "washed up." President Roosevelt O.K.'d a treaty rectifying many past abuses and settling the most thorny points at issue. Gradually Panama beef and other products were sold in the Zone canteens, which were then limited to their original purpose—to supply cheap goods to the Zone personnel, not to compete with Panamanian business. During the war itself the need for supplies, owing to shipping shortages, became pressing. The need for labor broke down the old near-boycott of Latin Americans. Workers were drawn in large numbers from Panama, Colombia, Ecuador and Central America.

Plenty of sore points remain. Latin American workers and travelers, nearly all of whom must funnel through the Zone, are always outraged at the preposterous harassment, complicated regulations and even the arrogance of immigration and customs officials. They invariably grow outraged at the "silver" scale of lower wages paid for work exactly equal to that performed by higher paid North American "gold" employees, and the humiliation of having to use "silver" drinking fountains (there rarely are any) and "silver" toilets and stand in line in the post office at a "silver" window. Such incidents rankle long.

But at least, through the breakdown of many of the Canal Zone's improper economic privileges and its boycott, Panama has been helped at long last to develop rapidly in new directions. This, too, has been part of a determined policy first started under Panama's most able President, Harmodio Arias, back in the thirties.

Previously bananas provided eighty-five per cent of Panama's exports. This made the entire country dependent on one highly competitive product and on a single foreign company—a very unhealthy state. Interventions, armed dictatorships, widespread poverty were some of the answers.

Rice—half of which had to be imported ten years ago—is now the chief farm crop, and production is so near sufficient that imports have been prohibited. Today the new sugar industry supplies more than half the country's needs, will soon supply all. A large alcohol industry has sprung up. Cacao exports have increased. Coffee is now all home-grown. A scientific plantation has been laid out at Boquete, and a million trees have been planted in the Volcán region above David near the Costa Rica border. Roads have been built into the area.

Cattle growing, especially on the fine savannas of Caclé and Chiriquí, has increased, and export of meat (to the Zone) and of hides figure in trade totals. The Nestle and Anglo-Swiss milk companies now supply all Panama's canned milk. New plantations produce cube (for rotenone), kapok and abacá. By 1944 abacá-fiber export amounted to 22 per cent of the total. Rubber, coconut, balata and tortoise-shell gathering is pushed. Lumbering grows steadily. All these enterprises have stimulated the building of new highways.

Banana exports, though not decreasing, now account for only forty-five per cent of the total. The rich multiple resources of all Panama are coming into better use. The country has ceased to be merely a dirty back alley of the Canal Zone.

D. Brazil

In Brazil the war called forth an incredible number of new farms and forest developments that have forever tumbled coffee from its former proud exclusive position. Cacao—Brazil has long been the world's second largest producer—has boomed. Rubber, lumber, balata, quinine, fibers, vegetable oils and waxes helped make up the wartime loss of Asiatic supplies. Permanent new industries were started. Extensive plantings of jute, abacá, sunflower seed, rubber trees, etc., were made. The government took over the great Ford rubber plantation in the Amazon basin. The United States wartime "good-will" search for rubber was a costly, unpleasant fiasco, a near international scandal and disgrace, but the production of plantation rubber with new disease-resistant strains promises long-range profits and the possible re-establishment of Brazil as a factor in the world market. Babassú oil, obtainable in unlimited quantities from more than fifty million trees, is increasingly exported. At home it now drives Diesel engines, tractors and autos in a land where petroleum is only beginning to be developed. This great diversification better cushions all agriculture and makes possible a stronger, more stable country.

Even before the World War new enterprises, some now greatly expanded, such as harvesting timbo for rotenone, tapping turpentine trees, growing tea, cultivating silkworms, had been started. Brazilian silks now appear in New York department stores—perhaps a worse blow for Japan than the loss of a dozen islands. Castor-bean oil production expanded two and a half times from 1940 to 1943. A million and a half tung-oil trees have been planted in Paraná; half a million in Rio Grande do Sul. The 1944 production of edible oils was in the neighborhood of a hundred thousand tons. Sugar-cane growing, long a dispersed, disorganized industry, has been drawn into a national pattern, with enormous new refineries and a fantastically large production of industrial alcohol. Rice has become an export product.

In eight years, instead of importing large quantities of tomatoes, canned tomatoes, ketchup and so on, Brazil has come to export those products to thirty countries. By 1941 this was more than half again the amount previously imported even though domestic consumption has grown vastly. Citrus and other fruits are increasingly exported. New air services all through the Amazon basin are rapidly opening up new farm and cattle centers.

Cotton

One could tell of the development of quinine and abacá in Guatemala; new fibers in Honduras; cube for rotenone in Haiti, Honduras, Peru and Panama; African palm oil in Honduras, Costa Rica and Haiti; cohune nut oil in Mexico, Central America and Colombia; Japanese luffa gourds in Cuba; sesame in Ecuador and Colombia; barbasco and tea in Peru; carnauba wax in Brazil; lemon and citronella grass in Mexico, Honduras and Brazil; new drugs, such as belladonna in Argentina (one hundred thousand pounds) and in Guatemala; ipecac from Central America and Brazil; many other drugs from Brazil, the Caribbean, Argentina, Chile and elsewhere that were not exploited to any degree before the war.

But let us turn to one highly competitive crop—cotton.

The world's largest growers are the United States, India and the Soviet Union. Brazil is now fourth. There acreage is far more fertile, gives from three to five times the yield of eroded, soil-exhausted Georgia and is potentially equal in extent to the whole cotton area of the United States. Labor costs are far lower.

Starting from scratch, in four years—by 1941—Brazil was picking 2,500,000 bales. Even before the war we saw the handwriting on the wall. In 1911 the United States produced three-fifths of the world's cotton; by 1939 less than half. In 1911-12 we exported over 11,000,000 bales; in 1938-39 only 3,327,000. With depression, decline in fertility, acreage curtailment, plowing under and artificial price boosting, United States cotton, despite its long-staple quality, found ever-harder sledding in a barter, gold-poor world. Cotton growing in Brazil, the Chaco and elsewhere south, as in Africa and India, rapidly expanded to undersell our product. Large North American brokerage houses moved bag and baggage down to Rio and São Paulo.

In Peru, this last trip, we sat among the crumbling Inca ruins and bleaching bones of ancient Pachacamac atop a coastal sandhill and looked across broad acres of yellow-flowering cotton from the Andes to the sea. By 1941 Peru was shipping out 382,000 bales, grown in addition to increased amounts needed for new textile mills. The following year, in that lush boondoggling period when public funds were not under inspection, United States taxpayers' money was used to subsidize Peruvian growers to restrict acreage. This clownish, antieconomical procedure in a foreign country could not be kept up and the industry is again expanding.

In the meantime Argentina exports surpassed those of Peru. Today every South American country except Uruguay is striving for full cotton self-sufficiency. All except Chile—which hopes to develop cotton lands by desert irrigation, particularly back of Arica—have about attained it. Most will export. In October 1947 Perón visited the Chaco of inner Argentina (which through recent colonization has grown enough to become a province instead of a territory) where he crowned a cotton queen.

The southern countries foresaw postwar dangers long before peace came and sought to reef before the storm by pushing products in demand in neighbor countries, in Australia, South Africa and other remaining free markets, and to create broader self-sufficient agricultural foundations.

In this they hoped to offset the loss of markets in eastern Europe, now behind the iron curtain of the Soviet closed trade system, the loss of markets in the Orient and the greatly reduced market in the remaining western portion of Europe due to economic decline resulting from the war. Some Latin Americans fear that the Marshall Plan will direct most European purchases to the United States and leave the southern lands out in the cold.

More self-sufficiency, more specialized production, more inter-American trade are sought as partial solutions. In all Latin America the road now being followed to greater economic independence—which in the long run will benefit them and us—has been precisely toward greater diversification, larger home consumption, more extensive trade within the continent.

Colombia, for instance, during the war and postwar worked out a far-reaching "Agricultural Development Plan," since farming accounts for sixty-five per cent of the country's production. In spite of her vast fertile acreage, Colombia long has been obliged to import many food-stuffs that could be grown at home. The main stress of the plan, there-fore, has been to promote diversification and more self-sufficiency. Self-sufficiency and possible export, it has found, can be easily attained in copra, cacao, sugar, corn, beans and rice, and, with more effort, in cotton and wheat. The operation of the plan was started in 1945. It calls for soil conservation and health projects, improved farm techniques, mecha-nization, free distribution of seed, development of consumer markets.

All such new developments will strengthen the southern countries and provide better ballast against the storms of fluctuating world prices, totalitarian controls, economic nationalism, subsidies, international car-tels and the great iron empires that now make free trade and free enter-prise in most of the world a complete myth. For Latin America the World War made a necessity out of a virtue.

The lack of adequate markets beyond the Americas, the lack of needed machinery and replacements as yet unobtainable in the United States in part due to the concentrating of all available American aid in Europe and the Orient, also the inflation in the United States which makes so many commodity goods even more expensive to Latin America than to us—these and other factors force a continuation of that virtu-ous necessity. Though peace is piling up monumental difficulties, it is accentuating the whole continental wartime trend of healthy farm growth and the building up of many new crops.

The agrarian plan of the new Betancourt government in Venezuela stresses (1) the opening up of the rich southern hinterland of plains, mountains and jungle by resettlement, farming, industry and immigra-tion; (2) agricultural self-sufficiency through greater, more varied pro-duction. Betancourt had laid down in detail a whole new farm policy for the country in 1940, long before it seemed he would ever come into power.

"How are Betancourt's plans for new crops getting along?" I asked a prominent Venezuelan.

"I can tell you this: in the next war or the next depression, our people will eat. The long oil dictatorship and Gómez' seizure of nearly all land in the country made us literally a slave people. We raised no food, scarcely any. Nearly all had to be imported at high prices. Since only a few thousand Venezuelans had jobs in the oil fields, this meant that the mass of the people had no income to buy enough food. Then during the war there was none to buy. The tankers could keep on taking out oil, but they couldn't bring anything in, and no other shipping came our way. When war ended, most of our people looked as though they had just come out of a Nazi prison camp. But from now on we shall eat, and we shall eat well."

In spite of the gloomy state of the world, this change in South America is important, for over much of the region the "Curse of Cain," the one crop, sweatshop feudal system, is being rubbed off the brows of the nations and the peoples.

V Dynamo

Dressed Fleas

Most persons have heard of Mexico's dressed fleas. Examined under a magnifying glass, the tiny creatures wear folk costumes, bright embroidered huipiles or blouses, scarlet sashes, miniature leather sandals. A couple may be decked out in billowy wedding gown and silk topper. Infinite patience and artistry go into this subvisual effort.

It would be easy to write a whole chapter on the psychology of flea dressing. Is such useless effort an attempt to escape from life's realities by a people long broken, for whom life has had little to offer? Certainly it provides an outlet for mordant satire. The stomach at the palace gates may be empty, but fleas are always free. In the Soviet Union the circus clowns were the only ones who safely lampooned Stalin and the terror. In Mexico under former dictators flea dressers enjoyed similar immunity. The lords of loaves and fishes, all the mighty who ran State affairs, the glittering pompous gold-braid generals, the clerics, the police—what could they do about being bitingly caricatured as a dressed flea? To take action against such seditious nonsense would have laid them open to universal derision.

Dressing fleas may be the art of frustration, but other types of hand art are vital to the well-being and happiness of many in rural communities. All over the Green Continent handicrafts have long had an essential place in the scheme of things. They provide a perfect union of utility and creative pleasure. This may partly account for the widespread sensitivity to form and color, the instinctive good taste even on poverty levels of the sunland dwellers.

Along with art and utility, such activities also provide a marked social rhythm, almost a religious rite. Whatever the spur of necessity, the fabrication of hand objects—woven goods, pottery, jewelry, decorative clothing, toys, furniture, hats, mats, basketry and so on—was never really a commercial art. This was its strength—but now its weakness in a supercommercial era. Though the maker, utilizing free time between

97

farm tasks, is usually hopeful of profiting enough to buy gadgets and supplies, he rarely calculates time or gain on a strictly commercial basis. His time has been handed to him free by God and the cycle of the seasons. To use that leisure in a creative way gives him spiritual joy. Since the soil gives him a minimum security, he does not feel the lash of haste—the enemy of all perfect creation. Countrymen coming to city markets never set a fixed price but bargain for anything above actual cost of materials. This whole process of conceiving, producing, journeying to market, mingling with other villagers, gossiping, telling yarns, exercising the wits in clever repartee when bargaining—these are all more important for pleasure and social health than any profit.

Many times this author has encountered peasants on mountain trails, loaded down with pottery or mats, serapes or fowl, bound for a distant city market. Often an offer to buy will be turned down flatly. The main thing for such vendors is not disposing of the product but the excitement of the trip, participation in a satisfying social rhythm.

Once in a town near Mexico City I wanted to buy an Indian woman's entire stock of oranges, spread out on a packing case under a tripod awning.

She flounced her bright red skirts and refused to sell. "What then, pray tell," she demanded hotly, "would I do all the rest of the livelong day?"

This attitude, however quaint to most North Americans, holds in it deep kinship with nature, the ability to find pleasure in daily tasks, the sociability and gregariousness of human beings, a desire to maintain the texture of life unmarred. The accent is on leisure and freedom, not on profit; on living, not on earning a living. For such people life, not hacked into such definite time units as with us, has an onflowing quality and texture: each part with its due measure of beauty and concentrated interest, but all linked together and suffused throughout with religious consciousness. Life is not, as we make it, broken up into separate unrelated compartments: a fixed workday period, a fixed religious day, a fixed daily playtime. Instead, in the spiritually richer Latin world the whole process of living is more woven into one pattern. Each part strengthens the other. Each part belongs to the other. There is unity.

The machine has accomplished the fragmentation of the human soul and the emotions, and for all its manifest blessings, its gift of higher living standards to more people, its grant of wealth and power, it has destroyed certain sides of the human spirit, or at least dulled or debased them. This loss of simple honest workmanship, this haunted glance at the clock for quitting time, this loss of pride and artistry in producing individual objects, this regimentation of work forcing mind and emotions into identical mass patterns of behavior, often victimized by propaganda, demagogues and fascists, this separation of joy and art from daily tasks, the fevered effort to find amusement in ways wholly unrelated to life's duties—all this has much to do with man's abandonment of religion in modern times save as a fetish, a get-ahead club or a parroting of one's neighbors. It lies at the root of the general decline of community taste, for the machine relegates the exercise of taste to groups of specialized designers subordinated to commercialism and tawdry motives, who impose their artistic merit, or lack of merit, on whole nations through the manufacture of cheap mass products. This closing of the doors of individual creative satisfaction in daily tasks lies deep at the root of the general governance of ideas and the spiritual emptiness that gnaws at all men in machine-made cultures.

No screed is meant against the machine or the inevitable, but an indication of some of the meaning of the machine's introduction into Latin America—perhaps on a slightly better basis. The author favors more, not less, machinery: its fullest use in a creative way to tame nature to mankind's needs and give him more leisure with which in time he may recover the arts and spiritual integrity temporarily dimmed.

Unfortunately the superb hand art that brightened the whole face of countries south of the Rio Grande is being debased in many places or driven out by the inevitable march of so-called progress and the overpowering machine.

To carry water it becomes easier to stick a handle crossbar in a five-gallon oil tin than to make a beautifully designed and tinted olla, more likely to break. Some years back I used to smile at the trophies of tourists who came back proudly with hand-woven textiles from Oaxaca—machine-made German imitations of handicrafts.

Handicraft designs in Mexico and Guatemala are frequently inferior to those of only a few years ago. The local arts have suffered by being torn from their natural village setting and their utility, and by being handed over to the Moloch of commercialism. The large city tries to convert them into images of its more sophisticated but uprooted taste. The tourist, blind to the life and the impulses producing such arts, having no such impulses within himself, flies like an arrow to buy the shoddiest examples and thereby creates a demand for more shoddiness. Today in Texcoco and Oaxaca the serapes worn by local people are far superior to those they sell to the undiscerning tourist. But there, as elsewhere, the obligation to produce unworthy art is destructive to the artist. The appearance now of such handicrafts on New York department-store shelves spells more rapid doom: the full substitution of mass-market commercialism for village utility, sociability and unique expression, the imposition, by the gross, of an outside taste wholly counter to the inner spirit of the objects. For such general sale objects become neater, better-tailored, more uniform, but the basic art content diminishes with standardization, and further evolution on the handicraft level is frozen. The spiritual wellsprings are dried up.

The machine is now coming to Latin America more than it ever has. In a few places it is being adopted with safeguards for individual and national welfare. Thus it is to be hoped that it may not wholly destroy the taste and creative sensibilities of human beings as in so many drab European and North American centers. It is to be hoped—though there is not much reason to hope—that the fine handicrafts in certain countries south may also survive. It is amazing how well those arts have endured for four centuries among peoples conquered and broken, reduced to poverty and inferiority. People like those of the Guatemalan highlands, who have been able to keep on turning out such breathtakingly beautiful objects, must indeed be great.

Who can help reveling in the love of art, the fine individual workmanship, the deep appreciation for form and color and composition, that animate the fine textiles of Mexico, Guatemala, Bolivia, Peru; the excellent rugs of Temuco, Chile; the exquisitely wrought silver work of Yucatán and Huancayo; the wood carving of Los Altos; the lacquered gourds of Tehuantepèc and Uruapan—all the beautiful artifacts still produced in the highlands of the Americas?

These and the life they reflect are still part of the glory of the Americas. They still provide vital activities for millions of persons, are truly a large part of the picture of Latin American culture. Not to know them and appreciate them is to know little of some of the moving forces of the New World. That side of Latin America may gradually wither away, but much of it undoubtedly will survive in the attitudes, the emotions and the taste of the peoples.

In Guatemala we sat cross-legged on a mat beside a handloom worker, who improvised his colors and designs as he went along.

"How can you be so sure it will come out right without a pattern?" we asked him.

"I have woven cloth this way since I was six years old. Surely I have had time to learn something. The general pattern is fixed, but the inner designs and colors—we combine those as we like while we go along. Between jobs I get to thinking how this change will look, how this spot of yellow—" he poked his brown finger at a blazing diamond shape he had just woven in—"will do, just that single splash, to bring out all the other colors. Then when I am weaving I get excited and do new things on the spur of the moment. Fresh ideas grow right out of the doing. It is very much like improvising a song. You make it up as you go along, and it makes work easy, and always you want to keep on and on."

Such opportunity is wholly denied an auto assembly-line worker. He can originate nothing. He is a robot. His spiritual and artistic instincts have been amputated from his work, leaving only the scarred stump of automatic efficiency, and, as a by-product, a dull dog-bone struggle over wages. One yellow spot and he would be fired.

Down in Uruapan, Mexico, we walked through a cactus lane around the side of a big adobe tiled house. On a sunny terrace, spread out to dry on all sides were lacquered gourds, big ones, little ones. Other gourds were freshly cut, others had been scraped ivory-smooth, still others had been traced with designs for carving. Some had been transformed into lovely long-necked birds. One young fellow was rubbing color into the grooves. Another was polishing with oil and fine river sand. Even the tiniest children were busy, important and happy.

"The way to do it, the way to carve, to put on paint, to polish—those skills have been in our family for generations," we were told. "Each of us does what he likes best to do. That way everything is better done. Don Miguel here—" a grinning moonface of eighteen—"likes to gather roots and minerals out of which we mix the colors. In the end no two gourds come out exactly alike. That would be utterly boring and silly. No two gourds are shaped just alike. No two human beings are exactly alike. What pleasure would there be in trying to make two gourds exactly alike? And who would want to own one exactly like somebody else owns? Nobody."

To myself I thought, Old Lady, you live a long way from the Rio Grande or you would not utter that "Nobody" with such sublime assurance.

An old toothless fellow heeheed. He was holding a gourd with his bare toes and carving it ad lib. He pointed scornfully to the gourds on which patterns had been penciled.

"That's the way they have to do it now. No talent. No confidence. When did we old-timers have to do it that way? I don't, even now when my hands are not so sure, my eyes dim. No, I have to get the feel of the gourd in my hands, in my toes; then I know right off how to dress it up. I know the proportions, what designs will do, how big they must be, how they will fit together. I fly when I design." He spread his thin old arms like some gaunt bird.

Gold

Mining by hand. Mining by the most modern machinery. Those two methods go on side by side all over Latin America. Mining, whether by men picking emeralds out of rubble or tapping off gold ore by individual hammers, or by some of the most complicated machinery and scientific methods, is one of the major occupations of Latin America, as it was before the Spaniards arrived.

The burning thirst of the Spaniards was for gold—first for the vast accumulated stores being used for art and religious purposes by the Aztecs, Mayas, Chibchas, Quechuas, Araucanos and other indigenous peoples. When those stores had been looted and divided up among the captains and the soldiery and the Royal Fifth shipped off to Spain, the conquerors sought for the sources of the gold and silver in the mountains.

When Hernán Cortés smuggled himself into Cuba in 1504 and was offered a large land grant, he said scornfully: "I came to get gold, not to till the land like a peasant." And when he moved to conquer Mexico, he told Tehuitle, the first Aztec chieftain with whom he dealt: "The Spaniards are troubled with a disease of the heart for which gold is a specific remedy." When emissaries of Montezuma conferred with him in Vera Cruz, he gave them a helmet with the request that it be returned filled with gold.

In Chile, Conquistador Pedro de Valdivia placed such onerous gold tribute on the Araucanos below Concepción that when the Spanish captain was captured by the dashing young *toqué*, or chieftain, Lautaro, the latter is said to have put him to death by pouring molten gold down his throat. "He is so greedy for it, let him have plenty of what he wants."

Soon after the Conquest great mines began pouring forth endless treasure, and from that day to this the capacity of the Old World to drain off the wealth of the New World seems never to have diminished.

The Spaniards worked the mines with Indian slaves, usually chained, branded, lashed to their tasks. Babes were even torn from their mother's breasts and branded for life. When these toilers dwindled in numbers from brutality, undernourishment and disease, Negro slaves were brought in. If, thanks to the work of the priests and monks and later enlightened Crown provisions, such conditions eventually were improved, the harsh methods the first Spaniards imposed in their mines throughout Latin America smack of those in vogue today in the slave camps of the Soviet Union.

Even so, brave legends and much romance hover over Spanish mining ventures in the New World. The daring men who sallied forth into dangerous areas to discover the mines, the fabulous hauls some of them made, all their risks and adventures, provide a seldom equaled epic. The story is told of one Guanajuato mineowner who for a wedding paved fifty yards of the street with silver and lined the bridal chamber with the same chaste metal.

One of the truly great yarns still to be told is that of the fantastic mining prospector and promoter, Frenchman De la Borda, who reamed out millions in silver from Guanajuato, then discovered the rich lodes around Taxco. Much of the beauty of that little showtown is due to his donations and efforts. It was he who laid out the famous La Borda gardens in Cuernavaca, which later became the rural retreat of Maximilian and Carlota.

Potosí, in the Bolivian highlands, where perhaps the greatest silver deposit on earth was discovered, became in its day one of the largest cities in the world. It stimulated the rapid growth of adjacent regions, the upper Argentine cities, Salta, Jujuy and Tucumán; it drained away the fruit and grapes of Tacna Valley in Peru; it brought Arica on the coast of Chile into prominence as a shipping port; it started plantations in the Cochabamba Valley in Bolivia. Likewise it drew produce, textiles, skills and labor from the great pre-Spanish capital of Cuzco and from the new Peruvian settlement of Arequipa. The latter soon spread out under its triple snow peaks with beautiful churches and buildings and is to this day one of the most attractive cities of the Americas. Sugar, fruit, wine and liquors, clothing, blankets, olives, almonds, cereals, meat, leather goods and every sort of luxury were in great demand in Potosí and fetched boom prices.

Pedro Cieza de León in his chronicles tells how some Spaniards returned to Spain wealthy merely from supplying Potosí with *chuño*, frozen potatoes in the Quechua style. The Potosí market, open from dawn to dark, outrivaled even the vast market at Cuzco. The turnover —and most of the trade was among the Indians themselves—was from twenty-five to forty thousand gold pesos each day. "I do not believe," he related, "that any market in the world equals the trade of this one." Another chronicler tells how "many Spaniards grew rich . . . just by having two or three Indian women do their trading in this market." Constantly great llama pack trains, "without any guard or protection," plodded across the Andes and down to the coast, seventy leagues to Arica, with bars of refined silver, and "no silver whatsoever was ever missing."

Something of the excitement of those years shines through the account given by André João Antonil of the discovery by the Portuguese of the rich Minas Geraes mines in Brazil:

"The insatiable thirst for gold stimulated so many people to leave their homes and to brave the rough roads . . . that thirty thousand souls are busy, some seeking, some directing, the search in gold-bearing streams; others in business, buying and selling, not only necessities, but luxuries, more so than in the seaports. . . .

"Portuguese and foreigners come in fleets, bound for the mines. There, from the cities, villages, inlets and back country of Brazil go Whites, Browns, Blacks and many Indians in the service of the Paulist monks . . . persons of every mixture and condition: men and women, young and old, poor and rich, nobles and plebeians, laymen, priests and monks. . . ."

The gold of Goiaz was discovered when a Paulist monk observed gold nuggets in the ears of Indian women on the Araguaya River. He cut off their ears to prove his story. Within ten years after the mines were located, Goiaz, previously unknown, had become a provincial capital and was buying the finest silks and luxuries.

Mercury was essential for gold and silver mining, key to the control of the whole industry. Spanish officials, favored by large mining concerns desirous of monopoly, used quicksilver to win more favors, squeezing out independent miners by allocating it to the more privileged and powerful.

One main source was at Huancavelica high in the Peruvian Andes, which, according to Manuel de Mendiburú in his *Biographical Dictionary*, provided the Spaniards, up to the time of Independence, with more than a million quintals.

We revisited this remote city. After a whole day's run over the highest railroad in the world, from Lima over the crest of the Andes and on to the great Indian market town of Huancayo, we took the narrow-gauge train on up to lofty Huancavelica, set on a barren mountain. It is a quaint, pinkish town, the central buildings constructed of the same rosy cinnabar from which mercury is extracted.

The mines are no longer exploited on the big scale of colonial times. Today it is a sleepy overchurched place, half decaying under tall limber eucalyptus trees.

Most of its simple people live almost exactly as their forebears must have done centuries before the Spaniards. We talked with an old Indian about the faded glories.

He smiled. "We are ignorant folk, Señor," he said slyly, "with none of the great wisdom of you reasoning beings who come so far to seek this curious black liquid—turning pink stone into heavy black ink, not good to drink, not even good for writing—but some of us are happier in our fields than those who work so hard and long for so little in the mines. See!" His hand swept over a circle of planted land. "Corn and potatoes grow here, right against the sky, and we eat, and God be praised! One of my sons worked in the mines. He did not live long. But the rest of us, we live too long, Señor, quite too long."

Chuqui

The old filibuster days of North American capital in Latin America are pretty well over: those adventurous, gambling days of gaudy concession hunters, of grab, fight and rule, the days of such daring condottieri and builders as Minor Cooper Keith, Henry Meiggs, Edward Laurence Doheny, William Braden, William Wheelwright and William Russell Grace. The last flare-up of this sort of grabbing activity, though of different complexion, was the loan buccaneering right after World War I.

The game has changed. Wildcat industries, such as petroleum, have been consolidated, organized. Big business has taken over the reckless individualism of earlier days, in nitrates, mining, plantation crops. Order has come into the helter-skelter picture—less romance, occasionally more justice. Government regulations more and more control such activities. A spirit of nationalism everywhere makes foreign enterprise suspect, to be forced into plans for local welfare and national growth. Labor pushed into the picture as another organized force.

Most big North American companies have learned, a few the hard way, to change with the spirit of the times.

Very recently a large company had over the doorway of its social club: "All Peruvians keep out!"

What would be the reaction in a United States city if a great foreign concern put up a sign over the company club: "All Americans keep out!"

This author suggested to the management that that single insulting sign would eventually cost the stockholders hundreds of thousands of dollars. It came down. The Peruvian people, like those in the rest of Latin America, are no longer in a mood to tolerate nasty nonsense of that sort.

Most foreign companies in Latin America are operating today on as an enlightened a basis as anywhere in the world and mostly pay wages superior to local firms. Initial arrogance and race discrimination have generally gone by the boards. Government regulations have forced the hiring of local citizens, not merely as menial underpaid labor, but as technicians and administrators. Some companies now actually give precedence to citizens of the country if any are able to do the job.

Of course in most southern countries this is now a legal requisite. In Mexico ninety per cent of all employees must be Mexican, and their pay must equal that of foreigners, bracket for bracket. Cuba and Colombia have similar laws. In 1945 Guatemala required that henceforth at least seventy-five per cent of all workers must be Guatemalans, and seventy-five per cent of the total pay roll must go to Guatemalans.

In Argentina the new government Industrial Credit Bank lends only to Argentine firms in which at least seventy-five per cent of management and employees are Argentinians.

In Chile at Chuquicamata, the greatest copper mine in the world, a progressive paternalistic policy has gradually been worked out. In years gone by the Chileans wrote terrible things about Chuquicamata, but today it is one of the more model enterprises.

North Americans, terrorized by big foreign words and ever too much in a hurry to let a poetic-sounding word roll lingeringly over the tongue, have shortened the name to brusque "Chuqui" (Chew-key).

The copper of Chuqui was mined long before the Incas conquered northern Chile, long before the Spaniards. One-eyed Conquistador Diego de Almagro stopped there to shoe his horses with copper. During the succeeding four centuries the deposits were pecked at. Now all necessary supermodern techniques, science and machinery are concentrated there in a desolate corner of Chile.

Compare those methods with some primitive mining still surviving. Such contrasts, living on side by side, between the prehistoric and the most complex modern setups, give zest to any over-all survey of Latin America.

Near Putaendo we visited a gold mine still being worked in the same way as before the Conquest. The barefoot Indians descended by the shaft of a tall pole notched in the fashion that pre-Spanish Araucanos made ladders. Up and down this pole—now, in this the twentieth century—barefoot workers ran agilely with heavy bags of rough ore or water, for the mine was partly flooded.

At Chuqui, on the other hand, the dynamited ore (highest grade is green; the worthless, red) is scooped up by machinery from a great open cut a mile and a half long and a quarter of a mile deep and dumped onto electric trains. At the crushing mills, two miles distant, two cars at a time are picked up by a gigantic metal hand and shaken out like bags of marbles.

Reduced to gravel, the ore is dumped into sulphuric acid leeching vats. The solution, in volume about two per cent of the original ore, is piped into a long building with hydrolytic baths that gleam iridiscent green and blue. There the pure metal builds up on thin sheets called cathodes. These cathodes are then thrust by the ton into great furnaces. After twenty-four hours, molten copper runs out to be formed into wire, bars or ingots for shipping.

It is a stupendous stamping, roaring, flashing spectacle. By day great clouds of dust and smoke and steam rise high into the sky. By night the heavens flash with green and violet light. One almost expects to see Moses and the Chosen People march over the majestic ridges to the call of God to the Promised Land.

This huge enterprise, started by the Guggenheims in 1915, sold to Anaconda in 1923, straddles the whole width of Chile, and it straddles the whole consciousness of modern Chilean life. Its water supply in that barren region comes sixty-five miles from the eternal snows at the Bolivian border, high to the east. Here, in a region only sixty miles in diameter are more than sixty snow-crowned peaks, some over twenty thousand feet, and all—not to mention smaller giants—higher than any mountain in the main United States. The power for Chuqui comes from the coast port Tocopilla from what is said to be the largest coal-driven plant on earth; and huge steel towers, with long swaying strings of many-petticoat insulators, step over burning desolation and up more than nine thousand feet, where the copper is scooped out of that gigantic wound in the mountain flank, to be stamped, powdered, dissolved and refined.

The trans-Andean train from Antofogasta, Chile's largest city on the nitrate coast, moves across the desolate plain over great glass-smooth *solares*, beds of nitrate or borax, through a region without a blade of grass, where no animals dart away, where no bird wings wheel their moving shadows. Alongside is the huge water pipe, bound to Antofogasta and Tocopilla. Here and there are lonely white property monuments. Here and there are dusty broken windows in abandoned nitrate *oficinas*, long ago pushed to the wall by synthetic nitrates and by the concentration of all that is left of the industry in the mighty Guggenheim refineries of María Elena and Pedro de Valdivia near Tocopilla.

The mine stop is at Calama (Chileans nickname it "Calamity") on fertile Rio Loa, the only stream in north Chile that survives desert heat to reach the sea. Calama is a verdant oasis of irrigated fields, lush alfalfa, truck farms, many fruit trees. Here, Indians from primitive back villages clear into Bolivia and Peru, bring in yareta blocks, which burn like coal and are universally used for heating throughout the mine region. Here, gauchos from Argentina, driving cattle through lofty passes, fatten up their animals before disposing of them to the mines, *oficinas* and towns.

Chuqui is ten miles away across an empty plateau against the red Andean foothills. From a distance the biggest thing is a great hill of gray-blue tailings, discard from leaching vats. Beyond this man-made eminence is a dismal dusty town stretching along Nature's own mountainside.

Here are mills, factories, endless tracks, great vats and tanks, and long rows of wall-to-wall company houses, each supplied with free water and electricity. On the main plaza is a not bad-looking church. There are movies and refreshment parlors, bookstores and company stores, a boys' school, a girls' school and an adult night school. The workers' club and recreation center has a baseball court and soccer field. The pride of the town is a two hundred-bed company hospital, equipped with labs, X ray and an iron lung. All workers are given free medical and hospital care; their families pay a fee.

Somewhat better clubs and centers exist for better-paid Chileans, the white-collars; still better ones for United States employees. So this town of twenty thousand is divided into three distinct class communities that have little truck with one another. The most tawdry section is for workers; next, better-paid Chileans; the best, for non-Chilean employees. In practice no Chilean visits the Chilex Club, reserved for North Americans. Nor is there social contact in homes. The American personnel is about as isolated as though on Mars. The women from the United States mostly learn just enough broken Spanish to order house servants about; few take any interest in the people, their life and culture, though Chile's accomplishments would be fruitful for any investigator.

But compared with twenty or so years ago, Chuqui has made great progress in employer-employee relations, in public relations with the country where it works, and in other salutary directions.

Novels of the most critical sort have been written about Chuqui, pamphlets and books have made blistering attacks. The harshest onslaught was made by Ricardo Latcham, ex-Rector of the University of Chile, in *Chuquicamata, Estado Yanqui*, in 1926, which ends with the blanket accusation: "The United States looks out confidently over the world and, guided by a greedy and reckless oligarchy . . . thrusts itself over the future in a sort of drunkenness without alcohol." Most irritating of all, he declares, is "the Yankee self-sufficiency in arrogating to themselves the title of superior race, and the contempt with which they look upon everything Chilean, except that from which they can extract material gain. . . . This hatred and disdain are seen in all spheres, from highest management to the last Yankee foreman. . . ." The Chileans are said to have "all the vices, all the backwardness, all the lack of intelligence and all the imperfections of a savage barbarous people."

Such attacks, which date back pretty far, should be taken with a grain of salt. Chile herself has been the most imperialistic country of all South America. She seized the whole nitrate and copper coast by a brutal war of aggression which sealed Bolivia away from the sea and appropriated a large chunk of Peru. Chile today is by far the most militaristic and chauvinistic of southern countries.

Also, since Latcham wrote, Chuqui has endeavored to obtain North American employees with experience and a friendlier attitude in dealing with Latin Americans. Chuqui wages compare favorably with the miserable best paid in Chile, plus free health care and other advantages. For years now, after initial labor tussles, the company stores have provided food supplies at lower than cost. In addition, the extensive social legislation adopted in Chile, following the Arturo Alessandri political upheaval and the new 1925 constitution—such things as minimum wage, cost-of-living wage adjustments, automatic annual wage increases, social security, workers' compensation, job tenure, health and safety protection, etc.—have reduced labor strife and brought about better living conditions.

Something of the change over the years may be seen in the housing. Older houses had drab interiors, only one kitchen faucet, no inside toilet, no conveniences. The new houses, if of the same dreary row type and too small, only two rooms and a kitchen, are more attractively finished, have sinks, toilets and showers and, except for Chile's new government housing, are better than most workers enjoy.

Chuqui, like similar enterprises in the Americas, gradually has become something more than a little piece of foreign empire carved out of Chilean soil to cater to outside needs regardless of the effect on Chile and the Chileans connected with it. Today it grows more rooted as a Chilean institution, contributing more to the well-being of the country. Eventually it will probably become entirely Chilean.

Oil

The gold of the twentieth century has been oil. Its discovery and exploitation in the Americas repeated much of the wild romance, greed and cruelty of the Spanish gold search four centuries earlier. Into the jungles of Mexico, Venezuela, Colombia and elsewhere rode the Saxon conquistadores of the new power age.

Men died there in the jungles from disease and bullets. Pitched battles were fought. Bandits were hired to fight governments and rivals. Men refusing to sell their titles were murdered. Children were kidnaped till they came of age. Legitimate children were made illegitimate. Illegitimate children were made legitimate. Parish records were destroyed or doctored. Men and women found themselves suddenly married or divorced—all by artificially yellowed, faked documents and records. Gambling and whorehouses flourished.

Oil brought tremendous risk and courage, laughter and romance, tragedy, skullduggery, greed and brutality. It also brought about important new developments, new opportunities, new cities, new ports. It contributed to revolution and civil war. It brought long-term dictatorship, cruel as sharks' teeth, to Venezuela. The oil rivals of two foreign corporations brought to Costa Rica the only revolution and dictatorship it had known this century. No oil—whereupon peace, no dictator, order, democratic practices once more. Oil lay at the very core of the Chaco War.

This is not the place to untangle those stirring events. Gradually the oil frontiers were defined. Gradually the oil resources of the continent came under the control of large British and North American corporations or else became the property of various governments. More order and stability have come into the industry. Today the oil business, paying more taxes, better royalties, concerning itself with local education and welfare, contributes far more than formerly to the places where it operates.

Thus the oil concession pending for part of the north Peruvian coast contains provisions for royalty, tax payments, wage conditions and so on, never contemplated even a few years back. In it are agreements concerning health, schools, clubhouses, roads and what not.

Today the continent seems on the threshold of oil development undreamed of since the days when Edward L. Doheny got hold of Cerro Azul and pumped more than a hundred million dollars out of a single well. Behind the Andes in the foothills of Peru has been discovered the Blue Goose Dome, which some believe one of the richest and most extensive oil regions on earth. It probably stretches from Ecuador clear to Cape Horn. To this field during the war the United States government built a trans-Andean highway. New areas were discovered in the Paraguayan Chaco, and a big concession secured. Here, too, the United States government spent many millions in public works and highways, much of it through Nelson Rockefeller's Co-ordinator's Office. Only a few years ago Brazil was believed to have no oil; now the geologists hold that half the country is floating on oil.

The Chilean government recently drilled the southernmost oil well in the world. The derrick rises in the rolling sheep meadows of Tierra del Fuego—Fireland—below the historic Strait of Magellan. About the near-by ports of Porvenir and Punta Arenas in bars and gambling joints you see the booted, sheep-jacketed oilmen, a breed previously unknown hereabouts.

"Hell," said one touslehead, "The whole Isla Grande floats on oil."

Isla Grande, the largest island in the Fireland Archipelago, is twice as big as the Netherlands.

A freckled Scotch sheepman spoke up. His burred accent clashed against the soft Spanish like changing gears. "With my own eyes I've seen chapaote [tar seepage] down near Cape Ewan, a hundred miles on south."

"They'll be drilling wells right out in the Loma Bay mud flats!" exclaimed the other. "Ever see the rainbow scum at sunrise?"

Fireland these days is full of such conjectures.

A Jugoslav storekeeper in Porvenir on the Strait—and mostly it's a Jugoslav town—shook his bullet head knowingly. "You come like I did twenty-three years ago to a bleak empty place, and it's been hard, but look at the little burg now! The guys who first came here and called this wilderness spot Porvenir—Future—knew their onions. The country is filling up, population doubled in ten years. And now, with oil and a few other things . . ."

The nearest wells to the new Chilean field are four hundred fifty miles north in central Argentine Patagonia—the great Comodoro Rivadavia field on the Gulf of St. George at the edge of sheep and ostrich plains that stretch west to the snow-draped Andes. All the Rivadavia derricks gleam silver on the plain with fresh aluminum paint—typical Argentine neatness and pride.

Since the Fireland strike many technicians believe the whole intervening region may produce oil. Argentina, hard pressed for fuel during the war days, brought in new wells fifty miles south of the established Rivadavia field and boosted national production thirty per cent. Just north of Argentina's beautiful lake country lies the Neuquén field in the northwest corner of Patagonia. And this is in the same foothill Andean region, but thousands of miles south, as the Blue Goose Dome of Peru.

Chilean government experts believe also that much of Pacific Coast Patagonia has oil. There are signs all through the storm-lashed south archipelagos, on Chiloé Island and near Puerto Montt. The oil is deep but apparently is there. The new Springhill well in Fireland came in at 7,280 feet—a light oil, rich in gasoline and lubricants.

That strike caused more excitement than a new comet. Never again, cried the newspapers gleefully, will Chile have its transportation paralyzed in wartime. Now, whatever happens to copper and nitrates, Chile will be sitting pretty and can use its foreign credits for machinery and consumers' goods instead of for fuel. There was a gambler's flavor to the talk, for Chileans, next to the Chinese, are the world's most passionate gamblers. "Good luck always smiles on Chile in her darkest moments."

It will take years and much capital, however, to develop the fields. Part of Argentina's loan of $175,000,000 to Chile is earmarked to develop the Springhill field with Argentine technicians.

The new Springhill well is at the seat of one of the enormous sheep ranches. From Springhill on three sides can be seen the slate-purple water of Magellan Strait, the four big winking lighthouses on the First Narrows, the short pipe line snaking northwest where tankers come. Small black and white dolphins frisk in front of steamers rushing in on the roaring fifty-foot tide. The Alacaluf Indians say the dolphins are children of the moon, trying to leap up to their mother who abandoned them to run after the sun.

Oil is part of the pattern of the new developing frontier of south Patagonia. The blood of civilization is flowing into the cold extremities of the southern continent, one of the great new frontiers of the Americas.

And so it is that the rhythm of oil in Latin America keeps pace with the world tempo, and it is keeping pace with the new industrial upsurge of the southlands. It is flowing forth to turn the dynamos of this new era.

Big Bend: Brazil

Before World War I Brazil produced only a small portion of its own basic industrial goods, almost no iron, steel, coal or cement. All industry was embryonic. Coffee and cacao usurped the stage.

But hardly was World War I over than Brazil, so long retarded by Portuguese restrictive policies and by tropical and geographical handicaps, began to put on another face. The country proved a refuge for much European capital, labor and technical skills. By 1920 there were 13,336 manufacturing establishments employing more than a quarter million workers as compared with less than 3,000 plants in 1907.

The principal new lines were food processing, textiles, ready-made clothing, toilet articles, chemicals, drugs. A rising standard of living created still more demand. Increasing use of electrical appliances caused expansion of power facilities. Little by little electrical goods came to be manufactured. In 1920 Brazil, though one of the world's leading potential sources, had only 356 power plants. By 1939 there were 1,300; by 1942 nearly 3,000; and now eight major valley projects are under way that will transform the land and do much toward making Brazil the world's greatest industrial nation next to the Soviet Union and the United States. Today the Usina de Cubatão, which supplies São Paulo, is the world's fourth largest hydroelectric plant.

In the late thirties manufacturing really began to step up, so Brazil entered World War II with a much bigger productive backlog: a steel and iron output of 350,000 tons; the mining of 1,500,000 tons of coal. Three quarters of a million tons of cement were chuting down into Brazilian-made bags. The number of industrial establishments by 1940 had topped 70,000. By then the value of industrial production had edged above agricultural output.

This meant that politically the coffee kings no longer could rule the whole roost. No longer would collapse of the coffee market bring national disaster and revolution. From 1911 to 1943 all industrial production increased 5,473 per cent. This growth was nothing compared with what took place during the war. . . .

Brazil has been held back all through its colonial period except in lines not competing with Portugal. Although iron was forged as early as the sixteenth century near São Paulo, and soon after shipyards were built in Bahía when gold was discovered, the mother country, wishing to bend the labor supply to that one activity, made all industrial enterprise a criminal offense.

The first real effort to establish industry, once Independence was won, came in the fifties, as it did in Chile, largely due to the foresight and energy of Viscount Mauá, one of South America's greatest economic geniuses. All during the period 1850-70 small new factories were set up. Ever since, São Paulo has forged ahead steadily as a great industrial center and today is probably the fastest growing city on earth.

In the more modern industrial trend that grew out of World War I the first big expansion, as is usual in belated countries, came in textiles and food processing. From 1914 on, the average percentage of new capital going into manufacturing as compared with agriculture increased two and a half times.

The recent World War greatly expanded such investment. Brazil seized the opportunity—arising from the closing off of manufactured imports, the clamoring home market, the financial and technical assistance of the United States—to push all types of basic industry. General government promotion was put under the National Council of Industrial and Commercial Policy. Speaking in 1942, Dr. Francisco Silva, Director of the Brazilian Government Trade Bureau, stated that the three main immediate objectives were: expansion of steel, cement and paper, the raw materials for which exist more abundantly in Brazil than in any other country.

"Brazil," he added, "needs steel for rails, for tools and basic industry. Brazil needs cement for roads, factories and booming towns. Brazil needs paper for the education of Brazilians; paper for all tasks of political and industrial organization; paper for most industries. . . ."

During the war new factories mushroomed overnight on all sides in all lines—chemicals, drugs, dyes, machine tools, motors, radio, paper, rubber goods, refrigerators, washing machines, gas ranges, steel office furniture, bathroom fixtures, electrical supplies, aluminum and many other metal products, steel rails, airplanes, autos, ships.

Today one of the biggest industrial empires in the world, rivaling DuPont, Farben and so on, is the I. R. F. Matarazzo, S.A., which has a greater income from its myriad enterprises from raw products, agriculture and industry, than any Brazilian State except São Paulo and is nicknamed "Brazil's Second State." IRFM offices, a marble edifice on Ipiranga Avenue in São Paulo, are ornately embellished with inlaid floors, rare tropical woods, pigskin and all-mirror walls. The concern was founded by a poor Italian immigrant who eventually became a multimillionaire and a count. Prior to the war, certain officials of IRFM were accused of having contributed heavily to the Green Shirt Fascist movement, subsidiary companies forcing all employees to give. In any case, it is a mighty empire and has done more than any other single financial force to bring about the industrial era in the country.

In 1939 two Italians, the Arnstein brothers, efficiency experts and engineers, who had long been harassed by the fascists, removed themselves and their capital to Brazil, and with a Belgian electrical engineer set up CEMBRA, an electric motor plant. The first small motor was successfully turned out in 1940. The concern now produces two thousand motors a month up to all sizes. It has five competitors. All Brazil's needs in the field, except for special types, are supplied, and an excess is exported. An X-ray apparatus plant and surgical instrument factories have been set up.

In 1941 the first really big modern pencil factory (Fritz Johansen), which also manufactures all its own tools and machinery, was put up and now exports to every Latin American country. The war saw two airplane plants started. In 1945 the first one hundred per cent all-Brazilian auto—every bit of steel, plastic, glass, every screw and bolt, made inside the country—was pushed out. It was mostly a stunt. But in that year a local corporation, the Brazilian Auto Industry, was organized to use Volta Redonda steel, motors from the National Motor Company, Brazilian-made batteries, aluminum and glass.

Auto tires are now widely exported. Seventy-four rubber factories, which make about everything, now supply ninety-five per cent of all rubber goods.

Sixty mills spin silk yarns; 82 turn out silk fabrics, thread, ribbons, stockings. Three hundred seventy-five cotton mills and 162 knitting mills not only supply all domestic needs, but export to every Latin American country, to Africa, Australia, Ireland and Scandinavia. Woolen textile and felt production have been stepped up. Between 1937 and 1939 linen goods and caroá fiber production jumped up 551 per cent. Four thousand three hundred seventy factories turn out hosiery, handkerchiefs, bed and table linen, shirts, nightgowns. Today Brazil is the greatest exporter of textiles in the world after the United States and Britain, and presently it will surpass the latter. Thirty jute factories supply all needs for burlap and bags. There are 3,600 leather-goods factories. Forty-seven million shoes and 9,000,000 hats are made annually.

The chemical and drug industry, scarcely known ten years ago, has multiplied guinea-pig fashion. Duperial (DuPont and British Imperial Chemicals) interests have long been active. They put up wartime plants and are building others to supply nearly all basic industrial chemical requirements. The Liquid Carbonic Corporation has started a carbonic plant.

Since the Amazonas supply nearly all plants used in medicine, the country may someday lead the field. New jungle products are being discovered daily. Also Brazil has unlimited resources for paper products and plastics. Thirty-eight paper factories have been put up, and Brazil exports cellulose on a big scale. Plastics are made even from surplus coffee.

Glassware and pottery output expanded about 150 per cent in the 1930-40 decade. Brazil formerly imported, now exports. In 1941 thirteen new glass factories were opened, and in 1943 factories with sufficient capacity to fill all window and plate-glass orders were set up.

Owing to Brazil's lack of oil wells, a new law required that a percentage of domestic oil had to be used in all combustion engines and automobiles. Sugar-cane alcohol production, only 19,000,000 liters in 1932 jumped to 320,000,000 in 1939, more during the war. Thus Brazilian self-sufficiency in nearly all basic lines is at hand. Many advanced manufactured products are exported. The country now produces 80 per cent of all her newspaper pulp, soon will have a surplus. Though Brazil was formerly a big cement importer, 98 per cent of home demands are met—demands that grow tremendously each year. Forty per cent of basic machinery demands are met and over 80 per cent of demands for all agricultural hand tools.

During the war was started great Volta Redonda—Big Bend—steel plant, with the aid of North American technicians and a $45,000,000 United States government loan, the $20,000,000 remainder being put up by the Brazilian government and local private capital. The initial capacity of 300,000 tons of rolled steel and 50,000 tons of pig iron (eventually to be four times that amount) was expected to double existing output from all other mills. Actually even before Big Bend started pouring, Brazilian steel, iron and sheet-iron output from other mills had reached 675,171 tons.

Brazil will soon have a steel potential equal to that with which Canada entered World War II and more than those of a number of European steel countries. This is only a beginning. Since Brazil has nearly a fourth of the entire world's known iron deposits, plus enormous coal beds, plus the world's second largest source of manganese—in spite of the difficult location of those resources in terms of present transportation facilities—her industrial future seems wholly assured and well-nigh limitless. Often iron and coal are moved far greater distances in the United States. Bethlehem even brings in iron ore from Venezuela and Chile, five thousand miles away, then again transships it.

The Big Bend plant is situated at a large loop of the big Paraíba River on the main rail line between Rio and São Paulo. A branch line runs down to the near-by port of Angra dos Reis.

The de luxe Rio-São Paulo train, Cruzeiro do Sul (Southern Cross), pulls out of the Central Railway station in Rio and passes across a drab dusty plain into rolling hill farms of fruit and eucalyptus groves. Then it climbs across the wooded coast range, the Serra do Mar, to the deep-slashed river valley of barren red mountains, where stands the huge mill and the new town of more than twenty-five thousand inhabitants.

The iron must come by rail from Minas Gerais deposits 240 miles away, a state where already are located twelve smaller reverberating pig-iron mills and seven Siemens-Martins steel furnaces. Coal after reaching Laguna on the coast is shipped 500 miles by sea to Angra dos Reis, then by rail to the plant.

Several of the American engineers on the project had previously worked on the Soviet Magnitogorsk establishment, similar to that at Big Bend. The Soviet plant, they said, was built with convict labor, without proper food, clothing or shelter, only a shack town. At Big Bend a new model city was put up. The Brazilian mill was erected with free though sadly underpaid labor (about $1.15 a day) in a country of almost Chinese inflation, but the more than twelve thousand workers were given better living quarters than they had ever known, houses and buildings cool with thick walls and provided with conveniences and sanitation. Also, the workers were exempted from military service.

Big Bend is the heart of Brazil's thrust into the power age. This undertaking was the great insistent dream of Dictator Getulio Vargas, who rode into power in 1931 as a depression product with the words: "The army's major problem is matériel. Clearly that problem can be solved only by establishing a national iron and steel industry."

More pacific folk see steel rejuvenating and extending Brazilian railroads, used for bridges on new highways, for new skyscrapers in Brazil's booming wonder cities, for industries far and wide.

Colonel Macedo Soares, the tall, curt military man who has directed Big Bend construction and operation, has stated that Brazil will succeed splendidly in its plans despite the gloom of foreign sociologists and economists, such as Burnham in his *Managerial Society*, who pontificates that Latin America cannot develop industrially but must remain an eternal supplier of raw materials to the rest of the world. Such allegations disturbed Colonel Soares not at all. "Brazil is now alert, trying to find, through better use of her resources, the elements for creating a magnificent civilization in the tropics. The dream is now becoming reality." Though outsiders from great industrial powers invariably have smugly assured themselves that Brazil's industrial accomplishments would always be negligible, "our capacity," the colonel declared, "is great and our ideal honest and sensible. Nothing will stop us . . . nothing will block the way to the nation's evolution."

The truth is, Brazil is in a position to become, along with the United States and the Soviet Union, one of the world's greatest industrial nations. Her resources are more varied and abundant than those in the United States.

Her greatest lack has been fuel oil, which foreign geologists long declared did not exist. During earlier years of oversupply foreign oil companies never wanted Brazilian oil developed and put on the competitive market. There are lurid stories of geologists who had reported favorably on Brazilian oil being killed, their reports destroyed.

But over the years Brazil has put in some $20,000,000 in research prospecting and test wells. She now has forty-odd producing wells and some small refineries. In any case the great new fields of the inner Andean region—such as the superrich Blue Goose Dome in Peru—assure her of plentiful adjacent supply, even if the Chaco oil goes wholly to Argentina.

Lately North American experts, working for the Brazilian government rather than for foreign companies, declared that prospects are tremendous, that more than half Brazil's vast area, or more than 3,250,-000 acres, has good surface indications. The most favorable prospects are in the Acre rubber territory, east of Peru; the upper Amazon basin; Marajó Island, big as all Denmark, at the mouth of the Amazon; large areas in the states of Maranhão, Paiahy and Bahía; the big Paraná River basin. At present a fight is on whether to let foreign capital move in or, as the army demands, hold and develop oil on a strictly national basis.

One industrialist told us that Brazil's steady expansion, which has meant more national wealth, in some cases improved living standards, has been as great proportionately, though not in certain basic industries, as that of the Soviet Union.

"Though we have had greater geographical handicaps and fewer technical skills to start with, we have accomplished this under a relatively free economic system as compared with the slave-labor terrorism and wholly bureaucratic methods of the Soviet Union."

This smugness has to be qualified. The Vargas regime was not a candy bar by any means, and little freedom of speech was ever allowed. Unions could organize only with police permission and had to meet under police surveillance if at all. And that free labor of Brazil—it is even worse off, has far lower living standards, than the workers of the

Soviet Union, which is saying that they are about as low as they could be.

Even the São Paulo industrialists have taken note of this: Brazilian industrial expansion cannot continue with people too underfed to work well and with such low general purchasing power that the domestic market is woefully limited. The São Paulo Industrialist Federation pointed out to the government several years ago that growth would be blocked unless Brazil creates a domestic market. Per capita consumption in the country, it asserted, was at least one twenty-fifth what it was in the United States. They demanded a national distributed income of at least 200,000,000,000 cruzeiros within fifteen years.

Mexico

The cornucopia-shaped country just south of the United States border has produced most of the world's silver, much of its gold, much of its oil. At one time it produced nearly all the sisal for binding twine. From the Quintana Roo jungles comes a large part of the United States supply of chicle. That industry alone is epic in its thrilling risks and adventure.

As with most of Latin America, Mexico's early industrial development was blocked in nearly all directions by arbitrary Crown edicts. After Independence the feudal plantation groups, with no interest in industrial enterprise, held the country in a tight grip, broken only with the 1910 revolution. Also, until recently the concentration of nearly all national energies on purely extractive industries—oil, metals, tropical plantation products—prevented the country's full development.

But today Mexico has made up its mind to industrialize, an idea become almost a religious crusade with all classes. This is the main goal of the present Mexican government. Even labor and capital have joined hands. The head of the labor movement, Lombardo Toledano, has warned his followers not to expect wage increases till the country produces more and frees itself "from foreign economic chains." With what corresponds to our Merchants and Manufacturers' Association he signed a ten-years' pact to work together to hasten industrialization and free Mexico from dependence on imported manufactures, a pact practically outlawing strikes.

Mexico's third Six-Year Plan calls for far-reaching industrialization, proposals worked out technically over some years by the Federal Economic Planning Commission, set up August 12, 1942, by President Avila

Camacho. This for the first time has had local collaboration through Mixed Councils of Regional Economy in each state.

Like Brazil and Argentina, Mexico has been greatly changed by the war. Much escape capital from Europe and the United States and the Orient has flowed in. It has been estimated that more than a billion dollars of North American private capital has sought outlet there, to gain advantage of low labor costs, escape taxes, and for other reasons. Since Mexican law now requires that over fifty per cent of all stocks ownership must be in Mexican hands, this has meant a new type of co-operation with local capital.

In 1939 a new law made special concessions to manufacturing in new lines: (1) five-year exemption from import duties on machinery and materials whenever not domestically obtainable; (2) five-year exemption from nearly all taxes; (3) exemption from all export duties.

Under this umbrella 285 new factories were put up in 1940. Over half were metal and chemical establishments. In all, that year showed a net gain of forty-five per cent over all previous capital investments in manufacturing.

In addition to the expansion of existing steel mills in Monterrey, Piedras Negras and Mexico City, a large new mill capable of rolling heavy armament plate was built at Monclova in Coahuila, just south of Eagle Pass, Texas. Today Mexico's present basic steel needs are about covered without imports. In all, Mexico has 115 metallurgical plants. A coal distillation plant is being built. The Continental Can Corporation has put twenty per cent of the capital into Mexican Envases Generales Continental and has provided the technicians. The canned-food industries of Mexico have boomed. Libby, McNeill and Libby have put money into one of the largest concerns.

A calculating-machine factory, set up in Guadalajara, now turns out 450 machines monthly.

The famous San Rafael paper mills near Amecameca, in the foothills of the snow mountains, and ten other large mills (47 all told) have now been supplemented by a big all-Mexican plant at Alenqueque in Jalisco which will utilize the timber on the slopes of Colima volcano, right up to the edge of the flames and lava.

The small glass factories, which have long made most Mexican glassware collectors' items, are being supplemented by a 3,000,000-peso neutral glass plant, using Corning Glass patents on a royalty basis. An exportable surplus will be turned out.

Nine ultramodern cement plants meet all national requirements, greatly expanded with new industry and the building boom. Future needs will be guaranteed by four huge new factories which will more than double present output.

An asbestos plant, which turns out various building materials, is part-owned by Johns-Manville.

The Celanese Corporation of America has put up, on a 51-49 basis, a big rayon mill, 6,000,000 pounds capacity. This and another big plant under construction, supplementing the existing 252 smaller plants, will supply all present needs. As the first rayon yarn mill was not erected until 1942, these developments are striking.

Mexico has 200 cotton mills, 11 cotton and woolen mills and 31 woolen mills. Cotton-goods output increased fivefold in value between 1940 and 1944; exports to Latin America, tenfold.

Shoe and hat production has improved in quality and quantity. The three-story Tardán hat store on the Zócalo in Mexico City, run by the biggest Mexican hat manufacturers, claims to be the largest store on earth devoted exclusively to the sale of headgear. There one may buy almost any head covering known—standard Mexican brands, those of the United States, Great Britain, Spain, Italy and France: a discreet business hat, a Texas sombrero or a vast Zapatista sombrero four feet across, of heavy black felt spangled with silver.

"Is there still much demand for these enormous toadstools?" I asked the manager and pointed to one that wouldn't go through any ordinary doorway.

"More than ever," he replied. "The country has been prosperous, and more people now can put out three to five hundred pesos for a hat. They come in droves up from the hot country. You know, with a Mexican, his hat is his greatest pride. It sets his status, as an automobile or a bathroom or a basement bar does with you North Americans. Maybe you have noticed how many barefoot beggars, though they own nothing else in the world, nearly always have a huge sombrero that once cost a pretty penny."

Mexico was long self-sufficient, except for certain categories, in army rifles and cartridges, shells, machine guns and clips, artillery, etc. Now it is self-sufficient in footwear, clothing, auto tires, light bulbs, canned fruits, perfumes, matches, soap, most paper needs, certain chemicals, ordinary drugs, glassware, pottery, paints, varnishes and lacquers.

Mexico now manufactures much of its plumbing and electrical

apparatus. Shipbuilding yards have been set up in Vera Cruz. Farm-machinery plants, with the aid of McCormick, have been built. Industria Eléctrica, in which Westinghouse holds a minority interest and provides technical knowledge, turns out electrical appliances. An aluminum plant has been erected right outside Mexico City. It also turns out tin and lead foil (6,000,000 pounds per annum).

Most of these industries did not even exist twenty years ago. Two decades ago even such a simple product as vinegar had to be imported. All bottles then had to be brought in. You couldn't find any home-grown soap except the coarsest laundry brands. Today the finest toilet soaps are made. Even Palmolive soap is turned out locally on a leased patent right.

Chemical industries have grown tremendously, and there are now seventy large drug factories. Many standard North American brands are made locally on licenses.

Today, utilizing considerable native guayule and tree rubber (millions of new trees have been set out) Mexico maintains fifteen rubber factories.

The government has invited Dr. Lee De Forest, famed scientist and inventor of the vacuum tube, to work on plans for joint government-private enterprises, including a powerful television transmitter, a television and radio-set factory, and to establish a great educational center for study and research in electronics. This last would admit about five thousand students from all over the continent, a clearinghouse for all Hispanic countries. Among other private participants, the National Cinematographic Chamber is putting in half a million pesos.

All told in Mexico, from 1935 to 1940, there was a seventy-one per cent increase in the number of manufacturing establishments. During the late war growth was more rapid and continuous.

We had a long talk with our old friend Ramón Beteta, a graduate of the University of Texas, who was President Miguel Alemán's campaign manager and is now Minister of Finance. Beteta, an alert, incisive man, sharp as a new blade, often cleverly sarcastic, is determined that Mexico henceforth shall shape its own destiny. His own star and monetary fortune have risen with that cause. Few leaders in any country are better informed on all phases of life and government; still fewer have the courage to speak and act in accordance with their findings and at the same time work realistically with people of different convictions and contrary purpose.

He gave us details of how the latest Six-Year Plan was drawn up and the procedure being followed in stepping up industrial development. He cited various industrial conferences being called, some attended personally by the President.

In Zacatecas a national mine conference was held to advance the interests of the industry and increase production. To it were invited the heads of the industry, smelting and affiliated enterprises, local bankers and businessmen, Chambers of Commerce heads, railroad men, social and health workers, local and national union leaders, the best government specialists. Everyone made suggestions what management should do, what labor should do, what the government should do. The findings were summarized, pros and cons checked off. Agreement by all parties was about ninety per cent. That ninety per cent has provided the government with a working chart for action that would win full co-operation from everybody. The ten per cent disagreement will be threshed out later, ignored, arbitrated or settled by government fiat. In this mutually helpful, modern and scientific spirit, considerably different from the days of dictatorship and blind special privilege or later days of revolutionary bitterness and violence, Mexico is now forging plans.

VI Blueprints

Peru Looks Ahead

THE author was on the floor of the Peruvian Chamber of Deputies as the guest of Congressman Luis Alberto Sánchez, Rector of the University of San Marcos, when he received a phone call to go to see Haya de la Torre, the popular leader, head of the powerful Apra party which only a few years back was outlawed but which is now the majority force in the country. Haya was at the office of *La Tribuna,* the daily newspaper of which he is nominally editor.

I had known him well in exile days in Mexico, when Peru was wholly in the hands of the army and the Civilista feudal reactionaries. I had seen him later when he was in hiding from the police in a suburb of Lima after having been released from a long period in the Panóptico wing of the penitentiary. Now he has become the most potent figure of his country.

Sitting at his desk in a busy editorial room, Haya appeared considerably stouter, but was as genial and eager as ever, even more agile in thought and body. As usual he was considerably more than one jump ahead of his opponents in his ideas: a man of much vision, always pushing a constructive plan rather than some easily won maneuver.

Haya always loved blueprints with which to reinforce his ideas in an easy visual fashion. In the outlaw days of his party, the blueprints were often diagrams for the proper organization of the various propaganda cells. Now the wall beside his desk was plastered with blueprints of the new Peru in the making—from the planning to make Lima the best organized, best serviced and most beautiful city anywhere, on to plans for dams, electrification, roads, railroads and industry. His early blueprints came true. Will his new ones?

His central blueprint was a chart of the proposed new Economic Council, the legislation for which has already passed the Apra-controlled Chamber of Deputies. This council will be made up of private

125

capital, labor and government, and will proceed with the full development of the country's great resources as rapidly as possible.

According to Haya the trouble with Chile's great Corporación de Fomento, a similar organization which has already done much to develop that country so rapidly, is that it lacks both adequate labor representation and foreign-capital representation, is too much an all-government enterprise and hence does not always win full co-operation.

One great trouble with foreign capital in Latin America, Haya declared, has been that, in spite of its large interests, it has had no direct representation in the countries where it operates, so that whenever it has felt its interests menaced, it has had no recourse except to intrigue, to buy propaganda, to corrupt lawyers and officials, to start armed uprisings and to appeal to diplomatic protection which has invariably strained good relations. Under Haya's plan, capital, whether foreign or domestic, would be accorded voice and vote in the council according to its share of national production. Direct participation, he believes, would lessen need for antipatriotic maneuvers; but, even more important, it is hoped that this will bring better co-operation and influence foreign capital to contribute resources, knowledge, skills and experience for the general upbuilding of Peru.

The new council will map out essential projects, preference to be given to basic industries and utilization of Peru's actual resources. Private industry will be encouraged to take on what it can efficiently and profitably carry out; where it cannot or will not act, the government will proceed. Some undertakings, Haya believes, can be carried out by workers' co-operatives.

"What we want is results," he insisted, "not theories: production and more production—the full development of Peru as a prosperous country, everybody's rights protected, better living standards for all. We plan no extremes. Any imitation of Soviet methods, even if desirable, would be absurd, not cut to Peru's needs. Our workers are in no sense prepared to run industry. We cannot even imitate England in socialization. We lack the knowledge, skills and capital. Our great need is new industry, more production, more jobs, better wages, more national wealth. Whoever can do a given task best—private industry, the government, or any other agency—let that party do it and get it done for the benefit of all and the country as a whole."

The Apra plan—still blocked by the feudal Civilistas who are now opposing North American capital, and by the Communists seeking more power—is not yet in operation, though many great undertakings, above all the Santa River power project, are under way. Major features of the Apra plan have been copied by Colombia, Venezuela and other neighboring lands. Also, new industry has pushed in, textile, paper, rubber, processing plants. Numbers of new joint United States-Peruvian concerns have been set up. Thus, in September 1946, the General Shoe Corporation of Nashville, Tennessee, which has been going into various Latin American countries, made a deal with the largest existing Peruvian shoe company to double operations by putting in new capital, machinery and technical assistance.

Trouble and Change

The mushrooming of Latin American industry has been the result of domestic demand, world shortages and determined planning. Nowhere has it been wholly a hit-or-miss anarchic development. Growth is part of popular and national will, translated often into direct government action. Everywhere south, industrialization and national economic independence are an integral part of the program of all new popular movements and of government thinking and planning. There is a widespread desire to escape the hardships resulting from two world wars and an intermediary depression of terrific proportions, a feeling that Latin America has paid and suffered in the war and got nothing much to show for it and less security than ever before.

Many governments have shown far more initiative in promoting and developing new sources of wealth than is customary in the United States, with its hands-off philosophy. But only by such government aid was it possible for most South American countries to make the grade at all. The handicaps of geography and climate, the existing one-crop system, the long-intrenched agrarian feudalism, the large use of labor for merely raw-product exports, the dominating position of foreign capital, the lack of technicians and local capital (and what capital there was, largely without experience) long made it well-nigh impossible for much new industry of any importance to get under way.

Foreign capital, more interested in supplying the home country than serving the land where it worked, did not often respond to local desires. Often capital expansion south was directed toward securing the raw materials necessary for manufacturing in the United States but did not promote, and frequently hampered, new enterprise abroad. Thus the big Ford rubber plantation on the Amazon was started, not to satisfy Brazilian needs or build Brazilian auto factories, but to supply Detroit. The powerful steel corporations, which have got hold of most of South America's iron resources, keep that ore in tight reserve—as for instance the enormous deposits in Cuba—or if they do exploit it, ship it clear north to United States mills. They have frowned on setting up local mills. California knows a bit about such policies. Brazil long tried to interest North America companies in setting up a modern steel mill, finally had to do it by government initiative.

Thus Bolivia, depending for ninety per cent of all exports on tin concentrates and ore and on allied metals, still labors under a terrific handicap. It cannot develop other resources properly, although they are among the richest of any South American country, greater, except for agriculture, than those of Argentina. As a result of this overriding dependence on tin exports under foreign control, revenues are meager, political stability is impossible, communications are deficient. Democracy is repeatedly aborted.

England long controlled a world tin-refining monopoly. Thus Bolivian ore was sent—and still is—nine thousand miles to England to be refined, then nine thousand miles back to Argentina and Uruguay to have meat put in the tins; then the tinned meat must travel another nine thousand miles back to England and Europe. A fleet of freighters did nothing but cart tin and tin products in both directions to and from South America. Nice business if you can get it—and keep it. The erection of a wartime United States refinery, though it is not fully equipped to handle straight Bolivian ores properly, modified the situation; but in general the world tin cartel still operates to the detriment of Bolivians, ordinary Englishmen and the world in general. It is even a menace to United States security. Even in wartime certain Washington officials played the tin-cartel game instead of looking after the legitimate interests of the United States. A vice-president of the Patiño tin corporation became an assistant co-ordinator in the good-will efforts. This made Bolivia and some other countries south right happy.

No proper solution for Bolivia's problem could be found till either Bolivia or near-by Argentina set up their own tin refineries. For obvious reasons this has not been easy to do, but Argentina has now built an electrolytic refinery at Córdoba and in 1947 raised the ante on the price to outbid the United States for a large share of Bolivian tin. This will greatly change the picture in the far south countries—and for the better.

In general, foreign capital, long averse to taking the risks of setting up manufacturing on the local scene that would compete with the products they manufactured at home and shipped in, began to do so to a slight degree only when government protection was given native industry—especially in the drug, automotive, cosmetics and textile industries. Today, also, there is a considerable movement in this direction by European and United States escape capital seeking to avoid increased regulation (in some instances, nationalization or Communism) and high taxes due to war.

Argentina and Brazil, for instance, were greatly benefited by much German escape capital after World War I, which brought know-how and put up hardware, textile, electrical goods, chemical, drug, shipbuilding and other establishments. Most of this capital became resident, not absentee, capital.

Among this author's acquaintances are three Belgian brothers, large textile manufacturers who in World War I lost everything in the German invasion. They fled to Mexico and with what meager funds they had left started a small shoddy factory. After the war the Belgian government offered to reimburse their losses and help them re-establish their factories, but by then they were already forging into the millionaire class again in Mexico, with big mills and holdings of timberlands to provide their own pulp.

One Lithuanian manufacturer arrived at that time in Mexico in such penury that he had to sell silk stockings on the streets. But he had the operating experience and today he is running a silk knitting mill and makes the stockings which others peddle and which previously had to be imported.

World War II has sent even more capital fleeing into the southern countries from all sides, this time even from the Orient. One of the biggest present-day operators in Mexico is a millionaire from China, who managed to get most of his capital out.

But in many instances new Latin American industry simply could not be put on its feet except by governmental promotion, by organized land settlement, by the opening up of new regions and towns, mines and resources, by costly new communications and by strong protection against cheap foreign mass production. In some cases profits from undertakings which are desirable, even necessary, for the country and its welfare, promised to be too small or the realization too many years in the future for private capital to take any interest. In general the measures invoked have been very similar to those resorted to here in the United States when infant industries first stepped forth.

Three major events changed the needs, methods and outlook of Latin America in these matters: World War I, the world-wide depression of 1929-37, World War II.

If World War I provided the first strong impulses, the more powerful persuader was the depression ten years later. In fact some countries, like Cuba and Chile, stepped right into catastrophic collapse almost as soon as war was over. The blows south were often worse, for the governments there could not afford costly doles and subsidies.

Depression conditions were aggravated also because the United States had ended World War I with nearly all Latin America's trade tucked in its pocket, a favorable situation that endured as long as private loans and investments—to the tune of six billions—were poured into the southern republics. But the Great Depression did two things right off the bat, besides shaking confidence in the stability of United States economy and prosperity: it dried up all credits and investments overnight at the very moment most urgently needed; also it dried up United States buying power. Thereafter for a number of years the United States bought less from a number of countries than it had at the beginning of the century. For Latin America, with all its trade eggs in the Yankee basket, this was utterly devastating. Seventy-five per cent of all Chilean enterprise stopped dead in its tracks.

Seventy-five per cent of the people of any nation, cold and hungry, simply will not twiddle their thumbs. Revolutionary upheavals hit every nation south except Venezuela, still booming with oil, still under the brutal Vicente Gómez dictatorship.

Unfortunately, so far as popular liberties went, better governments did not always result. Democracy is a luxury of prosperity. But all governments, whether Right or Left or in between, whether dictatorial or democratic, began laying far-reaching plans for revising economic life. From that day to this the promotion of diversification and manufacturing, as security against wartime, depression and shortages has steadily gained momentum.

Remedies

There is a striking similarity throughout the continent, regardless of the type of government, in the various plans put forward to meet the depression and revolutionary conditions.

In 1934, with the election of President Lázaro Cárdenas, Mexico enthusiastically put forth her new Six-Year Plan. It was in the early thirties that Argentina began elaborating her famous Pinedo Plan, which a decade later would come to fruition in Perón's Five-Year Plan and with the collapse of the British financial empire down there could really be pushed energetically. It was in the thirties that the Carlos Dávila plan was put forth in Chile and its application now is in full swing. It was in 1930, from Europe, that exiled Haya de la Torre laid down his party's program for the over-all reorganization of Peru's economic life. An echo of this was heard in the Peruvian Constitutional Convention of 1931, which, though under the dictatorship of the feudal Civilistas, created the National Economic Council. This is now to be widened into an overriding instrument of national policy.

It was in the early thirties that the "Electric Power" dictator, Gerardo Machado, was overthrown in Cuba, and plans for diversification were pushed by succeeding governments. Some of those plans were temporarily stymied by the Hull-Caffery reciprocity treaty, but again are in motion. Before the war Cuba imported nearly all cotton textiles, but has come to manufacture sixty per cent of the national needs. When some arable lands are recovered from foreign control, Cuba will likely go into cotton growing. Rice growing, a new industry stalled for the time being by the treaty, has expanded. The new government made it compulsory to use in bread a certain percentage of Cuba-grown yucca flour with all imported wheat flour—the end result was a fluffy and tasty loaf. Lard processing was started. More vegetable growing supplemented Florida imports. And of course the war saw the establishment of new manganese and copper-refining plants and many other new businesses.

It was in Brazil in 1931 that chunky little Dictator Getulio Vargas, after prolonged bloody civil war growing out of the collapse of the world coffee market, rode into Guanabara Palace in Rio at the head of his Rio Grande do Sul cowboys and the tough miners of Goiaz. After a strenuous period of crimson purges to consolidate his authority and center all power in his personal hands, Vargas proceeded to drive through a steel and iron industry, to start myriad manufactures and to open up innumerable new resources.

It was in the early thirties that President Harmodio Arias started to win back Panamanian rights, and freedom from intervention, and pushed a far-reaching program for developing the interior.

The carrying out of these new programs of greater self-sufficiency and economic independence was pushed with varying degrees of enthusiasm, according to the sincerity of the particular government, the obstacles encountered, the resources available. In some countries, Chile for instance, they did not really get under way till the eve of the war or later.

Preparations for new war filled Latin America with much strife as the various European nations hauled at it seeking to gain investment or trade advantages, seeking to shape governments that would be sympathetic. At the same time Latin American trade began to zoom upward as the various nations started laying in stock piles of strategic materials.

The United States sought to strengthen its inter-American system, and in wartime to promote strategic transportation and industry on a truly continental scale.

Not at all sure that, before the world fracas was over, Latin America might not become a battleground, the United States worked hard at building new railroads, highways and airfields, to develop new resources, to replace lost East Indian production with new crops in the Americas and to start industries. Much of Latin America welcomed such wartime aid. What most countries tried to get out of it was basic industry and better communications, and Brazil, Mexico and Chile now have large steel mills to show for this good-will effort. Peru and other countries have tire factories. Aluminum, chemical and metallurgical plants were scattered around. All sorts of new enterprises attest to the inexhaustible energy of United States money and agents, who were often laughingly referred to south as "the second band of conquistadores."

The end results were varied and, as in all human efforts, ranged from fine success to complete flops and scandals, from honest endeavor to wholesale graft, the latter induced by the copiousness of money poured forth and the iron curtain of secrecy maintained.

Health efforts and the building of new hospitals were mostly carried out efficiently. Here, too, many were placed not solely for their help to the war effort but also as an aid to the holders of new raw-product concessions. There have been some fine hospitals put up in remote jungles that are far better than those you will find in most of Georgia and Mississippi.

Some roads—especially those built by the army—cost the American taxpayer a pack of gold mines, and some couldn't even be used when the engineers pulled out. But a few good and important highways were built.

Latin America is now dotted from end to end with fine airfields and airports, even out in remote jungles, put in by the United States government. Those useful for commercial purposes have since been turned over to Pan American Airways.

Much of this effort was to get out necessary strategic products without which the war could not have been won. It did not wholly benefit the southern countries. It did prevent unemployment, and they shipped more goods abroad than ever before in history.

But mass buying plus wartime monopoly of all world markets by the United States and England kept Latin American products down to a low, almost prewar price level. Due to this required wage freezing and the outlawing of strikes—in some cases of all labor unions—living conditions, already at a coolie level in much of the continent, were driven still lower by spiraling inflation in the limited amount of commodity goods imported and by the splurging of much free money by the "Lend-Lease" millionaires who were created. The unstinting self-sacrificing war effort of most South American peoples, who went without things more than North American citizens, provided the United States with strategic materials without which the war would have been prolonged many years, might have been lost.

The southern countries were unable to get more than a dribble of machinery and consumer goods in relation to what was needed. Even these shipments were mostly tied down in many places to United States government projects and corporations, or else were luxury goods benefiting chiefly the upper classes able to pay outlandish prices. But it must also be added that only thoughtful action by the United States saved a number of Caribbean peoples from acute hunger, for nearly all the world's vessels, in North American or British hands, were being used elsewhere.

Thus the war wholly reinforced the earlier will of the various countries to gain more productivity and independence. The suffering caused by lack of shipping has caused most of the southern lands to work hard since then to build up their own merchant marines. Argentina now has a big fleet. Venezuela, Colombia and Ecuador have joined hands to launch the large intergovernmental supermarine, the Grancolombiana. Among other things it now handles all Colombia's coffee shipments. According to officials it has already "broken a forty-year monopoly by United States shipping interests." The State Department has made formal protests that the new concern discriminates against United States shipping. This merely called forth riots and stoning of the embassy and consulates. The new fleet is obviously necessary and beneficial for the three countries.

Potent reasons (despite deep-rooted isolationist and neutrality sentiments of the whole people) why Argentina did not come into the war until the tail end were: the general boycott against her, without continental consultations, on metals, oil and rubbers by the United States; and the State Department's refusal to send needed drilling and refining equipment to the government fields there unless the private American company operating in Argentina was allowed to receive a fair share of such shipments.

Elsewhere, to get Latin America to produce much, sell cheap, freeze wages, let working conditions get worse, do without machinery and consumer goods, the various countries were promised that economic co-operation would be continued after the war, that necessary factory, railroad and farm equipment would flow south.

This promise has not been kept. A few of the countries were wise enough to protect themselves with contracts that ran over for several years after peace would be declared. But postwar economic co-operation never materialized. Instead the good-will agencies in the United States were quickly liquidated, thus imparting to that noble policy—as many Latin Americans point out—the taint of having been merely a wartime ruse. The sign-off came with the Chapultepec inter-American conference at war's end when southern delegates were told their countries could count for no appreciable economic help beyond the limited funds of the Export-Import Bank, which had already earmarked most of its effort for Europe. In fact aid was cut off sharply, like a dead corn. In the first two years after the end of the war, of the twenty-odd billions tossed abroad, Latin America received exactly the fifteen million dollars already pledged.

The economic situation, with such a brutal policy shift and lack of needed goods, had grown decidedly worse by 1947. But at the Rio Conference in 1947 Marshall and other North American delegates resolutely resisted all efforts to discuss economic matters, even though these are the crux of any bona fide defense of the continent and might greatly assist in aiding Europe and thus reduce strain on the United States people. Global recovery certainly has been whittled down, the bulk of world trade forced onto a narrow one-way street and a government monopoly at that.

Before all else basic Western Hemisphere defense depends on economic stability and growth, whereas, if inflationary conditions continue to the south, widespread revolution may yet shake the better part of the continent, as has already occurred in nine countries.

A serious feature is that the reduced amount of postwar materials Latin America has been able to obtain from the United States has cost from fifty to five hundred per cent above wartime prices. Since Latin America built up the credits for such goods through much wartime abnegation by selling her own materials at near prewar prices, this has been a mighty tough break. It has rapidly exhausted dollars and has prevented the securing of much coveted machinery. It is the traditional squeeze—low-priced raw products, high-priced consumer goods—always suffered by colonial lands, but never before has it been so gross and glaring, so gigantic and callous.

So quickly has this difficult trading situation struck some countries, so rapidly have dollars been drained off, that today half of the governments have forbidden nearly all except basic imports. Cuba, with dollar credits from sugar, and Venezuela, with dollar credits from oil, have been exceptions. Radios, autos, frigidaires, electric appliances, furniture, cosmetics, all luxury items (and many items normal to ordinary North American life are considered luxuries to the south) have been among banned products. General licensing of imports has become the rule in nearly all the countries, plus stern exchange controls. The red tape a mere stranded tourist must now go through in most of them just to get a few dollars will make his hair crinkle the rest of his born days. Our policies are driving them rapidly into barter and excessive economic nationalism. Only Argentina has been somewhat successful in building up a healthy free-trading area in the southern half of the continent.

In certain quarters there is much smouldering anger. Friends of "democracy" feel let down. Communists and fascists are playing on this. The pro-Franco conservative and feudal landholding elements are crowing: "We told you so." Some southern businessmen have joined the chorus of "Yankee imperialism." High government officials, dizzily trying to solve tough problems and unable to face their people with the rising inflation, join the same chorus. The better chorus at the moment would be "Yankee neglect," too great preoccupation with bankrupt declining Europe.

One Foreign Minister told us: "The United States needed us in wartime. Now we are given the brush-off. All the minor allies—though without their help the war could scarcely have been won—were arrogantly shoved to one side by the final settlement of world affairs. Everything was to be ruled so wisely by the Five Big Powers. One of those Big Five, China, was already a myth in power terms. The Big Five became the Big Four, became the Big Three, is now the Big Two, and so is now the Big Nothing. This is the worm befouling the core of the apple. We have hopes that before it is too late this whole concept will change. More and more the United States is seeing the wisdom of taking into account all peoples. You can't ignore world opinion in a highhanded manner. It will not be long now before you really try to strengthen the inter-American system, almost knocked out by unilateral browbeating of Argentina by Spruille Braden. Who are you anyway to arrogate to yourself the right of running Argentina affairs? Somebody's head needed a longer, brighter soaking in lasting suds. The recent Rio Conference was a fine beginning once more. Its scope was quite too narrow, too much the same old stuff of using us for a front for your own Old World policies. A world constructive plan is in order, certainly some sort of a hemisphere plan, one that is not just a selfish power plan, not merely countercontainment plans, not merely a European plan—for there is no longer any Europe."

Another high official said: "We don't like this rearming of our countries. Mutual defense—that is fine. But the implementation of it must be worked out better than it ever has been. We still have a few nasty dictatorships down this way. Are you going to bolster them up at the expense of the people? Create more of them to saddle us at this hour with outworn surplus armaments, the same sort of costly dumping that went on after World War I, which started such corruption, disorderly revolution, discord and war throughout the continent? That will merely weaken not strengthen defense. Resources needed for expansion will be used up in nonproductive enterprise. We don't have the surplus fat that your country has. We are lean peoples. What we put out for your castoff war clothes will reduce our buying capacity for what we really need. It will further intrench remaining military dictatorships, give the instruments for new dictatorships to arise, will hinder progress and undermine or destroy democracy. What we truly need now is machinery, machinery, more machinery."

All these difficulties, whatever the pros and cons, confirm the Latin American idea, built up so strongly during depression and war years, that even more strenuous efforts must be made to achieve greater national self-sufficiency, that the South American countries must pool their resources and trade to ward off impending blows. Actually, therefore, the stoppage of North American credits, whatever the temporary hardships, the laments and the difficulty of getting materials, may prove a blessing in disguise. It affords a certain protection for new industries. It stimulates new industries.

After World War I, with a great flood of bankers' and investment credits (six billions) pouring into the twenty republics, the peoples were prone to rest on their oars. Complacently they let the new capital be used for raw-product industries that threw the local economy out of shape, and they bought types of North American goods they could easily have produced themselves. They floated on the stream of great postwar boom, with no eye for the coming rapids of "bust."

This postwar they have received little and no credits are in sight. Wartime credits built up by so much abnegation have been sponged away in the bat of an eye by inflation. Expected goods have not been forthcoming. Although considerable private United States capital has been edging in nearly everywhere, even it is partly stymied by the near-boycott trade quotas for Latin America. By and large the tossing of all United States aid into the European drain, the Greek-Turkey credits, the Marshall Plan—this means the southern countries must now sink or swim by their own muscles. From now on, Palacios Rudas, General Comptroller of Colombia, told the people as early as September 1947, you will have to develop the fatherland "with our own resources." Difficult as this is, the wartime trend of industrialization is thereby being fortified by the peace.

Old plans have been pulled out of cubbyholes. Blueprints are being scanned anew. Earlier plans are being revamped, amplified, tested, pushed ahead once more in accordance with present possibilities. In spite of all, a new era has been set in motion for the countries south. It is a continental revolution in nearly all lines and in all places, and it will increasingly have its effect on the shaping of the world tomorrow. a world far different than that envisaged by either the Soviets or the United States.

VII New Wheels

Chile Takes Stock

"CAN Chile ever really industrialize?" was the question we put to business men, government leaders and others.

"Why not?" was the invariable answer.

Said one: "Chile is more than twice the size of Italy, nearly six times the size of England, with more natural resources than either. We export eighty percent of all minerals and metals sent abroad from South America."

Another reported: "We have to become more industrial or remain a poverty nation. Chile does not have enough good land even to provide its present population with adequate food."

A businessman said: "Of course we can never compete with a big industrial nation like the United States or the Soviet Union but we can specialize like Switzerland, develop unique skills in tune with our resources, and we can manufacture more of the goods we require. Every day we are doing so. Many such things can be made in Chile as cheap or cheaper than imports. We've been too long wholly dependent upon exports of nitrate and copper, and that spells periodic disaster."

"Aren't isolation and self-sufficiency the curse of the world?"

"To have an economy broad enough to stabilize employment and be independent of the whims of outside governments and companies, that does not spell isolation. The more diversified a country's production, the larger its trade with other countries. That's not isolation."

One Chilean said: "The real trouble, Chile has been isolated too long. It came into the world's main trading orbit only recently—after the Panama Canal was opened. What actually most isolates Chile is the failure to produce more of its own requirements. The Chilean peasant earning only thirty or forty cents a day is isolated from all civilized goods."

The present attitude in Chile is similar to that of its earliest economist right after Independence. At that time, the notable scholar and business-man, Manuel Salas, advocated large industries, carefully planned for the harmonious development of all resources. Had his advice been followed Chile might have been saved many subsequent headaches.

In 1846 famous Cabinet Minister Camilo Vial formulated govern-ment policy toward industry in wise terms, but after a short period of expansion, his advice was forgotten as Chile went into the nitrate and guano booms and became merely a provider for outside powers. "Far from believing," said Vial, "that a people in order to be wealthy, needs to produce everything, nevertheless I am convinced that to be prosperous, free and civilized, it must possess an extensive, if possible, diversified in-dustry. What have the purely agricultural countries been? . . . Such a fate threatens us also if we do not promote industry with firm hand and constant determination."

Chile has the advantage of possessing large coal and iron deposits and much potential electric power. The Corral steel mill, established as early as 1906, was given special privileges.

With the 1929 depression, Chile, prostrated since right after World War I, was driven into revolutionary upheaval. Determination then crystallized to industrialize the country to get away from dependence on fickle raw products. In 1933 the Corral mill was revamped with the most modern Swedish electrical furnaces, and until recently was able to supply the country with all needed iron ingot and about forty per cent of steel plate. Now, a still larger modern mill, government-owned, is going up at Talcahuano with the aid of United States money and technicians.

City Hotel in Concepción near there was abuzz with North American engineers and technicians and their families. Busily they were seeking houses in a city rebuilt from scratch after the 1938 quake and still shy of housing.

One engineer told us the new mill site is perfect: close to major naval establishments, on a rocky tongue of land at the mouth of Chile's broadest navigable river, the Bío-Bío, and at the head of the rich Lota coal region where the mine galleries even run out under the ocean floor. The iron will be brought from the rich El Tofa field north of Coquimbo where the Bethlehem Steel Company scoops it out with great electric excavators, runs it over an electric railway to one of the most efficient ore-loading ports in the world. Other even richer fields are located near by. The new mill with a 180,000-ton capacity, will turn out girders, rails, fine light steel, tin plate—will supply all Chile's present needs.

New developments in good part have been the result of definite joint planning by government, business as well as labor.

As one leader put it: "Chile has had a century-old struggle against meager resources, backward development and extreme poverty. No private interests, for instance, would build our trunk railroad because the cost was too great, population too small, possible business for many years too limited. What private company in its right mind would put in thousands upon thousands of miles of track in a strip of difficult country along a coast cut up by mountains, rivers and canyons, a strip half the width of your state of Indiana and in most regions inhabited by far fewer people?

"But the roads simply had to be built if we were to tie ourselves into a nation—not just a collection of remote villages lost in primitive squalor. We had to serve such isolated communities, and we needed the lines for national defense. Were we to go without railroads because foreign capital could not build them? They were built and they are the best in all South America. Over the years they have more than paid for themselves, if not in direct bookkeeping, by making modern life possible in this strangely shaped land of ours.

"The same hurdles exist for many enterprises very profitable for the country as a whole though at the beginning unprofitable for individual companies. Besides, foreign capital has been interested only in banks, utilities, nitrates and copper—the monopoly fields—not in producing consumer goods for a relatively small market. Our feudal elements are interested only in land monopoly and primitive, underpaid, underfed peasants. But new enterprises were absolutely necessary to strengthen Chile, provide employment, get Chile free from such overwhelming dependence on one or two products. Nitrates and copper, which provided most of our income and revenues, were industries employing very few Chileans: fewer today with modern methods and mechanization than they did a century ago when output was considerably smaller.

"Now, thanks to our determination to give all Chileans productive work and bring more wealth to the land, the government has pushed a hundred new activities. As a result, there is far more private business, big and small, than there ever was, and mostly it is Chilean business, not foreign monopoly. There is more of everything. Today Chile is something more than a fenced-in foreign mine and a fenced-in feudal plantation. The last twenty years it has emerged from the terrible revolutionary period of the thirties to become a modern civilized country.

With each step forward we discover new possibilities we had ignored or, rather, had no means before of exploiting."

Facing the Dilemma

During the revolutionary depression period of the thirties President Carlos Dávila, though he headed a short-lived regime, marked out a constructive course for the country and set forth what is generally known as the "Dávila Plan."

Chilean life at the moment was utterly paralyzed by the mining collapse. Nitrate production, because of synthetic manufacture, could never hope to regain its privileged position in the world market. Never again would Chile supply ninety per cent of man's nitrate; in fact the percentage was to drop down to eight. Chile could pull herself out of misery and chaos only by seeking new paths, finding new industries to provide employment—a firmer base for her whole national economy to make possible stable and progressive government.

Chile did force the foreign nitrate and mining companies and public utilities to hand over a large share of profits to the workers and the Chilean government, but confiscation and state ownership of existing properties, as occurred in Mexico, was ruled out as providing no solution. To seize and divide up the great feudal estates in the Vales of Paradise would, for a long time, merely lower efficiency and production in a period when Chile needed every ounce of food and had no foreign credits to buy outside. The evil was not in the form of existing ownership so much as in the lack of opportunities for Chileans; the need was for more and varied wealth—not taking over industries temporarily bankrupt, whose conditions, given the world situation, could not be improved.

Shortly after this I talked with Dávila. His attitude was: we don't have to fight foreign capital, but merely set to work developing the many untouched resources we have in the way we wish for the benefit of our people. Instead of confiscating foreign capital, we should supplement it.

The Chileans, more handicapped than most, worse off at that time than any present war-stricken European nation, set heroically to work without aid from abroad to mend their fences.

These various efforts finally crystallized in the government Corporación de Fomento, started April 1939 by the Aguirre Cerda Popular Front administration.

Its stated objectives were: to procure machinery for Chilean manufacturing, promote consumption of nationally made products, get Chilean capital to widen out its investments and efforts.

A board headed by the Minister of Economy was set up composed of two senators, two deputies, five bank representatives, five government bureau heads, the President of the Chamber of Commerce and a representative of the National Labor Confederation. The members receive two hundred pesos (six dollars) for each meeting attended.

Fomento was started in a tragic hour of national bankruptcy, with half south Chile wrecked by earthquake and not even the rubble cleared away. That was one of Fomento's first tasks—scarcely a profit maker—to rebuild the devastated region, especially the country's third largest city, Concepción.

In spite of this handicap, in ten years Fomento came to handle many billions and has literally made over the whole face of Chile. Today almost everything the average Chilean touches—though he may not even know it—in some way is due to the impulse given by Fomento. When he buys a suit of clothes, builds a house, gets a tin of fish or a pair of shoes, picks up his skis to go to the snow slopes, visits a movie or buys a piano, he is getting a Fomento product or one from an enterprise helped by Fomento.

Results in every field have been impressive, failures few. Before 1931 sixty per cent of Chile's cement was imported. The Corporación secured machinery to produce 780,000 tons a year, and by 1944 less than ten per cent had to be imported.

The country now supplies nearly all its own tiles, bricks, porcelain, chinaware, glassware. The new Yungay crystalware finds favor abroad. More than a million dollars were invested in a drug corporation which now exports to all Latin America. Many millions were used to promote a domestic textile industry—wool, rayon, cotton, linen. The new Said mill in Quillota supplies 50,000,000 pounds of rayon yarn to more than 120 mills.

Coal production south of Concepción was boosted nearly 100,000 tons annually by a Fomento investment of 50,000,000 pesos in existing companies. Up-to-date machinery was secured, methods improved. Fomento has set up many metallurgical plants, one of the best being the Mademsa foundry. It has taken over bankrupt French copper refineries to produce enough for domestic needs and to rehabilitate smaller native Chilean mines forced to close down because unable to compete with the rich ores and great modern technical efficiency of the Chuquicamata and El Teniente mines. Lead and zinc smelters are being set up. Forty million pesos have been put into oil exploration and drilling. A scientific survey of lumber resources has been made and production boosted. When we were in Puerto Montt, the docks were piled high with alerce, coigue, pine, cedar and special Chilean woods, some of which are found in no other country. Half a dozen boats were being loaded to carry these woods through the Straits or up to central Chile. Reforestation has been pushed, 50,000,000 new trees have been set out. A cellulose plant near Valdivia proposes to process the turpentine tree. Plastic and paper factories have been built.

The electrical industry has been expanded to national self-sufficiency, and Fomento is installing new electric power systems in leading cities, with all-Chilean materials and technicians. We went over the fine new installation in Rancagua, Chile's seventh city.

Three billion pesos are being put out on hydroelectric development. New power plants have been completed at Pilmaiquén (50,000 h.p.), Suzal (120,000 h.p.) and Abanico (150,000 h.p.). All this type of work is handled by a ninety per cent government-owned company.

Existing shipbuilding companies have been heavily financed to expand facilities. Fomento has promoted shipping by improving harbors, docks, warehouse facilities. It has secured new planes for the National Air Lines (LAN); new vessels for the merchant marine; busses and streetcars for companies in Santiago, Valparaiso and Viña del Mar. It acts as purchasing agent for all government utilities, farmers, many private businesses.

A laboratory for livestock vaccines, it is estimated, has already saved stock raisers 300,000,000 pesos. New breeds of cattle and sheep have been introduced.

New crops have been started. A beet-sugar industry has begun. Production of flax and linen has been tripled and new uses found for the strong native cañamó fiber. The country has been made self-sufficient in vegetable oils and establishments to process them. Fruit and dairy co-operatives have been helped in a big way.

Much farm machinery has been purchased. Within six years the amount used in the country was doubled. Fomento rents and operates at cost machinery for small farmers unable to buy equipment.

One major active effort has been to build up the fishing industry. In this field Chile has great resources. Some of the finest shellfish in the world are here. The range is great, from the Torrid Zone 6,000 miles into the Antarctica whaling fields, with the greatest collection of inlets and islands, bays, waterways and fiords of any country on earth. West, the Chilean banks extend 400 miles to the marvelous lobster areas of Juan Fernández—Robinson Crusoe—Island, and on to Easter Island, 2,000 miles out in the Pacific. In all, Chilean waters contain at least 250 kinds of edible fish, from the 2-inch lamprey, considered a special delicacy, to the world's largest swordfish. In 1936 an 842-pound specimen was caught off Tocopilla.

A large fishery school has been established at San Vicente. Above Viña del Mar laboratories to investigate fish habits and diseases have been built. New fish have been acclimated. Large hatcheries are maintained, and Chilean rivers are now among the best stocked in the world.

Millions of pesos have been lent to individual fishermen and co-operatives for boats, nets and other equipment. The government maintains parent ships at distant banks so fishermen can unload their catch and replenish their supplies without having to return clear to port and perhaps lose fine opportunities when fish are running well.

Canneries, salting and smoking establishments have been erected. Much tinned fish is now exported. Railroads have been provided with refrigeration and plants have been set up in all main centers. That in Santiago cost 25,000,000 pesos.

As a result of these efforts, the Chilean fish catch has more than doubled, and the country hopes eventually to outrival Norway.

Fomento has greatly promoted the tourist trade, built modern ski runs, and opened up many new lake and hot springs areas. De luxe hotels, matching South America's best, have been constructed in the Andes, the lake country and at beach resorts. Customarily these are then leased to private management. Recently Fomento provided funds for hotels at the Andean ski pass near Portillo and at Lake Pirihueco, the latter to be one of the world's more luxurious hostelries.

Except for the big cream-colored Pacifico Hotel in Arica, the whole nitrate coast has been without a decent hotel. Even the largest port, Antofagasta, has only fourth-rate hotels or worse. In Iquique even the rats moved out long ago. Foreign companies, of course, maintain private luxurious quarters, but these are of little benefit to Chileans and most tourists. Fomento has planned, under construction or nearly finished a whole chain of first-class hotels along the whole nitrate coast. The new concrete structure in Iquique has just been completed. Others planned, or else being already put up, are those at Mamiña Hot Springs, Antofagasta, Ovalle, Serena, Coquimbo and Copiapó.

Where Chile Stands

The Corporación has become a direct active partner with private business right down the line. Its investments range from six to ninety-nine per cent. Jokers say: "That one per cent lacking is so no one can say it is government-owned."

When an industry was lagging, Fomento has moved in with money, experts, modernized equipment, has secured supplies at low prices, worked on marketing. Several smaller Chilean nitrate companies, obliged to cease operations because of inability to compete with synthetic nitrates and the supertechniques and machinery installed in the great Pedro de Valdivia and María Elena plants set up by the Guggenheims, were put back on their feet by developing a local fertilizer business, with which the Guggenheims never bothered. A Chilean brand name has been publicized. A big campaign was started among Chilean and South American farmers, and sales stepped up at home and abroad.

Once an industry is in a flourishing state, Fomento often liquidates its holdings to use them elsewhere.

The greatest hurdles, according to Fomento, have been:

1. Scarcity and high prices of raw materials
2. Inefficiency of many small establishments
3. Lack of technical knowledge and experts
4. The exaggerated individualism of certain large producers

To meet the first difficulty every effort has been made to produce and utilize whatever is available within the country. What is needed from abroad is now bought on a mass scale to secure lowest prices.

Given Chile's resources, terrain, population distribution and limited home market, much of her industry can be carried on successfully only in small units. Great effort has been made to increase their efficiency, introduce expert knowledge, provide better equipment, help distribution and better marketing. Such small enterprises now get the same low price on raw materials as that enjoyed by the biggest buyers.

The technical side is being met by getting large foreign corporations to give Chileans more opportunities to learn techniques by students being sent abroad and by the establishment of more technical schools. Early in the nineteenth century Chile took the lead in trade and craft schools and now has the largest network of such training centers of any South American country. Fomento has provided technical laboratories in four universities and institutes.

Resistance by large producers has been tackled through a co-ordinating bureau which works out plans for rationalization, helps lift marginal producers to an efficient profitable level, eliminates useless competition and unfair practices.

Much has been accomplished through publicizing the work and plans of the Corporación. Early fears that it meant to socialize all Chilean industry have subsided. Actually it has created more and better private business, and it has diversified Chile's whole economy. It has proved of great help to concerns needing capital, has increased their output by better organization, low-cost materials and modern equipment.

The Fomento has kept its nose pretty well to the grindstone of its task. The operating personnel, made up of trained technical men, has been pretty much left to work on its own without undue outside political interference. Fomento has particularly tried to aid small business.

Criticisms have not been lacking. One big new cannery almost closed down for lack of an expected catch, and others because Fomento had not guessed correctly that the shortage of tin would continue. In reorganizing the Corral steel mills, it was charged, Fomento bowed to union demands for padded pay rolls. However that may be, the Corral mills are doing better than they ever have and are confident they can now compete with the new superduper government mill being put up at Talcahuano by North American technicians.

Although in such a big setup as Fomento undoubtedly many mistakes have been made and there may be hidden graft, gradually it has sold itself to all classes by its concrete accomplishments and visible improvement of Chilean life. However badly or well any given task has been performed, the over-all picture is impressive.

When we visited an industrial exposition on Ahumada Street in Santiago, we were astonished at the range of goods now produced in Chile, most of which were imported a decade or so ago, such as farm and factory machinery; wood, gas and electric stoves, refrigerators, washing machines, motors, dynamos, transformers, bolts, screws and nuts, carpenter and plumber tools, electric lamps, black and galvanized pipe, malleable iron fittings, boilers, screw drivers, drills, bores, bits and braces, bus and auto bodies, faucets, grinding and polishing machines, meat slicers, saws, railroad locomotives and cars, streetcars, boats, bicycles, pianos, shoes, hats, every type of clothing, every type of canned meat, fish, fruit and vegetables; drugs and cosmetics.

Much in this Chilean achievement has been inspiring. In a moment of national chaos and disaster, with a bankrupt government, with the unemployed bawling in the public plazas, with world depression at the gates, the Chileans, against so many man-made and natural handicaps, gave a noble demonstration of what a determined people, not afraid to work and plan, can do to revitalize a country, open up new frontiers, produce new wealth, improve living standards and start a march toward prosperity.

In the postwar Chile is again hard hit. But no such national disaster, overwhelming violence or economic collapse has yet occurred as after World War I, for Chile now has a broad cushion of industry. This time, vanishing exports and fickle trade in copper and other metals, the lack of shipping, the uncertainty, have not prostrated the land or shaken down the governmental edifice. Conditions may change and political trouble may come, but, economically at least, the country is in better shape to face its problems than it ever has been.

Oil, Fish and Bananas

Both Ecuador and Colombia have established a "National Economic Council" to promote development. Ecuador's was set up in 1935, but economic and political difficulties have prevented much accomplishment. That of Colombia started in 1931, but did not become full-geared until the broadening act of 1940. Great progress has been made; in fact no country on the continent is experiencing greater growth.

Various agencies have been set up in Venezuela under Betancourt to lessen dependence on oil, and progress in all lines has been considerable. One of Venezuela's first steps, once it got a progressive government, was to fashion an over-all plan directed by the Minister of Development, Juan Pablo Pérez Alonzo, to push new farm, transportation and industrial development. Thoroughgoing financial and tax reform was pushed via a new Central Bank, which now controls most loan making and promotion. The general plan calls for immediate expansion of textiles, food processing, soapmaking, shoe and leather goods, chemicals and drugs; in the more distant future, an iron and steel industry to utilize the nearly two billion tons of known ore, now being exploited and shipped to the United States. One first step was to oblige the refining of at least part of Venezuelan oil within the national territory instead of on near-by Dutch islands. To finance developments, larger taxes and royalties have been obtained from the oil companies. Royalty is now taken in oil as this gives the government better bargaining power to get needed materials.

Nearly all postwar planning in Uruguay has aimed at the target of more industrial development, particularly that which can utilize the country's own resources and turn out what may most readily be disposed of in neighbor countries. One especial new effort has been the promotion of the fishing industry, the development of a fishing fleet, coastwise shipping and shipbuilding. A mission was sent to the United States and Canada to study fishing methods, and a mixed company has been set up. Plants completed or being built are for processing vitamin A from shark's liver and for freezing, salting and canning fish and using by-products.

Guatemala received a big shot in the arm during the war from United States money, Lend-Lease, the quartering of thousands of troops and bureaucrats on her soil. In proportion to its size few of the countries had so many United States officials carrying on so many activities. These efforts and money started many new undertakings.

Unfortunately the ruthless dictatorship, its jailings, killings and graft, scarcely jibed with the progress and enlightenment, but with Ubico's overthrow in 1944, Arévalo's popular government instituted new efforts on a wide scale to open up new territories, diversify farming, further improve communications and start small industries. Before the war Guatemala's chief export was coffee. Today, though she exports more coffee than ever, it is a much smaller percentage of the total. Thus Guatemala, too, is moving toward a broader economic base than she has ever had.

Argentina Breaks Chains

The first Argentine depression product in 1930 was the military coup of General José F. Uriburu, which overthrew the sixteen-year Radical Party rule of Hipólito Irigoyen and Marcelo T. Alvear and brought back into full power the great landed Conservatives in alliances with the army and British capital. But although democratic practices and honest elections largely went by the boards for fifteen years (until partly restored by Juan Perón) the military dictatorships and the governments that grew out of it—those of Justo, Ortiz and Castillo—soon found depression conditions could not be solved merely with bayonets. Far-reaching plans were evolved by more constructive minds. These plans today are rapidly making over the whole economic life of Argentina.

One idea was that Argentina depended too much on foreign trade for it to have a stable economy and stable government. More production for domestic use was essential. Better utilization of national resources would cut imports of raw materials.

A thoroughgoing survey of resources was made to find out what Argentina could most successfully produce rather than import. Fuels, building materials, metals, oil, possible new crops, manufacturing—nothing was overlooked. The general aim was economic independence, the greater prosperity of Argentina.

This whole program was largely developed and pushed by the brilliant Minister of Finance, Federico Pinedo, and clever young economists. Felix F. Weil, now of Columbia University, previously one of Pinedo's advisers, considered his "dynamic" chief to be "the ablest and most daring statesman Argentina ever had."

Pinedo, in the face of great opposition, especially from British interests, succeeded in implanting an income tax. Federalization of excise taxes increased government revenues forty-six per cent merely through efficient collection. He overhauled the financial system to favor Argentine rather than foreign capital, reconverted the national debt, stabilized the currency and established the Central Bank. Controls over loans directed them into basic enterprises, and large-scale crop financing was started. Exchange controls directed trade toward the building up of home industry, and in ten years the new exchange office brought in more than a billion pesos.

Besides these concrete accomplishments, the Pinedo Plan looked forward to the complete elimination of foreign-owned debt, the eventual purchase of British railways and all foreign-owned utilities, including the Standard Oil Company, to stop the drain of wealth out of the country. It proposed industrialization, the export of new types of goods to relieve Argentina of the disaster of meat and wheat price fluctuations. Many of these projects were blocked, but Pinedo did start the economic liberation of Argentina.

The country certainly needed such a reaffirmation of national policy to escape from the shackles of foreign capital. Up until World War I foreign capital quite dominated all Argentina production except agriculture—British capital to the tune of sixty per cent. Since Great Britain took from twenty-five to forty per cent of all exports, it could call the turn in every line. Most shipping facilities and business were monopolized by British firms.

The British railroads had long prevented—sometimes by agreements signed and sealed—the building of highways or railways to compete in any way with the British trunk lines. In 1929 the British protested sharply against Argentine plans to build direct roads between villages and cities rather than merely railroad feeders. In 1931 the British openly petitioned the government to stop such work. Subsequent agreements were forced on Argentina to halt development of communications and industries competing with British interests.

If more than ninety per cent of all industry in the United States, plus all banks and foreign trade, were in the hands of foreign companies with little interest in American welfare, blocking nearly all independent enterprise, interested only in profits for far-off absentee owners, and if such companies used American citizens only in menial positions to prevent them gaining the knowledge to better themselves, doubtless the American people would not long delay in trying to gain control of their own resources, finances, industry and trade. No method to do so would appear improper to them. A comprehension of this simple fact would bring more understanding of Argentina's long, painful predicament and her present efforts to make an Argentina for the Argentineans and provide for proper economic, political and military defense of the country— in short, to make it into a prosperous land not restricted merely to undertakings profitable to outside capital.

Argentina's national pride has been further compromised by the intervention at every turn of arrogant meddling diplomats whenever the slightest effort has been made to promote the true economic interests of Argentine people. This points up some local difficulties: how big foreign corporations carry on their pay rolls the more prominent lawyer-politicians, how officials have been bought and controlled, how legislation has been constantly twisted. A Senate investigation revealed that three former Presidents of Argentina actually had been on the direct pay roll of British and American power interests! Saavedra Lamas, the Foreign Minister of Chaco Peace and Nobel Prize fame, was an official of various foreign corporations, lawyer for others. When the 1943 revolution reduced light and power rates (among the highest anywhere) there was great outcry.

Then it was that diplomatic intervention by the United States to "save Argentine democracy"—never undertaken in wartime when the country was ruled by the reactionary elements—really hit on all cylinders. Its less obvious purposes never fooled Argentineans nor much of the rest of Latin America, and it seriously jeopardized the inter-American system so patiently built up for so many years.

Add to this the thirty-year drama of Argentina's struggle with foreign oil interests, the Chaco War and Peace, the machinations of the Bolivian elements of the tin cartel, the wartime demand on Argentina that American oil interests be allowed to expand at the expense of the Argentine government corporation; then add the breaking of the trade monopoly of the great North American meat-packing establishments—and there was certainly plenty of reason to worry about "democracy" in Argentina. The unilateral policy of coercion to combat those early Argentine acts was very unfortunate, for it was destructive of the international norms established by agreement with Latin America in various Pan-American Congresses. Fortunately it was thoroughly discredited and the mistakes were rectified, in good part through the efforts of one of the ablest diplomats the United States has ever had, Mr. George Messersmith.

For many decades Argentine tariffs greatly favored British trade over all other countries and at the expense of Argentina's own industrial growth. Import permits for machinery were always hampered by the hired lawyer-politicians; imports of finished British commodities were invariably given preference over basic machinery. Through such measures before World War II the United States was all but eliminated from the Argentine market. England, among other things, was given almost complete monopoly of all textile imports. Today, of course, Argentina is self-sufficient in most textiles. Both the Runciman Treaty of 1933 (in accord with the closed-empire Ottawa agreements of 1932) and the 1936 treaty with Great Britain hit Argentine industry right between the eyes by favoring imports of finished goods many of which were already being produced in the country.

Weil gives typical examples of tariff discrimination to keep Argentine industry from developing—tariffs put across by the lawyer-politicians and by the wheat and cattle interests. The duty on light bulbs used to be 1.28 gold pesos per kilo; that on materials for making light bulbs added up to 3.33 gold pesos. In 1939 the duty on steel and other materials for making trucks totaled six times that on finished trucks made abroad. Such was the whole complexion of the tariff schedule up until the 1943 revolution. This is what Weil calls "protection in reverse," to help foreign countries, not one's own. Yet the Hull reciprocity demands would have made these schedules even more onerous for struggling Argentine industry.

Technical education also remained more backward in Argentina than in Brazil, Chile, Uruguay or Mexico, and foreign companies have given Argentine workers little chance to learn special skills.

Finally, also, the great wheat and meat barons till lately, were not only bitterly opposed to building up Argentine industry but unwilling to invest their surplus capital in such effort. The middle class, small and squeezed, could provide no new capital. The banks, nearly all in foreign hands, were rarely willing to lend money to Argentine-owned industrial enterprise.

Thus the Pinedo Plan was hampered at every turn. In spite of this, after World War I industry plowed ahead. It came up the hard way, enjoying not so much governmental protection as discrimination and competition from mass production abroad. Even so, as early as 1935 industrial production actually exceeded farm production in value by 14 per cent; by 1943, 132 per cent.

Even by 1939 Argentina had become self-sufficient in a long line of consumers' goods. For some finished goods—particularly chemicals, drugs, cotton textiles, radios, electrical refrigerators, electrical appliances, rayon, plastics, steel products, etc.—part or most of the raw materials had to be imported. Nevertheless new types of goods are now being exported in quantity sufficient to arouse complaints and fears among United States exporters, a few of whom added their voices to the denunciation of Perón.

Thus with the Great Depression industrialism was really born in Argentina—the most significant turning point since the founding of the Republic. Then World War II provided automatic protection for new industry and provided markets in neighbor countries. Lack of competitive goods from outside caused a great spurt. Today, with a vigorous policy of protection and promotion, the expansion in many lines is surpassing expectations.

The Marshall Plan of all-out aid to Europe and the almost exclusive control of what is left of the European market, outside the Soviet zone, by the United States works many hardships on a country like Argentina. Yet it makes even more necessary local industrialization, and it provides automatic protection, plus adjacent markets wide open to Argentine business initiative.

In other words, in Argentina the new wealthy industrial classes (not those dependent on foreign capital) and the new urban proletariat, plus the discontented peasants (also aided by Perón), have won much of the power held exclusively by the feudal land and cattle barons closely allied always with British imperialism. The new regime has determined to free Argentina forever from foreign tutelage and the paralysis maintained by the old feudal classes.

All this, though more peaceful and less abusive, is very similar to the seizure some centuries ago of the British feudal state by the new industrial and trading classes that built up the empire, except that in Argentina it has from the start rested on a far wider democratic base. Certainly it is a civilized, generous process compared to the ruthless methods now used in Soviet Russia to industrialize that country. /

The 1943 Revolution

From the first the 1943 revolutionary regime set about revindicating Argentine rights as against foreign meddling. Previous tactical playing off of German capital against British and United States interests was soon abandoned in favor of a direct constructive policy. The new regime put the screws directly on foreign public utilities, lowered high rates, extended financial reforms. The tariff was revised from top to bottom to provide protection for all industries decided to be basic for national welfare and growth.

Presently Colonel Juan Perón, who emerged as the most purposeful personality, took over the new cabinet post of Labor and Social Welfare and put across far-reaching labor and peasant reforms, promoted health and sanitation—especially in the interior—built dozens of new hospitals, instituted price controls on basic living commodities and won the support of nearly all organized labor, of the rural working population and a considerable part of strictly Argentine business elements. On the side he purged the army of unsatisfactory and pro-Nazi elements, broke the JO, the young officers' group by which he had ascended to power, and plumped for breaking relations with the Axis.

He promptly won the hatred of foreign corporations, the wheat and cattle barons, the feudal elements and the most reactionary groups. However his friendly Catholic policy broke the solid Conservative front and later won him the majority vote in super-Catholic Entre Rios province. The more progressive elements of the Radical Party (big business-middle class) joined his ranks. The Socialist labor unions abandoned Socialist leadership en masse, and half the Socialist Party came over to him (in one province lock, stock and barrel) everywhere leaving old-line party leaders, already badly tarred by connivance with previous dictatorial regimes, stranded. Even the Communist Party was split wide open.

In the elections the pro-Perón Party put out a sweeping economic and social platform, vigorously facing all phases of Argentine life and containing the most constructive and progressive ideas of the day.

The opposition coalition of badly split old-line parties—the National Democrats (the most reactionary of the landed proprietors, mostly Franco supporters and pro-Nazis), the Conservative Party (pro-Church, pro-Franco, many pro-Nazi elements), Radical Party and Socialist Party—had as their only slogans "Beat Perón!" "Democracy!" and "Fair Elections!" The Communist Party, on its own but also whooping it up for a democracy it did not believe in, supported the coalition. Not by the wildest flight of imagination could their candidate, cattleman Tamborini, the bright flower of the superreactionary Jockey Club, be labeled a "democratic" leader. Anything like that was impossible, not merely because of his connections and views, but because of his previous affiliation with the antidemocratic governments that had issued from the Uriburu dictatorship. Tamborini in positions under those governments had followed policies that many Argentineans believed favored foreign capital to the detriment of Argentine independence.

Before the elections Perón repudiated the support of the Nationalist Party (the most militant pro-Nazi fascists). This left the so-called "democratic" coalition holding the bag with the support of all the Christian fascists, the large pro-Franco sector and the Communists. Such was the "democratic" coalition which the policy of Braden and the State Department tended to favor.

Even the opposition admitted that the elections were technically honest, probably more so than any previous elections in Argentine history, though freedom to campaign for them left much to be desired.

"The fact is," admitted a younger leader of the Radical Party, "even if we had had better campaign opportunities, the old-line party bosses wouldn't put out a labor or land program, no real platform at all. They kept mum. They had nothing to offer the people but traditional submission to British interests. All were holding jobs with such companies. So Perón stole all the thunder."

There was plenty of demagogy on both sides, though neither suggested the people eat less meat. Whatever else Perón may be, he is a great personal showman, just as Roosevelt was, and he enjoys the antics of democracy if perhaps not always the essence. The Perón literature and posters never mentioned Tamborini, but read:

"PERÓN OR BRADEN?"

And after the elections Perón remarked: "As an Argentine, I detest Braden; as Juan Perón, I am wholly grateful to him, for without his opposition I might not have been elected."

Perón came out in favor of the *"descamisados"*—"the shirtless ones," *i.e.*, the poor and exploited.

The opposition branded this as "a fascist shirtless shirt movement," and called for freeing of Argentina from the Nazis, although their side probably had a bigger assortment of pro-Nazis and fascists than Perón's bunch.

Actually Perón was pro-Argentine; he was in the main current of the country's trends and in the main current of the whole Latin American trend, and he had a straightforward program.

Shortly after assuming the Presidency he told the country (the gist of his remarks as heard by this author):

"There seems to be a feeling abroad that the aims of this government are a dark, dangerous mystery, that we harbor unworthy secret intentions. There is no reason for anybody to be alarmed on that score. There is no mystery whatsoever. I shall set up a big blackboard right in the Casa Rosada (Executive Mansion), there in the light of day for all to see. Everything we intend to do will be chalked up there so all may know what we propose and no one need fear that we will go beyond that. As each thing is accomplished, we will cross it off so that all may see how well we have lived up to our announced program and whether we have been worthy of your confidence."

Subsequently he added: "All honest Argentineans can help in that work. We harbor no grudges against our late political opponents but hold out the olive branch to all who wish to co-operate in working for a greater, more prosperous Argentina."

That blackboard was the Five-Year Plan, to reorganize and develop the country—128 pages covering every phase of life in the Argentine.

This was little more than the Pinedo Plan brought up to date, pulled into a practical working pattern, popularized, dished up dramatically with far greater emphasis on social welfare, labor and peasant safeguards and national defense. Mostly it is a culmination of fifteen years of careful surveys, studies and honest effort by the best minds of the country.

The wisdom of most proposals can scarcely be questioned. That so much can be accomplished even with Perón's driving energy seems doubtful. In fact General Royal B. Lord, brought in to survey possibilities and direct much of the Plan, soon advised that it was too ambitious in so short a time to attempt so much, owing to obstacles of international trade, lack of machinery supplies abroad, labor problems, deficiency in technical know-how, etc. Perón thereupon announced that he had set a goal which might in some lines require not five but ten or fifteen years to reach.

The salient points of the Plan and of corollary policies, as indicated by public declaration by him or his ministers, are:

(1) *Financial Reform.* All bank deposits are to be rediscounted at the Central Bank. No bank is permitted to loan beyond its assets without permission. All loans are supervised for use in needed developments, not for fripperies or speculation. For the first time Argentine banks are to be put on an equal footing with foreign-owned banks.

These regulations and others so roundly denounced by newspapermen close to Braden, as tending toward centralized fascism, are little different from services rendered by the United States Federal Reserve Bank, by federal guarantee of bank deposits and loans. They are similar to our FHA procedure through private banks. The program does not go so far as recent United States legislation for small business loans. As a matter of fact no Latin American government is anywhere near so up to its neck in government banking and loan-making as the United States government.

Fears of the new Argentine measures were not shared by Ambassador George Messersmith or the American and British banks themselves, although the latter did not like all the provisions. At that time our embassy at Buenos Aires informed me that since no discrimination was involved and since the measures taken were similar to those invoked earlier in the United States to free itself from financial domination by European capital, no protest was indicated. In June 1947 the Irving

Trust Company of New York reported*: the new law "provides that all deposits are received for the account and risk of the Central Bank; that a bank cannot loan in excess of its capital and surplus without permission. . . . As far as the public is concerned, in its dealings with banks, no change of any kind has taken place. As the Central Bank grants satisfactory compensation for the service which its agents [the private banks] perform, profits are good. Banks are strong."

(2) *Elimination of the Foreign-Owned Debt.*

This has been wholly accomplished by the federal government and for all state and local governments. The federal debt has been liquidated: approximately $250,000,000.

(3) *Government Ownership of Foreign-Owned Public Utilities and Certain Basic Industries* to halt capital drain out of the country.

All British and French railways have been bought up, also North American and British light, power, traction and telephone companies. For political reasons Standard Oil, which the country has long tried to buy out, was left alone, but it must sell all its products to the government. This part of the Plan is almost completed.

(4) *Government Purchase and Sale of Exportable Surpluses* of wheat, wool, meat, hides, vegetable oils and seeds to be continued to meet mass government buying of such products by foreign governments. This is carried out through the Exchange Institute (IAPI), the profits of which in 1947 were two billion pesos. This finances the Five-Year Plan.

This is little different from the United States government wartime Lend-Lease practice, still carried on in a wholesale way by government purchasing for European relief, by army purchasing for prostrated Germany, by purchases to cover the interventions in Greece and Turkey. The great difference is that the United States government method results in federal one hundred per cent loss, not profit, that it is used chiefly for international policies rather than in legitimate free-trade exchange. In fact today the United States government, through its vast purchasing, licensing and trade controls, exercises far more control and administration over exports than Argentina. Also, Argentina pays more to the farmer, and more directly, than the United States, which buys through brokers who have already jacked up the price in half a dozen prior exchange manipulations.

---

* "Condition in Argentina, with Supplementary Background Material," Irving Trust Company, New York, June 1947. (Prepared by Vice-President J. W. Rowe, after personal investigation.) P. 2.

(5) *Government Monopoly of Purchases of Certain Types of Farm and Industrial Machinery and Raw Materials* (also through IAPI) in bulk lots to get better prices in this hour of scarcity and world inflation, to meet buying competition of other governments, as for instance United States government mass tin buying in Bolivia; also, to guarantee compensating purchases of Argentine goods.

During the war Argentina was faced with joint British-United States government purchasing, set up to hold down prices of Argentine meat and wheat. Great Britain, most of Europe, most of the world, continue this practice. This is similar to United States wartime commodity buying abroad—sugar, rubber, tin, etc.—which still continues with a long list of materials. One of the biggest buyers in the world today is the United States Army. Formerly it purchased through American companies; now it sends its own buying missions over the face of the globe to get what it wants, when and where it wants it. Foreign trade today is pretty well nationalized in the United States.

(6) *Continuation of Exchange and Import Controls to Promote Industrialization.*

These controls have been tightened to make use of foreign credits, especially dollars, for the purchase of basic raw materials, equipment and machinery rather than luxuries and nonessentials.

(7) *Fomenting Basic Industry.*

New metallurgical, plastic, textile and aluminum plants have been started. A new steel mill, near Tucumán, where coal and iron exist, is already in partial operation. It has fine suburban-style workers' housing with every modern convenience. Argentina's blueprints call for an immediate expenditure of $100,000,000 in steel expansion to give a minimum output of 350,000 tons a year, to be 90 per cent government, 10 per cent privately owned. Initial bids for a 150,000-ton mill brought an offer from one of the largest United States steel companies for a plant twice that size. Argentina's present steel consumption runs close to a million tons a year, but is expected to increase greatly.

A new penicillin plant has been authorized, via a five-year monopoly contract with a leading United States drug company. Many United States corporations have been offered big inducements, including short-term monopoly, freedom from taxes and other benefits, to set up new factories. In some cases new factories are built by the government, more often by government-private ownership. Bids have been authorized for a synthetic rubber plant.

One of the most salutary things for all South America, and particularly for meat-packing Argentina and Uruguay, and for tin-mining Bolivia, has been the erection of an electrolytic tin refinery in Córdoba. In 1946 Argentina outbid the United States for nearly half Bolivia's tin output.

Argentina oil output, despite lack of equipment, has been increased, and now meets 70 per cent of present national needs. Also, much aid has been given to Bolivia in the drilling of wells, laying of pipe lines, building roads and railroads to develop the fields in that country. A 1,100-mile pipe line is being completed from the oil field of Comodoro Rivadavia to Buenos Aires to supply natural gas and save much coal and electrical energy.

Production of armored tanks, artillery, machine guns, rifles and ammunition has been started. Existing plants have been expanded.

All-steel railroad freight, day and sleeping coaches and a few locomotives are being turned out.

(8) *Better Distribution of Industry.*

Wider regional development is planned; also the location of new industrial plants closer to raw materials. Plans for Patagonia, for instance, include new railroad development, coal and metal mining, new industries, particularly woolen mills and leather factories. A wholly new industrial city is planned for the lake region, near coal, minerals and unlimited water power.

Many parts of this plan are already being pushed. One of the most basic popular forces in the Perón "New Deal" was the "uprising of the interior provinces, both against their local feudal lords and also against the "imperialist, pro-European" port of Buenos Aires which, always absorbing far more than its rightful share of the public revenues, has kept its eyes cast overseas rather than on the land it was supposed to govern and develop. Few other governments in recent times in Argentina have ever called so extensively on the talents of people of the interior for government work, and no government has ever done so much so rapidly to build up the interior, distribute revenues more equitably and place the home-grown boys on a par with Buenos Aires.

(9) *Development of Argentine Resources.* The effort is to be made to discover and utilize all possible Argentine materials.

The search for minerals and metals continues. A large uranium deposit has been found near Tucumán. New, rich coal beds, 225 miles long and at least 6 miles wide, have been uncovered. Those in Patagonia on the Turbio River are already being exploited by government enterprise.

New roads are being pushed into timber areas, for Argentina has a much larger stand of timber than the main continental United States. Measures are being studied to make use of the big peat beds of Tierra del Fuego for fuel.

(10) *Extensive Highway and Railroad Construction.*

Budgets have been increased. New rail lines are being surveyed or constructed across the Andes and elsewhere. The purchased British and French lines are being reorganized into a unified network in conjunction with previous government lines to eliminate duplication of stations, personnel and overhead.

(11) *Water-power Development.* This is a "must" in view of Argentina's limited fuel-oil resources. The plan calls for sixty-nine major hydroelectric, canal and irrigation projects.

Numerous projects are already under way. An aerial survey has been made to determine the best sites.

(12) *Expansion of the Merchant Marine.*

By the end of 1946 the fleet consisted of more than thirty vessels, and Argentina is now the seventh country in the world in ownership of oil tankers (excluding Panama, which is mostly camouflaged United States registration to escape controls and labor laws).

Argentina has new vessels on order in England, Spain, Sweden and Italy, some in exchange for wheat and meat.

(13) *Expansion of Government and Private Air Services* at home and abroad.

New, better, more frequent services are in operation to outlying districts. Airfields are being multiplied, new ones abuilding. A billion pesos' worth of commercial planes have been ordered from Great Britain, many of which have already been delivered. There are many new international routes.

(14) *Large-Scale Immigration.*

Perón hopes eventually to bring in as many as ten million skilled immigrants. New immigrants are to be selected for special trades and skills, character and assimilability. Farmers are not wanted; agronomists and soil chemists are. Traders and commercial classes are not wanted; carpenters, masons, mechanics, air pilots, engineers, geologists *et al.* are.

Already Argentine immigration offices have been set up in Europe to screen applicants before aiding them to migrate. All immigrants are guaranteed prevailing trade-union wages and all social benefits accorded

Argentine citizens. The Dodero Steamship Company was awarded a contract to bring in over thirty thousand Italians by the end of 1947. These paid $280 a head (less for other members of families), repayable to the Argentine government in forty installments. Argentina is now making agreements by which various foreign governments will split the cost of transportation to bring in immigrants free.

This program serves as an example to other countries who talk so much about their marvelous world humanitarianism, who wish to force displaced Jews into Arab land, who keep hundreds of thousands of displaced persons rotting in concentration camps, but who will not accept any within their own borders. Recently a shipload of Jewish refugees, denied admission to Brazil, were at once invited to come on to Argentina.

(15) *Public Health*.

The Plan seeks to build up hospital and public medical services throughout the interior. According to Perón, in seventy per cent of Argentina half the people die without medical care or receiving a doctor's certificate. The rural districts have few hospitals, few doctors. This is one of his special hobbies.

Much has been accomplished.

(16) *Social Welfare*.

This part of the Plan involves: consistent improvement of worker and peasant welfare and living standards; price controls; elimination of speculation in land, rents and foodstuffs; better, more equitable distribution "to dignify labor and humanize capital."

Extensive labor and peasant legislation has already been put into effect. In general wages have doubled—more than the price increases. Labor now receives two weeks' vacation with pay, five national holidays with pay, and a month's pay bonus at the end of each year. Social security, worker's compensation, retirement and old-age pensions have been some of Perón's reforms. Instrumentalities for conciliation and arbitration have been set up.

All basic food and clothing are under price controls. This began to get out of hand somewhat in 1947, and a general ten per cent reduction was then ordered, including prices of meals in restaurants. All prices so fixed must be displayed in the windows. Since there is an abundance of all materials, there is little black market. Dealers, however, may charge what prices they wish for superior grades and materials. Toward the middle of 1946 this writer investigated price controls, visited numerous stores, meat markets and clothing establishments. Goods and materials at the government price rates, about the 1938 prewar level, were available in plentiful quantities. Official prices (United States exchange) were then:

Bread: 3 cents a pound.
Butter: 30 cents a pound.
Cheapest meat cuts, including round steak, stew meat, mutton, lamb: 3 cents a pound.
Cheese: 15 cents a pound.
Flour: 2 cents a pound.
Spaghetti: 15 cents a pound.
Soap: 2 cents a pound.
Olive oil and vegetable cooking oils: 10 cents a quart.
Table wines: 40 cents a bottle.
Alpargatas or work slippers: 30 cents a pair.

In August 1947 the government took drastic steps to curtail all loans for speculation, such as food corners, warehouse hoarding and land grabbing.

(17) *Development of Technical Skills*, with expansion of technical education, the sending of students and others abroad, attracting skilled personnel from other countries.

Several new technical institutes have been completed. Late in 1946 General Lord announced he was seeking a corps of one hundred United States engineers for special tasks.

(18) *International Economic Co-operation.* Perón seeks to level trade barriers wherever possible, while protecting new industries against the larger industrial powers. He has especially sought to wipe out barriers with neighbor countries where there is a possibility of true reciprocal trade. This is squarely in line with Pan-American agreements adopted at all past international conferences. In this direction Argentina has done more than any other member. Perón has frequently spoken in favor of and has acted in behalf of European relief. Besides the regular obligations in connection with the United Nations, many countries have been directly assisted.

A. Trade and passport barriers have been wiped out with Chile, Bolivia and Paraguay. Trade barriers have been greatly lowered with

Brazil, to a slight degree with Uruguay with which relations formerly were touchy. Negotiations are proceeding with Peru, Ecuador, Venezuela, etc.

Today it is easier for tourists to travel, with less red tape and more generous provisions, in Argentina than in any other country in the Western Hemisphere or anywhere else in the world. In comparison, for outsiders to visit the United States, Brazil, most of Central America, Peru, Chile and some other countries spells martyrdom. Nor does any other American country give such full protection and legal equality to all foreigners.

Typical of new-type trade agreements is that made with Brazil for a five-year period starting June 1, 1947. Argentina agrees to ship Brazil at least 1,200,000 tons of wheat annually. Brazil agrees to ship to Argentina 5,000 truck tires the first six months and 80,000 truck and auto tires each year thereafter; also to make annual shipments of 15,000 tons of pig iron, millions of yards of cotton textiles, such things as glass panes and various woods.

The new Argentine treaty with Venezuela provides for barter of wheat and manufactures for Venezuela's government royalty oil. Because of lack of tankers and the world gasoline shortage, Argentina has been handicapped.

B. Argentina has contributed more to European relief, officially and unofficially, than all the rest of Latin America. Buenos Aires has many voluntary centers for collection of food, clothing and money. The large Slav, Polish, Jewish and Italian population has contributed to arousing Argentine interest. In his tour seeking such aid ex-President Hoover found more hearty official co-operation in Argentina than almost anywhere else. The Pope has repeatedly thanked Argentina for its generous contributions. Large government gifts of wheat and other foods have been made to Italy, Spain, France and other countries. On May 10, 1945, Argentina gave 40,000 tons of wheat as a gift to Norway although that country, then under Soviet influence, had just fought Argentina's admission to the San Francisco UN conference.

C. Argentina has assisted many countries with large credits. In the case of the American republics this has helped greatly to tide over the sudden catastrophic freezing of nearly all United States credits to the Western Hemisphere. In contrast to the billions poured into Europe and the Orient, Latin America, during the two years following the war, was granted only $15,000,000 in loans—an almost brutal curtailment, doubly so in the light of promises previously made. Chile and Bolivia would have been in a bad way indeed had it not been for Argentine assistance. Oscar Ivanissevich, Argentine Ambassador to Washington, declared in this connection that his country had "a Marshall Plan for her neighbors." She has also helped Europe. Economic Minister Miguel Miranda pointed out in 1947 that in proportion to her size, production, wealth and population, Argentina has actually given more credits to Europe since the end of the war than did the United States.

Some of the loans:

Great Britain. Nearly a billion dollars, via frozen pounds sterling, has been converted into a low-interest long-term loan, likely never to be repaid. Six hundred million dollars has been given as a purchase price for British railways, plus other large sums for other British utilities. The national debt of $250,000,000, much of it held in Great Britain, has been paid off in cash, very tangible aid at a needed moment. Orders have been placed for a billion pesos' worth of passenger planes, plus orders for military planes; also orders for ships, machinery, motors, railroad equipment. Of course, a good part of the steel Marshall proposes to ship to England will be used for those orders. But in all Great Britain since the war has probably drawn from Argentina in one form or another $2,500,000,000. In proportion to size, resources and population, the total amount relatively is about six times United States government aid to Britain.

Bolivia. Nearly $65,000,000 has been lent for trade, investment and public works—greater than all previous United States government aid and on terms more liberal, with less overt intervention.

Chile. Largest single loan—$175,000,000—ever granted to any Latin American country, six times all wartime and postwar aid from the United States government to Chile; earmarked as follows: $25,000,000 revolving credit; $75,000,000 to promote new industries for export to Argentina, such as copper, iron, steel, nitrate, cola, oil, wood, electric power—enterprises to be pushed under a joint Argentine-Chilean company, presided over by a Chilean; $75,000,000 for public works. The treaty and supplementary agreements provide for merchandising insurance, increased exchange of motion pictures, branch banking in either country, mutual rights to build free ports in each other's territory and maintain resident personnel and officials thereon. Argentina agrees to erect no synthetic nitrate plants, to get its entire supply from Chile.

Both countries agree to respect and support each other's antarctic claims. (As yet this has not been ratified by the Chilean Congress.)

Paraguay. Sums far larger than United States government credits, not administered and spent by outside bureaucrats; terms more liberal.

Spain. $35,000,000. (The United States government lent Spain $50,-000,000 plus much other assistance.)

Italy. $175,000,000—partly paid over in meat and wheat; to be repaid in machinery, ships, etc.

France. $175,000,000, plus $46,000,000 paid for French-owned railroads in Argentina.

All these loans are for sound investment, trade and self-liquidating projects, such as roads, railways, oil and mineral development, factories, public works. None is for armaments.

(19) *National Defense.* Argentina's defenses lagged far behind those of Brazil, so long aided by the United States, though Argentina is much wealthier. The Brazilian militarization of her borders and the plotting on Brazilian soil during the war by Juan P. Justo filled the Argentineans with fear and led to universal demand by the army and the public that the country's defenses be put in shape. Justo, the former dictator, became the white-haired presidential candidate of the United States Offices of Strategic Services and of the State Department. Public platform honors were paid him by Dictator Vargas of Brazil, by Ambassador Caffrey to Brazil and by Ambassador Armour to Argentina. However, Justo's death put an end to such machinations. The sending of United States battleships to Uruguay and the pressuring of that country to permit the United States to set up military bases on Uruguayan soil, right on Argentina's doorsteps, also frightened the southern pampas land and created more sentiment in favor of adequate national defense.

Even now Argentina has far less mechanized army equipment, fewer planes and a smaller navy than Brazil. The Five-Year Plan calls for the establishment of basic war industries (at least to match those of Brazil), additional munition works, the mechanization of part of the army, the building up of a strong air force.

Of sums thus far spent the larger portion has gone toward raising the pay of ordinary soldiers and noncoms, in supplying the rank and file with proper clothing and living quarters and food. Except for show troops in the capital the army was always half-starved, ill-clad, poorly housed. That is true no longer. Jet planes have been ordered from England and Sweden, several delivered. Nearly two hundred reconditioned United States Army landing craft have been purchased, chiefly for passenger and cargo service on rivers.

Argentina with a seventy-five-year record of peace and the pacific settlement of at least three thorny boundary disputes, ceding territory to which she had a very secure claim, even today spends a far smaller percentage of her national income on war, cost of war and armaments than the United States. Far less per capita than some of her neighbors. Her outlays over ten years in proportion to her budget have been far less than those of Brazil, Chile and a number of smaller Latin American countries. December 15, 1946, Perón stated: "Argentina does not need more arms than those indispensable for its own defense. This is absolutely a pacifist nation, which can develop normally only in an atmosphere of peace. Argentina, therefore, does not have to prepare any aggression, but only to face any danger. . . . In the Americas there can be no 'leading' nations, only equally free and sovereign nations." Most other nations, he pointed out, including the United States, were spending far more of their income on armaments than Argentina planned to spend. What other nation on earth, he implied, had a longer, more consistent record of peace and no wars than Argentina? None on earth.

The Perón administration in Argentina may suffer from grave defects, but it is the majority choice of the people and today would be re-elected by an even greater, an almost overwhelming, majority in free elections. It is impossible to forecast its future, all its purposes, or in what direction it may veer. That is impossible to prophecy for most governments, including that of the United States.

It can be said, however, that in the first two years the Perón administration did more for public health, labor and peasant standards, improved living conditions, transportation, control of basic prices, industrialization and development of the country, international trade agreements, friendly relations with all neighbors, than any previous government in Argentina's history, and in some directions did more than was ever done by all past governments of Argentina put together. This is a better record than almost any existing government in the world and in any case is a pretty good record in a world of chaos, militarism and jealousies.

Already in not a few directions Argentina is surpassing all European countries. In the near future it will surpass them all except the Soviet Union in production, strength and general progress.

All these planned Latin American efforts add up to a continental trend. The goals are: more production, wider industrialization, more and better employment, improved living standards, economic freedom. These efforts are part of the New World's answer to the general course of international events and to the blind destructive power struggle now going on between Washington and the Soviets. They offer a new encouraging balance in world affairs. Here is a rich new area of the world rising into wealth and cultural greatness while Europe continues its inevitable decline. The continents of the Americas are on the march.

VIII | Wings over the Andes

Crossing America's Highest Mountains

THERE are many ways to cross the Andes—on foot, on mule or horseback, by car, by train or in an airplane—and all these modes of locomotion are constantly used.

The faster you go, the less you see, but that less is magnificent. By plane you get a stupendous bird's-eye view. If the plane zigzags through the Uspallata snow pass, great white peaks are lost in the sky above the frosted wings on either side. If you soar in a new Panagra, British or Argentine pressure-cabin plane over the crest at more than twenty thousand feet, a white wilderness spreads out below. Through the eternal drifts and glass-blue glaciers are scrawled the hieroglyphics of black ridges, swept by Andean storms.

You see considerably more by train. As the cars climb up through utterly barren foothills, then rack-rail against the side of cliffs, some of which stretch ten thousand feet in perpendicular majesty, you get a vivid sense of vertical as well as horizontal proportions. By rail you can go over the outer Andean ridge from Guayaquil to Quito in Ecuador. You can ride the highest railroad in the world (with an oxygen tank handy) from Lima on the desert coast up to the smelter town of Arroyo and on to the great Indian market center of Huancayo in the back-country valleys. Or you can go by branch lines up to Cerro de Pasco, the great North American copper mine, or up to Huancavelica, where are the age-old mercury mines.

Or you can go up from the Peruvian port of Mollendo to a junction where other rail lines split off toward Cuzco, the ancient capital of the Incas, or to Lake Titicaca, there to take a boat to another line into La Paz, the Andean, snow-circled capital of Bolivia, and eventually clear on to Argentina.

Still other lines run out of Chile to Bolivia and Argentina. One road climbs close to the Peruvian border up among glorious snow mountains to La Paz; another line runs out of the nitrate port of Antofagasta, past the greatest copper mine in the world, Chuquicamata, across great dried lakes of nitrate and borax, to a junction with the La Paz-Buenos Aires line. Finally there is the dramatic Santiago de Chile-Buenos Aires road, which leads up to the Uspallata snow pass under the white crest of Aconcagua, the highest mountain in the Western Hemisphere, and Tupungato, almost as high. Other lines are now building across the Andes which will reshape the trade routes of South America and mayhap the entire world.

Highways parallel some of these rail routes. By car you will see still more of the fantastic grandeur of the region. You can get up from the Ecuadorean coast to Quito and on to Bogotá through inner mountains; or from Lima to the central plateau, and even to Cuzco; or up from the coast below Chala to Arequipa, Cuzco and Titicaca. A road is being built around the lake which eventually will reach La Paz and Argentina via the highlands. Or you can go from Antofagasta through Socompa Pass, also overshadowed by great snow crests, to Salta in northern Argentina, a route soon to be followed by a railroad line now nearly completed.

There are several other northern but pretty rocky desert routes. Then there is the Santiago de Chile-Buenos Aires link, usually considered part of the Inter-American Highway, which more or less follows the railroad through Uspallata Pass. The traveler whips out of Santiago on a fine concrete highway. This presently turns to macadam and then to hard-packed gravel. It goes right over the crest beside the notable Christ of the Andes, the statue of eternal peace erected by Chile and Argentine following the settlement of the Andean border by arbitration rather than war.

There are several more auto routes, with regular bus service, farther south in Chile, the most notable being a combination auto-lake steamer route through Bariloche. If it is not raining—it rains 300 days a year—this is probably the most beautiful and spectacular tour anywhere on the globe, passing a dozen Lake Comos and fifty Matterhorns. For sheer grandeur it is scarcely rivaled anywhere. The nearest to it is in our own superb Northwest country.

Finally, at some risk of life or limb, you can go on horseback or on foot through some 300 snow passes, ranging from less than 3,000 feet in far southern Chile to 19,000 feet in northern Chile. All along the Chilean-

Argentine border these various passes are used for cattle drives; the rich herds of Argentina provide much meat used by the more arid Pacific country. Many trails are still used by mule and llama pack trains, even by porters on foot, plodding along with great loads strapped to back and brow. Through some of these passes ran the remarkable Incan roads, worn deep now by ten centuries of man and llama travel. The Spaniards got their silver and gold out that way. Such pack trains still come down into Arica and other coast towns from the Bolivian highlands.

The lofty Uspallata Pass also is still used by such elementary travelers. Even though planes whip overhead, even though rails have been laid through, and a great high tunnel pierces the solid rock walls between the two neighboring countries, even though autos loop along that lofty road, and trucks careen along the mighty precipices, the big-lung men still plod across with heavy loads on their backs.

The Incas, too, used this route steadily—it is in fact called "the Road of the Incas"—and they also knew of and used the various mineral hot springs high in the folds of the mountains where now stand fine hotels.

The first "modern" trans-Andean road was built by the last Spanish governor of Chile, Ambrosio O'Higgins, whose illegitimate son Bernardo O'Higgins liberated the country to become the George Washington of a free Chile. Along this road Don Ambrosio built brick tambos or refuges, modeled after earlier Inca wayside stations. These were kept stocked with firewood and provisions so that trans-Andean travelers might take refuge from sudden blizzards. Some still stand and are still used, though rather mightily perfumed now with the refuse of four centuries.

It seems incredible that the ancient, most primitive means of travel and portage can still compete, if on a minor scale, with modern auto, rail and air transport. But to this day there is a professional group of contractors who scout for freight on the little remote ranches and villages in the interior folds of the Andes, make deals for carting produce through the snow passes, then round up mules or llamas (which stand the altitude and cold better) or even human beings, to land the stuff at city markets. They carry back cloth, knives, hardware and salt.

Thus the old ways persist in the lands south, alongside the most modern methods. They will continue as long as labor standards remain so low that muscle is cheaper than metal. In Mexico City I have seen four men trotting along a city street with a piano on their collective heads. Head-bearers are still a common sight in the southern countries, from the handsome swaying girl balancing a stalk of bananas or a five-gallon tin of water, to the back-brow porters that make it a regular trade. So accustomed are the Indians of Guatemala to trotting over mountain trails with enormous burdens that when they have no such loads, it is said, they load up with stones in order to maintain the usual balance and make better traveling time. But I'll have to see it before I quite believe it.

River Travel

In jungle and mountain country the rivers become doubly important as a means of transportation. This is particularly true of Brazil, with the mightiest network of inner waterways of any country in the world. Ciro Alegría's remarkable novel, *Serpent of Gold*, tells of the hardy, reckless boatmen of the Marañón River at the dashing narrows where that great and boisterous stream breaks through the Andean wall to join the more placid march of waters through thousands of miles of jungle country to the Atlantic.

An intimate cross section of life is obtained by traveling by such elemental means on the inner ways of the continent.

Some years ago I went from Lake Nicaragua down the San Juan, which follows the border between Nicaragua and Costa Rica, through dense crocodile and flamingo jungles to Greytown on the shark-infested Caribbean Sea.

A gasoline launch towed a combination freight and passenger scow, half of which was protected by a hood against sun and tropic deluge. Our departure from the little port of San Carlos was announced by the blowing of a conch shell. On board were sacks of beans and brown sugar, heaps of banana suckers, a sewing machine, a number of pigs, chickens and turkeys, Indians, Negroes and whites, and a man just peeling from smallpox.

Our most dangerous and exciting passage was running the rocky rapids below El Castillo, a town where we had to sleep on the store counters. The most beautiful spectacle was the wide island-dotted juncture of the largest south tributary where we slept overnight on the boat under a rich tropical moon. But what was important about this trip was the chance to observe how people far removed from the bustle of modernity make a pattern of industrious happiness for themselves, how they manage to get around, communicate and trade their products.

Some of these more primitive means of transportation still feed out the products required by the outside world. Once, off the coast of Costa Rica and Nicaragua, I traveled in a combination motor and sailboat, one of the numerous little tramps of the Caribbean, which was loaded to the gunwales with coconuts from Cocos Island, to be picked up at a larger port for the glycerin, gas-mask and armaments factories of some far land. Down the inner streams of Guatemala and British Honduras float the chicle gathered deep in the jungles of Quintana Roo and Petén. Into Iquitos, Peru, on the upper Amazon, float big rafts of raw rubber, manned by the most primitive folk of the back country, even head-hunters. On these they build straw huts and bring along their whole family. As they drift downstream, they fish, weave hats and cook. In Iquitos or some other river port they barter their rubber for calico, glass beads, knives, guns and ammunition, tobacco and salt, then thread through the jungle back to their home villages.

The southern countries are all pushing new sea and river ports and are building up river and international water transport. Colombia, Venezuela and Ecuador have jointly started the new super Grancolombia merchant marine, which is now handling all coffee exports.

Nicaragua has the brand-new Somoza seaport. Venezuela has started on new port facilities for La Guaira and on some twenty-five river ports. The entrance to Lake Maracaibo is being dredged out to permit access by ocean liners and refining right at the oil fields. In Peru, less than ten years ago, the main port of Callao could be entered only by lighters; today great ocean liners can dock. Chimbote in the north is also being developed. The new port of Matarani has been built alongside Mollendo by the Frederick Snare Corporation at a cost of $4,000,000. Behind two enormous breakwaters, one nearly 2,000 feet long, a 1,350-foot pier with four fireproof warehouses and railroad tracks will accommodate three liners simultaneously. The champagne was broken over the new esplanade early in October 1947 by officials of Bolivia and Peru. This port will serve the highlands and Bolivian trade.

Many new ports of Latin America have more modern and efficient equipment than New York harbor. Even in what, a few years ago, was a swampy malaria-ridden stink hole like Buenaventura, Colombia, modern docks, loading equipment, warehouses and rail service have been installed. Vera Cruz, Mexico, began overhauling its port during the war.

Other main ports in South America have been vastly expanded and improved.

The Inter-American Highway

In most of South America modern roads have steadily improved and have reached many new places. In Mexico the Pan-American link from Laredo to Mexico City, a magnificent highway for its construction and scenery, reaching tropical lowland jungles and spiraling up over great mountains, passes through quaint villages now graced with candy-bar gasoline pumps and tourist camps. Gradually feeder links are being built, and other connecting highways are being pushed along the west coast and toward the United States at various points.

On south from Mexico City one can whiz down to the tropical Riviera of Mexico, the swank Acapulco resort with its swarms of magnificent hotels and modern chalets, right alongside colorful native life. Clear through Mexico City from north to south has been cut a super-boulevard for thirty miles that gives access to a new mountain short-cut speed highway to the swank Cuernavaca resort, a place of eternal warm spring, then on to the silver center of Taxco, one of the most picturesque towns of the republic, and over great sweeps of mountain and valley to the southern port.

Or one can drive over a fine mountain highway, close to the glaciers of the mighty snow volcano, Ixtaccihuatl, the White Woman, to Puebla and on to the Tehuacán hot springs. A poorer road continues on to Oaxaca, one of the less spoiled, spring-bright cities of Mexico. From there workers in the rugged mountains have just linked up the highway with Tehuantepec, "The Isthmus," one of the most exciting areas, where people wear elaborate and showy peasant costumes.

Farther south, in Chiapas clear to the Guatemalan border, we saw bulldozers smashing through coast jungles. Various towns are booming in anticipation.

One road project, scheduled for some years hence, will provide a ferry-highway route that will cut off thousands of miles for travelers motoring south from the Atlantic seaboard. From Key West, Florida, cars will be ferried across the 100-mile sea gap to Havana. From there a good highway runs through Pinar del Rio province to the southwest tip of the island. Another ferry will then bridge the 130-mile gap to Yucatán.

Another highway, parts already built, will take motorists along the blue spray-drenched sea cliffs of Campeche, up over the Chiapas highlands, with their beautiful historic cities, on to the Tehuantepec Isthmus. There one will hit the main north-south Inter-American route: northeast to Mexico City or on southeast to Central America, eventually clear to the Straits of Magellan.

This new highway-ferry combination will save those from the eastern part of the United States several thousand miles motoring southwest to Laredo, then back southeast to Mexico City; and if the destination is Guatemala and on southeast—since practically all South America lies east of New York—the mileage saved will be of almost continental proportions.

South—despite the enormous wartime sums for road building spent by our government—the waste and graft were so great in places that much of the Inter-American Highway is not yet greatly to be recommended. In Guatemala, though the highway is not impossible, it is deep in dust in summer, heavy with mud in winter, badly graded, narrow with sharp unguarded curves. The link from Guatemala City to the Salvadorean border, built some twenty-five years ago, is much better, though at times pretty dusty. It is wide, well-graded and graveled. We went over this in a station wagon, with rather startling adventures and difficulties.

It is now possible to get over some kind of road to every provincial capital of Guatemala, something that could not have been said even ten years ago. A new highway, to cost nearly a million dollars, is being built from the government's new Petén land colony clear down through jungle to Sweet Water Gulf on the Caribbean.

Even before the war Salvador had built a fine network of concrete highways all over the country. These have been improved and extended and are by far the best roads in all Central America.

In Honduras the picture is lamentable. Under the dictatorship of Tiburcio Carías most roads are far worse than twenty years ago. Although a few fairly good roads have been pushed for some miles out from Tegucigalpa, they soon break down into imitations of goat tracks. An excellent short stretch was built by the United States government around Lake Yojoa to eliminate existing ferry service. Not a few bridges were given and installed by the United States. Most of these have been christened "Carías" after the dictator.

The Inter-American through Nicaragua is in trim shape, well-graded and bedded, though except for paved stretches near Managua, the capital, it is merely gravel-surfaced, allowing for only forty miles an hour with safety. Its construction was featured by great graft; it has not come up to required specifications; and it was actually twisted off the surveyed route in order to service one of the dictator's many estates—a detour for which the American taxpayer shelled out plenty.

We met one Nicaraguan employee sailing along in a fine car. He had been a well-paid "spark-plug inspector."

He grinned. "When I had nothing else to do, I used to put my wife and kids in the car and go for a spin and look over some of the cars and trucks. I always changed all the plugs—on paper—and sold the new ones."

At present there is a thirty-mile malarial jungle gap between Nicaragua and Costa Rica, impassable for cars. United States army engineers did a fair job of fixing up the northern stretch in Costa Rica, but on the southern portion graft was tremendous. Existing surveys were ignored, unfeasible routes selected, and after the fantastic expenditure of millions, many Jim Crow insults to Costa Ricans (incidentally of the purest Spanish stock to be found in the Americas), the whole job was abandoned in such uncompleted state that, due to tropic rains, grading will be a total loss. The Costa Ricans are scarcely joyful about all this, even though the North American taxpayer does love to pay for such nonsense.

One can now motor nearly the length of Panama, particularly the western half. New roads are being built into the coffee country above David, near the Costa Rican border.

Thus by the time this is published, it probably will be possible to get by car from the United States as far south as the Costa Rican border. Some of the highway in Mexico will be in provisional condition. The roads of Guatemala, if inferior, can be easily traversed in the dry season and with some cursing in the wet season. The motorists will spin over Salvador in fine shape, past the innumerable volcanoes and fresh lava flow and the densely populated countryside, very lush with semijungle vegetation. However, he will have to stop at a police or army pillbox every three or four miles to give his pedigree, color of hair and eyes, number of legitimate children, the names of his mother and father and where they were born, his religion, age, all physical blemishes; swear that he is sound of health and limb and provide other fancy details. This will take about as much time as the actual motoring on the road.

Over the Lerma River he will cross the longest suspension bridge in Central America, Puente Cuscatlán, completed during the war.

He will have to slow down to nearly ten miles an hour over that bad stretch in Honduras which circles the beautiful Gulf of Fonseca with its gem islands, woods and slim volcanoes. But he will get on pretty well in Nicaragua. On south he will circle Lake Nicaragua, with its sleek island volcano of Ometepé—Twin Peak—but should be careful about taking a dip. This is said to be the only lake in the world that has fresh-water sharks—a fact of which Nicaraguans for some queer reason are inordinately proud. Then he will bump into the jungle wall of Costa Rica and stop.

South American Roads

In South America one can now drive over the famous Simón Bolívar Highway from Caracas, Venezuela, through Bogotá, Colombia, and on to Quito in Ecuador. This single majestic mountain highway has done more to unite the three countries into "Greater Colombia" than all the dreams and armies of the great leader of Independence time.

It is a stupendous scenic route, over and across purple mountains, green valleys, dark jungles, tawny deserts and rolling meadows knee-deep with lush grass. In some high barren mountains only thorny cactus and other pulpy, barbed dry-country vegetation speckle the harsh slopes. The road swings through transplanted African and Indian villages, where natives lounge in blue or crimson ponchos or wear striped green and black capes, baggy white cotton trousers, jaunty wool or felt headgear and gather in big markets, piled high with yellow and crimson fruit, Panama hats, rugs, blankets, pottery and basketry. Often the car passes whole armies of Indians laden down with such objects or it must pick its way through big herds of cattle, pigs, sheep, even cackling chickens and turkeys. In some places in Ecuador where the highway is paved with mountain stone the traveler will come upon llama pack trains.

Colombia, Venezuela and Ecuador are doing much road building in all directions. Typical of Latin American interest in better communications is the activity in Venezuela. About the only highways previously built were those to the great private estates of Dictator Gómez and one paved highway, "the curve-a-day" stretch with its 365 half loops through the mountains from Maiquetía on the coast to Caracas. One of its culverts, scarcely even a bridge, was dubbed "Puente de Oro," "Bridge of Gold," because it was rebuilt so many times for such fantastic prices by the Gómez henchmen that its total cost was nearly a million dollars.

In one year after the 1945 revolution 266 miles of new highway and 1,097 feet of bridges were built, and some 400 miles more surveyed. No charges of graft have yet been leveled. This effort is in accordance with a general plan drawn up after careful study by the National Transport Commission, which provides for the spending of more than $100,000,-000 on 6,671 kilometers of highways and stock trails. Since the 1945 revolution bus facilities have been increased for nearly a hundred thousand passengers daily.

At present the northern countries of South America have no adequate road connections with the rest of the continent, though important new highways are building. At some risk and difficulty a car might conceivably get through from Ecuador to Peru in the dry season.

Some years back, according to the Leguía and Benavides dictatorships, one of the notable achievements of their regimes were new coastal and Andean highways. In 1934 we found the Andean roads barely hanging to mountainsides, scarcely one car wide, without surfacing, merely toboggans of death and despair. We tried also the coast road in numbers of places, only to discover it to be an agonizing stretch across the desert. Here and there busses did manage to get through between several major ports, but almost invariably got stalled for hours or even days in the sand.

But today the whole length of Peru's coast has a well-ballasted and graded highway of which about a thousand miles have been surfaced with concrete or asphalt.

In the south, beyond the picturesque little fishing village of Chala with its sumptuous new tourist hotel, the highway becomes gravel-surfaced and is cut along ocean cliffs. It provides one of the most grandiose mountain-ocean drives I have ever been over. Here and there are some truly spectacular and hair-raising stretches, such as the seventeen-kilometer "Slope of Skulls," breathless corkscrew chute-the-chutes of unadulterated terror. But new and safe links are now being sliced through everywhere with modern road machinery, and it will soon be a completely safe and magnificent highway.

Often the road hangs over cliffs for thousands of feet, directly above the sea rocks. At one place, now being eliminated, it spiraled up and up great barren mountains for nearly ten thousand feet, then came out at a super-Grand Canyon, which would contain half a dozen the size of that of the Colorado. It wound along the edge of this many-tinted abyss back down to the sea—all told four hours of highly dangerous mountain travel just to get past a few miles of sheer stone ocean cliffs that here tower up about four thousand feet.

In Peru one may also drive across the Andes to Huancayo or Huanuco by a good road, or on to Ayacucho and even to Cuzco by a pretty nerve-racking road, and on down the magnificent Urubamba gorge past the lofty incredible Machu-Picchu ruins clear to Bolivian jungles. But the best route by land is from Chala up to Arequipa on to Juliaca where one road splits off to Lake Titicaca and Bolivia, and the other goes up through picturesque mountain towns to the old capital of the Incas.

One important wartime development with United States government money was the building of an extension of the Huanuco highway over the inner Cordillera, down the mighty slopes to the jungles at Tingo María—where a big good-will agricultural experiment station was erected—then clear on to the Ucayali River, a large Amazon tributary. From this point passenger vessels go on to the river port of Iquitos and to the Atlantic four thousand miles away.

By this highway, for the first time in modern Peruvian history, the three difficult regions of the country—desert coast, lofty Andean valleys and Amazon forests—long so isolated, were united by fairly easy travel. This in fact is today the only completed transcontinental route, except for those far south between Chile and Argentina, and it goes right across the widest part of South America.

A few years back it took months of arduous, dangerous jungle travel, scarcely ever attempted, to get from Lima to Iquitos. Now by highway and boat the trip can be made in three days; and of course by plane in a few hours.

Even during the first year after its completion this highway had valuable economic results. It gave access to the rich Blue Goose Dome, the new oil strike, and opened up an important farm, forest and mineral region. Already it has brought in many tropical products, cereals and fruits to the Pacific Coast region. It has also made possible the development of a new wild-animal leather industry—the export of peccary, deer and alligator hides.

There in the Amazon foothills and bottom lands Peru has one of the world's biggest stands of fine timber, but heretofore it has been cheaper to import all lumber from Sweden or the Pacific Northwest than try to drag it out of the back country. Ninety-five per cent of Peru's lumber needs were supplied from abroad. With the new road, in only six months new sawmills were able to supply sixty per cent of all needs from the trans-Andean forests. Except for special woods Peru now largely supplies all her own needs. Pulp and paper mills have been built, and in these lines, too, the country will soon be independent of outside imports.

Chile in recent years has done much road building and is now spending large sums. Even so, the northern Chile portion of the Inter-American Highway is far worse than that in Peru. Around central Chile, in the Vales of Paradise, there is a fine concrete network. Valparaiso, beautiful Viña del Mar, Santiago, Concepción and intermediary points are well linked. Good gravel roads lead on to Valdivia and clear to Puerto Montt on the southernly Gulf of Reloncavi. Many roads thread through the handsome lake region and to the numerous hot springs which abound in all Chile.

But in the long northern desert reaches there are few good roads except right around nitrate plants and mines. Between Arica and Iquique, though the distance is less than two hundred miles, and the plane does it in a few minutes, the combination freight-passenger buses go through a dust-drowning ordeal of from twelve to fourteen hours. Not even busses attempt the Iquique-Tocopilla stretch. But out of nitrate port Antofagasta, one of the big shipping outlets for Bolivia and Argentina, the roads are better and there are regular bus services in many directions, in fact clear up to Tocopilla. Also regular trucks and busses go clear through Socompa Pass to Salta in Argentina.

In Copiapó, when we tried to hire a car to go on to La Serena on the coast, we were eyed with astonishment. The price asked was almost equal to buying the car, so bad is the stretch. But from La Serena on south to Valparaiso, a fine new highway, not yet surfaced, has been carved out. In south Chile bus lines run over regular routes through the lake region and the Andes into Argentina—the world's finest scenery.

The 1942 road census gave Chile only 862 kilometers surfaced with concrete or asphalt, and 14,513 kilometers with macadam, gravel, sand or hard clay. There are nearly 30,000 miles of country dirt roads. In the rainy season fly or swim—but whatever you do, do not go in a car! Improvement, though, is steady. In 1921 Chile was spending only a little over a million pesos on highways; by 1945 it was dishing out 423,-000,000; and for some years ahead it plans to spend over a billion a year.

The government Agrarian Plan provides for building 3,500 kilometers of main concrete or asphalt highways and 15,000 kilometers of macadam. A number of new roads are being built in the Province of Aisén. A few years ago Puerto Aisén, in the far south rain region, halfway between Puerto Montt, the rail terminus, and the Straits of Magellan, didn't even exist, but it has been rapidly developed with new homesteaders.

Motoring in Argentina and Brazil

During the war, Argentina, which formerly depended on the British railways that had long blocked road construction, spent large sums pushing highways, and even larger expenditures are now being made. Among major truck highways under construction or completed in recent years are:

(1) The Inter-American into Brazil. In July 1947 the ribbon across the big new bridge over Uruguay River was cut in joint ceremony by Presidents Perón and Dutra. (2) The highway to the Bolivian border. Argentina is also financing and building the road on the Bolivian side clear to Sucre that will give access to La Paz. (3) Surfacing and improving the main highways to Córdoba and Mendoza where the trans-Andean highway takes off. (4) The super highway to Nahuel Huapi in the Parque Nacional, the major scenic and lake region of Argentina. This is a splendid route with clear views of the majestic Andean snow peaks: Tupungato, San José, Tinguiririca and dozens of others. This route passes over big new bridges across the Grande and Barrancas rivers, where hotels have been built, runs by important hot springs, such as Sosneado, where a fine hotel has been put up, and skirts the fine fishing lake of Llancanelo. (5) The excellent new highway 1,500 miles south clear to the Chilean border near the Straits of Magellan, giving access to Punta Arenas, Natales and the beautiful Payne Cordillera. (6) A new road to the Lake San Martín coal fields from Santa

Cruz and Gallegos. (7) From Salta in the north to the Socompa Pass and into Chile. (8) A main highway into the Gran Chaco and the Pilcomayo River and Paraguay. (9) A new highway through the Mesopotamia paradise to the Uruguayan frontier.

At present Argentina has more developed highways of every sort than all the rest of South America put together.

During the war the United States government spent large amounts in Paraguay partly for roads, where a vast new Standard Oil concession was secured. A supermodern highway was built for fifty kilometers southeast from Asunción along Lake San Bernardino and over the Cascupé Cordillera to Villarrica.

Another important United States-built highway was carved out from the rich Santa Cruz food basket of inner Bolivia up to Cochabamba on the Andean plateau, regions previously isolated from each other. This will help solve food and fuel-oil problems of upper mining towns.

Brazil has a fair network around Rio and São Paulo, the two largest cities. A mountain road goes up from Rio to the famed hill resort Petropolis and beyond. New motor roads have been completed from inner Bello Horizonte, a handsome mining and resort city, through large industrial Juiz de Fora to Rio, also to São Paulo.

An excellent highway follows the coast from Rio to Santos, two hundred miles south, the greatest coffee port in the world, and from there a fine scenic route leaps over the coast range to São Paulo, from which other smooth roads ray out on all sides.

The main south highway continues on to Uruguay and Argentina as part of the Inter-American. From this good roads branch off to the leading ports, Paranaguá, Ponta Grossa, Porto Alegre and Rio Grande do Sul.

Out of Porto Alegre a highway runs to Ponta Pora on the Paraguayan border, then north a thousand miles to Cuyabá on the far inner Matto Grosso plateau, now being opened up with new towns and industries, finally on to historic Diamantina. From there about a hundren miles have been thrust north into the Amazon headwater country toward Ribeirão Clara.

The two most ambitious highways under construction are those from Manáos, the rubber port two thousand miles up the Amazon. One goes through dense jungle, ten years ago not even explored, to Rio Branco on the frontier of British Guiana, about six hundred miles. The other, through even more difficult jungles, will reach for a thousand miles to the Colombian frontier. These, plus the new Peruvian Andean road to the Ucayali, will help bind the whole central and north portions of the continent together.

Golden Spike

Railroad building, though hampered by lack of materials, has been pushed steadily in most southern countries. Today both Brazil and Argentina are rolling steel rails, making locomotives and railway cars.

On our swank train down to the south lake region and on the international express to La Paz we found no sleeping cars dated earlier than 1943. This fine new equipment is built on comfortable European compartment models.

Of particular interest are new lines being laid toward new passes in the Andes.

When the golden spike was driven in to complete the first transcontinental road in the United States, Europe paid little heed. Yet in many ways it was more important for Europe than even the Franco-Prussian war which presently was waged. The rapid utilization of the free fertile lands of our West revolutionized Old World agriculture which in many lines could no longer compete. The whole economic structure of Europe was ripped apart. World industry, trade and power began to shift, and the final balance still has to be struck.

Today few self-centered North Americans fully appreciate, any more than did Europeans a century ago, that epochal changes now occurring in Latin American transportation will forever alter the economic and international relations of South America, of our own country and of the whole world.

All during the war South America was driving in, often with North American help, a dozen new golden spikes in air, roads, railroads. Some rail routes will bring regions and resources never before tapped into the world market, will penetrate areas separated off since the beginning of time. This will not only change the map of South America; it will actually affect the lives and the occupations of millions of people in the United States itself.

Thus over the 12,600-foot Socompa Pass in the most rugged tangle of the Andes is being carved out the 550-mile railroad to link Salta in upper Argentina with the Chilean port of Antofagasta. Bus and truck service already carry across the uncompleted portion of the line.

On the Chilean side new construction has already crossed the great Domeyko Cordillera to the foot of the still mightier Sierra de Almeida, and only 35 miles of track laying remain to slap the line into the pass. On the Argentine side the rails have now pushed beyond San Antonio de los Cobres, and only about 100 miles are still to be built.

Already this route has had a remarkable effect on international trade. The fertilizers of Chile, instead of going around Cape Horn for 6,000 miles to Buenos Aires, then for 1,500 more miles into the interior of Argentina, today land there in a few hours. Similarly now the temperate-zone products of northern Argentina—wheat, meat, wool, steel and iron products, leather goods, cement—move into north Chile.

With new links building on east this will provide the shortest route from Chile to São Paulo clear across the continent in Brazil. Soon across this route will come the tropical products of lowland Bolivia, the Chaco and the Brazilian jungles.

Incidentally this line also brings the heart of the South American continent, the rich inner regions of Argentina and the Chaco, thousands of miles closer to New York and vice versa. It not only brings Argentina much nearer to the eastern seaboard of the United States but also makes her definitely now a Pacific Ocean trading country also. This is helped by the new treaty with Chile giving Argentina free ports on the Pacific litoral.

Another important rail line is being built in far south Patagonia to the Lake Buenos Aires coal field. Other lines are being pushed through the Andes from the oil centers of Comodoro Rivadavia and Neuquén: one to the Bariloche trans-Andean route, the other directly to the Chilean port of Concepción and the new Talcahuano steel industry. Several more trans-Andean lines have been started.

Exciting has been the rivalry of Brazil and Argentina to thrust railroads into the rich oil, manganese and farm regions of southeast Bolivia, regions never before tapped. The Argentine line is pushing north from frontier Yacuiba toward Sucre, the official capital.

The Brazilian line, which was agreed on by the February 25, 1938, treaty and favored with wartime priorities, pushed from the Santos-São Paulo trunk line to Baurú, then over the Brazilian Northwestern to Corumbá and Puerto Suárez on either bank of big Paraguay River, a total stretch of more than 7,000 kilometers. In Bolivia trains are already rolling over 170 kilometers—the most difficult portion, with jungles, swamps and excessive heat—of the 414 kilometers needed to reach through the Santa Cruz plantations and oil fields to the inner Andean folds at Cochabamba. From Santa Cruz the new North American highway climbs on up to the plateau. From Cochabamba toward the lowlands the line has been constructed 60 kilometers as far as Araní. On completion this will provide the most important transcontinental route of South America: for its great length surpassing that of any similar trunk line in the Americas, for the incredible richness of the regions it traverses, for the vast empire it opens up, for its benefits to the largest number of countries. Brazil will then have direct access to the Pacific Ocean through Peru (at Mollendo) and Chile (at Arica), and all Bolivia will have direct outlet on the Atlantic.

All these transcontinental links are a necessary integration of the southern end of the continent. Imagine the plight of the United States had our country stopped dead at the Rockies and other strong independent nations occupied California, Nevada, Oregon and Washington. Not until the mountains, the tariff and political barriers had been surmounted, would any of the districts have been able to attain the economic growth and prosperity that now exist. This necessary unification is the real significance of many new South American developments in transportation and industry—not intemperate talk about "Argentine imperialism." Actually, of course, the United States took most of the western obstructing regions by force. The southern countries, on the other hand, are co-operating to wipe away the obstacles.

Thus the east and west portions of the continent, previously linked only by the trans-Andean route from Santiago to Mendoza, began to be pulled together during the war at many points, and this effort continues. All the new routes, road, railroad and air, will weld the whole southern end of the continent into much needed economic unity. They bring Brazil, Paraguay, Bolivia, Uruguay, Chile and to some extent Peru into a transportation web which will mean more rapid growth of some of the wealthiest but hitherto isolated parts of the inner continent. With energy and wise co-operation there is no reason why this area in time should not match the United States in productive capacity and prosperity.

Brazil and Chile

During the war Brazil got priorities on equipment to electrify the major lines. Eventually the whole state-owned trunk line, the Central do Brasil, 3,150 miles, will be run by electricity. We talked with the technical engineer of this project. He has worked out a blueprint manual so clear that even an illiterate workman earning a few cents a day can ask for the necessary materials and install any given section.

The rail line out of Ilheos, serving cacao country, is being pushed on into the rich Rio de Contas Valley. The lines into the Itabira iron-mining region, also to various other coal and mineral areas, are being improved and extended. . . . A coastal system of railroads clear from Uruguay to northern Belém is planned.

Chile claims the first railroad ever built in South America, from Caldera to Copiapó, originally projected as a trans-Andean route and eventually to be extended into Argentina. Over it ran the first engine ever exported from the United States. Most early roads, however, were built by various mining and nitrate companies, short spurs from mine to shipping points. North-south trunk railroads were delayed because of difficult terrain and sparse population; also because it was cheaper to ship by sea along the coast. Besides, most products in that earlier period were earmarked for shipment abroad, not to other parts of the country. But gradually short lines were merged, connecting links built, and today Chile has a trunk line that runs from the tiny nitrate port of Pisagua in the far north clear to Puerto Montt on the southerly Reloncavi Gulf. It is one of the most efficient and comfortable systems in South America.

With the terrible blows given the nitrate industry Chile is the one country of South America where actual railway mileage declined between 1930 and 1942, since many tracks laid to nitrate fields became worthless. Nevertheless, the government has been pushing new lines, in addition to the Socompa route, toward the Andes to meet Argentine roads and into new ports and to various lake tourist centers.

In south Chile a new line from Lanco up to Lakes Calafaquén and Panguipulli, two show places, is almost completed. The difficult bridge over the Leufacade River at Puritón was installed in 1946.

Ecuador has most ambitious rail construction projected or under way. A line is being pushed from the Andean garden city of Ambato at the foot of Mount Chimborazo over the inner Andes to Curaray River in the jungles to give access to the Napo and Amazon rivers and, for the first time, to link up the coast with the back jungle country.

Another line is being pushed down from lofty Quito, the capital, to the northwest port of Esmeraldas. Nearly 200 kilometers have been completed, and only a short stretch is left. Another line, 174 kilometers long, has just been completed from Guayaquil south to the port of Salinas, a resort center where salt, sulphur and oil are produced. From Simbabe junction on the Guayaquil-Quito line a branch has been run south toward Cuenca, the capital of Azuay province, a quinine and sugar center. It has reached Tipacocha and Azogues, 70 kilometers. Azogues (Mercury) is the place where nearly all Panama hats are finished for retail sale. This line will eventually run on south to Loja to connect with another new trans-Andean line, 75 kilometers of which have been completed out of the Puerto Bolivia to Pasaje beyond the gold-mining town of Machala. This route eventually will reach Zamora in the Oriente jungle region and give access to the navigable Zamora and Amazon rivers and the Atlantic Ocean.

Colombia has many exciting projects. It is building a new railroad from the end of the Amaga railway to the rich Cauca Valley. A much more ambitious project is the trunk line from the Pacific port of Buenaventura to the Atlantic port of Cartagena. About 44 kilometers of this have already been opened for service out of Cartagena as far as Gambota. Eventually it will connect with the existing Buenaventura-Puerto Berrios line.

The new Nariño railway being built by the government from Tumaco, Colombia's extreme southwestern Pacific port, to El Pato, capital of the Department, on the Andean plateau, is in operation for 92 kilometers between Aguaclara (Clear Water) and El Diviso. On completion this will give access to the Bogotá-Quito portion of the Simón Bolívar Highway.

A railway from Bogotá, capital of the country, is being thrust through the northeastern Andes to near the Venezuela border at Bucaramanga, capital of Santander del Sur province, rich coffee and tobacco country. This city lies on the Simón Bolívar Highway between Bogotá and Caracas and in time will link with the Venezuela line down to the Lake Maracaibo oil region.

At the North American end of Latin America Mexico is the only country building railroads. Though work has gone forward very slowly, one line will link up Lower California with Sonora. A line southwest across the Sierra Madre will tie the Mississippi Valley in with the Pacific coast area. In 1945 bids were opened. These involved the building of 126 tunnels. A new route south of Uruapan to the Pacific coast will open up territory long isolated, some of it still marked "unexplored" on modern maps. A difficult engineering problem, because of marshes and jungle, is the railroad connecting Yucatán and the Campeche rail lines with the Isthmus of Tehuantepec along the Gulf of Mexico.

Wings

All Latin America has taken to the air in a great way. Aviation has given a quick solution for passenger and freight services to former secluded areas that could not be properly assimilated into the national economy because of the prohibitive cost of roads or railways. Whole new districts have not only been brought to the doorsteps of the modern world; they have been put to new productive use; they have received the impulse of modern civilization.

The world's first commercial air line was started in Colombia. And that country now has one of the most elaborate systems on earth. Today South America flies many more air miles per capita than any other part of the globe. Its total air mileage is approximately three times that of the United States. The Taca line in Central America reports that since it started it actually has carried more air freight than was carried in the whole United States.

World War II gave great impulse to air travel on every side. Growth has been stupendous. Airfields, many built by the United States government and since mostly turned over to the various countries or to Pan American Airways—to the disgust of many independent companies—dot the continent from end to end, even on little islands in remote jungle centers. Today the world's largest airport is in Natales, Brazil. In general the chief airport facilities of South America are superior in taste, comfort and public service to those in the United States. In these respects the capital airports in even the smallest countries are away ahead of such unpleasant North American airports as those in Miami, Philadelphia and LaGuardia Field in New York.

More than 20,000 planes a year take off from the great beautiful Santos Dumont Airport in Rio. A whole mountain was sluiced down into the harbor to make it. In 1929 Brazil—which incidentally claims to have invented the first airplane actually to fly and to have made the first transatlantic solo flight considerably before Lindbergh—had only 4,529 miles of air routes. They now total over 40,000 miles.

Brazilian lines now push on to Argentina, Uruguay, Bolivia, Paraguay and over the Andes to Chile, into French Guiana and Venezuela. The new Linha Aerea Transcontinental Brazileira competes with Panagra all along the Amazon River and tributaries and soon will extend its services into Peru. Many previously inaccessible places in the interior, deep in the jungles, are on regular air routes. Fields have actually been built in spots that twenty years ago had not even been explored by white men. One was made by parachuting in men, equipment and supplies. A whole new empire, one of the richest on earth, has been opened up, and before long the world will realize that it is important, as rich a storehouse, as productive a dynamo, as all Europe put together. If the United States could put as much money into this region as it has poured down the European drain, the results would be fantastic and really benefit the whole world.

Argentina has encouraged aviation in a big way during the war years and since. A billion pesos' order was placed at the war's close with Great Britain for big pressure-cabin planes for the transatlantic and trans-Andean flights. Delivery was promised plane for plane with those allocated to British overseas routes. Today scarcely a corner of Argentina is without regular plane service. The Argentine Automobile Association even maintains planes and flying fields to service its members quickly on remote roads, fly in repairs or get passengers quickly on to their destination while car repairs are being made.

In the international field, two Argentine transatlantic routes are now in operation, to northern and to southern Europe. Three-hour flights are maintained between Buenos Aires and Santiago de Chile, a schedule met by Panagra and the British line. The Argentine trans-Andean route will be prolonged up to Ecuador and through all Latin America, with lines running on into the United States and Canada. Various Argentine lines already run into Uruguay, Bolivia, Paraguay and Brazil.

In addition Buenos Aires is served by the lines of numbers of other Latin American countries (especially Chile, Uruguay, Brazil and Venezuela) by Panagra, British, French and Spanish lines. Holland and Italy are preparing to join the parade. Various new North American companies have obtained concessions.

The National Air Lines of Chile (LAN), where international companies are forbidden to handle local traffic, extend from Arica clear to the Straits of Magellan. The service from Santiago to Punta Arenas on the Straits, a nine-hour flight, was inaugurated in 1946. Out of Punta Arenas there is a shuttle service with Porvenir on Fire Island.

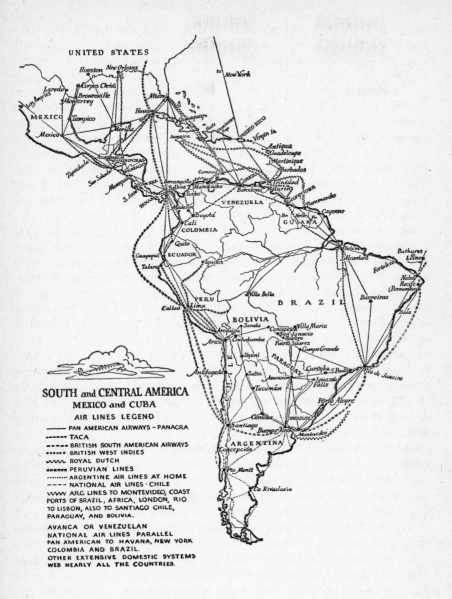

UNITED STATES

Houston · New Orleans

to New York

Laredo · Corpus Christi
Monterrey · Brownsville
Los Angeles

MEXICO · Tampico

Miami

Havana

Mexico · Merida

Jamaica

Mayaguez · PUERTO RICO

Virgin Is.

Antigua
Guadeloupe
Martinique
Barbados

Curacao

GUATEMALA · HONDURAS

San Salvador · NICARAGUA

Managua · COSTA RICA

Barranquilla · Maracaibo

Balboa · Manzanillo

Barcelona · Maturin

Trinidad

Georgetown

S. José · PANAMA

Turbo

VENEZUELA

Paramaribo

Medellin

Br. Nell·

Cayenne

Cali · Bogotá

GUIANA

COLOMBIA

Quito

ECUADOR

Belém

Guayaquil

Alcantara

Batkurst
Lisbon

Talara

Iquitos

Fortaleza

Natal
Recife
Pernambuco

Villa Bella

B R A Z I L

Barreiras

Baía

Callao · Lima

PERU

BOLIVIA

Sorda · Villa Maria

Arequipa · Concacion · San Ignacio

Arica · Cochabamba · Robore
Puerto Suarez

Campo Grande

Uyuni

PARAGUAY

Curityba · S. Paulo

Antofagasta

Salta

Asuncion

Iguassu
Falls

Rio de Janeiro

Tucumán

Porto Alegre

Córdoba

URUGUAY

Santiago · Buenos Aires

Montevideo

ARGENTINA

Concepción

Pto Montt

Pto Rivadavia

SOUTH and CENTRAL AMERICA
MEXICO and CUBA
AIR LINES LEGEND

———— PAN AMERICAN AIRWAYS - PANAGRA
········ TACA
- - - - BRITISH SOUTH AMERICAN AIRWAYS
∘∘∘∘∘ BRITISH WEST INDIES
∿∿∿∿ ROYAL DUTCH
∗∗∗∗∗∗ PERUVIAN LINES
·········· ARGENTINE AIR LINES AT HOME
- - - - NATIONAL AIR LINES · CHILE
∿∿∿ ARG. LINES TO MONTEVIDEO, COAST
PORTS OF BRAZIL, AFRICA, LONDON, RIO
TO LISBON, ALSO TO SANTIAGO CHILE,
PARAGUAY, AND BOLIVIA.

AVANCA OR VENEZUELAN
NATIONAL AIR LINES PARALLEL
PAN AMERICAN TO HAVANA, NEW YORK
COLOMBIA AND BRAZIL.
OTHER EXTENSIVE DOMESTIC SYSTEMS
WEB NEARLY ALL THE COUNTRIES.

189

The LAN service, which I used many times, is efficient, supercourteous and reliable. The Chilean lines now have pushed over to Mendoza in Argentina and will go to Buenos Aires. Future routes are planned for Bolivia, Peru and Brazil.

Peru now has three national domestic lines, private and government, and most of the inner Amazon region is well-covered by regular flights. Two lines go to Iquitos on the Amazon. One of South America's successful independent lines has been Aviación Fawcett. This was started when planes, illegally destined for Bolivia during the Chaco War, were detained in Peru. Fawcett now has an airplane manufacturing plant. In 1943 the government created a State-owned air corporation to develop new lines, construct airplane factories, produce airplanes and materials. Routes have since been pushed in all directions.

A new international Peruvian line (PIA) has begun flights south to Chile and north to Montreal, New York and Washington in competition with Pan American. At present it provides the only no-change, direct plane service from Canada and the cities named to South America.

Besides Panagra, or Pan American-Grace Airways, which covers all South America in conjunction with Pan American Airways, several other United States lines are preparing to go into Peru with international service.

Venezuela is building 38 new airports. Before the Betancourt government took over in 1945 Linea Aeropostal Venezolana (government-private ownership) had only 11 rickety, dangerous planes, with a top daily load of 96 passengers and 32,000 pounds of freight. By early 1947 it had 38 modern flying ships and was handling 700 passengers daily and 180,000 pounds of freight.

Four international routes are now maintained: Caracas (Maiquetía Airport) to New York via Havana; Caracas to Lisbon, Paris and Rome; Caracas to Trinidad; Caracas to Rio and Buenos Aires. Foreign companies Pan American, Taca and Avensa also operate to Venezuela. Two new private corporations have been started inside the country.

The Taca lines have long serviced all Central America with an intricate network. They fly into Havana, Miami, New Orleans, Mexico City, Panama, Colombia, Venezuela and Ecuador and have a subsidiary company in Brazil. They have just extended their service to Peru and are apparently determined to build up a complete continental network.

Mexico, besides many international services, has a dozen internal lines. Regular hourly service is maintained between Mexico City and

the resort center of Acapulco on the south Pacific. Frequent daily
flights are provided to Tampico, the oil center, to Yucatán and to the
west coast. Even minor Indian villages, formerly reached only after
days of horseback travel, are now regular air stops.

United States lines with permanent certificates to fly into Mexico are
Pan American, American, Eastern, Western and Braniff. In 1947 ten
Mexican air lines applied for permission to fly into the United States.

Pan American and Panagra completely web the whole hemisphere
with their services. Their silver wings fly down into every important
city of the Caribbean; from the west, central and eastern United States
into Mexico and Central America. Their planes crisscross Venezuela
and Colombia. In Brazil their subsidiary company, Panair do Brasil,
flies all up and down the Amazon basin and eventually will cover a
complete transcontinental route from Belém on the Atlantic to La Paz
in Ecuador. Already there is a transcontinental route, among others,
from Lima through Bolivia, with stops in the deep frontier jungle between Bolivia and Brazil, which goes on to São Paulo and Rio. A connecting route flies down to Paraguay and of course to Montevideo and
Buenos Aires.

Out of Lima, Peru, as a pivotal port, two routes are flown into Argentina, one via the west coast and Chile, then over the Andes to Buenos
Aires, with optional stops at Mendoza and Córdoba, and the other a
direct diagonal flight through La Paz, Bolivia.

Another flight ending at Buenos Aires leaves Miami, follows through
Cuba, Haiti, the Dominican Republic, Puerto Rico, the Lesser Antilles,
the French islands, the Guianas, the cities of coastal Brazil to Rio,
then to São Paulo, the mighty Iguazú Falls, Asunción in Paraguay
and on to its terminal. An alternative route passes through southern
Brazilian ports, Montevideo in Uruguay, to Buenos Aires.

Today, scarcely an island of the Caribbean is without some form of
air service. There, among other lines, converge Pan American, Taca,
British West Indies Airways and the Royal Dutch boats. The Cuban
"Q" line flies to Haiti, the Dominican Republic and on to Mexico.

Some flights in South America are quite impressive. The lakes, mountains, forests and coasts of Central America are a constant delight to the
eye, and the dip down Balboa Airport on the Canal Zone, over the red
tile roofs and gardens of Panama City, is a spectacular and beautiful
combination of bays, forests and mountains. The seven-hour flight from
Panamá to Peru, although occasionally there are impressive mountains

off the inland wing, is on the drab side—endless miles of open sea, then endless miles of green jungle, then endless miles of dun desert. An exciting interlude is provided by the descent into Guayaquil over the many mouths of the river, threading like silver ribbons through thick jungles.

Probably the most dramatic flying of all is in Chile under the rim of the great chain of snow Andes. For sheer grandeur few flights equal it: the multicolored desert beneath, the foam of sea rocks to the west, the great shoulders of snow pushing up to the east. Particularly impressive is the stretch from Copiapó to La Serena. Very beautiful also is the flight from Concepción south to Puerto Montt, especially in wintertime. Although the mountains there are not quite so high, they rise abruptly from the plain with few intermediary foothills, a majestic sweep of snow.

Rio de Janeiro with its great tropical harbor, flanked by modern skyscrapers, offers a magnificent spectacle from the air. But perhaps no panorama on earth is grander than the descent into La Paz, Bolivia, with its circle of snow mountains rising sheer above the great flat expanse of the sere upland plateau.

IX New Vitamins

Health for Freedom

GUATEMALA's leading writer, Rafael Arévalo, once said that his country's dictators were merely emanations of a nation sick with malaria. An unhealthy people could not hope to exercise democracy.

Back of disease lie poverty and ignorance. These evils are great in the Americas—this brave New World of ours. In spite of the gains made in so many parts of the continent, despite great resources, even so, social injustices, illiteracy, improper exploitation still keep millions in utter squalor. The old yarn about the Mexican being a beggar sitting on top of a silver mine has not been wholly belied by modern progress. There are in fact in these Americas probably more millions of people living in disease-ridden poverty and near-hunger—right on our doorsteps in North America and South America—than in all of Europe in spite of war, food shortages and breakdown.

Where in Europe even today will one encounter quite such hordes of sickly children as in Nicaragua? They are ready to pounce on the tiniest crust thrown from the car window—in a land where food has been ruthlessly monopolized by the dictator's crew and shipped out for the profit of a few officials. In what European city, except possibly in Germany, will one today see so many folk pawing over the garbage dumps and stuffing foul food into their mouths as in Tegucigalpa, the capital of Honduras, the realm of dictator Carías?

The handsome new cities of the Americas still have terrible slums; the contrasts still exist. The poverty shacks in the great new Mexico City have spread almost as fast as the old slums have been wiped out. What are more awful than the endless miles of *favelas* in Rio? Or the horribly lightless, unheated, waterless, toiletless *conventillos* of that incredibly fair city of Santiago de Chile, where half the people are

193

jammed up, giving that community eighty per cent of its t.b. cases and a tuberculosis death rate higher than anywhere else on earth?

The various governments in the last few years have been trying valiantly to make up for the centuries of neglect and exploitation. Chile has done an astonishing amount of public housing, but the cancer had rooted deep, and such conditions still make a mockery of even the most sincere health efforts, the whole battle for sanitation.

Ignorance, plus lack of medical care, runs a close second. Most rural folk of inner America, enjoying no doctors or hospitals, have had to depend on patent medicines, but more often on age-old lore. This includes much knowledge of herbs, roots and leaves, ofttimes knowledge not yet appropriated by science. A recent Peruvian study of survivals of pre-Spanish medicine indicates more than a hundred medicinal plants not yet named even by modern botanists, known only by their early Quechua names. Most rural people have devised locally made sweat baths. In Mexico there is an adobe Turkish bath called the *temascal* and known before the Spaniards. All sick folk are thrust in to die or to get well.

All such lore is usually compounded with gross superstition maintained by local *curanderos*, or curers. Healing, often more "psychological" than medicinal, may be accompanied by incantations, pin sticking, mouth sucking, charms, frog legs, human hair, coca leaves, "deereye" seeds, llama fetuses and what not. Witchcraft and voodoo still rule large areas remote from civilized contacts, just as in certain mountain and southern regions of the United States.

Medicine in Latin America has long been even more backward than the general level of development. Not only was it hard to impart modern hygiene to illiterate men with poor housing and diets, but cultural divisions made the task even harder. It is not always easy to convince poor Negroes, as in the Caribbean and Brazil, to accept scientific medicine rather than ritualistic cures, especially when they are aware a local doctor does not have adequate training. The same has held true with isolated Indian groups—in all, millions of people.

Sharp class division—the very rich versus the very poor, with little middle-class cushion: feudal groups living apart from peons—this has meant little interest in public health. The "aristocrats," able to pay for medical attention for themselves, long fought efforts to improve general health. Even though better workmanship might have resulted from healthier peasants, this would have meant higher taxes. The "aristocrats" closed their eyes to evidence that their own children, in spite of the best medical care, often were caught in epidemics due to surrounding poverty and lack of sanitation.

But everywhere industrialization, growth of cities, improved living standards, a larger middle class have now brought rapid advances. During World War II medicine made faster strides than in the whole previous history of the republics. Sanitation and health have become the constant preoccupation of all but a few backward dictatorial governments.

Part of this improvement has been due to lavish outlays by the United States for hospitals and improving water and sewerage systems in city after city. Malarial controls were introduced over wide areas. Often this work was to protect United States troops or personnel getting out raw rubber, quinine and other jungle products, but the local population received benefits.

We talked to a young Peruvian army captain, stationed for years in an unhealthy northern region. He could not help comparing the lack of decent water, toilets and medical care for his men with what the North American soldier enjoyed on a near-by air base. Returned sick to Lima, he is now furious at government neglect of the Indian conscripts, the army graft, the brass-hat indifference to the welfare of recruits. A few years ago he would have taken such abuses for granted.

In spite of the railing against foreign capital in many quarters, often United States business interests have done a great deal for the health of their workers, of the community, for medicine in general. The United Fruit hospital of Quiriguá, Guatemala, has made real contributions to knowledge of tropical diseases. The fine hospitals maintained by big mining companies, such as those at Chuquicamata and El Teniente in Chile, have helped workers and villagers and have raised standards for all other hospitals.

One fine aspect of the good-neighbor policy and various foundations was the bringing in of medical students to the United States. Many of these men, now practicing in their home countries, took back the best and latest methods. Thus Dr. Hernán Romer, a prominent lecturer and physician of Chile, was enabled by the Rockefeller Foundation to study industrial hygiene and epidemiology at the Harvard Public Health School. He returned to Chile in 1941 with five trunks full of medical literature and worked to extend the existing machinery of social medicine to include more preventive measures. Similarly Dr. Jorge Sarmiento of

Peru, head of the Anti-Tuberculous Mobile Dispensary of Lima, visited the United States and went back to work out better preventive methods.

In Guatemala we visited the big new Franklin D. Roosevelt Hospital being built with up-to-date architectural and professional knowledge from the United States. One American doctor felt that this project was too fancy for Guatemala, that it would have been better to scatter modern clinics widely throughout the country. But Guatemala lacks the medical personnel, and the new hospital will set standards and train doctors desperately needed.

The contrast with the old order was dramatic. We visited also the existing ramshackle general public hospital. It was without laboratories or decent equipment. Even most of the beds had been stolen by the minions of the Ubico dictatorship, and patients with pneumonia, typhoid, malaria and t.b. were sleeping in filth on the floor.

A North American official told us that the profession had co-operated marvelously with the free medical and dental clinics set up in Guatemala City. Local doctors and dentists, far from feeling this was an encroachment, eagerly contributed services for a pittance or gratis. But so-called landed "aristocrats" had bitterly opposed every step as improper coddling of the poor. Such efforts, they had insisted, should not be carried by the taxpayer, but by Catholic charity and private benefactions.

The public health interest in Guatemala is one of the most encouraging developments in that most beautiful of Central American lands. Today Guatemala is the most spick-and-span city on earth; it is getting more spick-and-span in a health sense too.

United States health work was carried on all through Central America. An occasional reminder of military occupation remains. Thus on a main street in San José, Costa Rica, only a few blocks from the red-light district, the authorities still maintain for the public the all-night prophylactic station installed by our army. It still carries the blatant wartime street signs in English.

In Venezuela, where the people until recently were the most downtrodden in the Americas, we found one of the most extensive malarial control projects of the continent.

Better health in the world, particularly in the Americas, has become more essential for the health of the United States itself. With the air travel of today poverty diseases, epidemics and their curse are right next door to each and all of us. The United States now finds itself merely one big house right on the world's main street of misery and disease. Sicknesses are flown in overnight, and the most rigorous frontier controls cannot keep them out. In Brazil, Chagas disease, a form of sleeping sickness often fatal, has been on the increase. This disease is little known in the United States, but the carrier, a parasitic insect called triatomide, is but one of many that now can stow away and travel north.

Mobile Hospitals

Public health is a particular hobby of President Juan Perón in Argentina. After the 1943 revolution strenuous efforts were made, largely at his instigation, to improve it, particularly in rural areas.

In a speech to the Argentine Medical Federation, June 21, 1944, Perón declared the first requisite for national health and hygiene was proper living standards: good working conditions, adequate diet, housing, decent wages. Already, he declared, the government had started constructing hygienic workers' housing. The immediate goal then was ten thousand new low-cost units. Unless the bulk of the population earned enough to get medical care, there was no possibility, he averred, of raising standards except through State aid.

The next great need, he said, was proper distribution of medical care throughout the republic. In seventy per cent of the national territory half the population "dies without medical attention." He promised that this situation would be done away with.

The technical aspects of sanitation and medical care fell directly on the shoulders of the profession, he said; but on its side the State had to see that all citizens received proper attention.

In other public addresses on the health question he has declared that his government intends to spend at least four million pesos on workers' housing; that social security, established by his efforts as head of the Department of Labor and Social Welfare, should be extended to include medical care. He has had experts studying the working of such legislation elsewhere, particularly in Chile. Workers' and peasants' legislation pushed through by him and his group has progressively included better health and working safeguards for employees, more access to medical treatment.

Eighty per cent of the country's doctors have been concentrated in Buenos Aires and Rosario. The doctors, he has declared, must have better inducements to practice in the back country. A redistribution is essential. Most of the sick people are in the country; most of the doctors are in the big cities, some unable to make a proper living.

One of Perón's first administrative acts was to reorganize the public health program and provide it with $250,000,000 for expansion. That would be considered a good deal even in the United States.

Medical students from the provinces have been given scholarships at home and abroad if they would agree to practice in their home communities for at least five years after graduation. To start the exodus of doctors into the hinterland, the government hastened to build new hospitals, not only for the public but so that physicians in such areas would have better economic security and access to modern facilities. A special chain of hospitals has been built for railroad workers. The first completed were these of Rosario and Bahía Blanca. Mobile hospitals have been installed on railroad trains to be rushed to any disaster or epidemic. Perón declares these to be "the first in America," although Chile had installed similar service some years ago.

Chile

The Chilean social-insurance law contains sweeping health provisions. Two per cent of all money from this source is devoted to medical care. Dental and medical clinics have been set up in all provincial capitals and in many departmental capitals. Special funds are set aside for preventive medicine as well as treatment. Low-cost workers' sanitariums and rest homes are maintained at four mountain and beach resorts. Mobile clinics have been installed on trains and trucks. Free regular health examinations are given to workers. By 1946 more than 600,000 persons had been examined, X-rayed, given free medical attention of some sort. Less than ten years ago no such facilities were available.

Health improvement is registered right down the line: deaths from typhoid and intestinal parasites have been cut from 68 per thousand in 1921 to 12 in 1942; typhus, from 49 to 1; smallpox, 49 to 0; measles, 60 to 15; whooping cough, 67 to 12; influenza, 334 to 65. Infant mortality, a few years ago nearly the worst on the continent and still five times that in the United States, has been tremendously reduced.

The great death reapers in Chile today are pneumonia, t.b. and other respiratory diseases. Though Chilean climate, both in the desert and rain regions, makes a higher than conventional rate almost inevitable, today's exaggerated statistics are chiefly due to poverty, bad housing, lack of winter heat, improper diet. That deaths from these causes have declined at all is due not merely to better medical attention but also to the government's nation-wide housing program.

Good-Neighbor Exploit

During the war United States official, also private, good-neighbor health efforts were extensive. It is rather startling to see a vast modern hospital, better than anything to be found in rural Mississippi, Georgia or Alabama, sitting deep in the Peruvian jungles. It has brought medical facilities to the folk of a vast region hitherto utterly neglected. The Rockefeller and other wealthy foundations contributed considerably. Particularly worthy of mention is a voluntary effort carried out by American Quaker boys at Paso de Oveja (Sheep's Pass), a hot-country village on the Mexico City-Vera Cruz highway in a bad malarial region where fifty per cent of the villagers had malaria; eighty per cent, hook worm. The Quakers volunteered to drain the area. A canal from three to seven feet deep and half a mile long needed to be built. Adjacent streams had to be channeled for better runoff of stagnant pools.

In February 1942 the Quakers rented a large house on the plaza, renovated it and supplied it with mosquito netting and cots for the volunteers.

The getting-up signal sounded at 5:45 A.M. Breakfast at 6:00 was followed by fifteen minutes of silent prayer and meditation. Trucks then took the volunteers to the job and brought them back at 2:30 in the afternoon. In their free time they studied, taught the people English, learned Spanish themselves.

The work, supervised by the town mayor, was not easy. Most of it had to be done in syrupy waist-deep water that sometimes got blisteringly hot from the tropic sun. Trees and roots had to be hacked away, and the boys had to be ever alert for tarantulas, poisonous snakes, centipedes, scorpions, even ferocious turtles.

They rounded out their job by building sanitary latrines for all the village homes. When everything possible had been done, they moved to the town of Coatepec (Snake Hill) to install a new water system. A single concrete effort of this sort undoubtedly creates far more good will than ten thousand official banquet speeches.

Health Co-ops

Cuba has solved much of its health program, especially for the middle class and better-off working groups, through voluntary co-operative effort in which the State has played little or no part. Dues for most of the big social clubs on the island provide full medical, dental and hospital care for the member and his family. Also, there are many special medical *quintas* or co-ops.

The customary fee for this full care is two dollars a month per adult, fifty cents for each child. The *quintas* maintain dental and hospital clinics, pharmacies to provide drugs at cost, X-ray equipment, laboratories. The various *quintas* show great rivalry in attracting the services of the leading physicians, dentists and oculists, who are paid a set sum to give part of their time to the *quinta*, and of course are available at any hour for emergencies. No member is required to accept any given physician but may choose among all those rendering services.

Certain *quintas* have such a high reputation that it is an added prestige for a doctor to be selected by them. Also, the doctor frequently has more ready access to X-ray and other equipment and facilities for laboratory experiment than he might otherwise enjoy.

Mexico

Mexico, once the Revolution had partly quieted down, began a big-scale war upon disease. Prior to the Revolution conditions were among the worst in the Americas. Mortality rates, even in essentially healthful spots like Mexico City, rivaled those of Calcutta and other pestholes of the Far East. Among the devastating exposés of the filth and disease that lay behind the fine international façade of the Porfirio Díaz dictatorship, was the brilliant study *Hygiene en Mexico* by Dr. Alberto Pani, who later came to head the Department of Public Health. Another powerful book, *La Camada—The Gang*, by Quevedo y Zubieta, told the story in fictional form of the utter corruption of the medical profession in that earlier period.

Beginning with the Obregón government in 1920, and still more rapidly thereafter, great progress was made in improving general health conditions throughout the country.

In 1931 we visited a big inland area of Oaxaca and Guerrero and bumped smack into a wholesale smallpox epidemic. This has always been a common disease in that part of the country. We found really pitiable conditions. There were villages where from twenty-five to sixty per cent of the population had been swept away, with no access to any medical care except home treatment or singsong witch chanters.

I recall the alacrity with which we jumped off the bed in the house of a peasant woman where we were resting after many hours of horseback travel while she prepared lunch for us. Her boy came into the dim thatched room to get the cooking oil from a shelf near the bed. He was just peeling from the disease and was still water-eyed and shaky on his pins. He had been sleeping in that bed until that very morning!

Even though we were properly vaccinated, we remained apprehensive as we proceeded through stricken village after stricken village.

The campaign against smallpox was just then getting under way and vaccine was being sent in rapidly. But often because of lack of trained personnel it was handled by persons with no idea of how to care for it properly. Thus, lying on the desk of the mayor of Malinaltepec, a town of tropic heat, we saw half a dozen glass vials of the vaccine. This meant that it was already spoiled and would not help those into whom it might be injected.

In some villages the rumor got around, since many people vaccinated came down with the disease, that inoculation was a diabolical plot of extermination by the federal government. In some places the villagers had to be rounded up by the army and forcibly vaccinated. Education would have been the proper civilized approach, but it is pretty hard to educate a person already dead from smallpox.

Since that time the disease has been practically outlawed from Mexican soil.

Other serious diseases also have been attacked. Publicity campaigns against venereal diseases have been staged repeatedly, and these ailments are treated free in public clinics. All known prostitutes are given physical examinations and are subject to arrest if they do not hold a stamped card showing they have taken their weekly checkup.

Much has been done to study, control and eradicate such tropic diseases as pinto and serious eye ailments. Various malarial and typhoid control projects have been undertaken.

Part of each Six-Year Plan has always been devoted to putting in new sanitary water and sewerage systems and other hygienic improvements in smaller communities.

Today public clinics are scattered throughout Mexico's larger centers. Prescribed medicines in case of need can be secured from the government at cost. All plantations and industrial establishments where outside medical care is not readily available must maintain clinics and a doctor. Workers' insurance now takes care of occupational injuries and diseases.

The major basic task of Mexico, of course, is not preventive medicine or curing the sick but the raising of the standard of living. The mass of the population, despite great revolutionary gains, does not have decent housing or proper instruction in personal and family hygiene. I have seen Indians coming down to the annual religious fiesta in Guadalupe, a place where dogs and chickens still run loose, scoop up water from the gutter and drink it!

Dr. Salvador Zubrirán, Undersecretary of Public Welfare, was still able to tell the Public Welfare Congress in Mexico in July 1943:

"The inhabitants of Mexico are a sick people, for endemic malaria is found everywhere along the coast. . . . Intestinal parasites, lack of proper nourishment, diseases caused by polluted drinking water, tuberculosis, leprosy and other diseases . . . continue to be the direct causes of high infant mortality and high disease rate found among the inhabitants of this republic . . . all of which makes Mexicans not only a sick people but a physically weak race and, as a result of these ills, a weak people from an economic point of view."

But whatever the deficiences and the problems, all over Latin America today good health has joined the march toward the future.

X The March of Books

Publishing Emigrates to the New World

ONE OF the symptoms of Europe's decline has been the wholesale transfer of publishing to the New World. This occurred long ago in the case of Brazil which early became a more important center of Portuguese intellectual life than Portugal. In the Spanish-speaking world the process was long delayed. But the Spanish Civil War, World War II and the Franco epilogue saw the publishing activities of the mother country shattered. Madrid, Barcelona and Paris had always been the great book centers for all Latin America. That is not true today.

Before the European holocaust a book published in Mexico had no general circulation in Argentina, and vice versa. There were no adequate distribution channels in existence. Inter-American solidarity was more of a myth than a reality. In ideas and culture the American republics were separated from one another, except for some exchange of more erudite publications among limited groups of intellectuals. For the most part there was no real overleaping of frontiers. The techniques of book publishing and continent-wide distribution were largely monopolized by Spain. Now this monopoly has been broken for all time.

Today the great intellectual capital of Spanish-America, if any place can be said to usurp that title, is Buenos Aires, which probably publishes more books and titles per capita than the United States. Chile is a hardy rival, and there has been a general renaissance over the continent. In all the countries, except a few still ruled by medieval dictators, there has been great expansion.

When we were in Buenos Aires, we stood on the magnificent river docks and watched a big freighter loaded entirely with books take off for Mexico at the extreme opposite end of Latin America, five thousand miles away. Such inter-American interchange means a real revolution in the life of the peoples. It is not only a gauge of new economic independence and growth but of greater intellectual independence, a real emergence from colonialism, and a very tangible inter-Americanism.

The Spanish Civil War not only broke the back of the great Peninsular editorial houses or drove them into exile, but subsequent Fascist dictatorship under Franco has so limited the range and freedom of publication that the mother country can no longer provide the intellectual nourishment demanded by the awakening New World countries, each with its own traditions and background and new needs. Spain has curled back into the womb of its feudal medievalism, in the darkness of a continent in eclipse, and the more virile New World cannot follow it there. Three of the largest Madrid houses have definitely migrated to the New World and are not likely ever to return. The most noteworthy is the great house of Espasa Calpe, today more Argentine than Spanish.

In addition, scarcely an issue of the Argentine magazine corresponding to our *Editor and Publisher* fails to reveal a new publisher's name in Buenos Aires or elsewhere. Today such important Buenos Aires houses as Espasa Calpe, Ateneo, Sudamérica, Sur, Tor, Losada, Claridad and the Socialist Vanguardia Press have dozens of hardy new rivals.

Franco's despotism also drove to the New World the best Spanish editors, writers, printers, bookmakers and technicians. The new western lands have reaped the benefit of their talents. In general the first-class editions of New World books are now better made, more attractive than the best ever turned out in Spain. The fine new art and camera books rolling off the Argentine presses have reproductions that rival the excellent work of Germany and France.

Chile got into the publishing field at the first jump. Owing to currency deflation that country for a long time was able to undersell all other countries and flooded the continent with millions of copies of cheap editions. This trade was largely concentrated in the hands of three major houses, Zig Zag, Ercilla and the smaller Nacimiento. Zig Zag has now forged ahead as one of the major editorial houses of the continent. It owns its own presses, in a fine new building north of the Mapocho River. In addition to books it prints seven magazines, the best in Chile, which circulate over much of the continent.

In Mexico the old-time houses of Botas and Porrua still publish and now, with the wider market, have expanded the number of titles issued. Many new houses have sprung up.

In Havana, Cuba, the number of concerns is astonishing. Recent volumes that have come into my hands have born such imprints as Minerva, P. Fernández, Monfero, Trópico, Montero, etc.

New Freedom

For the most part the growth of New World publishing forges ahead regardless of the nature of the government or the size of the given country. Though here and there dictatorial conditions have put on the brakes, even in some of those countries more books are now being put out. And some of the greatest writing has appeared in the smaller, more backward lands. For some years Ecuadorian novelists led the field.

But often considerable impulse has come from the achievement of larger freedom and more democracy. Thus, in Guatemala the overthrow of Dictator Jorge Ubico, who had stifled all free intellectual life, was followed by the founding of many new newspapers, magazines and cultural journals, the publication of an avalanche of new books. Not the least of these new volumes were a number of exposés of the bloody tortures and assassinations by the dictator, who during the war, through rigid censorship, was held up to the world as a great paragon of democracy and a true ally in the struggle for world freedom. The most powerful of those volumes, a devastating, hair-raising document, the dust jacket of which shows a murdered peasant held in a bloody hand, is *Ombres Contra Hombres*, which perhaps might be translated *The People Versus Men*, by Efraín de los Rios. He was jailed and tortured for visiting the United States Embassy where he went with a suggestion for a publication to promote the pro-United Nations cause and, though he had no connection with politics, for "plotting to start a democratic party." This occurred when the United States was pouring in money, Lend-Lease, machinery, equipment, sewer pipes, water pipes, clinics, hospitals, and thousands of soldiers and bureaucrats were on the scene.

The ending of the Vargas dictatorship in Brazil and partial lifting of censorship briefly stimulated new publications and new writings. Among the books which the dictator's harsh and pro-Nazi censorship, under the guidance of General Dutra since become President, would not permit to be translated were those by this author. In the movie world Steinbeck's *Grapes of Wrath* and scores of other fine films were suppressed.

In Cuba, also, the end of both the Machado and Batista dictatorships led to much renewed literary activity.

On the other hand, despite the harsh thieving Somoza tyranny in Nicaragua, the irrepressible Nicaraguans, secretly or in exile, have kept publishing some papers, magazines and books, and not all the terrorism has been able to stop their circulation within the country. The Ecuadorians, too, find ways to write, whatever kind of government they have—it is usually dictatorial. In Peru the rise of Apra, the people's movement, has stimulated a whole generation of strong writers, not merely propagandists but able novelists and social investigators. In the vicissitudes of Bolivia's tragically fluctuating struggle for freedom an increasingly freer, more original note appears in literature.

In Venezuela where, under Dictator Vicente Gómez, the whole country was merely a graveyard of culture, the literary growth has since been tremendous, especially during the last few years with Betancourt. Under Gómez' first two successors, who stemmed from his regime but who instituted some civil liberties, steady improvement was visible.

One significant work at that time was the volume *Problemas Venezolanos*, by Rómulo Betancourt. Though merely a casual collection of article reprints, it deftly probed the country's pressing problems: finance, transportation, oil, food, foreign monopoly, farm and land questions, diversification, industrialization, the need for a merchant marine. At that time Betancourt was the head of Acción Democrática, a minority faction. At this writing, he is President of the country, and a rethumbing of his book reveals how amazingly the program he there advocated has been carried forward.* Today Caracas, which a few years ago was merely a tomb of books, is now a flourishing editorial center and one of the best book marts on the continent.

War on Illiteracy

Another factor increasing sales and creating new demand has been the expansion of educational facilities during the past few decades, Mexico, of course, having taken the lead, although Chile has kept pace. In Latin America many more millions of people are literate than was the case twenty years ago.

In addition to increasing school facilities, various countries have staged dramatic crusades to stamp out illiteracy more rapidly. In this, too, Mexico has stepped out in front. The first nation-wide campaign was put on by President Obregón's Minister of Education, José Vasconcelos,

---

* Rómulo Gallegos, Venezuela's leading novelist, has since been elected President.

back in 1925, at a time when illiteracy was still close to ninety per cent. By 1946 it had been brought down to forty per cent.

In that year the new Minister, Torres Bodet, staged a similar but more thorough campaign with such slogans as "Each man a teacher" . . . "Everybody must teach at least one person to read" . . . "Help your neighbor to read and write," and so on.

Some methods may seem bizarre to us, but they got results. Every public employee throughout the country had to obtain a certificate that he had taught at least three people to read and write. If he did not do so within a given time, he had to buy a certificate for twenty-five pesos to provide money for someone else to teach them. No one was allowed to do business in any government office without presenting such a certificate.

The Department of Irrigation co-operated by setting up classes in the many regions where it works and as an inducement gave each pupil a quart of corn each time he attended a class. State governors offered prizes to the best voluntary instructors. The State of Oaxaca organized three thousand special classes and offered complete sets of band instruments to villages showing the best records—a great inducement in that music-loving state. One village mayor solved the matter easily by decree: "Every citizen, male or female, between the ages of six and sixty, who does not learn to read and write within six months, will be run out of town."

In Guatemala during his nearly two decades of dictatorship Ubico built scores of fine police and army barracks with bayonet labor, but no schools. Until the present Arévalo administration Guatemala, even in the capital, had scarcely any decent schools except for some private Catholic institutions. Previous Guatemala governments paid little attention to educating the children.

The Arévalo government started a campaign against illiteracy, and it soon became a national crusade. Communities, clubs, Chambers of Commerce, Rotary Clubs sometimes contributed far more money for the campaign than the government itself could afford—an unheard-of thing in that country. Businessmen and others volunteered their services to teach.

Much the same thing has happened in Ecuador, Haiti, Peru, Bolivia and Panama. In Venezuela, as part of a nation-wide campaign, the Betancourt government has formed mobile units to go from remote village to remote village to war on illiteracy. Twenty-four thousand adults were thus taught to read and write the first six months of 1947, and five more such traveling units were set up.

Book Stores

One is amazed today at the rash of new bookstores in all the southern countries.

In Mexico City the major local and foreign publishers maintain a great book center, known as the Crystal Palace, which extends a whole block between the National Art Palace and the central Alameda. It is surmounted by gaudy neon signs—the equivalent of about three long blocks of show windows. Here are books from all the world, though the bulk of the showing is from Mexico, Argentina and Chile.

All the famous bookstores, such as Botas, Porrúa, etc., have been modernized. New bookstores with the smartest up-to-the-minute display gadgets and modernistic chromium have appeared.

The story is similar in most of the Americas. Nearly every block of Buenos Aires' fashionable Fifth Avenue, the Calle Florida, has one or more large attractive bookstores. Two-story Ateneo is as large as or larger than Brentano's in New York.

Even the smallest communities of Chile have their bookstores. A small city like Valdivia, of only fifty thousand, has three large ones. Few communities of that size in the United States could say as much, and in our South many do not have even one bookstore—maybe "a Bible shop" or a corner of some business where a few novels and detective stories are displayed. In this direction it would scarcely be courteous to compare the lamentable situation in a state like Mississippi or in parts of Alabama with even the smallest, most backward, most dictator-ridden Latin American country.

Business interests are displaying much interest in cultural affairs. One of the large banks of Santiago de Chile maintains on its premises the leading art gallery of the country. The venture has increased patronage.

In Mexico the leading banks set up a trust, the "Economic Culture Fund," to be administered by a group of intellectuals, no strings attached, to spread economic, sociological and historical information. Among the first books published were those of leading American and European economists, and first of all the works of Karl Marx! The venture proved a happy and profitable one. A great collection of monograph books was also started, called Tierra Firme, which aimed to cover all Latin America; history, biography, geography, science, art and literature of all New World countries. Authoritative writers from each country were invited to contribute to the series. These books now circulate widely over the continent. They have helped the peoples of Mexico to know all her sister nations better; the same has been done for other countries.

One of the more recent volumes to come into my hands—No. 25 in the series—is *Political Ideas in Argentina*, by José Luis Romero. It is a fine survey of the political growth of Argentina and the thought and utterances of her statesmen. It is certainly too bad that such a lucid summary did not exist for the benefit of our correspondents and even a few of our diplomats who for some years now have so grossly misinterpreted the forces and the significance of events in that country—which after all is by far the easiest of all the Latin American lands to comprehend.

In 1947 the Fund started a new series, "The American Library," which it advertised as "a new editorial adventure" to consist of annotated texts of the best of the great Hispanic American classics "of all authors, of all times, and of all kinds." The first volume was the *Popol-Vuh*; *The Ancient Quiché Histories*: "The most important history of the primitive indigenous civilizations; a universal work for its literary beauty."

The second volume is the life of Columbus by his son Fernando.

"Modern Libraries"

One problem south has been that large numbers of the population, who have now become book-hungry, are unable to afford even the cheaper editions issued by regular commercial publishers. The governments have stepped in to fill the gap: (1) to provide cheap books for this group of citizens; (2) to issue books of great historical and cultural interest which otherwise would go unpublished because of the doubtful commercial return.

This has been done in various ways—by direct government publishing, by contracts with private publishers in which the government agrees beforehand to take a sufficient number of copies to guarantee the initial cost of publishing, or by joint government-private initiative and cooperation.

This, it will be recalled, was done by the United States during wartime, for propaganda, for books for the army and for the Latin American good-will effort. Also bureaus were maintained to translate the works of Latin American authors, thus eliminating a cost that often deterred publishers. Unfortunately much of this effort was vitiated by not too admirable political and propaganda purposes, and by censorship of books or authors not liked. Often shoddy books from Latin America got the green light over authentic literature.

Happily in Latin America the cultural purposes of publication rather than propaganda have been kept in the foreground. This has been achieved by putting well-known writers of nonpolitical character and of impeccable reputation at the head of the enterprises. In general the publishers have welcomed this government activity, for it catered to markets from which there was no profit, stimulated wider reading of books and created a larger book-buying public.

In some countries, as in Argentina and Chile, the private publishers have been able to do equally well themselves with cheap serial editions. Thus Zig Zag in Chile has dozens of different types of "Libraries." One series issued for the equivalent of about three cents is published with cardboard illustrated glossy covers in different colors: Red is for novels; green, plays; blue, poetry; purple, anthologies; brown, biographies and essays; orange, travel books. No. 28 in the travel series happens to be a translation from the French of M. Biard's famous *Journey to Brazil in 1858-59*.

Of these popular books in series one of the best is put out by the Mexican Ministry of Education. It is really a brilliant job. Each volume is about a hundred pages in length and is written by a leading author of the continent or an authority in the field. It sells for about five cents. A year's subscription of fifty books costs two dollars and a half. The series is now in its fourth year. Little Indian newspaper and candy stands sell the books.

Titles include out-of-print Mexican and Latin American classics, histories of various Mexican periods, the history and geography of each Mexican state (also of each Latin American country), biographies, novels, poetry, farm botany, etc. Thus *The Brief History of Chile* (No. 6) is written by well-known Chilean writer Enrique Delano. The history of the United States is No. 28 in the series. *Aztec Religion* (No. 38) is by Mexico's leading archaeologist, Alfonso Caso. *The Life of the Mayas* (No. 25) is by the chief North American authority on Middle American anthropology, Franz Blom.

A more highbrow series is put out by the department, called *El Pensamiento de América*, "Thought of America," library. Volume XXII is on the great Chilean nineteenth-century thinker José Victoriano Lastarría, whose tremendous integrity and originality reshaped the basic ideas and politics of his country.

In Colombia the Department of Education under the editorship of Daniel Samper Ortega, well-known novelist and critic, has published a hundred-volume collection of classics and contemporary writings and is now issuing the very cheap "Colombian Village Library" which is expected to total many hundreds of volumes.

With official assistance the National Publishing Company in Brazil has put out a series of more than two hundred volumes covering every phase of Brazilian life and culture.

The brilliant scholar Mariano Picón Salas, long exiled in Canada, Chile and elsewhere, heads the "Library of Venezuelan Culture."

In Peru Ventura Calderon is in charge of the official Library of Peruvian Culture.

In Quito a well-known novelist, critic and biographer edits the "Library of Ecuadorian Classics."

The Cuban Ministry of Education, under the editorship of Felix Lizaso, novelist and biographer, issues its famous "Notebooks of Culture," which now totals more than forty volumes. Its *José Martí Archives* are up to the tenth volume. The Ministry publishes one of the world's best quarterlies, *La Revista Cubana*.

The Municipal Government of Havana distributes the fine "Cuban and American Historical Collection," edited by Emilio Roig de Leuchsenring, an authority on Martí and Cuban international relations. Nearly every volume has had great documentary and historical significance.

These undertakings in making available the great works of each country, many of which have often been long out of print, help create pride in the past and its traditions, awaken a more general consciousness of cultural and national growth and also provide better ballast against the political demagogy of the moment. Most writers who survive the test of time have been lovers of liberty, and this makes for a free tradition.

Some of the governments south also assist in better distribution of books. Mexico for many years has maintained mobile public libraries, some in big vans, for rural districts. Cheap editions are often given away to all who come and ask for them. Other books are sold or lent. These vans carry big signs.

FREE BOOKS
WORKERS   PEASANTS
THIS IS YOUR LIBRARY
COME CLOSE AND SEE

The libraries travel to remote parts of the country on regular routes. This has been a great· boon to roadside farmers and distant villages where the cost of maintaining a public library would be too great and where few peasants have any means to travel to distant cities to get books even if they were so minded. The arrival of the rolling library has become a great event in the isolated places. People look forward to it as a break in rural monotony, and they crowd around with the excitement with which they used to greet a traveling peddler.

With the long prevailing class rule of Latin America books were considered the privilege of the elite and well-to-do, and little attention was paid to the diffusion of culture. With today's changing scene, one development has been the general increase in the number of public libraries. In all Chile in 1934 there were only sixty-six. One of the first efforts of the popular government which came into office shortly after was to expand library service. By 1942 there were more than six hundred public libraries, or nearly a tenfold increase.

New Opportunities for Writers

This widening interest in books and the shift of publishing to the New World have opened horizons and greatly stimulated home talent. Formerly Spain rarely bothered to translate books published in the United States. With the cutting off of Europe and the collapse of its culture, and with the good-neighbor policy, Latin America suddenly became greatly interested in discovering whether the United States had any culture at all. There came a strong demand for American translation. Today most leading books are promptly translated. Among American writers who have especially caught on are John Steinbeck, John Dos Passos, Ernest Hemingway, Erskine Caldwell, William

Falkner, Richard Wright, Upton Sinclair, Waldo Frank, Sinclair Lewis.

A few years back the literary agent of Margaret Mitchell got in touch with me to find a South American editor to bring out *Gone with the Wind*, which had appeared a few months previous. I had to advise her she was a bit slow. It had already been pirated, translated, published, put on the book stands—and was being reviewed in literary journals all over the continent! Subsequently the offending publisher made restitution.

As readers of Dickens know, at one time he was very bitter about the piracy of British books in the United States. This practice, since there was no adequate copyright protection, was common a few decades ago in Latin America. Today, with the rise of reputable publishers in most of the countries, cases of piracy are rare indeed.

Many North American classics are being republished. A good guess would be that more adult people in Latin America are reading Mark Twain, Edgar Allan Poe and Emerson—the three favorites there—than in the United States.

The shift of publishing to the New World has been a great boon to Latin American writers. The Spanish publishing houses used to turn up their noses at most New World authors. Only a few notables could get published in Madrid. A Latin American writer had to turn politician, become the friend of some minister in the cabinet, flatter him and get an allotment of paper or a subsidy to get his work published—only a few copies, no general distribution. He made no money out of it, and usually had to depend on some petty government job to survive. This automatically had the effect of subordinating thought and literature to the particular regime in power. Literature often was considered merely a stepping stone to a bureaucratic career. A book of poetry was nearly always good for a consular post.

Today the Latin American writer has a much more dignified outlet for his work. Although the various houses tend to publish the writers of their own particular countries, the demand for titles is so great that larger houses bid for writers all over the continent. Thus a Mexican writer, if he fails to get published in Mexico, often may find an outlet in Havana, Santiago or Buenos Aires.

This has had considerable effect on the promotion of liberty throughout the continent. Where publications have been suppressed in one country, the writers have a chance in any one of seventeen other Spanish-speaking lands to get their independent ideas printed.

The new literary inter-Americanism has also had an important influence on language. Words and expressions peculiar to a given country have become common coin all over the continent. Thus when Jorge Icaza of Ecuador wrote his best-selling novel *Huasipungo* (which a few years ago would have been peddled only in his own country in a very limited edition) and had many printings in three or four countries, the strange-sounding word, meaning "Thatched Hut" in Quechua, became the property of all Latin America. Gaucho expressions from Argentina are now current everywhere.

As in the United States, Latin American writers were long dominated by European trends and models, particularly those in France and Spain. From time to time, however, even from the first days of Independence, a few writers rooted their work deeply in New World soil—as for instance Joaquín Fernández Lizardi in his *Periquillo Sarniento—The Mangy Little Parrot*—a great picaresque novel richly textured with the intimacies of Mexican life.

But today, with greater national maturity and self-confidence, nearly all writers seek their own forms of expression and try to mirror the immediate life about them in their own communities. Few areas of the world have richer material to draw on. Geographically, racially, socially, nearly all the countries have an intricate diversified life. Few lands have had more dramatic histories. In fact, for a long time the very richness and multiplicity of the material at hand seemed to paralyze Hispanic writers of fiction.

A few years ago the notable Peruvian critic, Luis Alberto Sánchez, wrote a clever essay; "Latin America: A Novel Without Novelists," in which he contended that life in South America was so bizarre, so like fiction, that writers felt no urge to put it on paper. The secondhand edition seemed tame.

But living, however exciting, always needs interpretation and, increasingly, southern writers have turned to fiction as a means of understanding their own life. Today the Latin American writer generally remains more sensitive to universal ideas and outside literary development and is less encased in rigid self-satisfied patriotism and a one-language culture than are most United States writers. Yet all Latin American writers of any note find the true source of their material in the societies where they live and daily become more aware of the greatness and glamour of their own traditions.

No one can look at the over-all pattern of Latin American literature in our day without going back to *Ariel* by José Enrique Rodó, of Uruguay. It has subtly shaped, perhaps even poisoned, the thinking of an entire continent and a half. It was the first great call of our modern era to the youth of Latin America (Ariel) to create a free, spiritual, authentically American literature as opposed to the Old World patterns and particularly to the materialistic, utilitarian culture of the United States (Calibán).

Of all the countries Brazil most stands out, for that land has already produced one of the powerful literatures of all time—cultural achievement largely ignored by the rest of the world because the country has been so apart from the European main stream. However, some great Brazilian writers were hailed in Paris, so long the clearinghouse of the world's best culture. Brazil's greatest novelist, Machado de Assis, was well known there. Aluizo de Azevedo's great novel, *O Mulato*, was heartily acclaimed by Balzac, Zola and Flaubert. His greatest work, *A Casa de Pensão*, was popular in Europe.

What a powerful book is Alberto Rangel's *Infierno Verde—Green Hell*, compared with the sugar-sweet *Green Mansions* by Hudson, so much read in the English-speaking world, whereas Rangel's authentic work remains unknown! Who contributed more to shaping Brazil's legal and constitutional order than the great thinker and statesman, Ruy Barbosa? Who has interpreted the country better than José de Manuel Bonfim?

In the United States lately we have seen three important Brazilian works brilliantly translated by Samuel Putnam: *Os Sertões—Rebellion in the Backlands*, by Euclides de Cunha, one of the great classics of all time; Gilberto Freyre's powerful novel, *Casa Grande y Senzala—The Masters and the Slaves*; and *Terras do Sem Fim—Violent Land*—by Jorge Amado, a somber, blood-tinted, heavy-scented, steaming novel of ruthless cacao empires being carved out at the beginning of this century.

Even in Spanish-speaking South America Brazilian literature has never been well-known. A landmark was set recently when the Chilean publishers, Ercilla, brought out a history of Brazilian literature by Braulio Sánchez-Saez. Since then Zig Zag and other houses have published translations.

For a brief while after Vargas' fall there was a literary stir in Rio. Putnam, visiting there in 1947, compared it to the atmosphere in the United States along about 1936. In the confusion of the day there was a similar rush by many intellectuals to get on the Communist and proletarian band wagon, to go into politics, to head for various similar disillusioning goals. But, what is important, there was a general effervescence, experimentation, an eager exchange of ideas. Gilberto Freyre, probably the leading interpreter of modern Brazil, has become a leftist Congressman. Among other strong writers are José Amenco de Almeido, whose *A Bragaceira—Trash*—was an epochal turning point for present-day literature, and José do Rego, who wrote *The Sugar Cane Cycle*. A promising young novelist is Allegrio Meira Wanderly. An outstanding leftist is Garciliano Ramos for his *Angustia*. One of the finest contemporary poets is Carlos Drummond de Andrade.

Among North American writers those most influencing the Brazilians and Hemingway, Steinbeck, Caldwell, Falkner, Farrell and Dos Passos. Unfortunately the return of the Dutra regime to narrow police-state control has started to wither the new literary flowering, and once more ring down an iron curtain. This cannot endure too long, for the forces of growth are so powerful in Brazil that Dutra will soon have to backwater or be swept aside in revolution.

As in the United States, both Brazil and Argentina have their "Westerns." In Brazil these have been yarns about the intrepid *bandeirantes* who early invaded the backland. In Argentina there is a voluminous literature about the gauchos or *pampa* cowboys, which has ranged from the dime novel to the fine stories and novels by Sarmiento, Leguizamón, Lugones, Ugarte, Dávalos, Gerchunoff, Rojas Paz, and above all Ricardo Güiraldes, author of *Don Segundo Sombra*.

Domingo Sarmiento, one of the great New World literary pillars, was among the first true home-soil writers of the post-Independence period—authentic as the spurs of a gaucho. He lived an agitated political life, spent many difficult years in exile, then returned to become President and found Argentina's free educational system and its true democracy. In spite of so crowded a life, he found time to edit many papers and magazines and to write some eighty books, among them *Don Facundo*, a great novel of a gaucho dictator and one of the notable classics that stand out monumentally above the early literature of the continent.

There are a number of such Argentine literary pillars. Rex Crawford, for instance, in his excellent book on Latin American thought, picks out that fine and ardent Independence poet, Estebán Echevarría; that great political thinker, Juan Bautista Alberdi, who shaped the constitutional life and political thought of his country; and nine other writers. A more recent thinker, José Ingineros, who wrote vigorously in the fields of psychology, criminology, education and sociology, became one of the outstanding intellectual leaders of all Latin America.

In history, biography, geography, many fields of science, politics, economics, in poetry and fiction, the tree of Argentine literature is putting out foliage. According to critic Sánchez, not until better assimilation of the great immigration influx of 1880-1910 could Argentine culture express its real personality. But now the stamp of definite Argentine character is on nearly all writing. "After the United States," declares the Salvadorean, Juan Felipe Toruño in his *Poetry and Poets of America,* "Argentina has the strongest intellectual development in the Americas." The country is in the full tide of a literary renaissance.

"The great literary offensive of El Plata (Argentina)," declares Sánchez, "above all else is in poetry."

To cite a few new poets by name gives one an idea how rapidly various European nationalities have been absorbed into Hispanic culture, and how much they have contributed to the enrichment of Argentine literature. Present-day poets who stand out are: Blomberg, Buffano, Mellid, Pedrono, Leguizamón, Graffa, Lange, Roxlo, Wilcock, Calandrelli, Addler, Bunge, Sanguinetti, Gladyz Smith, Patrick Dudgeon. Among "the greatest" of the contemporaries is Enrique Branches.

In critical essays, such writers as Alberto Gerchunoff, an elegant stylist; José Gabriel, polemical defender of popular rights; Ricardo Güiraldes, protagonist of vernacular and gaucho speech; Ramón Doll, a bitter nonconformist, fill out but one important corner of the big canvas.

Alejandro Korn, mystic philosopher, though he appeals little to me, has wide influence over the continent. Widely heralded also is Eduardo Mallea, a seeker for the mystic Argentine soul, who writes poetically in an impressionistic mist.

Ever since the tragic Florio Sánchez, who was so poor he had to steal telegraph blanks to write his plays on and who died of t.b., the theater has flourished in Argentina more than in the other countries, although Chile, with its active League of Playwrights, its National Theater School, its Experimental Theater and its many good plays, is a close rival, in some ways doing more original work; and of late there has been a renaissance in Colombia and Ecuador. The most outstanding contemporary Argentine dramatist is Samuel Eichelbaum, author of *Bad*

Thirst, Nutshell, Solitude Is Your Name. There are several propaganda dramatists, such as Leonidas Barletta and Alvaro Yunque. Barletta—also a novelist—some years back founded the exciting People's Theater, a co-operative enterprise of writers, actors and technicians. After each performance the audience discusses the play it has just seen—a *polémico* that has become very popular. In summer the theater loads itself onto wagons and makes the rounds of poor districts and surrounding towns. Gradually the People's Theater has branched out with concerts, art exhibits, book fairs, movie making.

The Municipal Theater is subsidized to the tune of $75,000 a year, but in recent times has fallen into bad repute because it has got into the hands of charlatans and political quacks and has boycotted the best dramatists, playing favorites with third-raters.

In light satirical comedy the Argentines have often done clever work, a sort of cross between the traditional Spanish zarzuela and sophisticated piquant Viennese comedy.

It is impossible here to survey the vast new literature of Latin America on economics, sociology, jurisprudence, international relations, educational theory, psychology and science, beyond citing a few works that have come to my attention during the past year.

In archaeology and anthropology the Mexicans and Argentines have done the outstanding work of the continent, although Peru has the much disputed work of Julio Tello (just deceased) and of Luis Valcárcel who investigated so much of Sacsahuamán. The most startling work, which is still hotly discussed though it dates back, is Florentino Ameghino's *Antiquity of Man in the Plata.* Ameghino was torn limb from limb by the more conservative North American school, but recent investigations are beginning to bear him out more and more.

The land problem continues to excite attention everywhere: Alemán Bolaños' two volumes on Guatemalan agriculture; Alfredo Sanjines' *Agrarian Reform in Bolivia.* Much on this subject is being written in Argentina. One of the best little studies ever made was that by Luis Heysen, an exiled Peruvian leader. A very thoroughgoing analysis was made by Juan L. Tenenbaum in 1946, *Economic Orientation of Argentine Agriculture.*

Tin is always a big theme in Bolivia—in those rare intervals when the Rosca or tin-cartel lawyers are not in control of the country. Two excellent studies are those of W. Jaime Molíns and the brilliant Carlos

Montenegro, the man so falsely maligned by the State Department and forced out of the Villaroel government. Montenegro, in preparation for his work, made a personal firsthand investigation of the tin mines and refineries of the Far East.

Rather amazing, and somewhat futile in view of what the politicians are still doing to the universities and professors in Argentina, is the enormous three-volume superdocumented study by Gabriel del Mazo, *University Reform*, covering the period from 1918 to date.

Even more futile, for the moment, is the excellent volume entitled *The Social Meaning of University Culture*, by Justo Prieto, former Minister of Education in Asunción, for years now in exile in Buenos Aires, for his country is still engulfed in the blackest tyranny under Morinigo (so greatly assisted by the United States), and the slightest hint of culture is given a quick blood bath.

But José D. Crespo of Panama puts out *Fundamentals of New Education* in a land with one of the most enlightened and active Ministers of Education. And the many volumes on pedagogy, child psychology and philosophy by Juan José Arévalo seem to have considerable meaning—he is now President of Guatemala.

Leopoldo Zea, in his *Peak and Decadence (Apogeo y Decadencia) of Positivism in Mexico*, studies the philosophic trend by which the Porfirio Díaz dictatorship tried to justify its existence and policies.

Exceedingly valuable, exceedingly readable in many parts, but in other parts a somewhat hasty hodgepodge of research and information, is the four-volume *History of Mexico's Collective Evolution* by the veteran statesman, newspaper man and polemicist, Felix F. Palivicini, who played a cabinet role in the days of Venustiano Carranza. From a strictly Catholic and conservative angle Mexican history has been rewritten in three volumes by José Bravo Ugarte. In reading these two works one would hardly believe they deal with the same country.

Uruguayan history has been retold from a leftist, "materialist" point of view by Francisco R. Pintos in a short interpretive volume. A brilliant, frank book on United States policies and Pan-Americanism was written in Panama in 1945 by Juan Rivera Reyes, diplomat and Professor of International Law, *Un Mundo Nuevo—A New World*—with provocative proposals on inter-American relations.

Broad surveys of national and international literature are available in an increasing number of anthologies. Ercilla has edited a poetry anthology of each of the twenty nations (not completed yet). One of the finest poetry anthologies, covering all the countries, also the United States and Puerto Rico, is *Poetry and Poets of America* (1944) by Juan Felipe Toruño of Salvador.

Indians and Negroes

One definite literary trend, especially in the Caribbean and highland countries, has been the rediscovery of the life and culture of the Indian and the Negro.

In Mexico, in the days of dictator Porfirio Díaz, the Indian was scorned, his life was abused, his fine handicrafts were despised. An upper-class Mexican of those times would be seen dead before he would admit a serape or a fine piece of native pottery into his home.

In early days the Indians had a great defender in the man who became Bishop of Chiapas, and whose prose to this day lives with breathless passion and ringing conviction. This was Bartolomé de las Casas, famous for his efforts to abolish Indian slavery and protect the original people of the Americas. His arguments are set forth in his great story of the Americas and the Conquest, *General History of the Indies* and in flaming prose in his *Short Account of the Destruction of the Indians*.

He was born in Sevilla in 1474. His father had accompanied Columbus on his first voyage to the New World. On his return, he put his son in the University of Salamanca. After graduating in law, Bartolomé went with the 1502 Oviedo expedition to the New World. Eight years later he became a Dominican monk. In Cuba he could not stomach the misery heaped on the Indians by the *repartimientos* of lands and slaves and he went to Spain to protest.

The great Cardinal Jiménez decorated Las Casas, bestowed on him the title, "Protector of the Indies," and named him member of an investigating commission.

During his lifetime he crossed the ocean fourteen times to protest against abuses and made himself an eternal nuisance to the secular authorities. He was not above some political skulduggery, but, partly as a result of his labors, the famous Laws of the Indies were drawn up, one of the most enlightened colonial and labor codes in the history of man.

As Bishop of Chiapas at the age of seventy, Las Casas denied the sacrament to all landowners who kept Indians in slavery. His stern attitude made his position untenable, and he was obliged to return to Spain, where he continued to agitate in behalf of the New World peoples until his death at the age of ninety-two in the Atocha Monastery in Madrid.

But it took nearly four centuries to vindicate the good Bishop's position in a practical fashion. Following the Madero revolution in Mexico, which lifted the peon from serfdom, false sentiment often glorified the Indian as improperly as previously he had been abused. On one occasion I listened to a prominent Mexican politician, who happens to be of pure Spanish descent, pound his chest at a public meeting and shout, "We Indians must assert our rights!"

The theme of Indian redemption, played up so strongly in the revolutionary painting of the day, was also a constant theme of essayists and novelists after 1910. It threads indirectly through most of the work of the dean of Mexican novelists, Mariano Azuela, whose hard-hitting *Underdogs* became a continental best-seller and helped shape the thought and attitude of the whole region. Actually most of his themes deal with the collapse of the landed aristocracy, the dilemma of the middle class during revolution, the chaotic soul of the restless mestizo sweeping up into control of the Mexican State.

In 1944 Francisco Rojas González won the National Literary Prize for his *La Negra Angustias,* the story of a mulatto girl who led a motley band in the revolution. An uneven novel, it has vivid descriptions of bizarre types and keen dialogue.

In Chile writers, painters, sculptors and musicians have found deep inspiration in Araucano culture and never more so than today.

Chile's great classic poem, taught to every school child, is *La Araucana,* written by a Spanish captain, Alonzo Ercilla y Zuniga, during battle and bivouac right on the scene, in which he glorified the fight of the Mapuches or original people in defending their homes and liberties against the Conquistadores. He exposed the ruthless extermination practiced by the Spanish governor under whom he was serving, and said governor has been pretty much in the doghouse ever since.

One humorous result was that the governor, to clear his name and glorify himself and his battles, hired another poet, Pedro de Oña, to pen another epic in reply. The result was not happy. Although Professor Torres Rioseco of the University of California jumps off the deep end by calling Oña "the greatest epic poet born in the New World," Oña's verse, except for a few flashes, is pedestrian drivel, artificially straining at fake sentimentality and fatuous adulation. He even brought the Greek gods down in person to Chilean soil the better to puff up his patron!

Ever since Ercilla's day the great Indian heroes, such as Lautaro and Caupolicán have provided heroic themes for novels, plays, poems and public statues. Today the more intimate life of the Araucanos has been reflected in many good novels, plays and major symphonies.

Guatemala, the most Indian land of North America, has increasingly delved into this field, with such recent publications as Carlos Samayoa Chinchilla, *Cuatro Suertes (Four Fortunes Told)*, stories and legends and *Madre Milpa (Mother Corn Field)*; Luis García, *Indigenous Legends of Guatemala*; José Rodríguez Cerna, *Land of Sun and Mountain*; J. Fernández Juárez y Aragón, *Cuentos del Lar*; J. Fernádez Juárez Muñoz, *The Guatemalan Indian* (2 volumes).

In Ecuador some years back appeared three fine studies of Indian life and Ecuadorean institutions in general by Alfredo Espinosa Tamayo, Pío Jaramillo Alvarado and the Mexican Moisés Saenz. During the last ten years a bitter realistic school of fiction led by Jorge Icaza, with his continent-wide best-seller, *Huasipungo (Thatched Hut)*, has been turning out powerful vernacular novels and stories—Uncle Tom's Cabin tales of serfdom and revolt. They have ruthlessly probed the stormy character of the mestizo or cholo, the elegance and corruption of the landed aristocracy and the cesspool of militarism and politics. Among the best writers are Humberto Salvador, with a string of novels, and Humberto Mata, with his *Sanaguín* and other works.

In Peru writers of diverse tendencies have been rediscovering Cuzco, the old native capital. In recent years many novels, works on archaeology, anthropology, folklore and the social habits of the Quechua and Aimará peoples, who make up the bulk of the country's population, have multiplied. Luis Valcárcel, José Gálvez, Uriel Garciá, José Carlos Mariátegui (now dead), Enrique López Albújar, Clorinda Matto de Turner, the Mexican Moisés Saenz and, above all, Hildebrando Castro Pozo, who died in 1946, are leading names.

The same trend has developed in Bolivia. The little volume, *Tierras del Kosko*, by Gloria Serrano and Crespo Gastelú, is thrilling for its charming thumbnail sketches and lyrical prose, its intimate portrayal of the life and spirit and traditions of the highlanders. Interesting too, though oversentimentalized, is *Traditions and Legends of Bolivian Folklore* by Mercedes Amaya de Urquidi. One interesting novel about the Aimarás, by Victor M. Ibáñez, *Chachapama—The Lion Men*—was put out years ago. In 1946 José Felipe Costas published his *El Sol Se Iba—The Sun Was Going Down*—with the naïve title-page notation:

"This is the first Quechua novel in Bolivian literature." In Argentina, Fausto Burgos has made his name writing romantic Incan novels.

The theme of the Negro has attracted many writers in Brazil, Colombia and Venezuela—such men as Guillermo Meneses and, outstanding of all Hispanic American novelists, Rómulo Gallegos, in his *Pobre Negro!* and other works. A colorful exotic story, *Risaralda,* is by the Colombian, Bernardo Arias Trujillo. All Haitian literature and books on Haiti, of course, have to do with the Negro, for that is a Negro republic. Quite fascinating, a mine of information, is the *Negro of the Rio Plata,* by Ildefonso Pereda Valdés of Uruguay.

Numbers of Cuban novelists and students have concerned themselves with Negroes and mulattoes. Among important works of the continent must be mentioned the old-time classic, José Antonio Saco's four-volume history of slavery in the New World. Vivid is *Oh, mío Yemahá!* by Rómulo Lachatañeré, Negro stories and songs. The chanting poetry of Nicolás Guillén, a mulatto Vachel Lindsay, rings with the full beat and rhythm and mysterious chant words of the Negro soul.

The numerous Ñáñigo (Cuban Negro) studies by Fernando Ortiz, dean of Cuban scholars, delve into customs, folklore, sociology, psychology and African cultural vestiges. Ortiz is one of the giants of Latin American letters, not only for his scholarly Negro studies but for his examination of economic matters, the problems of tobacco and sugar, and polemics in behalf of political freedom which caused his exile during the Machado dictatorship. He stands out also for the numerous cultural magazines he has started, for the various international cultural institutes he has founded, for his unflagging aid and encouragement to new writers and students. Scarcely any phase of modern Cuban intellectual life, among the most alert and original in the lands to the south, is not indebted in some fashion to Ortiz. He is one of the truly significant New World figures of our day. Without implying the slightest criticism of the fine poetic talents (and the even greater humanitarian talents) of Gabriela Mistral, the Chilean Nobel Prize winner, Ortiz, it seems to me, had prior and greater claim.

Indicative of the present eager Latin American survey of the past, in the light of its new growth, is the Cuban literary preoccupation with the life and writings of their independence hero, José Martí.

Martí was a thinker and a great battler for Cuban freedom. His work and his ideas shine through the years with the same moral intensity as those of Mazzini, the European figure with whom he can most aptly be compared. The figure most closely approaching him in the struggle of the thirteen colonies is Thomas Paine.

Martí spent so many years exiled in so many countries that the task of reconstructing his life and recovering his writings from the many periodicals on which he collaborated—in Spain, Cuba, the United States, Mexico, Venezuela and so on—has required the co-operation of scholars far and wide. As an example of the place Martí fills in present-day Cuba, glance at the *Archivo Martí,* which in its fifth volume carries twenty-three solid pages of bibliography of books and articles written about him merely in the one year 1941. Leading biographers, aside from writers of numerous special brochures, have been Jorge Mañach, Felix Lizaso (two volumes), Dulce María Loyna, Roig de Leuchsenring. Even the President of Cuba, Grau San Martín, has written a small volume called *Martí and Democracy.*

In a similar way in Puerto Rico and Cuba have been pouring forth articles and books concerning another important writer, Eugenio María de Hostos, who fought so early, so many years, not only for the independence of Puerto Rico, but for the Dominican Republic and Cuba.

The government in Chile recently set up a national prize contest for the best biography of Bernardo O'Higgins, the George Washington of that country. This called forth works from the best-known writers. The prize was awarded to an exceedingly able study by Jaime Eyzaguirre.

A strong book is that by Rafael Arévalo Martínez, the most outstanding Guatemalan writer, *Ecce Pericles!,* the dramatic story of the long abusive dictatorship of Estrada Cabrera. His regime ended after he stole international funds sent to Guatemala when the capital was wiped out by earthquake. The enraged people rose unarmed and tore him from his throne.

All countries are busy writing new biographies of the great personalities of the past. A whole library of them, now numbering over thirty volumes, has appeared in Mexico. There is the great Espasa Calpe library of biographies of nineteenth-century Spanish and Hispanic American figures to which the leading writers of the continent have contributed. Among recent Argentine biographies worthy of mention are: Samuel Abud, *Rivadavia;* Manuel Gálvez, *Rosas* and *Yirigoyen;* and, of earlier date, Leopoldes Lugones, *Sarmiento.*

A leftist Costa Rican, Emmanuel Thompson, writes a *Defense of Carrillo,* an early dictator. Several new biographies of Filibuster Walker have appeared in Nicaragua.

Biographies of contemporaries are apt to be worthless eulogies and often amusing, like that by Lucas Paredes on Dictator Tiburcio Carías Andino, President of Honduras. The author actually compares the dictator to Jesus Christ, George Washington, Abraham Lincoln, Napoleon, Julius Caesar, Bismarck, Mussolini and Hitler. The dictator certainly got his money's worth out of that one! But another side of the coin is two terrific exposés of the life and times of Dictator Somoza of Nicaragua, by the ruthless pen of G. Alemán Bolaños. A very useful and excellent biography of the Peruvian popular leader, Haya de la Torre, has just been published by Felipe Cossio del Pomar, well-known Peruvian artist and author of a number of volumes on the history of painting in Peru and Chile.

The picture of present-day Latin American literature is indeed varied. There is a rich development of the historical novel, especially in Chile where it has been a preferred form ever since the great absorbing works of Alberto Blest Gana. Quite a tour de force, which I still have to read, is the recent enormous two-volume novel running to 1,300 pages, *Bajo el Chubasco—Under the Tropical Shower*—by Carlos Izaguirre, which covers half a century of Honduras' tragic history. Maybe Izaguirre could get so much paper because he has helped the dictatorship abolish elections and gag writers, but people tell me even so that it is a good novel. Quite lively is the Bolivian novel by Abel Alarcón, *Era una vez—Once upon a Time*—which is a tale of the great silver center of Potosí in the heyday of its colonial glory.

Fictionalized historical biography has become more common. Worth noting, though not recent, are the hasty but readable books by Peru's great literary critic, now rector of San Marcos University, Luis Alberto Sánchez, on *Garcilazo de la Vega;* the romantic *Perricholi* (who provided the heroine of the *Bridge of San Luis Rey*); and *Flora Tristán, Una Mujer Sola Contra el Mundo—One Woman Alone against the World*— that amazing girl who visited Peru and became a persecuted leader of the French labor movement.

Magda Petit of Chile has written *La Quintrala,* the story of the notorious wealthy female poisoner of the colonial period, who did a lot better than Bluebeard, and *Don Diego Portales,* the story of the early behind-the-scenes dictator, who cynically started the first war with Peru and Bolivia to cover up his personal peculations and who was so dramatically assassinated. When we were in Valdivia, the genial and charming novelist Fernando Santiván, who has a river farm there, told us he was just finishing a fictionalized biography of Bernardo O'Higgins.

The use of this type of novel for contemporary polemics is becoming more frequent. A powerful example, though in spots overemotional and rhetorical, is *A Sangre y Fuego—By Blood and Fire*—by Alfred Cantón, a Nicaraguan who relates the story of the patriotic leader, Augusto César Sandino, and his final assassination by the National Guard under Anastasio Somoza. Incidentally I was able to buy—bootleg—this book from under the counter in the dictator's own kingdom. A very bitter cynical novel of Nicaraguan abuses, dictatorship and moral degeneracy, by Manolo Cuadra, called *Almidón*, has somehow slipped past the censor.

As in other countries, for a time Latin America had its rash of dogmatic "proletarian" novels, and a bushel-basketful of novels attacking "Yankee Imperialism." While some are not entirely without merit, of more enduring literary value have been the regional novelists and impressionists, depicting the life of their localities in faithful and moving terms.

In Mexico, the life of Michoacán is charmingly reflected in the leisurely, nothing-much-happens novels of J. Rubén Romero. In Chile, Victor Domingo Silva brings us the harsh dreary tones of the nitrate coast, and Mariano la Torre, in overweighted descriptive style, the rich exuberance of the Maule River country.

In Brazil, Machado de Assis (Amazon), Oswaldo Cruz (Amazon), Alcides Maya (Rio Grande do Sul), Camara Cascudo (Rio Grande do Norte), Josquín Nabuco (Pernambuco), Carlos Díaz Fernández (Parahyba do Norte) and a host of other capable writers, past and present, have provided intimate pictures of provincial life in their particular stamping grounds.

In Bolivia, Augusto Guzmán has written numbers of works on the highlands, the Indians there, the regional beauties and sorrows. His latest is *La Sima Fecunda—Fertile Hollow*. Humberto Guzmán Arce has written colorful sketches of the jungle country entitled *Selva—Forest*.

Careful scientific or impressionistic regional studies have been appearing increasingly. In Mexico, Efraín González Luna has brought out *Michoacán Silhouettes*, and Jesús Romero two volumes of *Legends and Stories of Michoacán*. Rich as tapestry, warm and affectionate, is the account of *Tezulutlán*, in interior Vera Paz in Guatemala, by Manuel Chavarría Flores. Delightful also is the regional picture given by

Francisco Manzi, *El Viejo Taragüy* in Argentina. There is a flood of books on Patagonia, but most outstanding are the three fascinating and voluminous illustrated tomes by Aquiles D. Ygabone, published in 1945 and 1946. He has made writing about that region his principal lifework.

Among writers of rural plantation life, its fine agreeable quality and its peasant miseries, are: Moscoso Puello of the Dominican Republic, whose *Cañas y Bueyes—Sugar Cane and Oxen—*tells the story of life on the steaming plantations of the Caribbean; José Ramón Orozco of Nicaragua, whose *Cosampa,* with its weird plot, is as rich and glistening as the banana leaves and scarlet hibiscus of the coastland plantations; Humberto Salvador of Ecuador, whose various novels mirror the life on the cold harsh uplands and down on the boiling coast plantations; Rosendo Santa Cruz of Guatemala, whose *Cuando Cae la Noche—When Night Falls—*tells of the proud plantation family of the coffee region where the red berries ripen under the great guayacán trees; Fernando Santiván of Chile, many of whose fine novels describe the rural life in the Vales of Paradise under the snow peaks. In this genre, the chief, of course, is by Rómulo Gallegos, now President of Venezuela, and another logical Nobel candidate. His *Doña Barbara* tells the story of a powerful and beautiful woman who ruled lands, cattle and men with cruel, unerring (or almost unerring) instinct. This tale has become one of the imperishable classics of the whole continent.

Today Latin America has perhaps the greatest creative literary movement existing anywhere in the world.

XI New Pictures

Mexican Blood and Tears

THE major product of the Mexican Revolution, besides social reform, was the renaissance of painting. In the general decay of cultural values in the West after depression and two wars, the art movement of Mexico stands out now with even more vital meaning. Not only did it reflect a basically artistic people matching in fresh forms the hurricane of civil war and new economic and political freedoms, but it also re-established art in their lives as a basic need of a free people. It was an affirmation that the Mexican clamor was not merely for land and bread and effective suffrage, an end of arbitrary dictatorship and militarism, but also for schools; and for the food of beauty.

Unlike the Soviet upheaval, in Mexico the State did not attempt to cramp the artistic growth of its people into a narrow dogmatic formula or to use art crudely as a mere instrument of propaganda to coerce minds and souls. The Mexican government gave union house-painter wages and walls in public buildings to members of the Syndicate of Painters and said, "Go ahead!" Propaganda there was aplenty, of a direct anecdotal sort, especially in the Diego Rivera frescoes. But even this leading exponent of the theories of the new day lampooned the political shyster in the very government that hired him. He lashed out at many powerful upstarts of the Revolution itself, the scum that invariably clings to any new popular movement and rises to the top. He caricatured not only past feudal and ecclesiastical corruption, but took big bites in the legs of parvenu generals, opportunists, half-baked reformers and literary sycophants.

His art had guts, and in spite of aesthetic limitations and its almost flat brutality, it stands out as one of the significant products of our stupidly destructive era. In his great frescoes at the Chapingo Agricultural School, a fine free sensuousness combines with his driving ideas. Mood, inspiration and energy here met in happy combination reflecting the best in all of Rivera's painting.

228

His latest work in the new de luxe Plaza Hotel in Mexico, painted in 1947, if partly repetitious and in a more mellow reminiscent vein, shows renewal of the old fire and talent.

The finest résumé of Diego's life and work and the spirit of the time is *Portrait of Mexico*, by Bertrand Wolfe, who knows Mexico inside and out.

Diego studied many years in Europe, had a Russian mistress and girl child there, made extensive research into early Renaissance fresco techniques. He prepared his own colors and developed his own method of applying pigment right on wet plaster, an arduous procedure that often kept him working on the scaffold forty-eight hours at a stretch.

But he was never a hasty improviser. For merely one panel of one fresco he showed me a pile of diagrams, involved mathematical calculations, geometric tracings and preliminary sketches, nearly six feet high.

In one fresco Diego put a Spanish army marching with steel-headed lances. After this was finished, I came upon him late one night laboriously chiseling out each small spearhead. Unsatisfied with the precise shade of color, he would have to have each spot replastered and repaint it.

Diego married the beautiful and temperamental Lupe Marín, had children by her. For a time he went off to Moscow where he painted the Red Army clubrooms and other places. He returned to Mexico and married Freda Khalo, a remarkable painter in her own right. They built a modernistic double apartment house in front of San Angel Inn.

Once when Ambassador Morrow was at his Cuernavaca residence a local priest pried two thousand pesos out of him to paint his church. But as there was a feud on between Church and Government, the Ambassador feared his donation might be misinterpreted, so he hired Diego Rivera to put frescoes on the walls of the Palace of Cortés portico that looks toward the snow volcanoes.

Some of Diego's most magnificent historical frescoes resulted. Since his sympathies were wholly with the Indians and anti-Spanish, he depicted conquerors and priests as cruel and corrupt.

Morrow then became alarmed lest he had merely contributed more fire to the religious feud he hoped to patch up.

Looking up at Diego, painting aloft on his scaffolding, the Ambassador asked, "Don Diego, haven't you ever seen a nice priest?"

Diego, not even looking around, grunted a negative, kept on painting. Morrow persisted. "Haven't you ever known of one?"

Another grunt.

Morrow tried again. "Haven't you ever heard of one?"

Another grunt.

But a few days later Diego's huge frame came panting up the hill to Morrow's house.

"I just read about a nice priest!" he said.

And so it was that on one end panel Diego altered his original plan and put in the portrait of Motolinía giving aid to the Indians.

Diego's nearest rival is Clemente Orozco, and some people like his work better. He is a more impassioned but more uneven artist. In a few spots he reaches a sublime torture never achieved by Diego, but at other times hits a low of bathos and mediocrity never plumbed by Diego. Too often he is apt to present the agonies of his own soul-searching rather than produce those emotions in the beholder. Too great strain is nearly always present.

Personally he is an odd combination of kindliness, loneliness and harsh, angry bitterness. His shortsighted eyes glare from behind his thick-lensed glasses, but they soften readily. He is a one-armed man who has had to overcome many obstacles. He long had a great hatred for the United States, which in later years has largely eased away.

When he was a young half-starved artist, he started for New York to try to establish his reputation. With him he took what must have been some of his most brilliant work, of which only a few examples survive. These black-and-whites he entitled the "House of Tears Series." They were vigorous sketches of prostitutes and habitués of gin mills. At the Texas customs, an ignorant official pounced on them as being indecent, hence a violation of law. They were torn across, stamped on.

Clemente has done much fresco painting, but he finds it hard to subordinate his vast emotions and talents to the demands of architectural harmony. Diego has always been past master in this field, and if he may have jumped out of bounds in not fully adapting his frescoes in Rockefeller Center in New York to the aims of that edifice, his crime there was not so bad as that of the destruction of his great work by his patrons.

The difference between the two major Mexican artists is well seen in two large murals which confront each other in the Mexico City Palace of Fine Arts. The Orozco painting there, per se, is far superior, and Rivera suffers badly by the comparison, for this is one of his least talented efforts, on the dry mechanical side.

And yet, of the two, strictly as mural painting, Diego's is better. It more successfully matches the spirit of the building and is designed to make sense and to present a perfect composition from whatever angle it may be viewed. Clemente's more powerful, livid painting, a scarlet torture of the flesh, is quite out of tune with the building and, for all its flaming superdramatic quality, cannot be viewed and appreciated satisfactorily from any position the beholder may place himself in.

There are other striking artists who did their best work in that climactic period: David Alfaro Siquieros, who paints exaggerated oversize figures, though his work always reminds one of miniature painting; Roberto Montenegro, a formalistic, superdecorative artist; Xavier Guerrero, earthy and Indian; Rufino Tamayo, somber and original, a note of haunting emptiness; and above all, the strong work of Manuel Rodríguez Lozano.

For a time more powerful central painters seemed to blot out lesser artists, to numb their talents. There was a rash of "little Diegos" and "little Clementes," imitating the two masters. That era, apparently, is now gone, and the newer painters are seeking their own light.

One exception is Xavier Guerrero, who, after years of Communist propaganda over the continent, has taken up the brush again, more or less in the Rivera style, with a heavy though strong hand. Often he uses coarse maguey-fiber canvas or wrapping paper to get a more primitive feeling. In general, just as Clemente tends to put magnificent canvases into murals, so Guerrero tends to drag murals down into canvases—a certain monumental stolidity. But once in a blue moon he gets away from imitation and mannerism and the Diego touch, and produces something startlingly subtle and delicate. In his landscape painting, especially in scenes of his native Chiapas in southwest Mexico, he achieves a more mystic and poetic quality.

If the original pictorial outburst, almost as explosive as the Revolution itself, seems pretty well spent, the fresco tradition in public buildings remains strong. Art schools have multiplied throughout the country. Painting is stressed in all public schools, and children's exhibits are constantly held; the best work is taken on tours. Every year exhibits of paintings by penitentiary inmates are displayed.

Everybody in Mexico today seems to be painting as never before.

Among newcoming painters who show promise one of the most startling is Juan Soriano. He has a fantastic imagination, swift drama, breath-taking suspense, a mysterious and haunting composition, bold, lurid colors far different from the somber tones of most Mexican painting. He uses symbolism with the deftness of a rapier, and his original synthesis of anecdotal painting and surrealism is lyrical and romantic.

Raul Anguiano is more conventional but the best technician Mexico has produced in modern times. His work is severe, always strong, has an almost molded-clay quality to it. He is an amazing painter, getting into the very heart and soul of his subject with a great economy of details, yet his work always seems rich and opulent.

Ricardo Martínez is a powerful painter with a sense of great empty space in his landscape backgrounds, always touched with a small lonely figure or two. His painting "In Memory of My Father," a man standing naked beside an open doorway before a long reach of barren soil and sky, gives a sensation of great affection, great sorrow and great resolution. His "Tobias and the Angel" shows two distant small slim figures on a barren plateau under an undecorated sky, with a great convoluted maguey plant usurping the foreground, like some torture symbol of a divine message.

Other works of importance are the strange hobgoblin pictures of José Chávez Morado; the horror and brutality of Guillermo Meza's work; the fine rich engravings of Alfredo Zalce, which capture so much detail and affectionate reality; the heavy, labored grossness, combined with delicacy, of Olga Costa.

Peru

The Mexican movement not merely influenced the depression-period art of the United States but created fresh interest in fresco painting the world over. It had especial influence on the other Latin countries.

If some of them, still denied freedom, did not show the same creative upsurge as Mexico, gradually a general art movement has taken hold of the whole continent. Today, for instance, nearly all the governments have set up national annual prizes and help hold competitive art exhibits.

Even little Salvador, the smallest of all, though its government is no great shakes so far as democracy goes, in 1946 was staging an art competition with a big national prize offered. We talked with a number of artists who had been doing almost everything except paint but who were now getting busy with their palettes again.

Mostly, though, in Central America poverty has been great, opportunities have been limited, a comprehending public has been all too scant, and dictatorial rule the customary diet. Most creative artists, like Carlos Mérida of Guatemala, one of the very best, and Roberto de la Selva of Nicaragua, with his mahogany-wood panels, have found their opportunities and inspiration in the shadow of the Mexican school. In general Central American art is more decorative and bolder in color than Mexican.

A strong early movement was in Peru, which leans on one of the greatest colonial art traditions of the Americas, and whose people are universally dedicated to art and handicrafts. Early Cuzco produced magnificent painters and sculptors, and at the beginning of the nineteenth century Pancho Fierro (1803-1879) made water colors of the street scenes of Lima in a bold, free Goya style.

Of contemporaries, the work of José Sabogal, Julia Codesido, Camilo Blás and others has turned away from banal French imitations to probe the life and meaning of Peruvian culture.

All of Sabogal's work is strongly influenced by the stark, magnificent scenery of his native Cajamarca, where he was born in 1888, near the site of Inca Atahualpa's palace and baths.

His choice of Indian themes, stories of the peasants, village schoolteachers, colorful markets and gorgeous costume fiestas at first aroused great hostility, for Peru—despite the strong popular movement growing up—was still wholly ruled by the most reactionary feudal group on the continent, the Civilistas! That small upper class, despising nearly everything Peruvian, considered the native peoples merely dirt, to be flogged and driven to their tasks, and it was too much of a shock to find the country's most capable artist discovering beauty in such people and their ways.

But in spite of hostility Sabogal came to be recognized as the most important painter of the day. For ten years he headed the National School of Fine Arts. He has greatly influenced the whole course of Peruvian art; he has influenced also the attitude of the whole nation toward its humbler citizens and has opened up to the gaze of all the beauty of the highland culture. He has been a real force in the making of Peru's new democracy.

Camilo Blás has perhaps a more delicate touch, a finer sensitivity toward details of landscape, a greater sense of mood and of the loneliness in the isolated life of the harsh uplands.

Carlos Quispez Asín has painted indigenous frescoes of some merit.

Young Jorge Vinatea Reinoso, dead now, found splendor in the lives of the Titicaca boatmen, with their nets, their reed vessels and tinted sails, in the haunting golden light of the highland lake region.

Brazil

Brazil, which has a great and long art tradition, is far more bound to conventional academic European traditions than any other country. There was but little indigenous folk art, as in most Spanish-speaking lands, to draw on, though of late much of the fine sense of form and color and rhythm of the Negroes have been seeping into Brazilian work to give it more vitality. Owing to long imitation of Paris art—for France has been the preponderant cultural influence in Brazil—most art has remained imitative, apart from the rich sources of the homeland.

But painting is an important aspect of community life even in smaller places. In Negro communities one comes on vivid painted walls and bars, house doors and even carts, much as in Haiti. On the sophisticated level, annual salons are held in Rio, São Paulo, Porto Alegre, Baía and so on.

The only modern original trend, however, though the circle is now widening, springs from the São Paulo group. But most of these artists, even when they have tried to devote themselves more to the Brazilian scene, have usually done so in the style of Matisse or Renoir or Degas; they have insisted on portraying a Negro diamond digger with Cubism.

But Emiliano di Cavalcanti turned in an exuberant flamboyant fashion to painting Negro life. Paul Rossi Ossire paints still lifes, landscapes and São Paulo peasants in a stiff metallic style. Rebolo González achieves a sort of paradox by painting coarse, ugly Negroes in settings of delicate decorative patterns. Lasar Segall sentimentalizes Negroes in a soft haunting manner.

The one real trail breaker has been Candido Portinari. He long painted conventional subjects in conventional style, conformed to the banal standards of the Rio moneyed classes and won his first renown as a well-paid portrait painter.

But he could not keep away from the rich life and color, the energy and exuberance, of the people of his home province. He was born in 1903 in the interior village of Bradoquivi, and thereabouts he later found the coffee serfs, cotton pickers, workers in factory and forge—all the vital subjects that inspired his real success.

This more authentic work met with much opposition from the elite, horrified by his subject matter, even more by his forceful presentation of it.

"Why can't Portinari paint like that?" a Brazilian asked me, waving his hand at a luscious poster girl mincing her high heels down the Rua Ouvidor in Rio.

"What does he see that is beautiful in those Negroes and poor folk?" asked another of me at a gallery. "They are ugly. Look at that nose! Look at those broken feet! Why perpetuate misery in paint?"

But what grand rhythm, balance and power!

When in 1935 Portinari won a prize at the International Exhibition in Pittsburgh for a painting of a typical Brazilian worker, done with vivid color and his customary slight off-focus emotional distortion that helps drive home the impression, people in Brazil began looking at his work with new eyes.

He was invited to paint frescoes in the Ministry of Education's striking new modernistic building in Rio. There he set forth in epic style the story of the various regional activities and the races of Brazil. Later he was invited to make a series of murals representing Spanish and Portuguese America for the Hispanic Foundation of the Washington Library of Congress.

Caribbean

Cuba is producing strong, fresh painting, such haunting work as that by Cundo Bermúdez, although the artists there have received little public recognition and less official support. About the only regular showings are made at the clubrooms of the Women's Liceo of Havana. Now the government has pledged financial aid to organizing a new museum in Havana to replace the present moldy junk shop on Ajuar Street.

Bermúdez is perhaps the most thoroughly Cuban in spirit of all— full of dreamy suspense, high color, zestful, free brushwork, "with the unleashed splendour of an individual Cuban artist's vision." There is boldness in most of Cuba's new painting: in the lyrical work of Mariano Rodríguez; the vehement color and decorative exuberance of Amelia Pelaez; the fantastic fancy and symbolism of Luis Martínez that seems to search into some deep voodoo mystery; the more classic-determined but original work of Mario Carreño. Fresh strong work is also being done in sculpturing by Alfredo Lozano and others.

Haiti has a long, beautiful handicraft-art tradition but little on the sophisticated level. A few names stand out from the past, good vivid painters with a certain naïve primitive touch, though mostly imitative of foreign models, as Colbert Lochard and Edouard Goldman. With Petión Savain and Verguraud Pierre-Noël, two brilliant painters, the first real effort, though not in very original terms, was made to interpret Haitian life.

But until lately art in Haiti has had little encouragement. Then, during the World War came a surge of vitality. A good part of the credit for this growth and opportunity was due to an American teacher of English, De Witt Peters, who stumbled upon startlingly fine paintings stuck around in odd corners. With his own funds he started the Centre d'Art on the Rue de Revolution in Port-au-Prince. Later he was assisted with United States government funds, one of the most helpful and least meddling of the official cultural efforts of the period.

Haitians had always been painting pictures: on house doors and walls, on fences and outhouses, in little bars and restaurants. Among those pulled from such obscurity was Hector Hyppolite, so poor and starving he could afford only house paint and often had to beg that by the cup. The only paintbrushes he had were split chicken feathers, or else he painted with his fingers.

A saloonkeeper offered him two dollars and all the paint he wanted to decorate his establishment. Hyppolite filled the walls with flaming poinsettias, a kicking donkey, peasants, girls and flowers. Now he is recognized as one of Haiti's strongest and most beautiful painters. His work has been publicly acclaimed, and his earlier efforts have become collector's items.

Other painters, similar to Hyppolite in their untutored ability, their poverty and obscurity, found a place in the Centre. Most were quite illiterate and without professional training. Capable critics have gone on record as believing that some of these primitive but powerful works are the best thing being done in painting anywhere in the world today. Certainly a good painting has more to commend it than an atom bomb.

Wenzell Brown in his fine book on the Caribbean, *Angry Men, Laughing Men*, gives a vivid account of the whole Haitian movement. He tells of Philome Obín, one of the best new painters, who had been wielding a brush in a lonely shack for forty years without ever getting more than a dollar for a canvas. The primitive power of his famous painting of a prison stockade has been hailed far and wide. Antonio Joseph, who miraculously survived the horrible massacre a few years ago when 7,000 Haitians were slaughtered along the border by Dictator Trujillo, earns his living as a tailor's apprentice. In the paintings of Louveture Poissón, an aviation mechanic, every picture has "an open door through which can be seen the brilliant colors of the Haitian landscapes." Jean-Baptista Bottex' canvases are crowded with sinewy black Haitian bodies in faded dungarees and calico, with pink-walled huts and thatched roofs, red coffeeberries and the sharp needle mountains of Haiti.

These painters are really discovering the glory and beauty that is Haiti, its abnegation and secret power, its hopes and its challenge.

Chile

Since the movement toward economic and political emancipation in Chile that got under way from 1925 on, a great impetus has been given to painting. Chile, long a military colony and still the most militarized land in the New World, has had the scantest art tradition of any South American country, although the Araucanos had produced great handicraft art before the coming of the Spaniards and still turn out beautiful textiles, jewelry and carved leather.

In Concepción we stood in the big new railroad station and looked at the powerful, soaring frescoes of Gregorio de la Fuente. Though obviously influenced by the Mexican school, they have more open composition, are less crowded with detail. In bold lines and color, they told the story of Chile and of Concepción—simple, dramatic. One remarkable panel, considerably out of key with the rest but perhaps the most impressive, is a symbolical portrayal of the terrible earthquake that wiped out the city in 1938. On few occasions has the mood of the mystery, majesty and terror of Nature been more powerfully struck.

Probably at the moment in Latin America no other country has such an active art revival as Chile. The nation seems to wish to make up at one stride for its many centuries of comparative barrenness in art, for even in relatively late years it often ignored the fine art that it did have.

Although the National Art Academy was founded as early as 1849, painting never had great vogue and was pretty imitative. The best work was done by temporary foreign residents. Some really strong and charming work was done between 1834 and 1840 by a German, Juan Mauricio Rugendas, who left his mark all over South America. His "Battle of Maipó" is in the Museum of History, but better than his historic battle scenes are his folksy, sympathetic and vigorous studies of *huasos*, rodeos, convoy wagons, campfires, riding herd—a medley of vivid ponchos, curving knives, bloomer trousers, red meat and often, behind these figures, the towering majesty of the Andean cordillera.

But whatever the lack in the past, today few large cities in the world have so many art exhibits so steadily going on as Santiago. The year round, in the salons of the Bank of Chile, the National Museum of Fine Arts, in various university salons, the Ministry of Education, in the Alhambra Palace, in the Galerie du Parc and elsewhere, exhibits are constantly being staged. Every year there is a big national prize contest in the Summer Salon at the Viña del Mar coast resort.

The government offers an annual art prize of 100,000 pesos. Medals and prizes are given out by the National Salon. Large prizes have been established by wealthy businessmen. Recent prize winners have been Pablo Burchard, an anecdotal, impressionistic landscapist; Israel Róa, impressionistic and on the delicate side; Federico Zabala, Alfonso Vila, Hortensia Oehrens and Ana Correa. Ramón Subrercaseaux and Alberto Valenzuela are good, if romantically patriotic, landscape painters.

Chile's painters, conventional, balanced and restrained, and in general far less experimental and imaginative than those of the Mexican or Peruvian schools, concern themselves much with the stark Chilean desert, the wild southern coasts, the broken adobe streets, with the ragged *rotos* of the nitrate fields, the coal mines, the farms; the life of *huasos* or Chilean cowboys. It is all very disciplined and sober, like the Chilean spirit, economical in its color, lines and methods.

Fresco painting has not had the general encouragement that it has had in Mexico, but judging from the work by De la Fuente, Hermosillo Alvarez, Osvaldo Reyes, Luis Vargas Rosas and particularly the fine folk murals of Laureano Guevara, this promises to become one of the strongest sides of Chilean art, and one particularly in keeping with the severe, almost architectural Chilean temperament.

Chile has a much more extensive tradition of sculpturing. The public monuments of a number of important sculptors—Nicanor Plaza, Virginio Arias, Rebecca Matte de Iñíquez and others—dot the parks and boulevards. On the garden hill of Santa Lucía in Santiago towers the statue of the Indian chieftain Toque Caupolicán, by Plaza. Humorously, a replica of this in New York's Central Park is labeled, "The Last of the Mohicans." Delicious provincialism! The sculptor Samuel Román Rojas has interested himself in folk studies. Santiago has a fine museum and a fine school of Araucano handicraft arts.

In many ways the plastic arts reflect the American spirit even better than literature, which in some countries has had to wait on a reconciliation of many cultures and the evolution of the language itself. But art in the Americas springs full-bodied from a rich colonial tradition of nearly four centuries and from the artistic and creative sensibilities of people long devoted to handicraft art.

One Hispanic American writer has said recently: "Paris has moved to the New World."

XII New Forces

Industrialists

THE quickening tempo of development from World War I to the present has brought into being in most Latin American countries a strong new native industrialist class.

In Europe the rise of industrialist classes was featured by the Reformation wars, all the long struggles against feudalism, the Napoleonic wars and other disasters never before paralleled in history. The whirring machine stuck out its steel fingers and shook all peoples of earth by the scruff of the neck.

In the United States this change came about fairly smoothly, although by the long, bloody Civil War Northern industrialists gained the edge over the feudal slavocracy of the South. Certainly the struggles in Latin America have been no worse. In fact they were less disorderly and bloody than previous struggles in the rest of the world.

The breakdown of European feudalism was essential to free the serfs and make possible a free competitive labor supply for the new factories. But in Latin America the rise of the local industrialists has been far more difficult, fraught with more obstacles. The new elements have had not merely to break the exclusive monopoly of the landholding classes on government and national economy, but also to face foreign monopolies in raw-product fields and the competition of foreign goods from highly industrialized mass-production countries already having the technical know-how. Their third great handicap was that they were starting up when an organized labor movement was already in existence.

Thus in Mexico, following the land-water-schools revolution, a strong labor movement reared up at the very moment Mexican industry was struggling to be born. In fact the revolution had been staged by and for the peasants and the new proletariat. In the face of such multiple

240

obstacles, the new industrialists could not hope to get under way without state aid.

However, much of the new industrialization was undertaken by the leading revolutionary generals themselves, who laid aside the sword— not too far off—to become makers of steel and textiles, auto tires and light bulbs. These men had fought their way to power at the head of the Mexican disinherited to become powerful entrepreneurs. One needs only to call the roll of leading generals and politicians to name the biggest capitalists in Mexico: Obregón, Calles, Abelardo Rodríguez, Portes Gil, Almazán, Aarón Saenz, the Camacho brothers, the Cárdenas brothers, and now President Alemán. In spite of the humble origins of most of these, all became big businessmen. They are the "Millionaire Socialists," who talk straight Marxian lingo, push social and labor legislation, stand for the most progressive principles—and make money, lots of money.

The feudalists were broken by revolution and nation-wide land distribution. Foreign business was squeezed by tariffs, high taxes, rail rates hitting it harder than they did native business, militant labor demands backed by the government but not hurting home concerns, harassing court actions and inspections, and downright expropriation. Among this new governing clan the slogan "anti-imperialism" became one not merely of national liberation and patriotism but mighty good business besides.

Thus control of the State was temporarily shared by labor and native capital allied against both feudalism and the foreigner. An indication of this new nationalist front of labor and capital has been the postwar compact between Lombardo Toledano (the pro-Moscow labor boss of Mexico and the continent) and domestic capitalists, providing for a ten-year no-strike pledge and co-operation in a joint plan for industrialization. In practice this pledge does not apply to government-owned utilities, foreign business or jurisdictional conflicts.

Since the end of the war a new formula of 51 per cent Mexican, 49 per cent foreign capital has drawn in tremendous investments from abroad. Eventually this may break the capital-labor front. A more hopeful outcome would be for it to benefit everybody concerned.

In varying details and degrees the Mexican pattern repeats itself over the continent. This is also the story, in slightly different dress, of Perón in Argentina, as earlier of Vargas in Brazil, where the new local industrialists edged in behind the military to take over the State. In Brazil labor got few crumbs indeed, but in his revolt against the coffee barons to push industrialization Vargas set up the most personal absolutist regime ever known outside the Orient.

In Argentina the change-over could not be done merely with old-line militarists, so long tied up with the wheat, cattle and foreign interests. It needed the aid of labor and peasants—this to offset the unprogressive elements in the army itself. In the rapidly expanding economy there, labor and the peasants, also large industrialists not too tied in with foreign capital, could be satisfied and induced to lend support. The new-type industrialists have had a fairly free hand, either on their own initiative or as partners in government enterprises. On its side the government has knocked out foreign business monopolies in banking, insurance, railroading, shipping, aviation, oil, meat packing, wool packing and shipping, plus all public utilities. Here again, labor's militancy has been cleverly directed against large foreign concerns.

At the same time the drastic new peasants' legislation has hit the landed proprietors right between the eyes. They have been subjected, more than the industrialists, to government controls. All exportable farm products must be turned over to the government at a fixed price.

Much the same pattern was followed by Alessandri in Chile when he forced foreign capital into joint government holding companies with rigid allocation of profits, and pushed far-reaching social legislation. Since this change came at a time of universal unemployment, the big landholders of the country, though they lost their old monopoly over government to the progressive industrialists of the Radical Party and the more alert wing of the Liberal Party, were not hit as they have been in Mexico and Argentina.

A small industrial class appeared in Chile in the middle of last century. Toward 1900 the big mineowners and industrialists started the Radical Party. For a time in the twentieth century the new industrialists through intermarriage tended to amalgamate with the famous "600 families" long ruling the country.

But with the depression after World War I, with revolution rocking Chile on its heels, more drastic steps had to be taken. Then it was that more alert and daring business groups in the Radical Party, through an alliance with labor, swept into the halls of state and definitely took over from the feudal elements that had so long held back industry, transportation, sanitation and modern growth. In a few short years, despite great handicaps, the new business-labor alliance made over the whole productive map of Chile.

This general trend likewise illumines the present blue-prints of Haya de la Torre in Peru. This is part of the meaning—aside from popular unrest due to previous long-standing dictatorship and lack of all economic opportunity—of the new Betancourt regime in Venezuela. This explains the Conservative-Liberal alliance in Colombia. This was even part of the explanation of a ferocious dictator like Ubico in Guatemala. The subsequent inauguration of the Arévalo government widened the basis of the effort, now being carried on by a series of regional and industrial conferences of all elements—labor, technicians, government, civic groups and business—such as the fine and honest survey made in Escuintla in 1946. In other words, the effort moves on from dictatorial imposition to a broader co-operation of all groups.

What is really significant in all this seesaw is that new sources of wealth are being developed by local effort, and local policies are being ever more defined, with an eye to benefiting all classes so far as is possible and lifting the countries up from the previous morass of inferior colonialism.

Latin America does not intend—as things seem now—to follow the United States capitalist pattern or the Soviet totalitarian pattern, but some form of compensated economy. The countries are searching out their own paths in accordance with their own traditions and needs and remaining as much as possible apart from the unpleasant struggle engulfing the world.

The new industrialists are among the active shapers of these new policies.

The Middle Class

New factories, the remarkable growth of cities, plus many new opportunities, have resulted in the rise these past few decades of a middle class that now cushions the great gap between the old-time landowner and the hard-driven serf. This has helped break up feudal and military monopoly over government, as in the United States, softens the rule of the new industrialists and hence has helped the growth of democracy. In Europe war and depression drove the middle class into the shirted armies, on into the red path of war. In the Americas, with an expanding economy and a hopeful future, it is still a liberalizing force.

Besides its economic function, the Latin American middle class is far more of a go-between than in most countries. In South America—still so divided along Spanish Conquest lines, with deep-seated cultural conflicts—the mestizo, the man of mixed blood, has always had the temperament and talents best suited for all functions in this intermediary role. And the man of mixed blood has swelled the ranks of the middle class nearly everywhere. This has provided an additional way in which more pronounced Indian groups could be assimilated into modern culture.

The expanding middle class has demanded many new things from government. Formerly the landed aristocrat with his money and power could secure benefits for himself without regard to the public. He considered government money spent on education, sanitation, culture and so on utter waste—even dangerous. Hence there were few free schools. Even today public high schools in Brazil and elsewhere charge high tuition fees. Even in a big city like Lima the number of public elementary schools is very limited; the buildings are old, unsanitary, depressing, the teachers miserably paid, the classes jammed to the doors, so that everybody who possibly can is forced to send his children to parochial tuition schools, which receive the bulk of public funds. But the middle class has demanded more and better schools, and this has benefited rural areas as well. Free education is being brought within the reach of all. Talk of "democracy" was quite idle until this came about.

Sanitation, especially in towns and cities, has been pushed. Transportation facilities have been improved. Cobbles have given way to pavements. Previously libraries and museums were woefully neglected, and the general public had little access to them. Today such cultural activities in many of the countries are now well attended to. In Argentina and Chile, for instance, the museums are well-filled, well-equipped, catalogued and clean. A few years ago public libraries were almost nonexistent. Few loaned out books. But the number has increased nearly everywhere.

Also the middle class has brought about more bona fide political expression, more civil liberties, the right to form new parties, to have more honest elections.

Women

General emancipation has led to an improvement in the status of Latin American women. They now have better economic opportunities, protection of property rights in and out of marriage, labor guarantees, maternity safeguards in industry, new access to all the professions.

This changed all social relations and the attitude of both sexes. In Díaz' day in Mexico it was said there were only 500 women gainfully employed in Mexico City. Most were schoolteachers. Today government and business offices, stores and restaurants are packed with female employees.

This has made previous feudal restrictions impractical. Any male soon tires of escorting a woman home from work every day of the year at a set hour. She soon comes and goes as she pleases. Up to the early nineteen-forties in Mexico City it was still illegal for a woman to be on the streets unchaperoned after nine o'clock in the evening, unless she had a prostitute's registration card. But in 1946, in the new booming city, respectable girls were going unaccompanied to the movies; they now eat in public restaurants; they walk the streets at fairly late hours without danger of the type of police or male molestations formerly in vogue. Freedom of motion, freedom from constant chaperonage, freedom from economic subservience—these are some of the fruits.

Women have been increasingly granted the vote all over the continent, even by such an atrocious dictator as Trujillo in the Dominican Republic. In September 1947 Perón staged a great ceremony to celebrate the new law for women's suffrage in Argentina.

Women's influence in public affairs has steadily increased. Frequently now they are appointed delegates to important international conferences. Who would have ever thought, even ten years ago, that a red-sweater girl would be up on the rostrum in a Pan American conference, reading the Spanish texts of international agreements?

Here and there some women have been elected mayors or have been sent to congress. In 1947 the Vice-President of Panama's Congress was Señorita Gumersinda Paez.

The Inter-American Congress of Women has become a highly respected and influential body. Its findings carry weight over the continent.

The congress in 1947 was held in September in Guatemala City. These were its chief resolutions, widely publicized, usually on the front page, throughout all Latin America:

(1) Urge the Pan American Union and all member countries to break off relations with Dictators Trujillo, Somoza and Carías, "who constitute a disgrace for democratic countries."

(2) Break relations with Dictator Franco.

(3) Aid Guatemala in her just claims for the recovery of British Honduras and urge all governments to show solidarity with her in winning back that lost territory.

(4) General rejection of the Marshall militarization of the continent and utilization of the moneys instead for farm machinery and sanitation equipment.

Over the continent more and more women are engaged in business, the professions, art and literature. The first Nobel Prize for literature ever granted to a Latin American went to the Chilean poetess, Gabriela Mistral. The first woman in Mexico ever to take a medical course, only thirty years ago, had to fight the whole world, even carry the matter into the courts. Today, a woman manages one of the biggest shoe factories in Mexico. Another woman, the former secretary of President Calles, manufactures all medicinal cotton, gauze and bandages used in the country, a business she founded herself.

While women, even in the feudal past, sometimes played heroic roles, they were luminous exceptions to the general rule. No one in the United States can fully appreciate the tremendous revolutionary effect on all Latin America of the activities of Señora Eva de Perón, wife of the President of Argentina. We are used to women running around like that in our midst, but in Latin America to have a sort of combination of Mrs. Roosevelt and Clare Boothe Luce shoot across the heavens was a social earthquake. Whereas with us radio and theater talents, plus beauty, would have been points in such a woman's favor, in Latin America Señora Perón was subjected to every sort of unproved slur. She has been a courageous trail breaker, the like of which was never before seen down that way, and it has taken courage on her husband's part as well.

Originally women's servitude in the south was compounded because the Spanish conqueror, even when he married an Indian woman, considered her a concubine. It was more rigid because of the long Moorish domination in Spain. It was perpetuated into modern times because of the long feudal rule.

Today the old feudal era is passing away for women with the system of which it was a part. Less and less now are women literally locked in their homes to breed babies, cook and embroider, or allowed to go out merely to attend Mass and weep over the infidelity of their husbands. The conventional "Little House" is no longer pointed to with such pride.

It is also to be noted that many Latin American males, no longer condemned to the extremes of monotonously virtuous women on one hand and the concubine and the harlot on the other, are finding the sex revolution not without certain rewards.

Students

The student movement sprang up locally in Argentina during World War I and has remained part of the political pattern of southern lands ever since. It started as a revolt against professors appointed for political reasons, not for their knowledge and ability, and to reform the medieval, semiecclesiastical curricula.

The students did not want to study medicine under a hack politician meat chopper. They did not want to study canon law when the world was buzzing with industry and science.

All around the universities broad fields of *pampa* wheat were being harvested by the most modern machinery. Factory chimneys were rising. Roads were being built. Airplanes were whirling through the sky. But the universities provided little modern science, medicine or engineering to correspond to the revolutionary changes. Argentines had to go abroad to study about such things. Modern technical knowledge was restricted to the very wealthy.

The early student movement renovated the structure and life of Argentine universities and spread rapidly to other lands.

In Peru it centered at the University of Trujillo under the leadership of student Haya de la Torre, later the most potent figure in all the land. Much blood was shed. Victory was long delayed. In fact the reform of San Marcos University—closed for many years during dictatorial periods—was not achieved until it got its autonomous status in 1946, and Luis Alberto Sánchez, one of the first student leaders, was named Rector.

Everywhere students who fought for reform bumped directly into the State. The attempt to get proper professors hit at the prerogatives of the regime. The students soon found that to bring modernity into their institutions, they first had to modernize the government. If democratic methods did not exist, the only way was with rifle in hand.

They took up rifles and also began getting together in international conferences, laying down principles and programs for academic life, for politics and economic reforms.

So successful were they in shaking down some regimes that it has become axiomatic that the ruler who uses force against the students has cooked his goose. There is nothing quite so ridiculous and tragic as a dictator shooting students, however uproarious. Nothing so quickly arouses the anger of a whole people; nothing so quickly shames grown men into courage and action.

Student groups (among them, secret ABC cells, with which Batista of the army was affiliated) helped overthrow the Machado dictatorship of Cuba in 1933 and set up their own government. They stormed against the early Siles dictatorship in Bolivia and tossed it right out the window—just as they did again in 1946 with Villarroel, who was not only thrown out the window but also hung to a lamppost, Mussolini-style. They knocked down several atrocious dictators in Ecuador. They have played a very active part in Guatemala, Salvador, Nicaragua and Honduras and have much influence in Panama, where I had some long and pleasant talks with their leaders. Those young fellows made more plain ordinary horse sense than half the political leaders I saw over the continent.

In some places, and on many occasions, they have suffered greatly or have been killed. The fate of student friends of mine at the hands of the Carías and Somoza dictatorships has been quite too horrible to be told or believed. Some years ago, a score of Nicaraguan students, mostly from León, were seized by the National Guard. After prison tortures they were stripped to the waist and their belts taken away so they would have to hold up their trousers with their hands. Soldiers on horseback then whipped them on foot, backs bleeding, clear across the wild mountains to the Honduras frontier.

In 1946 my friend Carlos, who had been driven across the mountains that way, risked returning home. He stayed at the same hotel with us in Guatemala and left before we did. A week after we reached Nicaragua, about a month later, a small newspaper item said he had fallen off a high bridge outside León in a drunken stupor and had been killed. Carlos had never in his life touched any alcohol, not even beer. What happened? He was beaten to death, and his body tossed on the rocks.

The students began winning university autonomy, as in Mexico, Guatemala and Peru. They freed the national institutions from direct political interference and won the right along with the professors to choose their own administrative personnel. In many places also they won free tuition, opening the doors of higher learning to the new middle class, even to the proletariat—a basic democratic gain which has had much to do with promoting civil rights and more popular government.

Labor

A new balance wheel in public affairs has been the growth of organized labor. This, like the students' movement, by limiting monopoly of power by army and feudal elements, has helped lift the curse of militarism, has been a real contribution to the growing determination of the South American peoples to get away from rifle-rule and all its evils. It has produced a new civic force and has provided a larger body of politically conscious citizens.

Subsequent attempts to capture organized labor by Communists and outside nations, or for unworthy nationalistic ends, are another story. At the start the battle of organized labor, merely for the right to exist (not yet won everywhere) has given an additional chance for all other civic groups to thrive.

In countries where labor is still suppressed, as under Ubico in Guatemala, often not even lawyers, doctors or other professional groups are allowed to associate; the Rotary and Lions Clubs were permitted there only when they allowed themselves to be headed by a stooge selected by the dictator.

Labor unions began to appear in Mexico toward the end of the Porfirio Díaz period. In 1907 strikers at the Rio Blanco textile mills and Cananea copper refineries in Sonora were shot down. Future President Plutarco Elías Calles, a schoolteacher in Sonora, was one of the Cananea strike leaders. Another leader, sent to the underground Ullua Island dungeons, later became a cabinet minister.

In 1914 labor battalions of Vera Cruz and Tamaulipas helped Venustiano Carranza oust Dictator Huerta. When Carranza in turn began to clamp down on the "Workers' Houses," labor turned to Obregón. Labor battalions helped suppress the 1923 De la Huerta revolt. In Mexico City at that time I interviewed Luis N. Morones, leader of the labor movement and in charge of the National Munition Works. He gave me pictures of Plutarco Elías Calles, candidate on the Labor Party ticket, at the head of labor volunteers in San Luis Potosí.

It so happened that I heard Morones give orders to the head of his Palanca, or labor strong-arm gang, about how to handle Juan Field

Jurado, President of the Senate, who was helping the rebels, and Congressmen who were not playing ball.

When Calles came into office, all labor leaders were rewarded with government jobs. Morones became Minister of Industry, Commerce and Labor.

His star declined in 1928 when he backed the wrong political horse, General Francisco Serrano. Serrano revolted and was shot by Calles. After President-elect Obregón's assassination by a religious fanatic, Provisional President Portes Gil terrorized labor and peasants' organizations and set up the National Revolutionary Party, a totalitarian group, later liberalized.

Eventually, in conjunction with the campaign and administration of Lázaro Cárdenas (1934-40), Lombardo Toledano built up the Mexican Confederation of Labor (CTM), a more radical body. The CTM has since remained the official organization, rewarded with government jobs and subsidies.

The next strongest labor movement rose in Cuba. Under Dictator Machado only puppet unions were allowed, but after the 1933 student-sergeant revolt unions mushroomed and the Confederation began to play a role. The new freedom, on the heels of fifteen years of depression, misery and dictatorship, brought on a wave of strikes. Instead of being suppressed by armed force, these were negotiated. Collective bargaining was inaugurated.

Later on, for a period, Batista tried to put labor back into the strait jacket of complete government control. This Nazi process was unsuccessful, and when Grau San Martín was elected to the Presidency by legal ballot (1944) labor was again allowed full freedom. When we passed through Cuba late in 1946, it had come under full Communist leadership and was giving Grau plenty of headaches.

No bona fide labor unions have ever been permitted by Dictator Trujillo of the Dominican Republic. Only lately have they been allowed to function to some extent in Haiti. Jamaica, which toward the end of World War II was granted what is tantamount to free Crown Colony status, has now come under the almost absolute control of a demagogic labor leader, Bustamante.

In most of Central America unions long lived a precarious existence, mostly still do. When a Central American Labor Confederation was formed back in 1926, Dictator Orellana outlawed the Guatemalan federation and forbade any sessions of the Central American organization. All leaders fled to Salvador.

When I was in Guatemala City in 1927, I met a dapper check-suit Chilean salesman representing a North American machinery corporation. As he bore the identical name—"Castro," I believe—of one of the labor leaders sought by the police, he was clapped into prison. It took the United States minister many months to convince the Guatemalan authorities that he was not the dangerous quarry.

Later I met Castro the labor man in Salvador in a candlelighted cellar where the Salvadorean leaders, then in danger of their lives, were holding secret sessions. He turned out to be a mild-voiced Indian shoemaker.

Dictator Ubico continued to suppress unions, but since his overthrow (1944) the Guatemalan Confederation of Labor has enjoyed freedom under Arévalo's government. Unfortunately it responded to that freedom (thanks to Communist agitators) by staging three general "political" strikes in difficult moments against the most democratic administration the country has ever enjoyed.

President Arévalo told me calmly this was a natural impulse among workers long starved and persecuted, that the solution was not machine-gun suppression but the education of labor to its rights and obligations and better standards of living.

Repeatedly in Salvador union people have been mowed down by machine guns. In 1944 unions and peasant organizations helped overthrow the dictator. The army soon staged a countercoup, but when I was there in 1946, labor, in spite of much police brutality, enjoyed more liberties than before.

The high cost of human rights in Honduras was chalked up by a strike of airport workers asking a raise from sixty centavos to a peso a day. For coming to the defense of the strikers the chief daily paper of Tegucigalpa was destroyed. Dozens of arrests were made. The young strike leader, with whom I later talked many times, said he had eked out life for weeks in an underground latrine that served sixteen prisoners in the cell block above, and he had been tortured and flogged for several years. Dictator Carías, in spite of all the contrary evidence I gathered from hundreds of political prisoners, told me no prisoner had ever been maltreated by his government. When I asked him why labor unions were not permitted, he replied that wages were so high (the maximum about a dollar a day) that unions were not necessary.

In Nicaragua, Dictator Somoza alternately cajoled and terrorized labor. Briefly he played ball with the small Communist wing and recognized Soviet Russia. During this interlude other unions were maltreated. In September 1947 he declared war on Communists and all unions. This has meant the extermination of every brand of opposition.

Dictator Higinio Morinigo smashed Paraguayan labor down completely in March 1945. Seven hundred leaders were shipped off to a jungle concentration camp in the remotest corner of the Chaco, one of the worst hellholes on the continent.

During Vicente Gómez' days in Venezuela, a union card was a free ticket to the hereafter. Successive executives permitted some organization, with only a relatively few machine-gunnings. The workers (except for the Communists) backed the successful Rómulo Betancourt revolt against President Isaías Medina.

In Costa Rica, Colombia, Uruguay, labor unions have long been a dignified part of the social setup.

Labor has had cruel ups and downs in Ecuador, but was a main support, in coalition with the Conservative Party, in electing Velasco Ibarra President in 1944. Velasco restored all liberties but soon turned dictator, purged or ditched his labor following, outlawed the Confederation of Labor, then leaned wholly on army and Conservative support. This provoked a military coup of the more liberal wing of the army, but Conservative elements fought back into the Palace.

The attitude of both the Catholic Church and the army in labor matters is revealed by events in Ecuador and Costa Rica. In Ecuador the Archbishop threatened all who attended the 1945 labor congress with excommunication. But in Costa Rica the Archbishop, in return for educational concessions, joined hands with labor to push through a "Christian" labor code.

The small Costa Rica army keeps aloof from politics. The Ecuadorian army is the State, the court of last resort. When the army splits there is trouble. One army faction is now pro-labor, pro-democratic, pro-liberal; the other is controlled by the feudal Conservatives. This split explains the recent brief civil war.

Dictator Vargas wiped out the whole labor movement in Brazil. By 1918 organized labor had gained a membership of about half a million and was affiliated with the International Federation of Trade Unions. After that, Vargas permitted only "stooge" unions as part of his Fascist Estado Novo, or corporate state. Public labor meetings were taboo.

When a few civil liberties were for a short while restored on his downfall, labor organization grew quickly, especially in São Paulo. In November 1946 was held the first bona fide national trade union congress in fifteen years. Long repression, secret work by Communist agents and repressive legislation combined to cause many unions to turn Communist.

Onerous Vargas' fascist legislation still controls every phase of labor-union organization. The police and the Minister of Labor must be notified of any union meeting, which may or may not be allowed. All officers in every union must be approved by the Ministry of Labor and can be tossed out by the government, which can then itself run the union or abolish it. Strikes are illegal. All unions must pay taxes.

The labor movement in Peru, gathering headway only slowly under the dictatorships, never achieved national federation until the Mexican labor leader Lombardo Toledano appeared on the scene during the war. Now it is strongly organized. Control is divided between the Communists (south Peru, Arequipa and Cuzco) and the Apra, the Popular Party (Lima and the north).

Inflation has caused much labor trouble. In 1946, the North American Cerro de Pasco mines, 15,000 feet above sea level in the Andes, were hit by a strike. Haya de la Torre, head of Apra, told me how he had settled this strike by convincing the management that they should consider their scarce labor supply—the big-lunged Indians of the highlands—as much a part of their capital as the copper in the ground. Owing to more satisfactory opportunities in the new coast industries and the easier climate and conditions there, mine labor shortage is now so great that the company hesitates to open up a new vein considered one of the richest in the world. According to Haya, the workers were granted even more than they had demanded.

Because of the soaring cost of living a general strike broke out in Lima in 1947. The government resorted to martial law, a ruse, the Apristas claim, to prevent freedom in the Congressional elections. High-school students, joining the strike in protest over bad food and living quarters, were fired upon by the police, and one was killed. Public outrage was so great that the government saved itself only by forcing out the general in charge of police.

A strong labor movement grew up in Chile after World War I and gained headway during depression years. It forced the adoption of the most extensive social reforms of any country on the continent. Labor, now divided between Socialist and Communist leadership, has formed the basis of all popular regimes since 1938.

In 1946 Acting President Admiral Duhualde outlawed unions in North American mining companies. This provoked a general strike early the next year. Duhualde then machine-gunned a mass meeting at the Civic Center in great Plaza Bulnes in Santiago. The stones ran with blood. All leaders were ordered arrested. So horrified was the country that all parties, including the Radicals, the backbone of his administration, withdrew from his government, and he was isolated except for several army men.

Once asked how he became President of Chile, Duhualde replied cynically, "Easy. That took me only fifteen minutes. The hard thing is to become an admiral. That took me a lifetime." At this ticklish juncture it looked as though he had only the conventional fifteen minutes to lose the Presidency. He pulled out white rabbits.

Emissaries were rushed to Socialist leaders in hiding. They betrayed the strike and their fellows by jumping right out of refuge into the cabinet. The strike was broken, the labor organization split wide open.

This treachery gave the Socialists only one year of ill-gotten political spoils. Their own party broke in two. No one would accept them in any of the 1946 political coalitions. They finally ran their own candidate, Bernardo Ibáñez, for President but he won fewer votes than a garden club. One unfortunate result was that labor was driven farther into Communist control, under the leadership of Bernardo Araya. This gave the new President, Gónzalez Videla, an excuse to declare general martial law and arrest all leaders, as in the coal-mine strike in Lota in October 1947.

Labor was never well organized in Argentina, and until Perón's day that country was one of the most backward in labor legislation. Unions were restricted to Buenos Aires and a few other large cities. Peasants who tried to organize were always jailed or killed.

By 1939, the General Confederation of Labor, painfully struggling into life ever since World War I, still had only 270,000 members. Independent unions accounted for 150,000 more—these were "Socialist" or "Radical Party," anarchist-syndicalist or Communist. A Catholic woman's union, not for bargaining but for social contacts, had less than 20,000 members. The only farm organization was a small co-operative never allowed to bargain.

Following the reactionary Uriburu army revolt, union meetings were allowed only if police were present. Under "Christian fascist" President Ramón Castillo martial law was almost continuous, and labor was a main target. The number of labor-union meetings dropped to nearly half, attendance to a fifth.

After the 1943 revolution, which was soon actively supported by the railway workers and the General Confederation, new unions sprang up, membership was quadrupled. Peasant unions now cobweb much of the country. Proper legislation has been put on the statutes. As Minister of Labor and Social Welfare, Perón personally settled hundreds of strikes. Labor made great gains in wages and working conditions. Before running for President, Perón gave up his fashionable apartment and moved with his wife María Eva into a workers' residential district—one of his typical dramatic gestures.

Today the peasants and the Confederation support Perón wholeheartedly. After he came into office leaders were given jobs and organizations were helped with subsidies as in Mexico. Señora Perón spends all her free time visiting labor unions, and is so popular taxi drivers stick her picture up in their cabs.

Independent unions, though they have lost much membership to the Confederation, still exist. Six anti-Perón deputies under Cipriano Reyes, a bold political opportunist with few scruples, control a few of these. They even have some strength in the Confederation itself and have founded what they call an independent labor party.

This was happening when I was in Buenos Aires. At a small gathering of Conservatives, Radicals and Socialists, I got a vivid picture of the political mentality of Argentines who for so many decades have known few political rights.

One of the Conservatives remarked: "Perón will have to kill Reyes. It's one or the other now." And he added, though he himself was bitterly against the new President: "He'll be a fool if he doesn't." Most of the others around the room nodded.

But Reyes is still doing business at the same independent stand and thus far hasn't suffered a hand scratch.

The Reyes clique filled the A. F. of L. delegation to Argentina, early in 1947, with plenty of "bunk." Nevertheless the delegation was fair enough to report: "A great deal of attention is being devoted by the government and the labor movement to the problems of improving the economic conditions of the common people. We were impressed by the physical indications of economic progress and by the relatively advanced standard of living of industrial workers."

The C. I. O., also invited to Argentina, where their delegates might have learned something, declined the invitation with a a combination of ignorance and bad grace, declaring Perón had turned Argentina into "a corporate state along Nazi lines." This glaring falsehood smacks merely of loudmouthed Communist name calling.

The shift of Argentine labor into the Confederation was partly due to the bankruptcy of the Socialist Party as a trusted moral force because of its co-operation with previous dictatorial regimes. Even before Perón was elected, about two-thirds of the membership of the Socialist unions had deserted their leaders—imbued with rigid European dialectic—to enter the Confederation. In Santa Fé province the whole Socialist Party and its unions seceded and entered the Perón fold. Perón's present Minister of Finance, Miguel Miranda, a wealthy industrialist, is an ex-Socialist. A further shift to the Confederation occurred when Perón recognized the Soviet Union. The local Communists then ordered all their unions to disband and told the members to seek entry into the Confederation.

Various efforts to form continental confederations have been made.

The early Pan-American Confederation (PAC), formed in Laredo, Texas, in November 1918, was the outgrowth of an appeal sent to the A. F. of L. asking its support in getting the Pershing punitive expedition withdrawn from Mexican soil. The Confederation was chiefly an alliance between the A. F. of L. and the Mexican Regional Confederation of Labor, which under Luis N. Morones came to be the official labor movement of the Obregón and Calles regimes. A few "stooge" paper unions from dictatorial countries were roped in. The Pan-American Confederation pretty much went to pot when Morones lost control of Mexican labor.

When an international labor congress was held in Uruguay in 1931 the charge was made that the PAC was merely a "false front for Yankee imperialism." This effort was largely manipulated through the Soviet Legation in Montevideo, and the Mexican delegation was headed by the Mexican Communist painter David Siqueiros. The organization was short-lived.

A new confederation was built up by Mexican labor leader Lombardo Toledano during the war. His followers were pledged to no wartime strikes—then the Moscow countersign—and his efforts were aided by local Communists and smiled on by the Mexican and United States governments for the sake of uninterrupted production. International congresses were held in Montevideo, Cali in Colombia, Havana, Mexico City and, in 1947, in San José, Costa Rica. The C. I. O. loosely ties in with this group. John L. Lewis, when head of the C. I. O., attended a Mexico City conference.

In 1947 the A. F. of L. began casting around to set up an inter-American confederation to offset the Lombardo group, and a continental meeting was called for Lima on January 10, 1948. This was part of the reason for the A. L. of L. visit to Argentina, but the delegation decided that labor there was too controlled by the government. This statement irked the Argentine Confederation, which said that Argentina has a labor government, that the government is in the hands of labor. In any case, the A. F. of L. was willing to accept, in years past, the Mexican labor movement and others far more government-controlled than that in Argentina. Likewise, it apparently now will take in the Brazilian Confederation, which is not merely government-controlled, but police-controlled and police-run, and has fewer rights than unions enjoyed under Hitler. In addition, the new setup will likely include the Socialist segment of the Chilean labor movement and the Peruvian and Venezuelan confederations, which will likely slip out from under Lombardo's wing.

Hope Rainbow

Lombardo, though shakier than a few years back, remains on the ground floor of the continental labor movement. In 1946 he came back from a fresh trip to Moscow—where no labor leader not belonging to the holy of holies may enter—with new zeal and headed for a fresh crusade throughout Latin America.

With the end of the war, his policies, apparently obeying Moscow dictates, changed abruptly. This change was announced in the Esperanza Iris Theatre, in the center of Mexico City on Donceles Street—"The Street of Royal Pages"—beside the national Congressional Building. The theater bears the stage name of a famous Mexican actress now dead—"Hope Rainbow." Though a handsome gray-stone edifice, it has been outmoded by new super-de-luxe movie palaces dotting all Mexico City and is chiefly used for concerts, Soviet movies and labor rallies. The late Ambassador Oumanski is said to have leased it part-time through dummy fellow travelers for propaganda purposes.

There was great expectancy in that audience of blue-clad workers and white-clad peasants, for Lombardo's words would carry to every corner of Mexico and throughout the continent. The CTM, the Mexican Confederation of Labor, and the CTAL, the Latin American Confederation of Labor, both his offspring, would follow his orders.

Lombardo, sitting on the platform, was a slender, dark-haired olive-skinned man slightly over fifty, dressed in an ordinary two-button business suit and soft white shirt. His thin ascetic face with its regular features, smudge eyebrows and large forehead, wore a friendly frank smile, but his long dextrous fingers tapped nervously. Twenty years ago he was expected to depart from this world because of advanced t.b., but even in worst bedridden moments he always managed to do three times the work of an ordinary person. Ambition plus fervency have drawn forth such stores of hidden energy that his physical stamina has increased over the years.

One balmy afternoon back in 1923 I was standing with friends before the Ciudadela—the National Arms Factory—then being administered by the wealthy labor czar, the pudgy bediamonded Luis N. Morones.

In 1920 Morones had helped Alvaro Obregón oust President Carranza and become master of Mexico. All labor leaders then reached the banquet table of the powerful militarists. All members of the inner Labor Grupo Acción—of which Lombardo was a part—held lucrative government positions. Besides a professorship, Lombardo held two other sinecures (not legal) which gave him a handsome income.

But by 1923 Obregón faced a serious crisis. The De la Huerta rebellion ringed the capital around, and more and more generals were betraying the government. Even several high members of Obregón's own cabinet sympathized with the rebels.

In this dark moment as the De la Huerta forces piled victory on victory, the Mexican Congress blocked ratification of the Bucareli Agreements with the United States on behalf of the oil companies. The President of the Senate, Juan Field Jurado, boldly boasted he would not cede an inch and would remain in his post "until the victorious armies of De la Huerta entered the capital."

Morones' strong-arm gang, La Palanca, went into action. Lombardo, then a stripling in charge of the National Preparatory School, led machine guns into the patio of the Secretariat of Education to intimidate Minister José Vasconcelos, who sympathized with the revolters. Juan Field Jurado, whose life I saved for twenty-four hours, was shot down on his own doorstep. Six anti-Obregón Congressmen were kidnaped by the Palanca. Opposition to the Bucareli Agreements was broken. Ironically the temporary salvation of foreign oil companies was due to the direct-action tactics of Mexican labor leaders, among whom was Lombardo Toledano.

As the rebel armies were rolled back—with the aid of an oil-tax loan, with Russian-model rifles supplied by the United States government, and with worker and peasant battalions organized by Morones and the candidate for the Presidency, General Plutarco Elías Calles—state after state was left without a government. There was a bargain-counter rush to see how many Labor Party people could grab off the plums.

And so, as I stood before the Ciudadela at that particular junction in Mexican history, Lombardo rushed out.

"The big boss," he shouted, referring to Morones, "has ordered me to go take over the governorship of Puebla."

Boldly he lifted the pistol and cartridge belt off the hips of a friend and buckled them about his own waist. "May need this." With a number of cronies he jumped into a touring car that hurtled over the mountains to the rich Puebla plain on the other side of the snow volcanoes.

For several years he gave Puebla a good if radical administration, promoted education, pushed land reform, built roads and irrigation dams.

Puebla is Lombardo's native state. He was born in the village of Tezuitlán of middle-class parents, Spanish with some Indian admixture. When he took his law degree at the University of Mexico in 1919, he was dubbed one of "the seven wise men," a group of seven unusually brilliant classmates, all of them since prominent in public affairs.

After graduation Lombardo climbed quickly through the educational bureaucracy—law and philosophy instructor or professor in the National University; head of the National Preparatory School. He led radical students and professors in behalf of university autonomy. Once that was achieved, the university went right into the control of conservative elements, and Lombardo was kicked out, hand-bitten.

With a governmental subsidy Lombardo then founded the Gabino Barreda University, the Workers' University, still government-subsidized to the tune of fifty thousand pesos annually. Lombardo remains its titular head. The institution gives courses on labor, Marxian economics, international affairs, imperialism. Under its imprint are issued numerous translations of Soviet and Communist books. Its monthly illustrated magazine, *Futuro*, is an out-and-out hammer-and-sickle publication.

When President Portes Gil (1928-30) smashed all labor and peasant forces to establish a totalitarian party, Morones ordered Labor Party members to give up their government jobs in protest. Lombardo was the one and only labor leader who left Morones and his fellows in the lurch. He did not resign his lucrative posts.

Sometime later he formed the CTM, to participate in the PMR, the official government party, sustained by forced collections of dues from all government employees. Cannily he hitched his car to the rising star of General Lázaro Cárdenas, who in 1934 stepped into the Presidency for a six-year term.

Shortly after, invited to Moscow, Lombardo made his first hegira to the holy city of the Soviets, and ever since has rolled out his prayer rug in the direction of the Kremlin temple towers.

In the 1940 elections Lombardo guessed right again in supporting the more conservative Avila Camacho. By then world war was at the gates.

During the Soviet pact with Germany Lombardo's group ferociously denounced Roosevelt and Churchill, in the *Futuro* and the government-subsidized labor daily, as imperialistic wolves. The war was a capitalist war between rival oppressor nations. But in less than a week after the Germans smashed through Brest-Litovsk, Roosevelt and Churchill had sprouted lily-white wings in the holy crusade against bestial "capitalist" Nazism.

All during the war Toledano, in line with Moscow orders, was a staunch collaborator with State Department policy. He denounced Argentina and Bolivia; he eulogized Dictator Vargas of Brazil; he played ball with Dictator Somoza of Nicaragua. He held down strikes everywhere and pushed labor to augment production.

But he also built up his own fences. In Mexico "Red" organizations multiplied. Ambassador Oumanski sat on public platforms with Toledano. The latter organized a Marxist study club. Communist Youth, Friends of Russia groups, Red Aid, Labor Defense, the Free German Committee, the free Jugoslavs, the free Italy groups, etc., appeared.

Also, Lombardo utilized the war to tour all Latin America, to speak in behalf of the war effort, the Soviet Union and the United Nations, and to organize the new Latin American Confederation of Labor, the CTAL. In some countries, as Peru, Bolivia and Ecuador, he had first to create federations. He was welcomed by the illegal governments of those countries because they wished to break up the democratic movements which were threatening their existence. Dictators kept him out of four countries, but the organization won majority support of labor in sixteen nations, with an estimated membership of nearly five million.

His tactical somersault after the war was swift and complete. His speech at the Hope Rainbow, which has since echoed from the Rio

Grande to Cape Horn, once more stamped him as a fine orator. For over three hours he never once flagged, never once lost rapt attention. Wildly his hearers cheered every mention of the Soviet Union, Mexico, President Camacho, Stalin, the working classes, the unity of Latin America. They whistled derisively at Fascism, Trotskyites, capitalism, Yankee imperialism. His grand finale soared to the great glistening glass dewdrops of the massive chandelier:

"Comrades of the CTM, Comrades of the Miners' Union, Comrades of the Electricians' Union, Comrades of the Workers' and Peasants' Confederation, Comrades of the National Proletarian Confederation, Comrades of the Regional Confederation of Labor, Comrades of the National Peasants' Confederation, Comrades of the Workers' Federation, Comrades of the Government Employees' Federation, Comrades of the National Teachers' Union, Comrades of the Communist Party, Comrades of the Communist Youth Confederation—all organized women, soldiers and civilians, young and old—I address you with the voice of a Mexican, with the voice of a Latin American, with the voice of the international working class! Build the New Fatherland! On to the emancipation of Mexico! On to the emancipation of Latin America! Fight on that the war's bloodshed may flower in liberty and justice for the world!"

In his speech, Lombardo analyzed the world situation, then proceeded, with copious quotations from Marx, Lenin and Stalin, but not from any Mexican thinkers, to prove beyond doubt that his new alliance with Mexican capital for the prompt industrialization of Mexico was the quintessence of simon-pure revolutionary doctrine. Leaning wholly on the Bolsheviks, he laid down a program for Mexico, for Latin America, for colonial peoples everywhere, a program for a grand united *nationalist* front against capitalist nations, particularly the United States.

He explained that capitalism, weakened by World War I, was destroyed in a sixth of the world's surface by the Soviet Revolution. World War II saw capitalism's utter destruction beyond possibility of revival in Italy, Germany and Japan; it is now too weak to survive in France or the rest of Europe. Even England was going Socialist. The only powerful "capitalist menace" left was the United States. He argued for a united front of the world against the United States.

For colonial and semicolonial countries he recommends a united front of all classes against the Yankee imperialist. He defends this sharp new turn toward an all-class nationalism, so taboo during the war, as "the true revolutionary position for colonial peoples." The pattern of anti-American, anti-imperialist organization, worked out on hierarchical levels and wholly "Marxian," is to be:

1. A united front of workers and peasants in each country.
2. A Popular Front of Communists, Socialists and liberals: the workers and the middle class.
3. A national front of labor, the middle class and all native industrialists and business elements to fight United States financial and political encroachment.
4. A Latin American front to replace good-neighbor solidarity, and effect a counterbalance to the United States.
5. Complete and unqualified solidarity with the "nonimperialistic" Soviet Union.
6. An anti-United States front of Latin America, Canada, New Zealand and Australia on the theory that those peoples are tired of British rule and must not fall into the orbit of "American capitalism."

Part of this is merely a demagogic moon with a fence around it, but such is the message Lombardo now carries to all Latin America.

Successfully, as usual, he walks the tight rope between Mexican nationalism and support of the ruling regime there and the Soviet-Communist line, makes each seem different yet identical. He waves the red banner of the hammer and sickle. He waves the Mexican eagle and serpent. During the war he waved also the banners of the United Nations. But no longer. Today he speaks not of twenty-one Pan American brothers; he speaks of twenty enslaved sister nations that must combine for their very lives against Yankee imperialism. Now he sees the United States, not as he did during the battle—the great defender of liberty, but the great fascist menace of the world. And his voice carries far across the continents. . . .

Actually, except for being dressed up in Stalinist quotations, this new doctrine differs little from those of Corridini and the Italian Sempre Pronto Blue Shirt nationalists who helped Mussolini gain power. Mussolini always ranted about the capitalist nations that had to be fought by the proletarian nations. If the Browder line of Communist collaboration has been shelved in the United States, it has been continued and emphasized in Latin America. It is a doctrine of war, not peace and world reconstruction.

Lombardo's postwar efforts have contributed to decisive political changes in a number of countries. His unions, affiliated with the Communists and allied with the Catholics, put in President Teodoro Picado in Costa Rica. The latter's first official act was to recognize the Soviet Union.

Governmental overthrow in Ecuador was brought about by an alliance of Conservatives, Lombardo Unionists and Communists. The new government immediately arrested all Spanish bankers, industrialists and plantation owners and confiscated their properties. Foreign nuns and priests were kicked out of the country.

The Lombardo forces played some part in the overthrow of the dictators of Guatemala and Salvador, Ubico and Martínez.

Lombardo fulsomely praised Dictator Vargas of Brazil and in turn was permitted to hold practically the only labor mass meeting Vargas ever allowed. Lombardo hinted that Vargas would give permission to his "stooge" labor unions to affiliate with the CTAL. Later Lombardo and Prestes (Communist) sympathizers tried to keep Vargas in power by preventing elections.

Lombardo and his followers backed the established reactionary Medina regime in Venezuela. Two of his biggest pillars of support are the Cuban and Chilean Confederations, which have exercised tremendous political influence. The latter was instrumental in seating the Rios and González Videla governments in power. Peru became another strong Lombardo labor center. The course has been zigzag and opportunistic. With his out-and-out nationalist tack and the anti-Yankee bogey Lombardo has stilled some conservative fears and in other places has been able to join with downright reactionary forces, as in Nicaragua, Brazil, Ecuador, Peru and Venezuela, to get some sort of a foothold.

But the Hope Rainbow speech has not gone unchallenged, either in labor's ranks or outside. Not all of labor believes the pot of gold lies at the foot of any Kremlin rainbow. Not even the majority of Lombardo's own unions are dedicated to Communism. He merely seized the moment to paint his name on the side of the United Nations band wagon. He's off that band wagon now. There have been many straws in the changing wind right in Lombardo's own ranks.

In 1947 part of the Cuban movement revolted, and though Lombardo flew over to quiet the secession, he was not successful. Another big group of secessionists set up shop right in Mexico itself. In Chile, March 1947, Bernardo Ibáñez, head of the Socialist faction of the General Confederation, which is quite large, cabled Lombardo his group was withdrawing because the CTAL had "identified itself with the political interests of world Communism." In Peru the Apra or Popular Party influence is dominant in the unions and the confederation; in fact an Apra unionist head almost won enough votes in the 1946 international conference of the CTAL to take over Lombardo's post. The local confederation will also probably withdraw from the CTAL. Venezuelan labor refused to follow Lombardo and the Communists in fighting Betancourt and in its present opposition, so a break is likely. Nicaraguan labor, now so badly scourged, has little love left for Lombardo since his deal with Somoza.

Argentine labor will have little to do with Lombardo, an outspoken critic of Perón. At one time during the Farrell regime Lombardo claimed to have won control of sixty per cent of Argentine labor. Ten per cent would have been a handsome exaggeration, and much of that has since been lost, for the unions have generally joined the Confederation since Perón's labor laws and his election.

In Ecuador, Costa Rica, Nicaragua, Chile, the Executives, who as a rule were put in with the support of Lombardo unions, have now turned completely against their labor following. In Chile the Lombardo (Communist) unions provided the full 50,000-vote plurality with which González Videla squeezed into the Presidency, but in less than a year he began harassing them with fire and sword.

Unfortunately this type of martial-law suppression provides no real solution. The re-establishment of dictatorial terrorism in Brazil, Ecuador, Nicaragua, the Dominican Republic, Paraguay, Honduras and Chile, is a blow to all democratic forces and little help in developing a bona fide non-Communist labor movement.

In this changing scene Lombardo himself must be labeled an enigma. In spite of consistent adherence to the Moscow line, he has resolutely denied being a fellow traveler, claims he is merely a "Marxist." Of late he has receded considerably from his Hope Rainbow extremism and drags out the doctrine only with close followers or in the labor press. His position does not grow easier with growing co-operation between Mexico and the United States. There was open talk that President Truman's visit to Mexico was to urge President Alemán to put a crimp in Lombardo.

Milton Bracker wrote in the *New York Times*, March 2, 1947: "One of the unquestionably influential men in Mexico insisted privately this week that Mr. Truman's visit was tied to the decree to quash Communism in Latin America." All known Communists and labor leaders in Mexico were given stiff police warnings not to lift their heads during Truman's visit. Shortly after, a secession labor group was given the official green light. Similar developments occurred in Brazil on the eve of and after Truman's visit. Not only was the Communist Party outlawed, but labor unions were broken up by the police, and wholesale arrests made.

No one can feel too badly that the Communists receive the same sort of medicine they mete out to all non-Communists as soon as they achieve power. The real answer to Lombardo, the only way to accomplish a healthy labor movement that is not a spearhead of Moscow's imperialism but stands for the legitimate vindication of labor's rights, will be found, not in police coercion and persecution, but in improved living conditions and democratic guarantees for the great exploited South American masses.

In no country in South America are real wages lower, are people more exploited than in most of Brazil. Despite its handsome new cities, its new hard-driving industrial wheels, the progress and prosperity undoubtedly coming, what Brazil actually offers in human rights and decent living standards places it far down among the more backward Caribbean and Central American dictatorships. Until decent living conditions exist, until labor has freedom to organize in a democratic way, ordinary Juan Pérez is going to snatch at any catchword. Labor will continue to be the prey of fascist and Communist demagogues.

Communism

In September 1947 the Communist drive in Latin America took on additional significance in view of signs of a revival of the Comintern under the direction of the Soviet Communist Party's head and right-hand man to Stalin. This,though announced as a mere "information bureau," can scarcely help orienting and co-ordinating the propaganda and organizational work of the various Communist parties of the world.

Though Communism in Latin America has met with some spontaneous response because of low standards and anti-United States feeling, much of its progress results from a conscious power drive of the Soviet State.

Among southland peoples who have never known decent living standards or political democracy, Communism can scarcely mean anything worse than militarism, serfdom, despotism. In freer, more prosperous countries, such as Argentina, it has made little dent. Where it has been outlawed by force, where citizens have been machine-gunned by dictators, it has usually reappeared stronger than ever.

It also appeals to certain elements as a means to combat "foreign imperialism" and to limit the overwhelming preponderance of the United States, ever so feared in countries south. Such an international counterpoise has been frequently sought, both by rightist and leftist governments; in the nineteenth century, England; later Germany; then the Soviet Union. Today Communist parties, if not out of hand, are exceedingly valuable for all countries, for by pointing to "the menace," financial aid can be easily pried out of Uncle Sam.

The fomenting of New World Communism gives the Soviet State more leverage in world affairs and it has at least nuisance value for the United States.

The Communist anti-United States line, vociferously parroted by Latin American Communists from dawn till dark, makes dents on other groups, particularly bitter feudal elements seeing their authority slipping. Such accusations make headlines, as when on March 17, 1947, A. V. Georgiev, Foreign Editor of *Izvestia*, accused the United States of using "all means" to put Latin America "under United States domination." The war, he declared, had enabled the United States to take over Axis business and had squeezed England and other competitors out of the picture. Trade had been "Americanized." No machinery, control of export trade, blocking the growth of national industries—these were some of the instrumentalities. He charged that the Export-Import credits had been used to pressure the various economies, "hindering rather than aiding the development of Latin America." He cited the bank's refusal to give Chile a loan to develop its government oil fields. He told of the monopoly of Chilean copper mining, the securing of control of half the tin mines of Bolivia, new Standard Oil concessions in the rich oil areas of Paraguay, where dictatorship had been buttressed up. "Under the flag of anti-Communism, reaction is carrying on an offensive against the progressive democratic forces that are defending the individual development of their countries."

Since United States postwar loans to Latin America have totaled only $15,000,000—a drop in the bucket compared to what the Soviet Union itself received—and since the deluge of good-will aid south has ceased, it is hard to see how the Export-Import Bank policy has been directed toward dictating to Latin American economy except by absence from the scene. Previously the bank put up big funds for the state-owned steel industries in Brazil and Chile, to mention but two instances showing the bank's policy has not been ruled by any narrow dogma of private industry. What is more, the Chilean government never discussed an oil loan, never once requested one. And as for war on the democratic forces, who has warred more emphatically than the Communists against the democratic governments of Guatemala, Cuba, Venezuela, Peru? Who made deals with dictators Somoza, Medina, Vargas, Benavides, Batista, the reactionary elements of Ecuador? One gets pretty tired of such propaganda falsifications, but there is just enough truth in this type of accusation, however much distorted, to prick the old sore of anti-Yankee sentiment in the countries south.

It is not easy, at that, to assess the importance of Communism on the southern landscape. Not all the falsification is on the side of the Communists. As in the United States, often the word is bandied about in improper ways. This is particularly a trick of the dictators. Vargas of Brazil in his earlier days branded all opponents, even wealthy bankers, as Communists, well knowing this would blind the outside world to his jailings and martial-law system. When Alessandri was exiled from Chile, he was called a "Communist" though he was a member of the Liberal Party, which in Chile is considered a completely rightist group. When he returned to power, he branded the previous military Junta as "Communist." Somoza of Nicaragua, to cover up his smelly dictatorship and to murder all opponents, now calls everybody a "Communist." Trujillo of the Dominican Republic shouted loud and long that the punitive expedition from Cuba trying to unseat him was "Communist." The leaders, such men as Jiménez Grullón and Angel Morales, long striving to liberate their country from the debased rule under which it has had to grovel all these years, have never had anything to do with Communism. Dictator Martínez of Salvador at one time slaughtered more than 2,000 villagers with loud bellows of "Communists." Then he recognized the puppet state of Manchukuo and backed the Axis—till he had to shift ground. Those he killed were merely ignorant Indian serfs justifiably resenting inhuman abuses on German-owned *fincas*. They had never heard of Marx, Lenin or Stalin.

When I was in Honduras, Dictator Carías breathed hoarsely down my neck about the imminent danger of Communism which obliged him to use harsh methods. There are not a few Communists in Costa Rica and Guatemala; a baker's dozen in Salvador; in Nicaragua, a fair number, thanks to their being promoted for a while by the dictator himself. So now I checked most carefully on Honduras.

In Tegucigalpa, where the police are supposed to kill every Communist on sight, I easily discovered the Communist underground. It consisted of exactly eight persons, and none of them knew very much what Communism meant except that the Soviet Union was supposed to be a wonderful place. They'd got hold of some of the official Soviet propaganda being scattered about. Besides these, I found in all the city exactly four fellow travelers. Three of these were actually on the dictator's own pay roll! They were supporting the fourth, the owner of a little bookstore who occasionally mailed out a few typewritten copies of Soviet articles.

"Why don't the police pick him up?" I asked an official.

The official grinned. "What! We have copies of the letters he writes out. When the American Congressmen came through here to inspect the Pan-American Highway, we got them all hot and bothered about Communism so they wouldn't worry about the road. We showed them that guy's letters and read translations. What a blast a couple of them let out when they got back to Washington! Lock him up! We need him."

The Communist movement in Ecuador is largely confined to a few leftist novelists not overly active in politics and a few labor elements.

In many countries one discovers that such intellectual Communists are mere opportunists, using this temporary ladder to get a platform and eventually a job in the bureaucracy—those whom Manuel Seone, an Apra leader, in a brilliant pamphlet labeled "Creole Communists," meaning dilettantes or "parlor pinks."

Such a leader as Chilean poet Pablo Neruda, Communist deputy from Antofagasta, a brilliant and cultured man and a fine poet with whom I had many pleasant talks, hardly conforms to the party line in a way that would be required of him in Europe or the United States.

Although Communism, even with these reservations, is more widespread and stronger in Latin America than in the United States, much of it is merely an inchoate restless following, knowing little of Marxian theory, merely aware that the cost of beans has gone up.

But what points up these movements as dangerous is their control from outside. Nearly all outstanding Communist leaders, wherever you find them, have spent considerable time in the Soviet Union, being indocrinated, studying the technique of undermining the state and seizing power.

In all this intrigue and propaganda the Soviet authorities, during the nearly twenty years they have been messing around in Latin America, have, on occasion, been utterly ruthless with their own followers, turning the faucet of local Communist efforts on or off in accordance with the diplomatic strategy of the moment. They have even thrown these followers to the wolves when convenient for the aims of Russian national power. Most of the fanatical faithful have accepted this humiliating role without whimpering. On twenty-four-hour notice they have always been willing to reverse their stand on any given issue and argue quite as violently for the opposite side—a loyalty of complete self-abnegation and mental abdication, in which the search for personal dignity or truth plays no part.

The official Communist drive in Latin America began right after the Bolshevik Revolution. The Comintern appeared in 1919, and that very year the Soviets sent a stocky agent, well-heeled with Czarist jewels (lost en route), to Mexico on the pretext of buying henequén for binders. Actually his aim was to stir up revolution and disorder in order to keep the United States preoccupied nearer home in case the Soviets, then dominated by world-revolution theories, decided to carry the red banners of war into India. This brutal cynicism in trying to use other peoples as pawns, the callous disregard for the welfare of the Latin American people—this was typical of Soviet policy then as now.

The first short-lived Communist Party was founded in Mexico in 1917 under the direction of an exiled Hindu revolutionist, Rabindranath Roy, who paid for publishing the first Communist newspaper. Later he was stationed in southern Russia near the Afghan and Indian borders. Then he became Borodin's aid in China.

After 1925 Soviet efforts in Mexico were redoubled. Many outside Communist agents were utilized, from the United States, Peru, Chile, France and Italy. The tiny Communist sheet, *El Machete*, blossomed out into a big multicolored newspaper. Every sort of fellow-traveler organization was set up, from Communist Youth to Red Aid. A national peasants' league, headed by Urusulo Galván, affiliated with the Fromintern, the Moscow international.

Mexico had recognized the Soviet Union that year. Foreign Commisar Tchitcherin gleefully broadcast that Mexico would provide a Soviet base in the Americas. The first Soviet Minister, Petskovsky, a big bearded revolutionist, with tobacco-stained gnarled teeth, who had spent eight years in Siberian prisons under the Czars, met a frigid official reception. His tactlessness was astounding and typical. He attacked the official Mexican labor confederation (CROM) and its head, Luis N. Morones, a cabinet minister, and made the legation on Calle del Rín an active center for all radical forces opposed to the government. Labor and peasant leaders were sent in droves to Russia to be trained in revolutionary methods. There they and other Latin American protégés were housed under assumed names in the mysterious Hotel Lux. Among such was Hernán Laborde, railroad unionist, and the painter Xavier Guerrero, later a Moscow spearhead to Chile. Communist membership, hitherto insignificant, increased in Mexico and elsewhere.

Open Soviet aid in the form of a 50,000-ruble donation to striking railway workers, not members of the official labor confederation on government lines, was taken as a direct affront.

Madame Kollontai was sent to replace Petskovsky. She had been Minister to Norway, a famous revolutionist and author of *Red Love*—a charming cultivated woman. Though she played a most passive role, the Soviet Legation was raided and guests arrested.

By this time Soviet diplomacy had honey in its mouth. Socialistic nationalism had replaced revolutionary crusading abroad. Jewish Ukrainian medico Dr. Makar, who succeeded Kollontai, scarcely let a Mexican Communist step inside the legation and cultivated only the elite.

Toward the end of 1929 the Comintern ordered Communists in all countries to protest Mexican persecutions of labor and peasant leaders, who under President Portes Gil were being put through the wringer, shipped off to Islas Marías penitentiary and killed. Wild demonstrations before Mexican legations were staged the world over; windows were broken by stones; walls daubed with insults. When President-elect Ortiz Rubio toured the United States the Communists greeted his train everywhere with red banners, provocative placards and hoots.

Mexican Foreign Minister Genaro Estrada gave a statement to the press, ordering Makar out on the first boat. Otherwise he would be treated as an ordinary foreign citizen illegally in the country.

Makar, not directly notified or handed his passports, refused to take the insulting order seriously. He locked himself up in the legation, awaiting orders from Moscow. When he finally did try to sail from Vera Cruz, he was arrested for five hours. His baggage was seized and shipped back to Mexico City to be ransacked by police sleuths.

Soon both Catholics and Communists were being seized wholesale by the military commandant of the Federal District and stuffed into the military barracks. Among them was the painter David Siqueiros. Some prisoners were never heard of again, till pigs rooted up human bones beside a country road. The Communists were getting a real taste of tried-and-true Soviet methods.

The Assistant Soviet Commercial Attaché, left behind to liquidate about $5,000,000 of Soviet trade assets, was thrown into prison. There, his wife told me, his beard was yanked, his face spat upon. He was held incommunicado and secured his release only through the direct intercession of the United States Embassy, which for the Soviets must have been a pretty galling route to follow.

Under President Lázaro Cárdenas (1934-40) the situation changed. All organizations—Communist, fascist, liberal, reactionary—were once more allowed full democratic rights. The purgings and killings of the Calles and subsequent regimes were forsworn. The Communist Party came into the open again under the leadership of Laborde.

In 1937 the Communist Party tried to gain full control of the CTM, the new labor confederation, although this would have displaced fellow traveler Lombardo Toledano as its head. Failing, they forced the secession of unions with a combined membership of 300,000. But since this directly violated the new Popular Front tactics ordered by Moscow, Laborde found himself on the spot. Hastily he left for New York to confer with Earl Browder, United States Communist leader. Eating humble pie, Laborde confessed the error of his ways, and the unions, after disciplinary action, were readmitted to the CTM.

After World War II broke out, Russia was again recognized. The first incumbent was Constantin Oumanski, who set up a huge embassy staff in a palatial edifice, threw grandiose caviar and champagne parties with no trimmings lacking and put on a full-fledged propaganda drive up until his death, when the airplane crashed on which he was going to present credentials to Dictator Somoza of Nicaragua.

He rented propaganda halls, built a modernistic movie room at the embassy, provided radio stations and the press with canned Soviet cable news services, published magazines and literature, brought over Soviet musicians, poets, scientists, writers, world-tour bicyclists. Communist fellow travelers soon got control of various professional organizations of writers, architects, painters, et al.

Personally Oumanski demonstrated Soviet tractors and took orders for deliveries the Soviets could make as easily as they could hop over the moon. He and his associates, though it was still wartime, never missed an opportunity to sneer at the United States. After his death, activities were less blatantly pushed, and negotiations were opened with President Medina of Venezuela to permit the use of that country as the main Soviet propaganda center of the Americas.

The early Soviet diplomatic venture in Uruguay also turned sour. Likewise, Soviet trade offices—set up in Buenos Aires, kicked out of the country and re-established in Montevideo—came to nothing.

But if diplomacy failed, the Comintern still operated and the Montevideo legation had made much headway in propaganda with labor and cultural groups. Comintern agents continued to thread the continent— Communists recruited from all over Latin America, the United States, France, Italy and elsewhere. What with numerous military dictatorships and the general suppression of civil liberties in that epoch, the Communists mostly had to work underground. But denial of democracy plus depression provided them with increasing opportunities.

In 1938 the Popular Front candidate, Pedro Aguirre Cerda, was elected President of Chile with Nazi, Liberal, Conservative, Socialist and Communist support. Among other outside Communists present were the two Mexican painters Xavier Guerrero, long schooled in Moscow, and David Siqueiros, who had fled there after having been accused of misdeeds at the time of the assassination of Trotsky's secretary, an American citizen.

Chile was the South American country hardest hit before and during the world depression. Collapse had been complete and tragic. And that year of 1938 the Communists came to hold more seats in Congress than in any other country outside the Soviet Union.

In spite of an attempted coup by his Nazi supporters and constant friction with the Socialists and Communists, Aguirre Cerda, a quiet, compromise candidate, turned out to be, for all his mild manner, one of the finest and most levelheaded administrators Chile has ever known, a statesman of real stature.

In the next elections the coalition was widened to a "Democratic Front" to take in more progressive Liberals. Soon the new President, Juan Ríos, tried to swing to the Right, and all leftists, even most of the Radical Party, moved out of his government bag and baggage. But the Conservatives and most Liberals, whom he had hoped to attract, merely stood by delighted at the leftist breakup.

In the 1946 elections the Radicals, led by Gabriel González Videla, squeezed back into power by an extremely narrow margin—without Socialist or Liberal support—a mere plurality of 50,000 votes. These were provided by the Communist coal miners of Lota and the Communist nitrate and copper unions. The Communists were rewarded with three cabinet posts.

However, in 1947, about the time Italy and France purged Communists from their governments, González booted out his Communist ministers. Soon he declared martial law, arrested labor and Communist leaders wholesale, suppressed newspapers, got out the machine guns.

He was promptly faced by a stubborn coal strike. The government charged this was wholly political. The workers contended that, with inflation kicking up to New York levels, they could not eat on a dollar a day for ten hours' work in the undersea galleries.

A high light of the strike was the arrest and deportation of two Jugoslav diplomats accused of egging on the strikers. Relations were soon broken with Jugoslavia, the Soviet Union and Czechoslovakia. The army moved into the coal and nitrate fields and the North American copper mines.

Unfortunately this nation-wide destruction of civil liberties in Chile, the return to martial-law dictatorship, may throw the country into another open revolutionary period, with the likelihood of fascist or army elements seizing power; resulting, as in the thirties, in a full-fledged civil war. Unfortunately also, under the present dictatorial regime, the Communists, who in Chile have a strong secret setup, will continue to advance, while democratic forces will be increasingly emasculated.

During World War II, with the prestige of Soviet victory and the alliance with the United States, the Communist parties of Latin America grew considerably. Part of the reason was the freezing of wartime wages but no freezing of prices, so that inflation caused the cost of living to rise to unbearable heights. The Communists grew even faster underground in dictatorial countries, as in Brazil, than they did in the open. South American Communists at the time dutifully obeyed the Moscow countersign for war's duration, dutifully followed United States foreign policy, even to the extent of heaping high praise on dictators who had their jails full of Communists. In general, since the Soviet Union was an ally, the United States frowned on police suppression of Communists.

During the Soviet Alliance with Hitler, the war, for the Communists, had been wholly "imperialistic" and "capitalistic" against the people.

But with Soviet entry, overnight it became a holy crusade for "the proletarian fatherland," and Tory Winston Churchill became a noble leader fighting for the working class. Similarly in the democracies Stalin was no longer pictured as an ogre drinking baby's blood, but a nice fatherly man who loved to dandle poor orphans on his knee. At the behest of Washington, Dictator Batista in Cuba dropped tyrannical methods against Communists and took them into his government.

Right after the war the United States at Chapultepec tried to persuade all Latin American countries to recognize the Soviet Union. The Soviets, as Byrnes has pointed out, intended to keep out of the United Nations at the forthcoming San Francisco conference all countries who had merely broken relations with the Axis without declaring war, and were dead set against accepting any country that had no relations with the Soviets. Most South American countries hastened to recognize the Moscow government.

The Communist parties reversed their position as soon as the war was over and, even before tension arose, instigated a new wave of anti-United States propaganda. In Latin America the postwar Moscow mandate was for bigger and better collaboration with local dictators, businessmen, Conservatives, any element which would join in a common nationalist front against the United States and its "imperialism." This shift was well typified by Lombardo's Hope Rainbow speech.

The Communists now blamed the whole inflation and lack of consumer goods and needed machinery, not on the billions of aid the United States had sent and was sending to the Soviet Union and its satellites, but on the "fascist" Washington government which was boycotting Latin America—a deep-dyed "capitalist plot" to keep South America in eternal bondage.

The Communists for a time attacked Juan Perón of Argentina, and the Chilean Communists in the most cynical manner even faked up documents and false propaganda to prove that Perón intended to launch a South American war of conquest, a propaganda so cleverly done that it fooled even North American diplomats and newspapermen. They also gleefully pounced on Spruille Braden's intervention as a proof that Big-Stickism and imperialism had come back, that the inter-American system had been junked, that it was an intervention to help the Power Trust, Standard Oil and the meat packers. Most Argentines still believe these allegations. Even so, when Perón recognized the Soviet Union and played cat-mouse with a Soviet trade mission, the Communists tried to jump on his band wagon, with as loud shouts as they had used denouncing him. They even disbanded their unions, ordering members to join the Confederation.

Today, the biggest Communist movement due to previous dictatorship and to present terrible inflation—aside from aid from Moscow—is in Brazil.

There, during his first years, Dictator Getulio Vargas—originally supported in his illegal seizure of power by a tiny group of São Paulo Communists—labeled all opposition, even wealthy bankers, high army men and big Conservatives, as Communists.

Depression was so bad in Brazil, he actually was faced with one Communist-led revolt in 1935, although the military element involved probably knew nothing of Communism. The ramrod was Captain Luiz Carlos Prestes, who had been a revolter way back in 1929, then had hung out with Argentine Communists. In his 1935 attempt he was advised by a number of outside agents, among them Harry Berger, a German Communist, (who much later in the course of the war appeared as an organizer of "democratic" Free German organizations) and by Rodolfo Ghioldi, still head of the Communist Party in Argentina.

Vargas crushed this effort and instituted a general reign of terror. For a long time bullet-riddled bodies, by no means all of them Communist, were found in the woods near Rio. Some principals of the movement later turned up in Nazi concentration camps. Using this revolt and others as a pretext, Vargas suppressed elections and staged his totalitarian coup with the Green Shirt Integralistas.

Vargas' fifteen years of martial law, his complete uprooting of all democratic forces, removed all normal obstacles to the growth of Communism and it made steady progress underground. At the very end of his long reign, this hater of Communism, this lover of Hitler and Nazism, for so long the white-haired boy of the State Department, heaped with more good-will assistance than any decent ruler south, let Prestes out of prison and made a deal with those same Communists to try to hang on to power a little longer.

Prestes at once helped whip up the hysterical police-promoted "We Want Vargas" or "Queremista" movement and sought to stave off elections so Vargas could continue ruling, even though the country, sick of his personal dictatorship, wanted restoration of civil liberties, elections and representative government. Prestes and the Communists, however, were now allowed to address monster mass meetings in São Paulo, Rio, all over the country, meetings never before permitted. Most democratic groups remained disorganized or suppressed.

However, a reactionary military group, led by the two most ardent pro-Nazis of an earlier day, Generals Goes Monteiro and Eurico Gaspar Dutra, staged a coup in the name of "democracy." For a brief while a constitutional system was restored, some abbreviated liberties were granted. The inevitable harvest of Vargas' long suppression was an outpouring of 500,000 Communist votes and a Communist victory in various large cities.

This was the rather ironic aftermath in the country to which during the war the United States had given the most money, equipment, technical and military aid, where more troops were quartered and more cultural and economic enterprise carried on than in all the rest of Latin America put together. Somehow the glossy-print propaganda and the numerous North American representatives had failed to reach the masses. In fact, they stirred up considerable animosity because of failure to understand Brazilian psychology. Jim-Crowism at the army bases (where a dark-skinned Brazilian cabinet minister was shut out of the American officers' club), much splurging with North American officers' cars in a land devoid of gasoline, and in general the exclusive hobnobbing with only the upper strata—such things were not altogether popular.

Apparently, playing ball with dictators always has its ultimate price. Our wartime alliance with the Soviet Union has amply demonstrated that.

But in Brazil it also had a price for the Communists. Late in 1947 Dutra outlawed the Communist Party, and after Truman's visit seized an excuse to break off relations with Russia. Unfortunately this has meant not only the suppression of commerce but a restriction of everybody's liberties. Here again, happy as we are to see any spoke put in Communist aggression, the police methods now ruling Brazil play hob with all democratic elements. Only the Communists are able to carry on an underground struggle.

In Cuba, now having the third largest Communist movement (called "Popular Socialist"), the leftist leaders control the strong labor confederation.

Although entirely suppressed during the long Gerardo Machado dictatorship, the Cuban Communists kept alive a strong underground, a secret Communist Youth League and an Anti-Imperialist League. An

American Communist, who had organized students on university campuses, was sent down for a year to help in this secret effort.

Under the more democratic Grau (1933-34) before he was forced out by State Department and battleship pressure, the Communists came out into the open. It then grew evident that various labor officials were Communist. Apparently convinced the hour had struck to take over power, they carried on all sorts of disorder, called unnecessary strikes, seized factories and estates and did far more to overthrow a progressive democratic regime than they had ever done against Machado.

Grau lost patience. The police retaliated by massacring Communists parading with the ashes of Julio Antonio Mella, a young Communist assassinated in Mexico, some say by Dictator Machado, some say by another Soviet agent.

All the Communists succeeded in doing was to convince the United States government that Grau lacked popular support. The island was ringed around with thirty battleships, and another military coup by Batista became inevitable. As dictator, he gave the Communists jail or the firing squad for nearly ten years. But he crushed all democratic expression and the labor movement with equal ruthlessness. Not soon will I forget the burning alive by Batista's secret military police of my friend Octavio Seigle, a Conservative.

In spite of this harsh treatment by the dictator, the Communists largely boycotted the spontaneous 1935 general strike of workers, teachers, students, business and professional men—nearly the whole island—against Batista's brutalities and assassinations. When I reached there by plane, the harbor was utterly dead. Not a thing was moving—no cabs, no one to get my bags to the hotel. Had it not been for the Communists, Batista's harsh rule might have terminated then and there.

After that, ordered by Moscow to adopt the "popular front" line, the Communists suddenly sought the friendship of the exiled Grau and other democratic groups.

For a time Batista leaned toward the Fascists and Franco in Spain, but under State Department pressure, he suddenly went "democratic," restored civil liberties, permitted all parties to operate. The ban on Communists was lifted. Once more the Communist leader Poet Juan Marinello engaged openly in newspaper work, broadcast over the radio, held government posts. New York Communist publications then hailed Batista as a great forward democratic statesman.

After 1942 the local Communists were abetted by the Soviet Legation in Havana. The Soviets installed themselves in a luxurious building in the exclusive Vedado residential district, and their propaganda has since been consistent and intense. The fifty accredited members of the legation staff plus swarms of secret agents outnumbered all private Russian citizens in Cuba. As there are no Soviet property interests and no direct trade, the only reason for such an elaborate setup was propaganda.

The Soviet Legation gained control of Cuba's largest radio station—the only one allotted an international wave length. It spread propaganda literature, published excellent newspapers and magazines and provided free direct Soviet cable news to papers. Special relations were cultivated with all Cuban cultural organizations, all organized groups. Communist control of the labor confederation gave them direct access to the masses. This propaganda, even in the days of wartime alliance, emphasized the superiority of Soviet culture, freedom and power, the decadence of "capitalist" society, and handed out advice on how to combat it. Soviet armies on the front were not mercenary armies; they were "working-class" armies.

Right after the fall of Germany attacks from that source on the United States became open.

As early as September 9, 1945, R. Hart Phillips in the *New York Times* contrasted successful Soviet indoctrination of the Cuban masses through every conceivable organized channel with the meager, though more expensive, United States cultural efforts—usually carried on by folk not speaking the language, knowing nothing of Latin psychology and caring little about the people. Her remarks might be applied with equal force to every country on the continent:

"Little or no advantage has been taken of the channels already existing through which the various sectors of national life can be reached. Local organizations, endeavoring to promote friendship between Cuba and the United States complain they have received no co-operation from the Co-ordination Office. Propaganda has been directed almost exclusively to the upper classes. No concerted effort has been made to reach the masses." The United States' effort was handled as "a straight political job, which has had no penetrative effect on the Latin American people, has given them no sympathetic insight into the aims and ideas and feelings of the American people."

Today the Cuban Communists are among the best organized on the continent, and though President Grau has no love for them, he has had to make many concessions because of their control of the Cuban Confederation of Labor. Thus far he has resisted their demands for a key cabinet post. Their actual voting registration is 158,755 (as of October 1947), only about 8 per cent of the electorate.

Since the dictatorship of Gómez in Venezuela, the Communist Party there, well schooled in underground methods, has operated in the open. By the time of Medina, the Communists were making a deal with him to support the imposition of an official candidate, Ex-President López Contreras. Eventually this would have outlawed all democratic groups while giving the Communists a free hand. A move was on to make Venezuela, instead of Mexico, headquarters of official Soviet propaganda in the Americas. The 1944 Betancourt uprising nipped this in the bud. The Communists fought the Betancourt forces from behind barricades and were nearly the last elements to give in.

Today, despite new civil liberties and Betancourt's far-reaching social reforms, the Communist leader Bautista Fuenmayor and the "Marxist" Rodolfo Quintero label the government "Trotskyite" and "Social Fascist," mystic words that arouse great frothing at the mouth among the faithful. These have been repeatedly hurled at Betancourt by the Communist press of New York and in Moscow, where any chance to attack him is never missed—and if none exists, he is attacked anyway. His free and democratic regime has received a worse barrage of vituperation than any of the out-and-out dictatorships of the continent.

The best Communist allies in Latin America have been low standards of living, widespread poverty, the terrible inflation, the suppression of liberties by ruthless dictators, the failure to receive postwar commodity goods and machinery from the United States. Merciless governments, suppressing freedom and democratic institutions, even though in the name of fighting Communism, it is now amply clear, have fostered even more Communism than they suppressed. Communism has then ramified underground, through intrigue, secret plots and penetration of native organizations. It has gathered prestige for fighting a type of government loathsome to all, taking risks and daring where others do not. Most such underground resistance and propaganda methods are impossible for democratic elements, indeed are not democratic in principle. This has meant the destruction of the one sure barrier to Communism.

The whole Communist drive is closely connected with present world chaos and the failure of the world's productive life to get on its feet. But in spite of bad conditions in Latin America, and the appeal Communism has made to underprivileged groups, most people south have suffered too long from feudal oppressors, from militarism and dictator-ship, to be enamored of any system imitating such methods even for other ends. Communism of the rigid Moscow doctrinaire sort does not jibe with the Latin spirit. The long struggle for democracy and civil rights, still not victorious in so many places, is deeply rooted. People are far less regimented, more individualistic in their thinking, than in the United States. For more than a hundred years they have never stopped fighting for political and economic liberty. Only desperation might drive them to put on the new strait jacket of Communism.

In spite of the grave difficulties of the moment the industrial growth of Latin America within the past few years has been remarkable. It is an expanding, not a contracting world, and this can provide, through wise leadership, a steady improvement in standards of living, better wages, more public works, improved opportunities for the middle class, limitless possibilities for new industrialists. So long as the governments move toward a progressive enlargement of free institutions, happier living conditions, proper development of home resources, the Communist theater, in spite of the big stage provided by the present chaotic situation, will steadily shrink.

The greatest danger at the present moment is precisely the war being waged against Communism. The worst dictators of the continent, Somoza, Trujillo, Carías, have been the first to seize on this slogan to buttress up their shaky positions and impose new terror on the people. This is the sad road now being followed by Dutra in Brazil and González in Chile. The examples may spread. There is now even real danger of a night of black military oppression descending over much of the continent and destroying the great democratic progress made during the war and the postwar. If people are thereby made desperate, they may turn to Communism in earnest.

XIII Democratic Profiles

Joaquín García Monje

His post-office box is Lestra X, San José, Costa Rica. His office: two rooms on a side street. A small faded sign:

REPERTORIO AMERICANO
Joaquín García Monje.

The chief reason I stopped off in San José on my last trip through Central America was to see Don Joaquín, whom I first met over twenty years ago.

The street shutters were closed. It was still siesta time, but the door opened promptly, and there stood Don Joaquín in person. Except for a slight stoutness he looked as young as ever—medium height, neat suit, light skin, dark eyes, brown hair, firm, even features. There is always a dignified aloofness about him, as is true of most Costa Ricans, and he has a cosmopolitan intellectual manner, an air of competent intelligence—impressions strengthened the longer one knows him. Except for the setting he might be taken for a businessman, doctor, lawyer, engineer. He happens to be, among other things, a professor. So far as I know, he has never traveled outside Costa Rica, but he reads the chief languages and his mind belongs to the world. He is at home in all cultures. He has the universality of the best European intellectuals.

His humble office was helter-skelter, piled high with books, newspapers, clippings, paper, string, glue and tall tottering stacks of *Repertorio Americano,* the bimonthly magazine he has edited for thirty years.

For a decade or more he was head of the National Library, which with a limited budget he made over into one of the best organized institutions in all Latin America. He has always held a chair in the University of Costa Rica, and practically every student in that institution in the past thirty-five years has studied under him. Thus he has personally guided a generation and more of Costa Rican writers, intellectuals, statesmen and leaders, and I never heard one of them speak of him except with great respect and boundless affection.

But this influence extends far beyond the local scene. Few persons are better known throughout the entire Spanish-speaking world. No visitor to Costa Rica, who knows anything at all, fails to make a beeline to his door.

He founded *El Repertorio* at a time when there was little intercommunication among the various Latin American countries, and at a time of intense feeling against the United States because of marine interventions. His goal was continental understanding, the spread of continental culture, to bring artists, intellectuals and friends of human liberty of all countries together, make them aware of one another's creative efforts and stimulate them by a wider audience. Progress in one land should encourage them elsewhere. He has consistently attempted to promote cultural interchange and understanding, to make the whole continent conscious of itself. As a result the *Repertorio* became the one magazine of Latin America with international circulation and influence.

Soon he had contributors from every country. For three decades the magazine has carried articles, stories and poems from every outstanding leader of thought and progress in the Americas. He has been especially cordial to new writers, and many since become well known saw their first words printed in *El Repertorio*. Palacios of Argentina, Betancourt and Gallegos of Venezuela, Ortiz of Cuba, Icaza of Ecuador, Caso of Mexico, Sánchez of Peru are some of the important personalities who have graced the pages of Don Joaquín's magazine.

Mostly he has eschewed political controversy. "Politics always divide and embitter," he told me. "Culture, creative writing, the arts—such things unite the peoples."

Not that he has turned out a mere ivory-tower magazine. If at times Don Joaquín has been quite too generous with his space to third-rate poetesses and immature essayists, some of the great enlightened documents of the continent, which have set forth new goals, were issued for the first time in *El Repertorio*. He published many of the first writings of Haya de la Torre during his long period of exile.

If the magazine's chief emphasis has been on culture, he has ever had a ready eye for all worthy causes. He has been one of the continent's most consistent apostles of political and economic democracy. Thus he has always opened his columns to refugees escaping from various tyrannies. He has fought the ephemeral dictators of Latin America from beginning to end, has exposed them, has made their names anathema in all free lands. Somoza, Carías, Trujillo and the earlier fallen tyrants, Gómez, Machado, Ubico, Díaz of Nicaragua, have felt the lash of his condemnation. And throughout the continent that verbal punishment carried weight.

Although he has always supported the United States policies he considered wise, he was a staunch opponent of dollar diplomacy and marine interventions. He threw open the doors for any articles in favor of the Nicaraguan hero, Agusto César Sandino, in the battle against the Marines. On the other hand he was of invaluable help to the United States cultural attaché during the war.

But on this visit I found Don Joaquín a trifle sad and pessimistic. Maybe it's the state of the world and of Costa Rica where factional politics are growing steadily more bitter. "In Costa Rica," he remarked, "today you must be either a Communist or a Fascist, and sometimes you are called by both names."

He feels the United States is now missing great opportunities. During the war the attaché co-operated with him, and Don Joaquín worked day and night for the United Nations cause in a land recently poisoned by an unusual amount of Axis propaganda. But the new attaché who came down in 1946 never even looked him up. Nothing much is being done now.

Don Joaquín smiled wryly. "It gives you the feeling that the United States was interested in Latin America and good neighborliness only when it needed us during the war."

He does not wish cultural relations to slump. Latin America, he told me, wants to know much more about the United States than guns and warships, the eternal propaganda of the glossy print of the war period. "We've always known you are powerful, and it does not amuse us. We want to know more of your culture, which many down here feel doesn't amount to much. An article on Poe or Paine, Emerson or Whitman, he feels, would do more for good neighborliness than all those constant pictures of American tanks and planes. The United States ought to distribute more and better translations of its literature: the works of Jefferson, Thomas Paine, Henry George, Veblen, Steinbeck, Dos Passos, Upton Sinclair, Sinclair Lewis.

It was hard to imagine the State Department ever sending out the authors Don Joaquín mentioned.

If American embassies, he argued, would distribute liberal quantities of such translations free, such purchases would give the necessary underpinning for local publishers to bring them out, for booksellers to stock them, and many intellectuals, too poor to afford the books they need, would be benefited. Such books and the land in which they were written would be treasured.

According to García, the Soviet Union is now doing just that. Not only is it already flooding Costa Rica with propaganda in books, pamphlets and magazines devoted to the past history and the culture of the Russian people, but it is putting out in Spanish a great "library" of Russian classics and contemporary writers to be distributed throughout Latin America. Don Joaquín, though chary of political implications, indicated he was all in favor of such dissemination of thought and culture.

"But the United States is missing all such opportunities," he told me. He finds it hard to understand this is so. "We thought during the war that the United States really would stand up for democracy around the world. Now we are not at all sure. We have certainly been let down all over Latin America." He voiced a constant query one hears: "Why do North American diplomats invariably hobnob with known fascist elements, with the most reactionary elements, the powerful, the officials, and ignore the people, the writers, the arists, the professors?"

But Don Joaquín keeps hammering away at the old stand—as I write two issues of his magazine have just come through the mails. He keeps the light in the lighthouse burning that all the lands may see—his own metaphor. He has sought to create a great cultural empire, to promote peaceful inter-Americanism, to influence the more enlightened spirits of the continent. That has been his goal from the first—and that goal he achieved. Although the number of copies printed is not large, *El Repertorio* is read by most of those who write, who think, who lead. Its influence has been consistent and prolonged.

If any man in the Americas has better served the cause of democracy, of true internationalism, of enlightenment, and the growth of liberty and justice in the Americas, I cannot name him. In his quiet unassuming way, long ago, without fanfare, with no loud drums, with meager resources, Don Joaquín set to work to promote a widespread love of democracy and freedom, of free discussion and honest opinion. His efforts did much to prepare the southern countries psychologically for their role in the great conflict that so recently shook the world.

Much credit over this long period goes to Costa Rica and its various governments. Besides his public posts and his professorships, he received for a time a small subsidy for the magazine. So far as I know, no Costa Rican government has ever interfered with Don Joaquín or the ideas he has upheld or the articles he has published. His patient labor could not have been carried on except in a country as stable, as enlightened, as generally tolerant, as Costa Rica has been over the years. *El Repertorio*, over that long period, could not have appeared without interruption in any other land of Latin America except possibly Colombia or Mexico. Thus the consistent policy and the uninterrupted role of the magazine are an honor not only to García but for the land in which he lives.

Vicente Saenz

When I arrived in Mexico early in 1946, I received a phone call from Vicente Saenz, whom I had not seen for many years. Would I meet with him and a group of exiled Nicaraguan patriots at the eternal light of Mexico's Independence monument on the Paseo de la Reforma and there participate in a public ceremony of placing a wreath in memory of the Nicaraguan hero, Augusto César Sandino, on the anniversary of his assassination?

My acquaintance with Don Vicente goes back twenty years. Today he is the most saintly, determined apostle I know. He is respected (or disliked) by many governments; he is a force in the political life of the continent; and his Central American Union, with headquarters in Mexico City, has great influence everywhere.

When I first knew him, he was employed by a North American oil company in Mexico. One fine day he threw up his post and told me henceforth he was going to dedicate his life to free government in Central America.

He took this stand at the time of American Marine interventions, at a time of threatened war in Central America, at a time of absurd, unpleasant dictatorships holding those countries to a condition of terror and backwardness. His task seemed well-nigh hopeless. Except for his native land, Costa Rica, the region presented a dismal picture. But through the years he has worked patiently and persistently, and many of the seeds he sowed have grown into sturdy plants.

He started publishing articles, writing books, organizing groups to work for the freedom of the various peoples. He built up good will with the Mexican authorities for exiles driven from their homes. He opposed armed interventions. He fought the dictators.

His literary style is lucid and strong, his material always perfectly documented. Only by hard facts, he believes, can truth prevail and a good cause survive and go forward. There is not an ounce of demagogy in him. He is passionate in his beliefs but restrained and emphatic in his utterances, and always he is fearless.

When the Spanish Civil War broke, he saw that the rise of reaction in that country would delay his work in the Americas and perhaps make it unrealizable for a generation. He went to Spain, fought for the Republic, fought the Nazi-fascist intervention at a time when the statesmen of the democracies were fearfully temporizing. He wrote articles, made speeches, wrote a vivid account of the struggle and its implications for the freedom of the peoples and for the peace of the world.

The battle in Spain was lost, and he returned to Costa Rica to discover that a network of Gestapo and Franco intrigue had been thrown about his own country. A land long noted for its free institutions was falling under the spell of the doctrines of the so-called master race and all its hatemongering. He set to work to rouse his people to the danger that threatened their lives and security. He broke the Nazi ring. He swept Costa Rica into a passionate anti-fascist stand, and it was the first country in the Americas after Pearl Harbor—ahead of even the United States—to declare war on the Axis.

In Mexico Don Vicente married an American girl, born in Colombia, educated in France and naturalized in the United States. Both teach in the university and public schools, give lectures. They work together on writings and translations. Saenz founded the Central American Union and publishes a pocket magazine with the same name.

The headquarters of this organization, located on Nile Street in one of the quieter residential districts of the Mexican capital, is the center for all sorts of people from Central America, from all the five nations and beyond. It is lined with shelves filled with books and propaganda material. Here are held weekly dinners to which are invited distinguished visitors, newspapermen, writers, diplomats, statesmen. In 1946 the new Colombian Minister, who attended an honorary dinner there the same night I did, made it a point to visit the Union even before he had presented his credentials to the Mexican government.

In the Union problems of Central America are talked over, correspondence read, measures agreed on. The organization now has branches in all five countries, although in the dictatorial lands, such as Nicaragua and Honduras, the groups have to work underground or periodically remove their headquarters to some adjacent more friendly country.

The first aim has been to fight the dictatorial regimes and help install democratic government; secondly, to support and strengthen democratic trends in those countries which have made progress. The more distant goal is to bring the peoples of five nations closer together and to work for their eventual union. With the resultant reduction in governmental, diplomatic and military overhead, the wiping out of economic barriers and the creation of a large mass market for products, the industrial expansion of the whole area, and hence the improvement in the living standards of the people, would become a reality. In fact, such a Central America would be as large as Germany and have great resources.

At present this union is still only a remote possibility, but Saenz has used the theme to instill in all Central Americans a common regional patriotism and loyalty, to promote common ideas and hopes and to make all the peoples eager to co-operate in working toward free government and better living conditions. It is a task for all five peoples.

Saenz's efforts have born fruit. In Costa Rica he has put the brakes on new fascist and Communist trends, helped create a common democratic front and bolstered the traditions of free elections. A long-needed labor code was drawn up, an effort in which the Communists, the democratic elements and the Catholic Church co-operated. The efforts of Saenz and the Central American Union, its propaganda and educational efforts played a real part in the overthrow in 1944 of Dictator Martínez of Salvador. Although Martínez was able to put down an army conspiracy against his tyranny, he could not face the united unarmed protests of the people. As a result today one of the leaders of Saenz's local Unionist organization edits one of San Salvador's leading dailies, and his brother became a member of the Salvadorean cabinet. The battle for democracy in Salvador is far from won, but what progress there is has been in good part due to Vicente's efforts.

Similarly the Union played a real part in the overthrow of the Ubico dictatorship in Guatemala. That, too, was a massed unarmed people's strike against tyranny, and Ubico, despite his great array of guns, Lend-Lease tanks and planes, saw his power crumble away in the twinkling of an eye. Some of the cabinet members of the present democratic Arévalo regime were active members of the Union and still support it.

One of Arévalo's first acts was to celebrate a frontier conference with President Castañeda of Salvador to lay plans, pending amalgamation of all Central America, for a provisional union of the two countries, through the elimination of customs and passport barriers, a common central bank and identical currency, and a joint educational system. Though Saenz is not a Guatemalan, he was honored by the new government by being sent as a special delegate to the United Nations.

Saenz's plans for overthrowing Somoza in Nicaragua and Carías in Honduras, the two remaining overt dictatorships based on graft, terror and totalitarian methods, went awry, and the two lands for a brief spasm were engulfed in even more torture and oppression. But the two governments are now out of tune with the march of events in Central America. They cannot survive. They are dark blots on the fair shield of Latin America that Saenz is trying hard to rub out.

In his work Saenz has had the active co-operation of the Mexican government and most of the press, which has eagerly published all articles and news emanating from the Union center. The government has been friendly to Central American refugees.

In May 1946 the Mexican government sent a special emissary south to talk over the possibility of Central American union—to start with the governments of Guatemala, Salvador and Costa Rica. The obvious aim was to find a formula for the elimination of the Carías and Somoza dictatorships as a prerequisite for the democratization and freedom of the whole region. All democratic elements in the various nations were tipped off to make special propaganda efforts, hold meetings, pass resolutions favoring democracy and union.

There is little doubt that much of Central America has been and is a benighted, backward part of the Americas, though nature has endowed it richly and has provided it with some of the most beautiful scenery and most fertile land on earth. Harsher evils are far from eliminated even from the freer lands, although in only a few years progress in Guatemala has been amazing. But in Nicaragua and Honduras people are still starving and enslaved, progress stifled. In 1946 I found both countries, despite some new roads, many new barracks, a few public works, a few new crops, economically and morally as backward as twenty years ago, which is saying a good deal. They are dark islands in the general awakening of Latin America. In the United States we also have our dark islands, our Bilbos and Gene Talmadges, and can understand the problem.

But what progress, enlightenment and hope have arisen in Central America these later years are in good part due to Saenz's long persistent fight for freedom. He is known throughout the continent and is beloved by all who know him.

Victor Raul Haya de la Torre

We sat in the dark, our feet dangling, on the end of a little pier at the foot of a deep garden that fronts a cove of the sea in Miraflores, a suburb of Lima, Peru. The stocky man beside me was being hunted by the police. Most of his friends and fellow leaders were in prison or in exile. That was in 1934.

My friend was Victor Raul Haya de la Torre, head of the Apra movement of Peru. He had begun at the time of World War I as a student leader, his struggle for a free Peru had already cost him seventeen years of his life and here he was in hiding. Though he had the vast majority of the people behind him, though he had actually been elected President, at the moment the chances of victory seemed darker than ever, though one would not think so from Haya's easy laughter that night on the pier.

The brutal dictatorship of Sánchez Cerro had left bloody welts on the land. He had been assassinated, but the arbitrary rule of General Óscar Benavides, based on a military coup and without legal or constitutional sanction and operating without benefit of Congress or any popular representation, was in the saddle.

For a brief while, when I first arrived in Peru that year of 1934, the Apristas, the members of the People's Party, had had a brief taste of freedom, though Haya himself had had to remain in hiding. But now the police and the army were smashing up the Apra press, the People's Houses, the co-operatives and Apra restaurants, and were jailing or exiling all friends of freedom.

That night, with the sea silver under the moon and the waters slapping the sands beneath us, Haya talked over his plans for a democratic Peru, the liberation of the Indians from serfdom, their incorporation into the political and economic life of the country, the reform of the great plantation system. Despite the difficulties of the moment, the new persecutions, Haya was calm and good-humored, confident of final success, not at all disheartened. . . .

Thirty years ago, as a result of democratic doctrines of World War I, a student's movement, originating in Argentina, swept over the Latin American world. The center of revolt in Peru—back in 1918— was the University of Trujillo and Haya was the main leader. Later, in the days of Dictator Leguía, the movement spread to other institutions, including venerable San Marcos in Lima, the oldest New World institution. Probably few in those first years realized that most university reforms would require thirty years to implant and are still absent from much of the continent. Not until 1945 was Haya's Popular Party able to force through the creation of a law for university freedom.

Back in 1918 and for some years after students were massacred, imprisoned, exiled. For the next twenty-seven years Haya de la Torre, except for one brief period, was in prison, in exile or in hiding.

When dumped out of the country penniless by Leguía, he traveled through adjacent Latin American countries, the United States and Europe, including the Soviet Union. Most of the time was spent studying and writing in England, Germany and France. He completed his education, took graduate work in the leading universities of those three lands. Weimar saw him, the Sorbonne saw him, Oxford and Cambridge saw him.

In Paris he gathered together a small group of Spanish American exiles and founded the Popular Revolutionary Alliance of America— Apra—which in Peru is now called the Popular Party and controls Congress and a good share of all local governments. Then it was but a handful of visionaries far from their homeland, far across the sea from a continent of dictatorships which they faced only with their words and their hope.

The program laid down in Paris was militant though constructive. It was anti-imperialist, anti-Church, anti-militarist. It stood for revindication of Indian rights, for land reform, for labor's rights, for political democracy, for social welfare and for industrialization and progress. Haya wrote constantly on these themes for publication all over the continent.

Soon the organization spread over the whole New World, and its ideas have been a great leaven at work in Cuba, Venezuela, Colombia, Chile and various other countries. Carlos Hevia, provisional President after the first term of Grau San Martín, was an officer of the Apra Party in

Cuba. Other prominent leaders were at one time Apristas in various countries.

Haya had learned all that Europe could teach him just then, and in the twenties he moved back to the New World, closer to home base, finding refuge in Mexico, where he stayed for a considerable period. I saw a good deal of him there. At that time the Communists launched bitter attacks against him and his propaganda. The Cuban Communist, José Antonio Mella, also in exile in Mexico and later assassinated, was detailed to the attack and dutifully wrote a scorching pamphlet against Haya and the Aprista movement, which the Communist Party, the Comintern and the Soviet legations in Mexico and Uruguay distributed by tons throughout Latin America.

Haya tried to persuade the Soviet Legation to lay off and quit confusing and dividing the people in their struggle for freedom, but he got nowhere. Subsequently Communist leaders in Peru as elsewhere on the continent, co-operated with various reactionary governments; at other times they came running to Haya and the Apristas trying to wheedle them into a Popular Front. But Haya hewed his independent line and maintained his party stand throughout all those difficult days.

Not until Leguía's downfall in the early thirties was Haya able, after nearly fifteen years of exile, to return to Peru. By then Aprista organizations were publishing newspapers and magazines all the way from the United States to Argentina, even in Europe and in China. An international Apra news service (Colombia) had been developed. By that time Haya had world-wide reputation as a leader and writer. His articles were being eagerly reproduced everywhere. And in Peru the organization, though illegal, had taken root and had gained the backing of most of the population. On his return to his native land, Haya was received in the Lima bull ring by the biggest popular manifestation ever staged in Peru. Wherever he went he was almost torn to pieces by the people hungry for freedom so long blacked out.

He worked to organize his party better, borrowing ideas from his political observations in many countries. He built it up block by block, cell by cell, district by district. In every block in Lima was installed a household captain with full instruction for any contingency—a meeting, a demonstration, an election, a political crisis, a strike. He knew what to do, how to take command of the block, how to direct the people. This served Apra in good stead when it was driven underground again.

For it was still a difficult time. Haya ran for the Presidency and he and the rest of the ticket probably received an overwhelming majority. But power was seized by the upstart mulatto colonel, Sánchez Cerro, a man of daring and ignorance, who killed people right and left and tried to cement his dictatorship by stirring up war with Ecuador and Colombia.

Haya's followers and some military backers wished to start a revolution. But he calmed them down, forbade overt action, declared that if they kept on quietly organizing and educating the people, the partisans of democracy would eventually take over the country without the bloodshed and destruction. The curse of Latin America, he told them, had always been revolution. The winner was then faced, thanks to destruction and bitterness, with impossible tasks of reconstruction and often failed. Haya was a great admirer of Gandhi.

We talked about this the last time I saw him in Lima. "Over the years," he told me, "it has been a difficult decision to make—not to fight; to take unfair blows, to lose elections honestly won. It has been a question at times whether we would not be wiped out completely. Sometimes it was not easy to carry on with our work of educating the people. But that is what they needed—education, not more force. There were dark moments. It was not easy to counsel patience when we could have gambled and probably won by fighting. But look what we have won. Look what we have now, without bloodshed—democratic liberties, a free press, free parties, free assemblage. We have a five to one majority in the country."

Certainly under Sánchez Cerro's tyranny, the Apristas were subjected to frightful persecution—wholesale massacres of students, peasants, workers and others. For a time Haya was in prison and little hope for his life was entertained. Probably only world-wide petitions for his safety saved him. He had made firm friends, many in powerful governing positions in other lands all around the world. At that moment in New York I spent considerable time getting protest letters and cables sent off to Dictator Sánchez Cerro.

Two attempts were made to assassinate Sánchez Cerro, and the second was successful. When I reached Peru in 1934, after his death, General Óscar Benavides, a heavy-handed, not wholly unjust military man, had seized the Palace.

There was no doubt by then that Haya's party had become well-organized. Haya had softened his more negative ideas, particularly earlier attacks on the army and the Church. Younger army elements had begun to swing to Apra's side. Many humble rural priests became sympathizers. Aprismo had rooted itself in the imagination of the whole people. Every rock and wall and mountainside of Peru was daubed with the word Apra. In Trujillo I even saw dogs with their ribs painted "APRA." The Civilistas, the reactionary landholders and the clique of "aristocratic" families that had ruled Peru with the help of an obedient army since before Independence days were shaking in their boots. Soon, after a short interlude of freedom under Benavides, new persecutions came fast and furious.

I was in Peru when the Benavides government finally showed its teeth. The police began closing down newspapers, jailing Aprista editors, raiding Aprista People's restaurants, raiding the so-called People's Houses, or headquarters and meeting halls. In Lima the police gave to the press a picture of a cache of secret arms from the main People's House. It was laughable: a few wires, a flashlight, pliers, monkey wrench, some round objects labeled bombs but merely tin cans from the restaurant, a few cartridges, several rusty pistols and one shotgun.

Apristas were rounded up on every side. News reporter Ciro Alegría, after a spell in prison, escaped to Chile, where he came down with t.b. but won the Chilean national novel prize. Sánchez, already famous for his history of Peruvian literature and other brilliant works, also escaped to Chile, where he became head editor of Ercilla, at that time the biggest publishing house in Latin America. Manuel Seone, in 1946 a delegate to the welfare commission of the UN, shot his way out of the Lima stadium when two secret police tried to arrest him, and fled to Argentina.

Later Benavides decided to permit elections. The Apra Party, however, was outlawed, not permitted to participate. The Apristas thereupon threw their support to the lone opposition candidate, a writer and university professor with no political machine. To everybody's surprise, when the votes began to be counted, he was 'way out in the lead beyond Benavides' officially supported candidate, Manuel Prado. At once vote counting was halted. The government decreed that since the successful candidate had been secretly supported by Apra, his candidacy was illegal, and he could not take office. Benavides, who had been governing wholly without Congress, now called together a rump group which hastily declared Prado elected.

Again Peru quivered on the brink of revolution. But once more Haya held his impatient followers in check, counseled peace and patience.

Many followers grew utterly discouraged. People said that his tame submission spelled the doom of the movement.

Prado finished out his illegal, unconstitutional term, a President occupying a stolen office. Haya continued in hiding in Lima, secretly directing his party's efforts. Among Prado's supporters were many known Fascists and Nazi propagandists. Communist leaders accepted jobs in his government. Prado declared war on the Axis, but his support of the United States was lukewarm.

During this period Haya threw overboard his previous opposition to United States' "imperialism" and became an ardent supporter of the Allied cause. Soon he and his party were constantly prodding his government into more active efforts in support of the democratic nations. Soon he was a thorn in Prado's side. Prado's fascist deals were exposed, such as the illegal sale of government vessels to the Castillo government of Argentina. At the time Haya continued to demand the strengthening of democratic government in all the Americas. It would be a hollow victory if Peru won the battle in Europe, and all democracy were lost at home.

To everybody's surprise, in 1945 Prado permitted elections, but the Apra party still remained outlawed, though many of its members filled up the ticket for Congress and local offices in other opposition parties. The official candidate, an army general Eloy Ureta, of inadequate cultural caliber, with strong Fascist backing, was opposed by a well-known diplomat and teacher, Dr. Bustamante y Rivero.

In the final week of the campaign the ban on the Apristas was lifted. Haya and his followers then swept through the country, holding the biggest campaign meetings ever pulled together, in behalf of Bustamante. Their candidate won by a fivefold majority.

Since Prado himself had sat on a stolen throne for six years, nobody expected that the will of the people would be recognized. But to the surprise of all, Bustamante was allowed to take office without bloodshed. Legal and constitutional government was re-established in Peru for the first time since near the beginning of the century. Congress now had a full Bustamante majority and most of this was made up of Apristas. The Popular Party was given three cabinet portfolios: Agriculture, Finance and Fomento. Free newspapers and magazines sprang up. Free political assemblages were openly celebrated.

The Apristas abroad came home. They came flocking back from Mexico, from Panama, Argentina, Chile, Colombia, the United States, from the far corners of the world. For the first time in nearly half a century, the jails were free of political prisoners. One of those who came out—after being behind bars for fourteen years—was José (Pepe) Melgar, the student who had made the first attempt to assassinate Dictator Sánchez Cerro. I saw a lot of him. He had studied in prison, and emerged to hold a newspaper job and then an important position in the Ministry of Fomento. For all his imprisonment, he held no bitterness. He was free and easy and jolly with people and had made a perfect and amiable readjustment.

In 1946, in the office of *La Tribuna,* the leading Apra daily, I talked with Haya, who has declined any public office for himself. He was full of constructive plans for industrializing the country.

In May 1946 he journeyed to Chile to attend the second international conference of democratic and people's parties. This organization, now assuming permanent continental dimensions, had delegates from Argentina, Uruguay, Ecuador, Venezuela, Colombia, Peru, Chile and Guatemala. It included the official government party of Venezuela and the semiofficial party of Peru, as well as parties in the governing coalition of Chile. Haya has been working in close harmony with Betancourt of Venezuela, and both are fighting, along with other democratic groups, against the domination of Communists, fascists and the feudal Conservatives. Thus the new organization of parties represents a prodemocratic bloc on the continent, opposed to Communism, dictatorship, imperialism and militarism.

In this conference Haya was the leading personality, and though he is now more identified with strictly Peruvian affairs, his influence still retains continental proportions, perhaps even more than before. He was unanimously elected head of the permanent organization—a new confederation of democratic parties of the continent with headquarters in Caracas, Venezuela.

Late in 1946 Haya made a speaking tour through Latin American universities, north to Panama, Colombia, Costa Rica, Guatemala. Later he attended the *Herald Tribune* forum in New York.

Eventually Haya will probably stand or fall according to whether he finally wins the battle with the die-hard Civilistas in Peru itself and can carry out the promised labor, land and political reforms he has so long advocated.

Early in 1947 the issue sharpened, and the three Aprista cabinet ministers were obliged to resign. Though the Apristas have come out on top in nearly all off-year Congressional elections, greatly increasing their strength in the legislative branch, Bustamante—a very mystical character—has been drawing steadily toward the old army and reactionary cliques.

When we were in Peru in late 1946 this trend was already too apparent. The army general then in charge of police was a holdover from previous dictatorship, notorious for his abuses, and he was showing his teeth. The Foreign Office was also in the hands of an old-line reactionary, close to the Bolivian tin cartel. No nation on the continent had meaner, more trying requirements for outside visitors than Peru at the moment. Traveling in the country areas has become a torture.

Even in the days of the Sánchez Cerro and Benavides dictatorships Peru was a pleasant place to roam around in. But this time not even in Soviet Russia or Hitler's German Reich did we run into so much police unpleasantness. After long weary bus or train rides, however late at night we arrived, before getting a room, washing up, going to the toilet or eating, we and any other foreigners were forthwith marched off under guard to police headquarters and subjected to a long process of filling out forms and answering questions, sometimes with police standing over us with hands on their pistols.

It was already a time of mounting tensions. The Apristas are again in a ticklish position. They have the majority vote in the country. They largely control Congress. They control the university. But the Civilistas, the army, the old feudal elements are pushing hard, and in spite of Haya's long efforts to achieve a progressive democratic regime without violence, the Apristas may yet be forced into an armed fight.

Haya is one of the continent's outstanding personalities. His goal is a free, modernized Peru—a democratic Peru—free government in the Americas, and a Latin America united on a nonimperialistic basis and co-operating on a sovereign basis with the United States. It is the old Simón Bolívar dream. It is much nearer realization than it was a century ago.

XIV Mosaic

Regions

LATIN AMERICA is made up of twenty independent nations, plus Puerto Rico, a North American colony, and the Canal Zone. Imbedded in it are vestiges of earlier European imperialism, fragments of the British, Dutch and French empires, and the Virgin Islands. Implanted in it are military, air and naval bases of the United States. The whole area is approximately three times that of the United States; the population slightly less than that of the United States.

But Latin America, besides being made up of twenty nations, is a bundle of distinct regions. Sometimes national boundaries slash in different directions, but each of these regions has its own economic, geographic, climatic and sometimes racial unity.

First of all, South America has two major regions—the Pacific world and the Atlantic world, separated by the great Andean Cordilleras. The Pacific area of Chile, Bolivia, Peru and Ecuador, even the west coast of Colombia, long remained more isolated, less in contact with the western European world. The long trip around Cape Horn was always treacherous, especially in sailing days. Even in the Spanish era this portion of the continent was more tied in with the China trade, usually thought of more in connection with the Orient.

Not until this century was the West Coast yanked out of its semi-isolation. In 1914 the Panama Canal opened. The first boat through was loaded with Chilean nitrates for the battlefields of Europe. Not until this century was the first railroad pushed across the Andes. Not until this war did Peru have even a highway through to the Amazon region, the largest portion of the country.

Today, with new roads, railways and airplane services, the two southern half-worlds, the Pacific and the Atlantic, are no longer severed. The unity of the continent is being created; nature at last is being circumvented.

297

With new ties and communications between Chile and Argentina, Chile and Bolivia, Argentina and Bolivia, Peru and Bolivia, a new southern economic, semipolitical region is coming into life which has the combined resources for full prosperity and strength to become one of the great centers of civilization. Here, in a zone comprehending Argentina, Paraguay, Uruguay, Bolivia and Chile, and tied in closely with southern Andean Peru and southwestern Brazil, is a flexible area with reciprocal production, with almost every known product and every conceivable climate. The great breadbasket of Argentina and Uruguay provides for the food deficiencies of the other regions. The mines and tropical products of Bolivia, Paraguay and Brazil can feed the industries of Argentina and Chile. The iron of Chile, and eventually the vast deposits in Paraguay, can serve all the countries. The Chaco oil is a major world source, and more oil is being found in Argentina and Chile, clear down to Cape Horn. The gradual amalgamation and development of this region on a mutually profitable scale is inevitable and highly desirable.

Most of Brazil, the vast Amazon world, represents a region apart. Here is the only great full-fledged tropical nation on earth. The Amazonas, with their mighty expanse of forests, great stretches of meadowland, some larger than Texas, in all more extensive than the whole pampa of Argentina, is truly the world of tomorrow. Behind it are the Andean foothills with their fine healthy climate, full of mineral wealth and oil, destined one of these days to have some of the majestic cities of this earth. The Amazon region, with its network of waterways, its great potential of hydraulic power, and the adjacent areas probably have more basic resources than are found in any other country on earth except possibly Russia. This area certainly is called to a great future. To that future it will contribute one of the most interesting, versatile cultures yet known to man. Here is a gigantic creative new force. It will emerge fairly rapidly from now on, for man has all the necessary techniques to tame the entire region and make it wholly livable.

Another major Latin American regional division is that of highland and lowland, a contrast that extends from Patagonia clear to the United States. With the exception of the Maya culture on the flat limestone plain of Yucatán and the jungles of Petén and Quintana Roo, the great pre-Spanish cultures of the most populated and developed areas, having several cities as large as those in Europe, were in the highlands—the Aztecs in lofty Anahuac Valley; the intermediary Zapotec-

Mixtec culture in the springtime uplands of Oaxaca and Chiapas; the Maya Quiche culture in the balmy central American highlands; the marvelous Chibcha culture in the Colombian plateau; and finally the vast Inca empire stretching on clear to Argentina and Chile.

After the Spaniards came, here in most areas took place the greatest mixing and welding of the races, a process still going on, so that the highlands are generally Indian-mestizo in culture and energy. Practically all New World highland nations are mestizo civilizations: Mexico, most of Central America, to considerable extent Colombia and Venezuela, Ecuador, Peru and Bolivia.

The highlands of Peru were almost too much for the Spaniards. Except in the mining centers like Potosí and Huancavelica, mostly they settled on the coast and ruled from there. As a result the major language of the South American highlands is Quechua, with allied Andacollo and Aimará. The Indian element in the population is very large. Since the number of Spaniards in Ecuador was always small, their culture and control there were soon absorbed.

But in Colombia and Venezuela coast jungles were too unhealthy, and the Spaniards moved on into the highlands, so that those two countries today are more on the White side.

This highland-lowland regionalism explains many internal tensions of the various countries, even some major wars. Those differences go back into the dim past, long before Europe even knew the New World existed. Thus the major civilizations of Mexico developed in the south central highlands, and the lowlands became conquest areas. This permitted Cortés, after some cannon fire and cajolery, to gain allies in his conquest of the Mexican highlands. The lowlanders, with no love for the military Aztecs, soon gave their loyal ties to the new bearded horse riders from over the sea.

The Mayas, before the Spaniards came, had achieved a partial fusion of a highland-lowland area in Central America. To this day, however, in Guatemala, Los Altos—The Highlands—are distinct in climate, products, race and organization from the lowlands and the capital city of the land. Still basically Indian, enjoying the most healthy terrain, this area, though so long harshly ruled from the center in the spirit of Viceregal Conquest days, nevertheless has provided most of the virility, art, vision and daring of Guatemala. The best writers and painters have usually hailed from Quezaltenango. Most of the military leaders, liberators, dictators, pacifiers and troublemakers have come from that high area.

The highland mestizo region runs all along the backbone of the two continents. Everywhere it has something in common—a distinctive psychology and living habits.

Curiously—and this must have some relation to mountain dwelling, and both dieticians and psychologists could well study it—the highland folk at a certain altitude love hot foods. Thus, in Lima little seasoning is used; but in Arequipa, about the same altitude as Mexico City, the people douse their food with mouth-scalding chile. Still higher, little chile is used.

Geography, often more than men's brains, makes political issues. In the United States the Populist Movement of the nineties achieved its strength with few exceptions in the low-rainfall belt. So in Nicaragua, in prehistoric times, tribal plus geographical differences had created war-like feuds between the men around the Gulf of Fonseca and the León lowland region, on the one hand, and the men of the hill and lake region around what is today Granada, on the other hand. This has been perpetuated in bitter and deadly modern rivalry between the Liberal and the Conservative Parties, which center respectively in the same two areas.

This geographical difference is still marked in Ecuador, still influences the history of the country. There is a persistent rivalry between coastal Guayaquil and lofty Quito for domination. Involved are deep-seated racial and cultural differences.

Before the Spaniards came, the centers of power in South America were in the highlands; the lowlands were Conquest areas. In due time the powerful Inca armies moved down and took over the coast. They pushed on into flat northern Chile, trying to subdue the fierce Araucanos, who were to give them centuries of bloody resistance.

With the coming of the Spaniards to Peru the picture was reversed: the lowland area then became the conquering area, Europeans trying to dominate the highlands. Previous racial and cultural differences were thereby accentuated.

There were various seditious efforts, even by Spanish captains themselves, to set up independent kingdoms in the native Andean region. During Independence there was a similar shuttle. Throughout the nineteenth century the Peruvian highlands, allied with Bolivia, tried to conquer the lowlands or vice versa. The great liberators and dictators of that period usually came from the highlands—men like Santa Cruz—thus restoring something of the pre-Spanish Incan rhythm. Only when the

Spanish feudalists of the lowlands allied themselves with foreign capital and gained more powerful instruments were they able really to dominate the country anew as had the Spaniards.

This highland-lowland duality has engendered wars. Quite aside from the question of nitrates and guano, of copper, tin and oil—which have been tangled in most of the bloody struggles in this region—the basic quarrel of highlanders and lowlanders has always contributed its share of discord. The Chilean wars with Bolivia and Peru usually occurred when the confederation of the two countries was under highland rule. The Chaco War between Bolivia and Paraguay—quite apart from the overriding factor of oil which provoked the fireworks—was the continuation of a struggle that began long before the Spaniards appeared.

Only today, with new railroads, roads and rapid transportation is this duality in Peruvian life being bridged. The highlanders now are flowing into Lima, making it a cholo city; more coast people are moving into the highlands. With the greater economic independence and development of Peru the fusion of the two areas and their people is really taking place. One nation is really being formed.

Another great New World region is the Caribbean, with its white-black-green islands, set like precious jewels in polished purple-green sea, a semitropical world tempered by easy ocean breezes (except when hurricane season is on). This region eventually will free itself from foreign rule and perhaps achieve some sort of independent federation. At present it is a poverty district of bungling colonialism. Yet it yields rich products: sugar, coffee, cocoa, tobacco, fruit, lumber. More integrated and free—and its people are stirring as never before—it would become a much more prosperous and developed area. The great iron, copper and manganese deposits of Cuba have scarcely been exploited. Other islands have considerable mineral wealth. The possibilities of new oil discoveries—oil is now being produced only from a few small wells in Cuba but is present in Santo Domingo and elsewhere—have not been exhausted. In the economic and racial orbit of this region are the rich Gulf Coast areas of Central America and Venezuela, which in climate and population (mostly mulatto) are more akin to Caribbean life than the highland interior region. Also, here are the three Guianas, rich in bauxite and other minerals, lumber, forest and farm products, and today the major rice-producing region of South America. With a better unification of these areas many new industries could be started, which would be supported by adequate markets.

The Caribbean is predominantly a black world, a world awakening, stirring, now crisscrossed by air lines, that is rapidly developing its own ways of life, its own art and culture. It is seeking freedom with an intensity that ere long will resound.

Central America, Colombia and Venezuela, of course, predominantly belong to the highland mestizo world. They are far more akin to Mexico, which is also a region apart, one of the major regions of its continent—the third country in area, the second in population, and progressing more than ever before in its history.

Climate

Variations in climate enforce minor regional divisions.

Whenever I return from a Latin American trip, many people ask me whether I suffered from the heat.

"Nearly froze to death" is my answer.

Many times I have been amused by North Americans getting off the train or plane in Mexico City, tricked out in linen suits and Panama hats, women in chiffon or organdy, to hit near freezing weather. Such attire is practically unknown in that highland city at any time of the year.

A North American university professor has written a book declaring that Latin America is a tropical region whose people, devoid of vim and executive drive, can never have a great civilization, never achieve industrialization. They must always be doomed to the eternal role of sitting at the feet of wise Anglo-Saxons and providing them with necessary raw products.

This Nazilike theory suffers from fallacies. The rapid exhaustion of basic resources in the United States, due to two world wars and preparation for a third, will rapidly equalize the situation, will soon give much of Latin America the edge on resources. And how is it that the European countries, many far smaller than the smallest Latin American country and with inferior resources, have achieved high degrees of industrialization, productivity and prosperity? Argentina is almost as big as Europe outside of the Soviet Union. If she is not so plentifully endowed with minerals, they are right across her borders. Argentina certainly has a great productive future. Italy, with few resources compared with Argentina's, for a long time played a big productive role and attained to considerable world eminence. There is no valid reason why Argentina, almost wholly a temperate-zone country, ten times as large as Italy, with twenty times the amount of good land, with much oil and coal—which Italy lacks—with many other mineral resources, should not be many times more productive. Once the general productive level of South America begins to rise and markets expand, she will become more wealthy and powerful than any European country ever succeeded in being.

The next fallacy is that Latin America is a tropical area. In that vast expanse every climate known to man exists. Argentina, Chile, Uruguay, large parts of Mexico and Brazil are actually in the temperate zone. Even great areas in the tropical zone have fine agreeable climates, far better in fact than almost anywhere in the United States. Altitude and other special factors cause spring temperatures throughout the year. The altitude itself, with its wide daily fluctuations in temperature, gives the tonic vibrations that fortify the human organism in lieu of the more lethargic seasonal changes in the United States.

Mexico is divided into three climatic zones: hot country, temperate country, cold country. All through the 3,000 to 5,000-feet zone—where are located some of the most fertile and pleasant valleys—one gets an all-year springtime climate. Here are such delightful places as Oaxaca, Cuernavaca, Guadalajara, Uruapan, Morelos, Chilpancingo, Tlapa. The year-round average temperature range in Cuernavaca—and this often occurs in a single day, for nights are always zestful—is fifteen degrees. Up to 8,000 feet, daytime climate remains balmy, though nights in winter may frequently get down to freezing.

Except for a few spots the whole Caribbean, its heat tempered by the sea, is a most livable region. Even hotter months rarely reach high New York summer temperatures, and come nowhere near the heat of our Midwest. On these islands are mountains of considerable height, which provide another escape from warmer days.

It is true that parts of the coast of Mexico and Central America can be deadly. I remember one town on the Honduras coast where I had to get up at five in the morning to catch the bus. Even at that hour I was wringing wet with sweat, and as I walked across the hotel room to the washbasin, I left damp tracks on the floor. But the Central American highlands have a delightful all-year spring climate, fragrant, balmy, zestful with eternal sun and flowers.. If for several months they tend toward an overwarm midday heat, most of the day is delightful and nights are always cool. In fact I never felt colder in my life than one misty Fourth of July night in Quezaltenango, Guatemala.

Except for Managua, which is low and for several months terrifically oppressive, all the Central American capitals have a delightful climate on the all-year warm spring side. San Salvador gets a trifle hotter than the others, but except for a few hours of midday lassitude I have never suffered there even at the peak of the driest hottest months. Panamá City, steadily warm the year around, but tempered by sea breezes, is never so hot as New York in the summer. Guayaquil, right on the equator in the lowland, can get fairly hot part of the year, but Quito, like Bogotá and Caracas, is high and springtime bright and can even get downright chilly in winter.

The rest of the tropic West Coast of South America has its climate altered by another odd phenomenon, the icy Humboldt Current, which gives the western lowlands of Peru and Chile the finest of all-year-round climates, with perpetually clear days, for there is no rainfall in that long desert stretch.

Only in Lima, the capital of Peru, is the climate slightly annoying for about three months of winter. For some reason that small area of the coast is then blanketed with dense dripping fogs and the sun becomes a novelty. But even during that period I always sat at my typewriter in my shirt sleeves. For if at night it sometimes got down to about fifty, in the day it was never below sixty-five. The all-year average is somewhere in the low seventies. Those who do not like fog can jump in a car and in twenty minutes be enjoying subtropical weather 2,000 feet up at the Chosica mountain resort. Going just a little higher they can find perfect spring or can get right into winter. Once I left Lima on the coast in the morning of an extra warm summer day and by nightfall landed in a twelve-inch blizzard at the Cerro de Pasco mines.

La Paz, Bolivia, is only seventeen degrees south of the equator, but it is 12,500 feet above the sea, and in the dead of winter—if it can be called that—though nights are chilly, the roses and geraniums are in full bloom, tumbling over ancient walls in a riot of color.

Chile moves through a warm spring climate on the nitrate coast; a southern California climate in the Vales of Paradise; into a rainy Oregon and Washington climate. Then come the cold regions of ice and snow near Antarctica. Even so, Punta Arenas, on the Straits, has far warmer winters than the Connecticut shore line; the average winter temperature is around freezing.

Thus in Chile every range of temperature can be found except strictly tropical weather, although the interior of the nitrate coast away from the shore can be sizzling. But the coast itself is idyllic all year, with a shift of only a few degrees, clear satin skies, never any rain, rarely even a cloud, except over the Andean peaks in the interior. There a few thousand feet up in the Andes the air is fresh and balmy. Farther up one can start skiing. From almost any of Chile's main cities, with their fairly mild climates, in from thirty minutes to two hours one can get to all-year ski runs and winter sports.

The Chaco and all of Paraguay are pretty steadily hot. But Buenos Aires is about the same latitude as Norfolk, Virginia, and has about the same climate. Sidewalk cafés operate all winter. Once in a blue moon there is snow—maybe on the Fourth of July. Christmas, of course, comes right in the middle of the hot spell. In Argentina as in Chile you can range south to the icy Antarctic, where the government has just imported reindeer from Sweden, or north into the tropical blazing Chaco. Northeast in the highlands and along the Patagonia foothills and in the lake region you can hit New England winters.

Once, held up at the Bolivian border overnight because the revolution gainst Villarroel had just broken out and bullets were zipping across, we were forced to put up at a primitive heatless hotel in La Quiaca. When we got up in the morning the water in a pail in the patio was frozen solid.

The fine climate of southeastern Brazil is one of the delights of that country. The coast is tempered by the sea well up into the Tropic Zone. Everywhere the coast range rises immediately, giving very pleasant cool resort places. The winter climate through upper stretches of Catharina and Rio Grande do Sul can be pretty cold.

Much of the great inland Matto Grosso plateau region, although close to the equator and warm, is delightful, never so hot as summer temperatures in most of the United States. Even the great Amazon basin has been maligned. Only in a few stretches near the wide river is it swampy. Much of it has no dangerous insects. Between the various tributaries it is interspersed with low hills. There is much open meadow country, whole empires of grassland. Nights, even right on the equator, are usually fairly cool. Much of the year a light blanket comes in handy. In some places during part of the year night temperatures get down as low as forty degrees.

The great Amazon basin occupies a third of the total area of Latin

America, but all the rest, except for pockets, even though it lies mostly in the tropics, must be considered a temperate-zone area. Petén in Guatemala and some of the coast are hot jungle, but the West Coast of South America turns to spring by the washing tides of the Humboldt Current, and the plateau everywhere provides some of the finest climates known to man.

The Races

Most North Americans think of the New World south as merely an extension of Spain and Portugal. In spite of the overriding influence of institutions and languages imported from Europe, nothing could be more remote from the true picture. Latin America is a region of the most diverse racial and cultural composition. North Americans, used to great cultural uniformity and regimentation, find it hard even to picture the tremendous complexity of the southern lands.

The racial origins of the peoples of the New World have never been clarified. Even our best anthopologists and archaeologists, mostly subordinated to a western European outlook and mentality, with unconscious superior-origin theories, have been most dogmatic on the whole question. Other sciences, such as geology, botany, paleontology, have had to push in to jar them loose from their easily come-by, rigidly dogmatic conclusions. Younger men in the field now are endeavoring to look at the picture with straightforward scientific eyes.

All agree that immigration into the New World—though the necessary spadework has never been done to prove even this conclusively, or to set times and places—occurred at relatively late dates across the Bering Straits. For a long time this seemed to account for all folk and all culture. Until a few years ago no anthropologist or archaeologist would admit that New World cultures dated back more than a couple of thousand years, although the most cursory examination and awareness of the tempo of cultural evolution should have told them those autochthonous cultures could not possibly have been built up in under twenty thousand years. Man's settlement in the New World, it is now generally granted, dates back that far, maybe much farther. Ameghino of Argentina found arrowheads in the bones of prehistoric monsters. Human bones have been discovered in Patagonia, probably the oldest inhabited area of the Americas, with the two-toed horse, long extinct. Presently the antiquity of man in Patagonia may prove to be one of the astonishing "discoveries" by North American scientists, though it has long been argued by those from other countries. Remains twenty-five thousand years old have recently been found in Arizona and California.

We now know that some modern peoples of Siberia are derived from countermigration from the New World into the old. Scientists are beginning to take the stand that the Polynesian area was partly settled by migrations from the New World. We know that the Incas got together overseas flotillas. Recently the Norwegian scientist Thor Heyerdahl took a party on a prehistoric balsa raft from Callao, Peru, to the South Sea islands. Linguistic affinities of the Polynesian and Quechua have been pointed out.

There is still much to be clarified with regard to early migration across Antarctic islands during early ice recessions, and the possible entry of original Australian folk, plants and animals into Patagonia, and vice versa. North American scientists close their minds to this, but French, German, Argentine, Chilean and others—most of the notables—have found geological, botanical, linguistic and other indications. How else explain some of the similarity in the flora and fauna of Patagonia and the Indian Ocean?

The whole prehistoric relation of South America and Africa has yet to be studied. The Salvadorean Barbareña pulled a great deal of information together. There are interesting straws in the wind. Mostly these have been brushed aside by old-timers in the field. . . . But let us look at the races as we know them in modern times. . . .

We danced in a highland village with the Aimarás, a whirling dizzy dance of great beauty. This region is icy cold and the women wear dozens of multicolored woolen skirts—which flare out almost horizontally. The men wear woolen caps with earflaps and an elfin peak; the women have gray or black flat derbies, in some places tall white stovepipe hats.

These are the big-lunged people, allied to the Quechuas who made up the Inca Empire. They have a lung-capacity twenty-five per cent greater than other human beings. How many centuries has it taken to produce a race so biologically different? How many centuries are required to change basic bodily structure to attune itself to an environment?

These sturdy highlanders are an industrious, disciplined folk. Living at that altitude they have to be in order to survive. At a lower springtime altitude, say seven thousand feet, the folk can be more indolent and playful. Thus the upper highlanders are a serious, methodical people with very solid virtues. Their culture still dominates the highlands of Bolivia, Peru, Ecuador and part of Colombia, even parts of Argentina and Chile. Probably ten million people in South America speak Quechua and Aimará or allied dialects. Many also speak Spanish, but the dominant everyday language of the highlands is still the pre-Spanish tongue. As one moves north through the Andes one hits other spoken languages in Colombia and Venezuela, and still others along the coast. Many folk in Panamá, not so far from the Canal Zone, do not even speak Spanish. All through Central America are pockets of people speaking ancient languages, Pipil, Lacandón, Quiche, Mosquito and so on. Probably more than half the population of Guatemala speak Quiche or allied languages. In the areas of the runaway slaves of colonial times—the Cimarron kingdoms the Spaniards could never subdue, and with which the English allied themselves to get a foothold in the region—combination Indian-African dialect is spoken.

In Mexico there are still several million who do not speak Spanish; many more are bilingual. In one interior Guerrero town some people actually speak four languages! It was rather disconcerting to find an illiterate vendor of chile in the market place in Tlapa, Guerrero, taking for granted a linguistic erudition which in our own country is usually reserved for college professors.

Mexico has fifteen basically different languages, and some sixty dialects. The rich folklore, costumes, arts and habits of these various peoples add to the sum total of the complex of Mexico, making it one of the world's richest, most unique cultures, with wellsprings flowing in from many different sources.

Once we went out to a Ñáñigo ceremony in Cuba, a combination of voodooism and Catholicism before a holy altar adorned with odd objects, curious stones and a long black doll in red clothes, fiber and copper bell adornments. Ritualistic knife, bottle and other dances were staged, and lofty pledges of brotherhood written in rooster blood were exchanged. The Ñáñigo ceremonies at various times (especially during American military occupation) were forbidden as pagan and disorderly. Actually they are beautiful spectacles, often in costume, sensuous, artistic, pregnant with tradition and meaning. The Ñáñigo sworn oaths are noble statements of loyalty to other members and their families—a promise to see them through sickness and dire need on all occasions, whatever the sacrifice.

A large part of Cuba's population—even many Whites—speaks the Ñáñigo tongue, a composite of the African languages of former slaves.

As one roams through the Caribbean, one encounters many languages, telling of the polyglot origin of the populations: Papamiento, Chinese, East Indian, Arawak or Siboney, many dialects of French, Dutch, numerous African tongues, Portuguese, Spanish, Danish and so on. In the quaint English of Jamaica a dawn shower becomes "the pride o'the mawnin', Suh." A common language built up from all tongues is used by small boatmen from one end of the Caribbean to the other.

Portuguese is the dominant tongue of Brazil, but there are various other languages and peoples—Indian, African, Hindu, French, Dutch. Many along the borders of Brazil and Argentina speak a queer mixture of Spanish and Portuguese that is almost a new language.

The universally spoken language of Paraguay is Guaraní. Once I was with a Paraguayan Minister in a ticklish moment of an international reunion when a call came through from the Paraguayan representative in Buenos Aires. My host immediately rattled off a conversation in Guaraní.

In Chile about a hundred thousand speak Mapuche, the early Araucano language. Still other indigenous tongues are encountered in the upper Andean folds. A few surviving natives through the south islands still speak Patagón, Ona, Tehuelche, Yagán and so on.

The Araucanos cling to their original ways. They are a dashing race, martial in spirit, stern toward outsiders, hilarious among themselves. Their weaving and silverwork cast an artistic rainbow over the little city of Temuco in south Chile, a bright spangle on the rather unimaginative severe cultural pattern of all Chile. The Mapuche markets, the bright-skirted women swirling about the wool-weighing scales, the horse fairs are full of color. The Mapuche are a singing folk always with special songs for play, for love, for sickness and health, for home-coming, for death. They were never conquered by Spain or by the Republic and became peaceful only with justice. Chilean musicians, poets, writers, artists are now discovering that here is the richest mine in all Chile's cultural heritage, that which most sets it off as distinctive from other countries.

The great bulk of the population of the New World are now melting-pot folk, mestizos, variously called Ladinos in Guatemala, Cholos in Peru, and other names elsewhere. Little by little they have become the leaders, the rulers, in all the highland countries. The most thoroughly mixed nations, so far as Indian and Spaniard go, are Salvador and Chile. The Indian vestiges and admixture are far greater in such dominantly mestizo countries as Mexico, Guatemala, Ecuador and Bolivia. Peru and Bolivia are still in the process of passing from White to mestizo rule.

In Honduras, except for pockets of Indians and Whites, there is a three-way mixture of Indian, Negro and White. In Nicaragua the Pacific Coast is mestizo, the Atlantic Coast, as is true of most banana regions, is strongly mulatto. It fits into the over-all black-white pattern of the Caribbean.

The mestizo spirit, gayer than that of the Indian, more reckless even than that of the Spaniard, more versatile and cunning than either, and always more uprooted, amoral and opportunistic, has demanded and produced its own customs—a new culture now in the making.

The Chilean *zamacueca*, that vigorous rooster-hen dance of coquetry and conquest, is a true reflection of the mestizo spirit. The *China poblana* dance in Mexico, born of the Spanish *jota*, costumed by the opulent China trade of the Colonial epoch, touched with the stamp and shuffle of Indian rhythm—this circling, toe-and-stamp dance around the rim of the big sombrero which has enlivened rural Mexican life for centuries—is also a faithful reflection of mestizo spirit. What is more mestizan than Holy Week processions in Nicaragua, that almost fanatically Catholic land? In an almost boisterous rather than solemn spirit holy images are set to doing the *rumba* in the streets while confetti, water and worse are thrown about with hilarity.

The upper classes of Latin America, ringed about with stiff etiquette and formality, do not have nearly so much fun. At a strictly formal function the slightest deviation from set etiquette means social ruin. The fixed greeting, the precise repetitions of your own name, your address, the comment, "There you have your house," are typically Latin America, but the intimate national flavor is pretty well diluted out to the banality of universal customs. Men rarely mingle with the women between dances. The man must ceremoniously deliver his dancing partner back to her chaperon or companions. At such stately gatherings, though sex is more open and coquettish, more sly and daring, always it is more protected by fixed rules than in most countries. Latin jealousy is always watchful, and the wrong action may cause definite complications. Dance too many times with the same girl, and you may be asked about your intentions, or you may find yourself in real hot water with her *novio*.

Such groups pride themselves on their wealth and complete aloofness from *hoi polloi*. But inevitably more vigorous folkways, as in all countries, make their way upward. Some years ago the tango was considered a shocking underworld dance, product of the pampa gaucho spirit gone to the city, with contributions from all the elements that flow together in the dives of any great port of the world. One marvels that out of such a rough-and-tumble environment could come a dance so formalized, so precisely patterned, so satisfyingly aesthetic, so utterly sensuous, yet so divinely restrained, requiring so much apprenticeship and such instinct of grace. But there it was, with an imagination beyond the frequenters of formal snobbish balls, with an appealing grace they could not create themselves but could master and enjoy, with a stylized sophistication that matched the most rigid formality. Thus out of the open galloping pampa came riding into the more barren and sterilely dying White world of the southern countries the fresh beauty and spirit and tang of the tango. Something like that is always happening.

Even though such formal affairs differ little from country to country, difficulties sometimes arise.

In Chile, the word *chicha*, means a gem, particularly a pearl. At a formal dance in Mexico a visiting upper-class Chilean, looking boldly at the magnificent rope of pearls on the bosom of his very décolleté dancing partner, remarked, "What beautiful *chichas* you have!"

She slapped his face and left him. In Mexico the word *chicha* is a vulgar word for a woman's breast.

Thus in all the southland, though race discrimination does not exist, class discriminations do, and strongly. Owing to historical circumstance, races often join hands. The obstacle is not race, but wealth or social know-how. A Negro in Brazil is a pariah if he is dirty, uneducated, uncouth—and most are, because so recently out of slavery and still held in serfdom—but an educated Negro with money finds no doors of society closed to him. The same is true of the Indian in all the countries. Often in Latin America I have heard upper-class individuals of almost pure Indian blood speak contemptuously of "the dirty Indians," but the term is a class not a race criticism.

An almost full-blooded Negro cabinet minister in Brazil referred to the "ignorant, superstitious Negroes." It was a class verdict, not a race criticism.

Latin American class differences were accentuated by long feudalism with a vast desert between upper and lower classes. Now that this desert is being populated by a middle class, psychology and habits change accordingly.

In Mexico, the peasant—and nearly always he is Indian or a mestizo on the Indian side—is marked by the universal costume of a big straw sombrero, white "pajamas," and thonged huaraches. If he lives in a remote area, more Indian, he may have a more colorful addition, a wider scarlet sash. His women will wear full multicolored long skirts, or wraparound skirts, and embroidered blouses. They may have complicated lace headdresses, as the women of Tehuantepec. And all over Mexico, the badge of the poorer woman is the *rebozo,* the blue or brown woven shawl—a thing of grace and beauty, the use of which is a great art. It serves as head covering and embellishment to accentuate face, eyes, the lines of breast and hip, for better flirtation, for carrying bundles and babies, for warming hands on chilly mornings. A *rebozo* worn into church takes on lines of piousness and chastity, a demure retirement of body and soul into chastened humility. Worn at the carnival, slanted rakishly across forehead and cheek, it frames a vivacious coquettish face. It is one of the most adaptable, artistic pieces of attire ever developed by any people.

The new proletariat, if above the day-labor class, lay aside thonged sandals and put on clumsy shoes. Blue overalls replace the white pajamas. The only touch of color left is perhaps a red bandanna about the throat.

Similar dress distinctions, often very beautiful, exist in nearly all the countries among the races and the classes. The woolen clothing of the Guatemalan and Andean highlands, which the folk of high cold regions wear, is woven into bright colors and designs.

But all such dress distinctions, despite their racial origins, are more a sign of strong cultural integrity than of race or class distinctions.

With the new middle class all distinctions in dress tend to go out. They are the true children of the regimented machine age, the "parroters" of their betters, the users of mass products, the imitators of mass-imposed styles. They tend to sink into the general reservoir of machine-made banality.

Being mostly mestizan, which means having a soul torn by conflicting cultures and traditions, but stirred into confusion and ambition, and being also such recent arrivals on the scene, the Latin American middle classes, which have never known anywhere near the economic opportunity or the security of the same classes in the United States, have resorted to many expedients to achieve pseudo comfort. As a result they are the temporary repository of all bad taste in the southlands, preferring the most tawdry machine object to the most beautiful homemade. They have largely lost the standards of the two cultures from which they sprang and are still striving to achieve valid group standards of their own. Their homes are usually a hodgepodge of the least tasteful things. Only in larger cities, as is true in most cities of the world, is their innate lack supplemented by the superior-imposed good taste of machine-made mass-production objects.

It is slightly pathetic that this has to be so. The new middle class is a fine and necessary part of the southern lands today, for it represents a healthy breakup of the old feudal pattern. It brings to the scene fresh ideas of freedom and civic rights. It is behind the new drives for education, public works, sanitation. Still one may sigh a little that the price of such worthy effort should be banality and the loss of creative instincts formerly so strong in both Spaniard and Indian. Those instincts still vitalize other groups in the community which do not yet bow their heads to what man is pleased to call civilization—that industrial process which in all lands tends to defraud man of creative power in the name of leisure and comfort, bathtubs and gadgets.

The Nations

Like Europe, Latin America is primarily a great geographic and cultural expression, with many nationalities, all of them different, decisive, sharply defined.

There is a common continental heritage provided by the Conquest; also by the mixing of races, the accretions of Indian and Spanish and Negro cultures, though here, too, uniformity is not so great as imagined. Many things live on side by side. In Mexican villages I have seen couples married three times: by civil law, by the Church, finally by the elders in Indian ceremony—couples very well spliced! In Peru I have seen a man freed by the courts of the land, retried by the village authorities and punished. Everywhere national differences are striking and important.

Except for Brazil, Haiti, and some colonial islands, the common language is Spanish, for the most part admirably spoken. In most of the New World the average man speaks a purer Castilian than the average citizen of Madrid itself, which has a sort of "Brooklynese" dialect all its own. The worst New World speech-sinner is Chile, perhaps because of its long isolation and early continuous conflicts with the Araucanos. It is the least Spanish Spanish of the continent, the worst pronounced, the most heavily interlarded with native expressions. But we have already pointed out the many differences in tongues that distinguish each country from the others.

The New World lands are all Catholic, although pockets of other faiths are represented—Protestantism, Buddhism, Mohammedanism, Judaism, Greek Catholicism. There are considerable areas where Indian religions have survived, as with most Araucanos, and still greater areas where Indian and Catholic rites have been garbled together. In places African rites persist. Some of these, too, are semi-Catholic.

There is a fairly similar over-all political pattern. To colonialism and Spanish absolutism, grafted onto native Indian practices, were later grafted on concepts of the French social contract and the ideas of the United States Constitution which grew out of French revolutionary roots. Thus all countries are republics in name if not always in practice. Theoretically and constitutionally they are all democracies, however much social habits and political antics have mostly deviated from that ideal. Those deviations themselves hark back to class, racial and geographic differences. Even property titles are not wholly Spanish. In Mexico I have seen villagers bring in old Aztec picture parchments to establish their communal boundaries.

But over the continent as a whole there is a common cultural pattern, a complex of similar institutions, habits and psychology. All the countries have a background of recent conquest and feudalism. Almost all have similar unsolved racial and cultural conflicts, however much the political pattern may vary.

And yet each of the twenty countries is different—starkly different—and the differences, though the language is mostly the same, are often more pronounced than those found between most European nations. With the years those differences, rather than diminishing, grow increasingly more striking, more rooted.

Although some unknown traveler on your train or boat or bus may be dressed in a conventional business suit, anyone who has journeyed a great deal around Latin America and who watches the stranger's gestures, listens to his vocabulary and the intonation of his Spanish and looks at the shape of his head, the tint of his skin, the features of his

face, in a very few minutes is nearly always able to identify the nation
he hails from.

The racial differences in Latin America, from one nation to another,
are sometimes greater than between any two countries of Europe. The
difference between Indian Guatemala and Spanish Costa Rica is certainly greater than that between Italy and Finland. The mestizo world
of Mexico is vastly different from the transplanted European world of
Argentina. These race-cultural differences play their part, besides geography and historical accidents, in bringing into being twenty decidedly
distinct nations.

In part these national characteristics spring from political divisions
imposed by the Spaniards. Those boundaries obeyed every sort of opportunistic and administrative motive. Sometimes they were based on
previous indigenous political divisions, created by the Aztecs and other
groups. But sometimes they were deliberately intended to break down
previous native unity, an early process of gerrymandering. In this way,
the better to govern the highlands and break up Inca unity, the
Spaniards eventually gave Bolivia to Pampas Argentina, and Ecuador
to Colombia on the other side of the mountains. So these colonial divisions might be highly artificial, though in the main they answered to
the kinds of transportation then enjoyed—the horse and the sailing
vessel. Political boundaries were further determined by the problems
of rule by Spain so many thousands of miles away in an era of slow
communications.

After the Spaniards were tossed out some pre-Conquest factors re-
asserted themselves. Thus the Spaniards had united Central America,
but right after Independence it fell apart. The new countries were
largely subdivisions of Viceregal administration, but these in general
had obeyed earlier differences of race and politics.

Salvador largely comprehended the early Pipiles, who were Nahuas,
blood brothers of the Aztecs. They have given to independent Salvador,
the most densely populated country on the American mainland, an unruly fierceness not found in neighboring Guatemala, peopled largely
by the mild, pacific Maya-Quiche.

In Honduras, very early mixtures of Spaniards, Indian and Negro
became thoroughgoing, and this in turn stamped out a separate country,
with distinctive customs and habits, a people of quick, rich imagination,
fairly unruly, often extremely cruel.

Nicaragua, for some reason the most effervescent land in the Americas, has an unruly passionate people. Nowhere on earth will the outsider encounter comparable friendliness and (it may happen also) hate, such hospitality and boundless generosity. Few people are so fanatically loyal and so courageous, so firm in their convictions—and so utterly unpredictable as to what they will do from one minute to the next— drink, go fishing, or start a revolution.

By comparison, the Costa Rican, right next door, an almost pure European with only a trace of Indian, is a cold, formal individual, very rational, even-tempered, disciplined, less imaginative. National temperamental and character derivations in the Americas are wide indeed.

The early divisions set up by the Spaniards in South America caused post-Independence wars between Peru, trying to recover Bolivia, and Bolivia, the highland center, trying to rule Peru. Modern economic unity demands that Peru, Bolivia and Ecuador be one country; but there they are—independent, not overly harmonious nations, each extremely different from the other. The early Spanish political boundaries, based on horse travel, no longer match the demands of modern highway, railroad and airplane—but that is also part of the tragedy of Europe.

How will one explain all these differences: the gentler, brooding artistic quality of the Peruvian as compared to the harsh, severe, disciplined, somewhat unimaginative character of the Chilean; the fierce warlike Paraguayan compared with the more energetic but peace-loving Argentine.

Into the various countries have flowed varying mixtures of peoples. The Spaniards themselves were made up of many groups, and much of the result in the Americas was determined by whether a given country was settled prevailingly by Gallegos or Andalusians, Basques or Catalans. The original New World people were also markedly different in language and customs. Wide divergences existed in the physique, temperament, thought, culture and social habits of Aztecs, Mayas, Quechuas— to mention only three of the hundreds of pre-Spanish "nations."

The theme offers endless possibilities for observation and analysis. But strangely, though national characteristics grow constantly more pronounced, are stronger today than a hundred years ago, the various South American nations at present are closer together in every way than they have ever been before in history. To rule the various colonies the Spaniards made it almost impossible to travel from one to another. Each was tightly sealed off. With Independence, communications were still lacking, and there was little ready means of transportation and communication among the different lands. For nearly a century it was easier to go from any of the Central American lands to Europe or the United States than to get from one to another.

Only today with the transfer of book publishing to the New World, with the arrival of international cable services, with fast means of travel and communication, are the Latin American countries really beginning to know one another, to live and work together, to build up closer political and economic relations. This has all been very recent indeed. Only now is some sort of New World unity being developed. It was never possible before. Not until our day did inter-Americanism, the old dream of Independence leader, Simón Bolívar, become anything more than a dream—though how persistent and imperative over the century it has been! Now it begins to be a reality. Until the last few decades the bases for it simply did not exist. Now a continental system, based on different sovereignties and cultures and wider tolerance and understanding, has become a possibility and seems on the way to realization.

The United States occupies about a fourth of the New World area. It is part of the New World complex of nations. With Canada it forms a cultural bloc set off from the Latin American. Between the Anglo-Saxon and the Latin American cultures is a difference even greater than that existing between the various individual Hemisphere countries. All that difference has been bridged in many ways, and the reciprocal cultural pattern can serve to enrich and fortify both areas and both groups of peoples. Neither one has the key to all life's secrets, to all culture or all the arcana of the human soul—or even to exclusive world power. The inter-American system, therefore, is much more than a periodic meeting of governmental representatives in conference. It is much more than military defense. It can grow in stature only through the fair exchange of goods and of ideas: techniques, science, literature and art; through a full respect for mutual talents, a tolerance for all differences of race and culture.

INDEX

INDEX

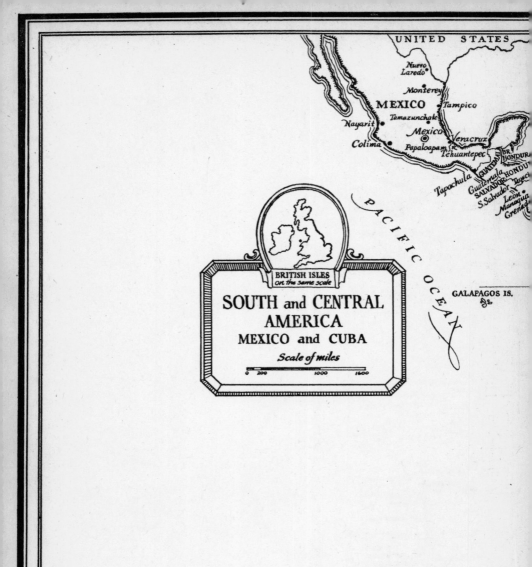

UNITED STATES

Nuevo
Laredo

Monterey

MEXICO · Tampico

Nayarit · Tamazunchale

Mexico

Colima · Papaloapam · Veracruz

Tehuantepec

BR. HONDURAS

Tapachula · GUATEMALA HONDURAS

Guatemala

SALVADOR

S.Salvador

Leon

Managua

Grenada

PACIFIC OCEAN

GALAPAGOS IS.

BRITISH ISLES
on the same scale

SOUTH and CENTRAL
AMERICA
MEXICO and CUBA

Scale of miles

0   200   1000   1600